CARROLL COUNTY
COMMUNITY COLLEGE CENTER

TWENTIETH CENTURY VIEWS

The aim of this series is to present the best in contemporary critical opinion on major authors, providing a twentieth century perspective on their changing status in an era of profound revaluation.

Maynard Mack, *Series Editor*
Yale University

RALPH ELLISON

RALPH ELLISON

A COLLECTION OF CRITICAL ESSAYS

Edited by
John Hersey

Prentice-Hall, Inc.  *Englewood Cliffs, N. J.*

Library of Congress Cataloging in Publication Data

HERSEY, JOHN RICHARD   comp.
    Ellison A Collection of Critical Essays

    'Twentieth century views) (A Spectrum Book)
    CONTENTS: Introduction: "A Completion of personality": a talk with
Ralph Ellison.—"The cost of being human": Warren, R. P. The unity of
experience. Bellow, S. Man underground. Chisolm, L. W. Signifying everything. Howe, I. Black boys and native sons. Hyman, S. E. Ralph Ellison in
our time. [etc.]

    1. Ellison, Ralph.   I. Title.
PS3555.L625Z7   818'.5'409   73-16224
ISBN 0-13-274357-4
ISBN 0-13-274340-X   (pbk.)

10 9 8 7 6 5 4 3

PRENTICE-HALL INTERNATIONAL, INC. (*London*)
PRENTICE-HALL OF AUSTRALIA, PTY. LTD. (*Sydney*)
PRENTICE-HALL OF CANADA, LTD. (*Toronto*)
PRENTICE-HALL OF INDIA PRIVATE LIMITED (*New Delhi*)
PRENTICE-HALL OF JAPAN, INC. (*Tokyo*)

Contents

RALPH ELLISON

Introduction:
"A Completion of Personality"

A Talk with Ralph Ellison

One of the most significant views of the work of Ralph Ellison happens to be his own. He is, as he himself says, a slow worker, and over the course of the years, while he was writing away at his second novel—and while Invisible Man *paradoxically refused to drop out of sight—Ellison granted a number of interviews, each of which offered some telling comments on the situation of a novelist who had been thrust into more gnawing fame than most writers would want in their own time. He reproduced three of the interviews in* Shadow and Act. *Two other valuable ones are noted in the bibliography of this book, and the vivid picture of Ellison by a younger writer, James Alan McPherson, also in this collection, originally included an exchange of letters between the two authors, in which Ellison further elaborated his predicament.*

For predicament it has been, and what is forced upon a reader of these interviews is a sense that the polemic-versus-artistic argument—the argument, as old as art itself, over the question: "What use has art?"—hounds Ellison perhaps more than any other first-rank novelist of our time, unless it be Alexander Solzhenitsyn. That argument dominates several of the essays in this book, and it hums in harmonic overtones over the rest of them.

It occurred to me as I assembled and read these various views that in the din of this argument we had never had a chance to hear much from Ellison about his attitude toward the actuality of his craft, about the processes of his creative ordeal, about what he thinks actually happens *when he writes, about the deep familial sources of his ways of being and doing, about how his mind works through problems of shape and dream and sound, and about the particular, idiosyncratic inner workings of his art which may have been molded by his existential past. Although it is entitled "The Art of Fiction," not even the* Paris Review *interview, reprinted in*

1

Shadow and Act, *goes beneath the surface of his struggle to achieve
an art worth arguing about as much as his has been.*

*And so, on a weekend that Ellison and his wife spent in my
home, we talked late into one night about all these matters, and
in the cool light of the next morning we had a conversation in
which Ellison, with extraordinary finish and economy, and yet with
a fabulist's deceptive randomness, too, synthesized and compressed
his views of his labor of choice. Here is what we said:*

HERSEY. You were talking about your mother last night, and as you
   talked I wondered how much she had been a force in moving you
   toward your calling as a writer, and even in supplying materials
   that you have drawn on.

ELLISON. She certainly had something to do with encouraging my
   interest in reading. She had no idea that I was going to become
   a writer, or if she did, she had more insight into me than I
   had into myself, because I thought I was going to be a musician.
   My mother always encouraged me to do *something*, and to be
   good at it—she insisted upon that.

   It was my father who wanted me to be a writer. I didn't discover that until many years later—he died when I was three—
   until after I had written *Invisible Man* and talked with an older
   cousin, who told me that my father had used to say, "I'm raising
   this boy to be a poet." Of course he had given me the name
   [Ralph Waldo].

   But my mother did feed my passion for reading. She brought
   home books and magazines. My concern with the Picassos and
   Stravinskys of this world started at an earlier age than usual
   because she brought home *Vanity Fair*. Here was a world so far
   from Oklahoma City, in any expected sense, yet it was shaping
   my sense of what was possible. And she understood that that was
   what was going on.

   And what I did get from my mother was an understanding of
   people. I was very quick-tempered and impatient, and things
   began to happen when I reached adolescence—and she would
   just talk about how people acted, what motives were, and why
   things were sometimes done. I remember being so outraged by
   something one of her friends had said that I didn't want to see
   her or her husband anymore. At thirteen I went to work as the
   husband's office boy and this close friend of my father was so delighted with having me around that his childless wife was upset.
   Her reaction was to spread the word around that she suspected

that I was actually her husband's child—Oh, boy! When the gossip reached me I was outraged—and not only over what it implied about my mother, but because of my love for my father. I had learned to walk at six months and had been his companion from that time until his death, and I was so far from accepting the reality of his death that I was still telling myself that any day he would reappear to take his place as the head of our family. Now I suspect that my fondness for my employer-friend and my vague awareness that he was, in fact, something of a father-figure added to my shock and outrage. At any rate, when I went to my mother about this matter she proceeded to calm me down.

"Well now," she said, "you should understand what's happening. You remember your daddy and you've been around and seen a few people and have some idea how they act. You've been working in drugstores and barbershops and at that office and since you've been around . . . and . . . as much as you have, you must know that she's crazy. So use your head. She doesn't have to be put in an institution, but you have to understand and accept the fact that she isn't responsible."

It was a rather shocking notion for me and I didn't want to surrender my anger, but I realized that my mother was right. What's more, I realized that very often I could save myself a lot of wear and tear with people if I just learned to understand them.

Beyond that, although she was religious, my mother had a great tolerance for the affairs of the world which had nothing to do with religion, and I think that that helped me to sort of balance things out, so to speak. The great emphasis in my school was upon classical music, but such great jazz musicians as Hot Lips Paige, Jimmy Rushing, and Lester Young were living in Oklahoma City, and through her allowing me to attend public dances and to maintain a certain friendship with some of them, even though she watched what I was doing, she made it possible to approach the life of the Negro community there with some sense of its wholeness instead of trying to distort it into some hoped-for religion-conceived perfection. As it turned out, the perfection, the artistic dedication which helped me as a writer, was not so much in the classical emphasis as within the jazz itself.

She also helped me to escape the limitations of trying to impose any in-group class distinctions upon the people of my community. We were very poor, but my father had been a small businessman who sold ice and coal to both whites and blacks, and since he and my mother were pioneers in a young state, my mother knew some of the city's leaders; they were my father's friends and remained as my mother's after his death. So she didn't strive to be part of the social leadership of the black community; that was left to the wives of professional men, to teachers and preachers. Her background and attitudes were such that all kinds of people came into the house, or we visited their houses. That was one of the enriching parts of my experience, because I knew people who went right back to the farm and plantation, along with those who had gone to college and medical school. Thus my sense of their stories and life-styles, and so on, was never very far from mind. My mother had grown up on a Georgia plantation herself, she was a farm girl; and then she left and went to live in Atlanta. It gave me a sense of a past which was far from narrow.

She liked to talk. She never allowed me to lose the vividness of my father, and she told me all kinds of things that he had done—that he had run away from his own father in South Carolina when he was quite young, and had become a professional soldier, and had been in Cuba and in the Philippines and in China. He was with our troops that fought against the Boxer Rebellion. Afterwards, he and his brother had operated a candy kitchen in Chattanooga. He had also operated a restaurant—always trying to get at something—and then had become a construction foreman; that was how they came West to Oklahoma.

There was also her overt and explicit concern with political conditions. There was never a time when I was not aware of what these were all about. When I was in college, my mother broke a segregated-housing ordinance in Oklahoma City, and they were throwing her in jail, and the NAACP would get her out, and they'd come back and throw her in jail again. This went on until my brother beat up one of the white inspectors, then she decided that it was about time to get out of that situation before he got himself shot. She had that kind of forthrightness, and I like to think that that was much more valuable than anything literary that she gave me.

HERSEY. The creative drive seems always to have been strong in you, ever since childhood. You said once that you couldn't remember a time when you hadn't wanted to make something—a one-tube radio, a crystal set, a toy; a little later you had an urge to compose music. Where do you think this drive came from?

ELLISON. I don't know where it comes from. Maybe it had something to do with my father's working as a construction foreman, building buildings. It certainly came from some of the boys that I grew up with, as a child. They were always *doing* things. I always admired the guys who could make things, who could draw. This was something that gave me a great deal of pleasure.

But maybe the desire to write goes back to a Christmas gift. One Christmas my mother gave me—I must have been five—a little roll-top desk and a chair, not a swivel chair but a little straight chair, oak, and a little toy typewriter. I had forgotten that. We were living in the parsonage of the old A.M.E. Church, Avery Chapel, which the leaders of the congregation turned over to my mother after the new minister turned out to have his own home. "Why don't you be the janitress of the church and live in the parsonage?" they said. And we did, and that's where I got the desk and the little typewriter. I was also given a chemistry set. Now this might have been unusual in such relatively uneducated families—I think my mother went to the eighth grade in school —but she felt that these were the kinds of things that her boys should have. She was also very explicit, as we grew older, about our economic condition. We knew why we could not have a bicycle, why we could not have this, that, or the other. She explained that we could not have such things because she didn't have the money, and we had to accept that fact. So what did we do? We learned to do other things. Instead of playing with store-bought toys, you made your own. You fished and hunted, you listened to music, you danced and you spent a great amount of time reading and dreaming over books.

When Mr. Mead, next door, taught me the fundamentals of playing an old brass alto horn, my mother bought me a pawnshop cornet. She could afford that, and owning the instrument made it possible for me to acquire enough skill to get into the school band. So she did what she could, and in addition to encouraging my interest in reading she encouraged my interest in music, and so on.

But the desire to make something out of my imagination and to experiment was constant. In one story of mine there is an incident taken from life, where my brother and I took baby chickens and made little parachutes and got up on top of the chicken house and dropped them down. The lady next door told my mother, and we caught hell for that. We didn't kill the chickens, understand, we just floated them down. We did that, you see, because we had learned to take iron taps and tie strings to them and then attach the strings to pieces of cloth. When we threw these into the air we'd get a parachute effect and imagine that the taps were parachutists. We just took it a step further.

HERSEY. What would you say was the starting point for your new novel?

ELLISON. I guess it started with the idea of an old man being so outraged by his life that he goes poking around in the cellar to find a forgotten coffin, which he had bought years before to insure against his possible ruin. He discovers that he has lived so long that the coffin is full of termites, and that even the things he had stored in the coffin have fallen apart. Somehow, this said something to my imagination and got me started. You can see that it could go in *any* direction. But then it led to the other idea, which I wrote first, of a little boy being placed in a coffin, in a ritual of death and transcendence, celebrated by a Negro evangelist who was unsure whether he was simply exploiting the circus side-show shock set off by the sight of a child rising up out of a coffin, or had hit upon an inspired way of presenting the sacred drama of the Resurrection. In my mind all of this is tied up in some way with the significance of being a Negro in America and at the same time with the problem of our democratic faith as a whole. Anyway, as a product of the imagination it's like a big sponge, maybe, or a waterbed, with a lot of needles sticking in it at various points. You don't know what is being touched, where the needles are going to end up once you get them threaded and penetrated, but somehow I kept trying to tie those threads together and the needle points pressing home without letting whatever lies in the center leak out.

HERSEY. How soon after *Invisible Man* was published [1952] did you start working on the new novel?

ELLISON. I was pretty depleted by *Invisible Man,* so I didn't start on another book immediately. I played around with various ideas and spent some time trying to salvage material I had edited out of *Invisible Man.* It was in Rome, during 1956, that I began to think vaguely about this book and conceived the basic situation, which had to do with a political assassination; this was involved with the other patterns—the coffin business.

HERSEY. This was before the Kennedys and King were assassinated, of course.

ELLISON. Yes, this was before. Almost eight years before. One of the things which really chilled me—and slowed down the writing—was that eruption of assassinations, especially the first. Because, you see, much of the mood of this book was conceived as comic.

Not that the assassination was treated comically, but there is humor involved, and that was rather chilling for me, because suddenly life was stepping in and imposing itself upon my fiction. Anyway, I managed to keep going with it, I guess because there was nothing else to do. I know that it led me to try to give the book a richer structuring, so that the tragic elements could contain the comic and the comic the tragic, without violating our national pieties—if there are any left. Americans have always been divided in their pieties, but today there is such a deliberate flaunting of the pieties and traditions—of others, anyway—that it's become rather difficult to distinguish what is admissible from that which is inadmissible. Even the flag and motherhood are under attack.

HERSEY. With such fast-moving reality so close at hand, how much in control of your fictional characters can you feel that you are?

ELLISON. Once a logic is set up for a character, once he begins to move, then that which is implicit within him tends to realize itself, and for you to discover the *form* of the fiction, you have to go where he takes you, you have to follow him. In the process you change your ideas. You remember, Dostoievski wrote about eight versions of a certain scene in *The Brothers Karamazov,* and in some instances the original incidents were retained but the characters who performed them were changed. I find that happens with me. I get to the point where something has to be done and discover that it isn't logical for the character who started out to do it, to do it; and suddenly another character pops up. In this book there is an instance wherein McIntyre has to interview the man who burns his Cadillac. This man is being held in the observation cell of a hospital because the authorities believe that a Negro who burns his own Cadillac has to be crazy. So for McIntyre to see the man there has to be an intermediary—so suddenly I found myself dealing with a new character, a Negro employed by the hospital, who gets McIntyre past the barriers and to the car-burner. This fellow wasn't foreseen; he simply appeared to help me get on with the form.

HERSEY. About motive—what gives you the psychic energy to take on a massive work and keep at it for a very long time?

ELLISON. I guess it is the writing itself. I am terribly stubborn, and once I get engaged in that kind of project, I just have to keep going until I finally make something out of it. I don't know what the something is going to be, but the process is one through which I make a good part of my own experience meaningful. I don't mean in any easy autobiographical sense, but the matter of drawing actual experience, thought, and emotion together in a way that creates an artifact through which I can reach other people. Maybe that's vanity; I don't know. Still I believe that fiction does help create value, and I regard this as a very serious —I almost said "sacred"—function of the writer.

Psychic energy? I don't know, I think of myself as kind of lazy. And yet, I do find that working slowly, which is the only way I seem able to work—although I write fast much of the time —the problem is one of being able to receive from my work that sense of tension, that sense of high purpose being realized, that keeps me going. This is a crazy area that I don't understand —none of the Freudian explanations seem adequate.

HERSEY. As to the short range, you used a phrase last night that interested me. You said you wanted to keep the early morning free "in case the night before had generated something that could be put to good use." What did you mean by that?

ELLISON. I never know quite what has gone on in my subconscious in the night, I dream vividly, and all kinds of things happen; by morning they have fallen below the threshold again. But I like to feel that whatever takes place becomes active in some way in what I do at the typewriter. In other words, I believe that a human being's life is of a whole, and that he lives the full twenty-four hours. And if he is a writer or an artist, what happens during the night feeds back, in some way, into what he does consciously during the day—that is, when he is doing that which is self-achieving, so to speak. Part of the pleasure of writing, as well as the pain, is involved in pouring into that thing which is being created all of what he cannot understand and cannot say and cannot deal with, or cannot even admit, in any other way. The artifact is a completion of personality.

HERSEY. Do you experience anything like daydreaming or dreaming when you are writing? Do you feel that the writing process may involve a somewhat altered state of consciousness in itself?

ELLISON. I think a writer learns to be as conscious about his craft as he can possibly be—not because this will make him absolutely lucid about what he does, but because it prepares the stage for structuring his daydreaming and allows him to draw upon the various irrational elements involved in writing. You know that when you begin to structure literary forms you are going to have to play variations on your themes, and you are going to have to make everything vivid, so that the reader can see and hear and feel and smell, and, if you're lucky, even taste. All that is on a conscious level and very, very important. But then, once you get going, strange things occur. There are things in *Invisible Man*, for instance, that I can't *imagine* my having consciously planned. They materialized as I worked consciously at other things. Take three of the speeches: the speech made at the eviction, the funeral address in Mount Morris Park, and the one that Barbee made in chapel. Now, I realized consciously, or I *discovered* as I wrote, that I was playing variations on what Otto Rank identified as the myth of the birth and death of the hero. So in the re-writing that conscious knowledge, that insight, made it possible to come back and add elements to the design which I had written myself into under the passion of telling a story.

What should also be said in this connection is that somewhere —it doesn't have to be right in the front of the mind, of the consciousness—writers, like other artists, are involved in a process of comparative culture. I looked at the copy of *The Lower Depths* on the table there this morning, and I remembered how much of Gorki I had read, and how I was always—not putting his characters into blackface, but finding equivalents for the experience he depicted; the equivalents for turns of phrase, for parables and proverbs, which existed within the various backgrounds that I knew. And I think that something of that goes on when a conscious writer goes about creating a fiction. It's part of his workshop, his possession of the culture of the form in which he works.

HERSEY. You once said that it took you a long time to learn how to adapt myth and ritual into your work. Faulkner speaks of a "lumber room in the subconscious," where old things are kept. How do you get at the sources of these things deep down in your mind?

ELLISON. I think I get at them through sheer work, converting incidents into patterns—and also by simply continuing at a thing when I don't seem to be getting anywhere. For instance, I wrote a scene in which Hickman is thinking about the difficulty of communicating with someone as constituting a "wall"; he thinks this as he is drifting off to sleep. Well, later in my work I suddenly realized that the damn wall had turned up again in another form. And that's when that voice in my unconscious finally said, "Hey, *this* is what you've been getting at." And looking back, I saw that I had worked up a little pattern of these walls. What the unconscious mind does is to put all manner of things into juxtaposition. The conscious mind has to provide the logical structure of narrative and incident through which these unconscious patterns can be allowed to radiate by throwing them into artful juxtaposition on the page.

HERSEY. Do you, as some writers do, have a sense of standing in a magic circle when you write?

ELLISON. To the extent that unexpected things occur, that characters say things or see things which, for all my attempts to be conscious and to work out of what I call a conceptual outline, are suddenly just *there*. That *is* magical, because such things seem to emerge out of the empty air. And yet, you know that somehow the dreams, emotions, ironies, and hidden implications of your material often find ways of making themselves manifest. You work to make them reveal themselves.

HERSEY. Do you, when you are writing, sometimes find yourself so totally engaged by a character that you are carried away outside yourself by *his* feelings—are literally beside yourself?

ELLISON. I find myself carried away and emotionally moved, sometimes quite unexpectedly, and my tendency is to distrust it, feeling that perhaps I'm being sentimental, being caught in a situation which I am not adequately transforming into art. So I put it aside and wait awhile, maybe months, and then go back, and if it still works after I've examined it as well as I can, as objectively as I can, I then perhaps read it to Fanny, and if she doesn't indicate that it's slobbering sentimentality, in bad taste, or just poorly achieved—then I leave it in.

HERSEY. Would you say that, by and large, when you have had these surges of feeling the writing does hold up in the long run?

ELLISON. Sometimes it does, sometimes it doesn't. I won't be able to say about this book until it has been read by enough objective readers. I won't be able to judge until then because it has some crazy developments.

I found myself writing a scene in which Hickman and Wilhite, his deacon, go into a strange house in Washington, and find a bunch of people in the hallway who are very upset because the police won't tell them what has happened in the apartment of one of their neighbors. Then one of the women goes hysterical and pretty soon she's outraging the crowd by talking about the most personal matters as she addresses herself to a bewildered Wilhite and Hickman. Not only was I shocked to discover myself writing this unplanned scene, but I still have questions about how it functions. ⌐et, for all its wild, tragicomic emotion—there it is! Now when your material takes over like that you are really being pushed. Thus, when this woman started confessing, she forced *me* to think about Hickman's role as minister on a different level; I mean on the theological level; which was something I hadn't planned, since I wasn't writing an essay but a novel. Finally, Hickman came to my aid by recognizing that the woman had been unfolding a distorted and highly personalized dream-version of the immaculate birth. To me she sounded merely irrational and comic, but Hickman, being a minister, forced himself to look beneath her raving, even though she is without question a most unacceptable surrogate for the Virgin. After that, I was forced to realize that this crazy development was really tied in with the central situation of the novel: that of an old man searching throughout the years for a little boy who ran away. So I guess it sprang from that magic circle you referred to, from that amorphous level which lies somewhere between the emotions and the intellect, between the consciousness and the unconscious, which supports our creative powers but which we cannot control.

HERSEY. I have wondered about the ways in which your musical experience has fed into your writing.

ELLISON. My sense of form, my basic sense of artistic form, is musical. As a boy I tried to write songs, marches, exercises in symphonic form, really before I received any training, and then I studied it. I listened constantly to music, trying to learn the processes of developing a theme, of expanding and contracting and turning it inside out, of making bridges, and working with techniques of musical continuity, and so on. I think that basically my instinctive approach to writing is through *sound*. A change of mood and mode comes to me in terms of sound. That's one part of it, in the sense of composing the architecture of a fiction.

On the other hand, one of the things I work for is to make a line of prose *sound* right, or for a bit of dialogue to fall on the page in the way I hear it, aurally, in my mind. The same goes for the sound and intonation of a character's voice. When I am writing of characters who speak in the Negro idiom, in the vernacular, it is still a real problem for me to make their accents fall in the proper place in the visual line.

HERSEY. Which comes first for you in writing, hearing or seeing?

ELLISON. I might conceive of a thing aurally, but to realize it you have got to make it vivid. The two things must operate together. What is the old phrase—"the planned dislocation of the senses"? That *is* the condition of fiction, I think. Here is where sound becomes sight and sight becomes sound, and where sign becomes symbol and symbol becomes sign; where fact and idea must not just be hanging there but must become a functioning part of the total design, involving itself in the reader as idea as well as drama. You do this by providing the reader with as much detail as is possible in terms of the visual *and* the aural, *and* the rhythmic—to allow him to involve himself, to attach himself, and then begin to collaborate in the creation of the fictional spell. Because you simply cannot put it all there on the page, you can only evoke it—or evoke what is already there, implicitly, in the reader's head: his sense of life.

HERSEY. You mentioned "making bridges" a minute ago. I remember that you once said that your anxiety about transitions greatly prolonged the writing of *Invisible Man*.

ELLISON. Yes, that has continued to be something of a problem. I try to tell myself that it is irrational, but it is what happens when you're making something, and you know that you are *making* something rather than simply relating an anecdote that actually happened. But at the same time you have to strike a balance between that which you can imply and that which you must make explicit, so that the reader can follow you. One source of this anxiety comes, I think, from my sense of the variations in American backgrounds—especially as imposed by the racial situation. I can't always be certain that what I write is going to be understood. Now, this doesn't mean that I am writing for whites, but that I realize that as an American writer I have a problem of communicating across our various social divisions, whether of race, class, education, region, or religion—and much of this holds true even within my own racial group. It's dangerous to take things for granted.

This reminds me of something that happened out at a northwestern university. A young white professor said to me, "Mr. Ellison, how does it feel to be able to go to places where most Negroes can't go?" Before I could think to be polite I answered, "What you mean is: 'How does it feel to be able to go places where most *white* men can't go?' " He was shocked and turned red, and I was embarrassed; nevertheless, it was a teaching situation so I told him the truth. I wanted him to understand that individuality is still operative beyond the racial structuring of

American society. And that, conversely, there are many areas of black society that are closed to *me* while open to certain whites. Friendship and shared interests make the difference.

When you are writing fiction out of your individual sense of American life it's difficult to know what to take for granted. For instance, I don't know whether I can simply refer to an element of decor and communicate the social values it stands for, because so much depends upon the way a reader makes associations. I am more confident in such matters than I was when writing *Invisible Man,* but for such an allusion—say, to a certain type of chair or vase or painting—to function, the reader must not be allowed to limit his understanding of what is implied simply because the experience you are presenting is, in its immediate sense, that of blacks. So the writer must be aware that the reality of race conceals a complex of manners and culture. Because such matters influence the shaping of fictional form and govern, to a large extent, the writer's sense of proportion, and determine what he feels obligated to render as well as what he feels he can simply imply.

I had to learn, for instance, that in dramatic scenes, if you got the reader going along with your own rhythm, you could omit any number of explanations. You could leave great gaps, because in his sense of urgency the reader would say, "Hell, don't waste time telling me how many steps he walked to get there, I want to know what he *did* once he got there!" An ellipsis was possible and the reader would fill the gap.

Still, I have uncertainty about some of the things I'm doing, and especially when I'm using more than one main voice, and with a time scheme that is much more fragmented than in *Invisible Man.* There I was using a more tidy dramatic form. This novel is dramatic within its incidents, but it moves back and forth in time. In such a case I guess an act of faith is necessary, a faith that if what you are writing is of social and artistic importance and its diverse parts are presented vividly in the light of its over-all conception, and if you *render* the story rather than just tell it, then the reader will go along. That's a lot of "ifs", but if you can involve him in the process his reading becomes a pleasurable act of discovery.

HERSEY. Do you have in mind an image of some actualized reader to whom you are communicating as you write?

ELLISON. There is no *specific* person there, but there is a sort of ideal reader, or informed persona, who has some immediate sense of the material that I'm working with. Beyond that there is my sense of the rhetorical levers within American society, and these attach to all kinds of experiences and values. I don't want to be a behaviorist here, but I'm referring to the systems of values, the beliefs and customs and sense of the past, and that hope for the future, which have evolved through the history of the republic. These do provide a medium of communication.

For instance, the old underdog pattern. It turns up in many guises, and it allows the writer to communicate with the public over and beyond whatever the immediate issues of his fiction happen to be. That is, deep down we believe in the underdog, even though we give him hell; and this provides a rhetoric through which the writer can communicate with a reader beyond any questions of their disagreements over class values, race, or anything else. But the writer must be aware that that is what is there. On the other hand, I do not think he can manipulate his readers too directly; it must be an oblique process, if for no other reason than that to do it too directly throws you into propaganda, as against that brooding, questioning stance that is necessary for fiction.

HERSEY. How do literary influences make themselves felt concretely in your work? You have spoken often of Joyce, Eliot, Dostoevski, Hemingway, Stein, Malraux, and others as having influenced you early. How do the influences manifest themselves? How have you transformed them for your own ends?

ELLISON. It is best, of course, when they don't show themselves directly, but they are there in many ways. Joyce and Eliot, for instance, made me aware of the playful possibilities of language. You look at a page of *Finnegans Wake* and see references to all sorts of American popular music, yet the context gives it an extension from the popular back to the classical and beyond. This is just something that Joyce teaches you that you can do, and you can abstract the process and apply it to a frame of reference which is American and historical, and it can refer to class, it can refer to the fractions and frictions of color, to popular and folk culture—it can do many things.

On the other hand, a writer makes himself present in your work through allowing you to focus upon certain aspects of experience. Malraux's concern with the individual caught up consciously in a historical situation, a revolutionary situation, provided insights which allowed me to understand certain possibilities in the fictional material around me. From him I learned that the condition of that type of individual is essentially the same, regardless of his culture or the political climate in which he finds his existence.

Or again, some writers—say, Dostoevski, or even Tolstoy—will make you very much aware of what is possible in depicting a society in which class lines are either fluid or have broken down without the cultural style and values on either extreme of society being dissipated. From such writers you learn to explore the rich fictional possibilities to be achieved in juxtaposing the peasant's consciousness with that of the aristocrat and the aristocrat's with the peasant's. This insight is useful when you are dealing with American society. For years, white people went through Grand Central Station having their luggage carried by Ph.D.'s. They couldn't see the Ph.D.'s because their race and class attitudes had trained them to see only the uniforms and the dark faces, but the Ph.D.'s could see them and judged them on any number of levels. This makes for drama, and it is a drama which goes right to the core of the democratic faith. So you get your moral perception of the contradictions of American class and personality from such literature, even more, perhaps, than from psychiatry or sociology, because such novelists have always dealt with the drama of social living.

HERSEY. You once had some very interesting things to say about the similarities and differences of the stances of black and Jewish writers in this country. It seems clear that Russian novelists have had a special kind of access to the deeper resources we were talking about earlier, access to primary feelings. Do you think there are particular ways in which Negro writers have had a corresponding access to those deeper resources—different in kind or degree from that of the Jewish writer, or the white Protestant writer in America, say, or the Russian writer, or the English writer?

ELLISON. You will have to be very careful about that, because writers are individuals, each unique in his own way. But I would think that the access to primary feelings that the great Russian novelists had grew out of the nature of their society and the extreme disruption of hierarchal relationships which occurred during the nineteenth century. Then you had a great declassed aristocracy, with the Tsar still at the top, and an awakening peasantry at the bottom. On one hand, society was plunging headlong into chaos, and on the other there was a growing identification on the part of many declassed aristocrats with the peas-

antry, an identification across traditional hierarchal divisions
which was sustained by the unifying force of Russian Greek
Orthodox Christianity. The friction generated by these social
unities and divisions in that chaotic scene made possible all kinds
of intensities of emotion and aggravations of sensibility. The
belief in the Tsar as a sacred "Little Father" remained a unifying force, but was no longer strong enough to rationalize and impose order upon the expression of primary emotions—class
hate, greed, ambition, and so on. Such disruption of the traditional ordering of society, as in our own country since 1954, made
for an atmosphere of irrationality, and this created a situation
of unrestrained expressiveness. Eyeballs were peeled, nerves were
laid bare, and private sensibilities were subjected to public lacer-
ation. In fact, life became so theatrical (not to say nightmarish)
that even Dostoevski's smoking imagination was barely able to
keep a step ahead of what was actually happening in the garrets
and streets. Today, here in the United States, we have something
similiar, but there's no point in my trying to explain Russian
extremism, or the genius of the great nineteenth century Russian novelists. Not even Dostoevski was able to do that.

Anyway, for all its expressiveness and chaos, the Negro American situation is something else, both in degree and source. Except
for the brief period of Reconstruction, when we helped create
the new constitutions of the Southern states and attempted to
restructure society so as to provide a more equal set of relationships between the classes and races, we were *below* the threshold
of social hierarchy. Our social mobility was strictly, and violently,
limited—and in a way that neither our Christianity nor belief
in the principles of the Constitution could change. As the
sociologists say, we were indeed disadvantaged, both by law and
by custom. And yet, our actual position was ambiguous. For
although we were outside the social compact, we were existentially
right in the middle of the social drama. I mean that as servants
we were right in the bedroom, so to speak. Thus we saw things,
and we understood the difference between ideal assertions and
crude realities. Much of the rhetorical and political energy of
white society went toward proving to itself that we were not
human and that we had no sense of the refinement of human
values. But this in itself pressured you, motivated you, to make
even finer distinctions, both as to personality and value. You *had*
to, because your life depended upon it and your sense of your
own humanity demanded that you do so. You had to identify

those values which were human and preserving of your life and interests as against those which were inhuman and destructive. So we were thrown upon our own resources and sense of life. We were forced to define and act out our own idea of the heights and depths of the human condition. Because human beings cannot live in a situation where violence can be visited upon them without any concern for justice—and in many instances without possibility of redress—without developing a very intense sense of the precariousness of all human life, not to mention the frailty and arbitrariness of human institutions. So you were forced to be existential in your outlook, and this gives a poignancy and added value to little things and you discover the value of modes and attitudes that are rejected by the larger society. It also makes you terribly brutal and thick-skinned toward some values while ultra-sensitive to others.

Now this background provides the black writer with much to write about. As fictional material it rivals that of the nineteenth-century Russians. But to the extent that other American writers, writers of different backgrounds, understand this material, or can implicate it in their own experience, they too have a way into what is currently known as "the black experience"—which I prefer to call "the *Negro* American experience"—because for for it to be worthy of fictional treatment, worthy of art, it has to be meaningful to others who do not share in its immediacy. I'll add that since it is both my own and an irrevocable part of the basic experience of the United States, *I* think that it is not only worthy but indispensable to any profoundly *American* depiction of reality.

To repeat myself, this society has structured itself so as to be unaware of what it owes in both the positive and negative sense to the condition of inhumanity that it has imposed upon a great mass of its citizens. The fact that many whites refuse to recognize this is responsible for much of the anger erupting among young blacks today. It makes them furious when whites respond to their complaints with, "Yes, but *I* had nothing to do with any of that," or who reply to their demands for equal opportunity in a racially rigged society with, "We're against a quota system because *we* made it on our individual merits"—because this not only side-steps a pressing reality, but it is only partially true. Perhaps they *did* make it on their own, but if that's true the way was made easier because their parents did not have to contend with *my* parents, who were ruled out of the competition. They had their

troubles too, but the relative benevolence of democracy shared
by their parents, and now by them, was paid for by *somebody*
other than themselves, and was being paid long before many
of them arrived on these shores. *We* know that as the nation's
unwilling scapegoat we paid for much of it. Nor is this knowledge a matter of saying, "Pay us off," or saying, in the words of
the old joke, "Your granddaddy kicked my granddaddy a hundred
years ago, so now I've come to collect the debt, bend over."
That's not the point. The point is one of moral perception, the
perception of the wholeness of American life and the cost of
its successes and its failures. What makes for a great deal of black
fury is the refusal of many Americans to understand that somebody paid for the nation's peace and prosperity in terms of
blood and frustrated dreams; that somebody now denied his
proper share helped convert the raw materials into the sophisticated gadgetry. I don't mean to imply that only the blacks did
this; the poor southern whites, the Irish—and numbers of peoples
did. They, too, underwent the crudities and inequities of democracy so that the high rhetoric could retain some resonance of
possibility and truth.

HERSEY. How much is anger a motive force for novelists of all
kinds? Does the artist start with anger more than with other
emotions?

ELLISON. I don't think that he necessarily starts with anger. Indeed,
anger can get in the way, as it does for a fighter. If the writer
starts with anger, then if he is truly writing he immediately translates it through his craft into consciousness, and thus into understanding, into insight, perception. Perhaps, that's where the morality of fiction lies. You see a situation which outrages you, but
as you write about the characters who embody that which outrages, your sense of craft and the moral role of your craft demands that you depict those characters in the breadth of their
humanity. You try to give them the density of the human rather
than the narrow intensity of the demonic. That means that you
try to delineate them as men and women who possess feelings
and ideals, no matter how much you reject their feelings and
ideals. Anyway, I find this happening in my own work; it human-
izes *me*. So the main motive is not to express raw anger, but to
present—as sentimental as it might sound—the wonder of life,
in the fullness of which all these outrageous things occur.

HERSEY. Have you felt some defiance of death as a writer—in the
sense that what you are making may possibly circumvent death?

ELLISON. No, I dare not. (*He laughs*) No, you just write for your own time, while trying to write in terms of the density of experience, knowing perfectly well that life repeats itself. Even in this rapidly changing United States it repeats itself. The mystery is that while repeating itself it always manages slightly to change its mask. To be able to grasp a little of that change within continuity and to communicate it across all these divisions of background and individual experience seems enough for me. If you're lucky, of course, if you splice into one of the deeper currents of life, then you have a chance of your work lasting a little bit longer.

The Unity of Experience

by Robert Penn Warren

In the preface to *Shadow and Act*, Ellison says of his struggle
to become a writer:

> I found the greatest difficulty for a Negro writer was the problem
> of revealing what he truly felt, rather than serving up what Negroes
> were supposed to feel, and were encouraged to feel. And linked to
> this was the difficulty, based upon our long habit of deception and
> evasion, of depicting what really happened within our areas of
> American life, and putting down with honesty and without bowing
> to ideological expediencies the attitudes and values which give Negro
> American life its sense of wholeness and which renders it bearable
> and human and, when measured by our own terms, desirable.

In other words, the moral effort to see and recognize the truth
of the self and of the world, and the artistic effort to say the truth
are regarded as aspects of the same process. This interfusion of the
moral and the artistic is, for Ralph Ellison, a central fact and a
fact that involves far more than his literary views: for if "truth"
moves into "art," so "art" can move backward (and forward) into
"truth." Art can, in other words, move into life. Not merely, Ellison
would have it, by opening our eyes to life, not merely by giving us
models of action and response, but by, quite literally, creating us.
For him, the high function of technique is "the task of creating
value," and in this task we create the self. This process is a life-
process—a way of knowing and experiencing in which is growth:
a growth in integrity, literally a unifying of the self, of the random
or discrepant possibilities and temptations of experience.

Now, "ideological expediency" would have Ralph Ellison formu-
late his "difficulty" somewhat differently. It would prompt him to
slant things so that the special problems of the Negro writer would

"The Unity of Experience," by Robert Penn Warren. From *Commentary*, Vol.
XXXIX, No. 5 (May, 1965), pp. 91–96. Copyright © 1965 by Robert Penn Warren. Reprinted by permission of the author.

be read as one aspect of the Negro's victimization by the white man. A very good case—in one perspective, a perfect case—can be made out for that interpretation. But Ellison refuses that gambit of the alibi. In various ways, he repudiates the "Negro alibi" for the Negro writer. For instance, in the essay "The World and the Jug," he says: ". . . when the work of Negro writers has been rejected they have all too often protected their egos by blaming racial discrimination, while turning away from the fairly obvious fact that good art—and Negro musicians are present to demonstrate this— commands attention to itself. . . . And they forget that publishers will publish almost anything which is written with even a minimum of competency."

Ellison is, in other words, more concerned with the way a man confronts his individual doom than with the derivation of that doom; not pathos, but power, in its deepest inner sense, is what concerns him. He is willing, pridefully, to head into responsibility. But in the last sentence of the above quotation from the preface to *Shadow and Act,* Ellison flouts even more violently "ideological expediencies" which dictate that the Negro advertise the blankness, bleakness, and misery of his life. Instead, Ellison refers to its "wholeness," its desirability, and elsewhere in the same preface he refers to "the areas of life and personality which claimed my mind beyond any limitations *apparently* imposed by my racial identity."

This attitude, which permeates Ellison's work, comes to focus in two essays which are probably destined to become a classic statement; they were written as a reply to Irving Howe's essay "Black Boys and Native Sons." [1] Howe's piece takes Richard Wright's work to be the fundamental expression of the Negro genius. The day *Native Son* appeared, he says, "American culture was changed forever. . . . A blow at the white man, the novel forced him to recognize himself as an oppressor. A blow at the black man, the novel forced him to recognize the cost of his submission." Though Howe admires the performance of both Baldwin and Ellison, he sees them as having rejected the naturalism and straight protest of Wright, as traitors to the cause of "clenched militancy"; and then, to quote Ellison, Howe, "appearing suddenly in black face," demands: "What, then, was the experience of a man with a black skin, what *could* it be here in this country? How could a Negro put pen to paper, how could he so much as think or breathe, without some

---

[1] The two appeared orginally in *The New Leader* (December 9, 1963, February 3, 1964), and now in Ellison's collection of essays are fused under the title "The World and the Jug." Howe's essay had appeared in *Dissent,* Fall 1963.

impulsion to protest . . . ?" And he goes on to say that the Negro's very existence "forms a constant pressure on his literary work . . . with a pain and ferocity that nothing could remove." [2]

This, to Ellison, is the "ideological proposition that what whites think of the Negro's reality is more important than what Negroes themselves know it to be"; and this, to Ellison, is Howe's "white liberal version of the white southern myth of absolute separation of the races." That is, the critic picks out the Negro's place (i.e. his feelings and his appropriate function) and then puts him in it. "I fear the implications of Howe's ideas concerning the Negro writer's role as actionist more than I do the state of Mississippi," Ellison writes. Howe's view is another example of a situation that "is not unusual for a Negro to experience," as Ellison says in a review of Myrdal's *An American Dilemma,* "a sensation that he does not exist in the real world at all—only in the nightmarish fantasy of the white American mind." That is a violation of "the basic unity of human experience," undertaken in the "interest of specious political and philosophical conceits":

> Prefabricated Negroes are sketched on sheets of paper and superimposed upon the Negro community; then when someone thrusts his head through the page and yells, "Watch out here, Jack, there's people living under here," they are shocked and indignant.

We must not fall into the same error and take his attack on the white liberal's picture of the Negro to be Ellison's concealed version of the common notion that no white man can "know" a Negro. By his theory of the "basic unity of human experience," which we shall come to presently, and by his theory of the moral force of the imagination, such a view—except in the provisional, limited way that common sense dictates—would be untenable. What Ellison would reject is the violation of the density of life by an easy abstract formulation. Even militancy, if taken merely as a formula, can violate the density of life. For instance, in "The World and the Jug," he says: ". . . what an easy con game for ambitious, publicity-hungry Negroes this stance of 'militancy' has become." He is as ready to attack a Negro on this point as a white man. In a review of LeRoi Jones's study of Negro music, *Blues People,* he says that Jones "attempts to impose an ideology upon this cultural complexity" and that even when a Negro treats this subject "the critical

---

[2] This is, of course, a totally abrupt and therefore necessarily distorted summary of Howe's essay, but the present concern is with the significance of Ellison's response taken in itself.

intelligence must perform the difficult task which only it can perform."

The basic unity of human experience—that is what Ellison asserts; and he sets the richness of his own experience and that of many Negroes he has known, and his own early capacity to absorb the general values of Western culture, over against what Wright called "the essential bleakness of black life in America." What he is saying here is not that "bleakness" does not exist, and exist for many, but that it has not been the key fact of his own experience, and that his own experience is part of the story. It must be reckoned with, too:

> For even as his life toughens the Negro, even as it brutalizes him, sensitizes him, dulls him, goads him to anger, moves him to irony, sometimes fracturing and sometimes affirming his hopes . . . it *conditions* him to deal with his life and with himself. Because it is *his* life, and no mere abstraction in somebody's head.

Not only the basic unity, but the rich variety, of life is what concerns him; and this fact is connected with his personal vision of the opportunity in being an American: "The diversity of American life is often painful, frequently burdensome and always a source of conflict, but in it lies our fate and our hope." In many places, Ellison insists on his love of diversity and a pluralistic society. For instance, in "That Same Pain, That Same Pleasure": "I believe in diversity, and I think that the real death of the United States will come when everyone is just alike." The appreciation of this variety is, in itself, a school for the imagination and moral sympathy. And, for Ellison, being a "Negro American" has to do with this appreciation, not only of the Negro past in America, but with the complex fluidity of the present:

> It has to do with a special perspective on the national ideals and the national conduct, and with a tragicomic attitude toward the universe. It has to do with special emotions evoked by the details of cities and countrysides, with forms of labor and with forms of pleasure; with sex and with love, with food and with drink, with machines and with animals; with climates and with dwellings, with places of worship and places of entertainment; with garments and dreams and idioms of speech; with manners and customs, with religion and art, with life styles and hoping, and with that special sense of predicament and fate which gives direction and resonance to the Freedom Movement. It involves a rugged initiation into the mysteries and rites of color which makes it possible for Negro Americans to suffer the injustice which race and color are used to excuse

without losing sight of either the humanity of those who inflict that injustice or the motives, rational or irrational, out of which they act. It imposes the uneasy burden and occasional joy of a complex double vision, a fluid, ambivalent response to men and events which represents, at its finest, a profoundly civilized adjustment to the cost of being human in this modern world.

Out of this view of the life of the "Negro American"—which is a view of *life*—it is no wonder that Ellison does not accept a distinction between the novel as "protest" and the novel as "art"—or rather, sees this distinction as a merely superficial one, not to be trusted. His own approach is twofold. On the one hand, he says "protest is an element of all art," but he would not limit protest to the social or political objection. In one sense, it might be a "technical assault" on earlier styles—but we know that Ellison regards "techniques" as moral vision, and a way of creating the self. In another sense, the protest may be, as in *Oedipus Rex* or *The Trial*, "against the limitation of human life itself." In yet another sense, it may be—and I take it that Ellison assumes that it always is—a protest against some aspect of a personal fate:

> . . . that intensity of personal anguish which compels the artist to seek relief by projecting it into the world in conjunction with other things; that anguish might take the form of an acute sense of inferiority for one [person], homosexuality for another, an overwhelming sense of the absurdity of human life for still another . . . the experience that might be caused by humiliation, by a harelip, by a stutter, by epilepsy—indeed, by any and everything in life which plunges the talented individual into solitude while leaving him the will to transcend his condition through art.

And the last words of this preceding quotation bring us to the second idea in his twofold approach to the distinction between the novel as protest and the novel as art: the ideal of the novel is a transmutation of protest into art. In speaking of Howe's evaluation of his own novel, Ellison says:

> If *Invisible Man* is even "apparently" free from "the ideological and emotional penalties suffered by Negroes in this country," it is because I tried to the best of my ability to transform these elements into art. My goal was not to escape, or hold back, but to work through; to transcend, as the blues transcend the painful conditions with which they deal.

And he relates this impulse toward transcendence into art to a stoical American Negro tradition which teaches one to master and contain pain; "which abhors as obscene any trading on one's own anguish for gain or sympathy"; which deals with the harshness of existence" as men at their best have always done." And he summarizes the relevance of this tradition: "It takes fortitude to be a man and no less to be an artist."

In other words, to be an artist partakes, in its special way, of the moral force of being a man. And with this we come again, in a new perspective, to Ellison's view of the "basic unity of experience." If there is anguish, there is also the possibility of the transmutation of anguish, "the occasional joy of a complex double vision."

For in this "double vision" the "basic unity" can be received, and life can be celebrated. "I believe," he says to Howe, "that true novels, even when most pessimistic and bitter, arise out of an impulse to celebrate human life, and therefore are ritualistic and ceremonial at their core." The celebration of life—that is what Ellison sees as the final nature of his fiction, or of any art. And in this "double vision" and the celebration which it permits—no, entails—we find, even, the reconciliation possible in recognizing "the humanity of those who inflict injustice." And with this Ellison has arrived, I take it, at his own secular version of Martin Luther King's conception of *agapé*.

If, in pursuing this line of thought about Ralph Ellison, I have made him seem unaware of the plight of the Negro American in the past or the present, I have done him a grave wrong. He is fully aware of the blankness of the fate of many Negroes, and the last thing to be found in him is any trace of that cruel complacency of some who have, they think, mastered fate. If he emphasizes the values of challenge in the plight of the Negro, he would not use this to justify that plight; and if he applauds the disciplines induced by that plight, he does so in no spirit of self-congratulation, but in a spirit of pride in being numbered with those people.

No one has made more unrelenting statements of the dehumanizing pressures that have been put upon the Negro. And *Invisible Man* is, I should say, the most powerful artistic representation we have of the Negro under these dehumanizing conditions; and, at the same time, a statement of the human triumph over those conditions.

Man Underground

by Saul Bellow

A few years ago, in an otherwise dreary and better forgotten number of *Horizon* devoted to a louse-up of life in the United States, I read with great excitement an episode from *Invisible Man*. It described a free-for-all of blindfolded Negro boys at a stag party of the leading citizens of a small Southern town. Before being blind-folded the boys are made to stare at a naked white woman; then they are herded into the ring, and, after the battle royal, one of the fighters, his mouth full of blood, is called upon to give his high school valedictorian's address. As he stands under the lights of the noisy room, the citizens rib him and make him repeat him-self; an accidental reference to equality nearly ruins him, but everything ends well and he receives a handsome briefcase contain-ing a scholarship to a Negro college.

This episode, I thought, might well be the high point of an excellent novel. It has turned out to be not *the* high point but rather one of the many peaks of a book of the very first order, a superb book. The valedictorian is himself Invisible Man. He adores the college but is thrown out before long by its president, Dr. Bledsoe, a great educator and leader of his race, for permitting a white visitor to visit the wrong places in the vicinity. Bearing what he believes to be a letter of recommendation from Dr. Bledsoe he comes to New York. The letter actually warns prospective em-ployers against him. He is recruited by white radicals and becomes a Negro leader, and in the radical movement he learns eventually that throughout his entire life his relations with other men have been schematic; neither with Negroes nor with whites has he ever been visible, real. I think that in reading the *Horizon* excerpt I may have underestimated Mr. Ellison's ambition and power for the following very good reason, that one is accustomed to expect ex-

"Man Underground," by Saul Bellow. From *Commentary*, Vol. XIII, No. 6 (June, 1952), pp. 608–610. Copyright © 1952 by the American Jewish Committee. Reprinted by permission of the author and publisher.

cellent novels about boys, but a modern novel about men is exceedingly rare. For this enormously complex and difficult American experience of ours very few people are willing to make themselves morally and intellectually responsible. Consequently, maturity is hard to find.

It is commonly felt that there is no strength to match the strength of those powers which attack and cripple modern mankind. And this feeling is, for the reader of modern fiction, all too often confirmed when he approaches a new book. He is prepared, skeptically, to find what he has found before, namely, that family and class, university, fashion, the giants of publicity and manufacture, have had a larger share in the creation of someone called a writer than truth or imagination—that Bendix and Studebaker and the nylon division of Du Pont, and the University of Chicago, or Columbia or Harvard or Kenyon College, have once more proved mightier than the single soul of an individual; to find that one more lightly manned position has been taken. But what a great thing it is when a brilliant individual victory occurs, like Mr. Ellison's, proving that a truly heroic quality can exist among our contemporaries. People too thoroughly determined—and our institutions by their size and force too thoroughly determine—can't approach this quality. That can only be done by those who resist the heavy influences and make their own synthesis out of the vast mass of phenomena, the seething, swarming body of appearances, facts, and details. From this harassment and threatened dissolution by details, a writer tries to rescue what is important. Even when he is most bitter, he makes by his tone a declaration of values and he says, in effect: "There is something nevertheless that a man may hope to be." This tone, in the best pages of *Invisible Man,* those pages, for instance, in which an incestuous Negro farmer tells his tale to a white New England philanthropist, comes through very powerfully; it is tragicomic, poetic, the tone of the very strongest sort of creative intelligence.

In a time of specialized intelligences, modern imaginative writers make the effort to maintain themselves as *un*specialists, and their quest is for a true middle-of-consciousness for everyone. What language is it that we can all speak, and what is it that we can all recognize, burn at, weep over; what is the stature we can without exaggeration claim for ourselves; what is the main address of consciousness?

I was keenly aware, as I read this book, of a very significant kind of independence in the writing. For there is a "way" for Negro novelists to go at their problems, just as there are Jewish or Italian "ways." Mr. Ellison has not adopted a minority tone. If he had done so, he would have failed to establish a true middle-of-consciousness for everyone.

Negro Harlem is at once primitive and sophisticated; it exhibits the extremes of instinct and civilization as few other American communities do. If a writer dwells on the peculiarity of this, he ends with an exotic effect. And Mr. Ellison is not exotic. For him this balance of instinct and culture or civilization is not a Harlem matter; it is *the* matter, German, French, Russian, American, universal, a matter very little understood. It is thought that Negroes and other minority people, kept under in the great status battle, are in the instinct cellar of dark enjoyment. This imagined enjoyment provokes envious rage and murder; and then it is a large portion of human nature itself which becomes the fugitive murderously pursued. In our society Man—Himself—is idolized and publicly worshipped, but the single individual must hide himself underground and try to save his desires, his thoughts, his soul, in invisibility. He must return to himself, learning self-acceptance and rejecting all that threatens to deprive him of his manhood.

This is what I make of *Invisible Man*. It is not by any means faultless; I don't think the hero's experiences in the Communist party are as original in conception as other parts of the book, and his love affair with a white woman is all too brief, but it is an immensely moving novel and it has greatness.

So many hands have been busy at the interment of the novel— the hand of Paul Valéry, the hands of the editors of literary magazines, of scholars who decide when genres come and go, the hands of innumerable pipsqueaks as well—that I can't help feeling elated when a resurrection occurs. People read history and then seem to feel that everything has to conclude in their own time. "We have read history, and therefore history is over," they appear to say. Really, all that such critics have the right to say is that fine novels are few and far between. That's perfectly true. But then fine anything are few and far between. If these critics wanted to be extremely truthful, they'd say they were bored. Boredom, of course, like any mighty force, you must respect. There is something terribly impressive about the boredom of a man like Valéry who could no longer bear to read that the carriage had come for the duchess at four in the afternoon. And certainly there are some notably boring things to which we owe admiration of a sort.

Not all the gravediggers of the novel have such distinction as Valéry's, however. Hardly. And it's difficult to think of them as rising dazzled from a volume of Stendhal, exclaiming "God!" and then with angry determination seizing their shovels to go and heap more clods on the coffin. No, theirs unfortunately isn't often the disappointment of spirits formed under the influence of the masters. They make you wonder how, indeed, they *would* be satisfied. A recent contributor to *Partisan Review,* for instance, complains that modern fiction does not keep pace with his swift-wheeling modern consciousness which apparently leaves the photon far behind in its speed. He names a few *really* modern writers of fiction, their work unfortunately still unpublished, and makes a patronizing reference to *Invisible Man:* almost, but not quite, the real thing, it is "raw" and "overambitious." And the editors of *Partisan Review* who have published so much of this modern fiction that their contributor attacks, what do they think of this? They do not say what they think; neither of this piece nor of another lulu on the same subject and in the same issue by John Aldridge. Mr. Aldridge writes: "There are only two cultural pockets left in America, and they are the Deep South and that area of northeastern United States whose moral capital is Boston, Massachusetts. This is to say that these are the only places where there are any manners. In all other parts of the country people live in a kind of vastly standardized cultural prairie, a sort of infinite Middle West, and that means that they don't really live and they don't really do anything."

Most Americans thus are Invisible. Can we wonder at the cruelty of dictators when even a literary critic, without turning a hair, announces the death of a hundred million people?

Let us suppose that the novel is, as they say, played out. Let us only suppose it, for I don't believe it. But what if it is so? Will such tasks as Mr. Ellison has set himself no more be performed? Nonsense. New means, when new means are necessary, will be found. To find them is easier than to suit the disappointed consciousness and to penetrate the thick walls of boredom within which life lies dying.

Signifying Everything

by Lawrence Washington Chisolm

Ralph Ellison loves language with an intellectuality which sets extraordinarily high goals for his fiction. Other poets have mused on words with a playfulness as serious as Ellison's. Other novelists have created social worlds with more scenery and with actors we know more about. And occasionally writers have tried to convey some sense of what it is like to live amid swiftly changing conditions, but it is much more difficult to locate a life in the fluid Somewhere which is change than in the more stable though falsified Nowhere which placates readers everywhere. For a novelist concerned with change the problem is to create human identities implicated as fully in the chaos of emerging conditions as they are defined by more familiar patterns of order carried out of the past. Ellison's distinction is that he names the problem and faces it without evading the difficulties. He accepts as the writer's task nothing less than the creation of forms which can render the process of change intelligible and significant. *Invisible Man* is such a form; divided vision the crucial perspective it nourishes—divided in the sense of made aware that only ambiguous vision is clear enough to rely on. The essays of *Shadow and Act* remind us that the word magic which animates *Invisible Man* proceeds from a systematic conjurer who puts words under the pressure of experience and raises the pressure until the words become unstable, until they actually move, their transits shaping meanings for change itself. Ellison's battle against confusion is a battle for clear naming, for names which suit reality precisely because they are ambiguous. Ellison at his best puts so much reverse English on words like "yes," "light," "up," "fate" that their transits of meaning in *Invisible Man* spin out actual shapes of change. Bliss Proteus Rinehart, that "Amer-

"Signifying Everything," by Lawrence Washington Chisolm. From *The Yale Review*, Vol. LIV, No. 3 Spring, 1965). pp. 450–454. Copyright © 1965 by *The Yale Review*. Reprinted by permission of the author and publisher.

ican virtuoso of identity who thrives on chaos and swift change," is so confident a con man because he is closer to reality than everyman; his many shapes must be recognized before he can be signified. The clues which Ellison's essays offer about the shapes of his own struggles as a writer in America deserve close attention.

The significance of the essays gathered in *Shadow and Act* is autobiographical, or so Ellison asserts. Yet they say little about his life in any conventional biographical sense. On the face of it they are occasional pieces (the earliest published in 1942 and the most recent [in 1964]) which divide reasonably under three headings: literature (mostly American); jazz and blues; and social commentary (mostly on "the Negro American subculture"). The essays are autobiographical in a special sense: they both demonstrate and assert that man's conversion of experience into symbolic action *is* life and that the artist's role in creating a language for this conversion is fundamental, especially in a society undergoing rapid change.

Ellison continually emphasizes the freedom of perception rather than the limits of circumstance. In describing his family he introduces more ancestors than relatives, a playful distinction which serves his philosophical thesis. Ancestors, particularly spiritual ancestors, can be chosen, whereas relatives are simply given. Ancestors project ideal possibilities; relatives are Fate. In this sense ancestors can be conjured from anywhere and everywhere whereas relatives present limits which must be acknowledged. (Henry Adams' *Education* proves the rule.) When Ellison names ancestors and relatives he is making several points, and all at once, as usual. Melville and T. S. Eliot are his ancestors as are Pound, Joyce, and Hemingway, Homer, Leonardo, and Henry James (William James belongs there, somewhere), as well as André Malraux and Kenneth Burke. Richard Wright is part ancestor but mostly relative—a distinction that Ellison insists that critics should make. Wright is an ancestor because he reverses Negro withdrawal underground and presents an unavoidable face; Wright is a relative because Bigger Thomas is not big enough, because Wright's characters are prisoners and in the end his writing has added to social confusion by ignoring changes.

Curiously, Wright is the only "relative" that stays in mind. Ellison was three when his father died; the paternal legacy is a poet's name, Ralph Waldo, transcending all disguise. Ellison's mother is present but in the shadows, a nurturing figure recalled as idealistic—a socialist before Irving Howe had ever heard of Marx. In general, the landscape of memory is unusually free from relatives.

Ellison remembers his childhood in Oklahoma in the twenties as free and dreamy. His heroes were everybody's heroes, his models the usual outrageous variety of movie stars and stuntmen, gamblers and scientists, soldiers, knights, and jazzmen, their essential powers and skills assembled in imaginary identities—merging for Ellison in the figure of a "Renaissance Man." He reminds us, gently, that children's imaginations are unaware of incongruities, irreverent even toward caste. When social analysts deny this possibility in their deterministic theories, they add to social confusion. As a case in point, commenting on the Negro student sit-ins, Ellison asks, "How do you account for the strength of those kids?" Certainly there was no answer at the time in the extensive sociopsychological writings on "Negro personality."

Speculations about the roots of this special integrity might well begin by considering the role of jazzmen as models for finding sustenance in chaos. Jazz was clearly crucial in the development of Ellison's own sense of free life. Jazz virtuosos showed young Ellison how the discipline of music opened a world for expressive play. Part of the beauty grew from tension between the limits of traditional musical forms and techniques and the limitless goal of humanizing sound as the voice does. And this artistic tension had a social counterpart in the complex ironies of the jazzmen's relations to Negro and white respectabilities and evasions. Ellison's extended musical apprenticeship to writing gives weight to his flat judgment that "Negro musicians have never, as a group, felt alienated from any music sounded within their hearing."

In fact, nowhere do Ellison's reflections suggest alienation. He stresses the special advantages of growing up as a frontiersman in the social chaos of Oklahoma City amid a strange mixture of attitudes, naïve and sophisticated, benign and malignant, affording a "wide and unstructured latitude" to imagination. "Isn't one of the implicit functions of the American frontier," asks Ellison, "to encourage the individual to a kind of dreamy wakefulness, a state in which he makes—in all ignorance of the accepted limitations of the possible—rash efforts, quixotic gestures, hopeful testings of the complexity of the known and the given?" Yes, agreed, and the real frontier is the edge of perspective, we add, only to find that Ellison has been making that point all along. "The American novel," he declares at the close of an interview, is "a conquest of the frontier; as it describes experience it creates it." The Negro frontiersman of

Oklahoma jazz, by reverse English, has turned Turner's frontier into an American ambiguity—no dilemma, just ambiguity.

Like Walt Whitman and William James, Ralph Ellison is in love with possibilities. The central excitement of his essays is their enactment of a progressive discovery that words can set men free. Ellison's accounts of this discovery pivot around the idea of discipline, a discipline of double vision which reveals reality and connects man to it at the same time detaching him from it and enabling him to act freely, that is, to create. Because this disciplined doubleness works so magnificently in *Invisible Man* the elaboration of Ellison's views in *Shadow and Act* deserves analysis, even at the risk of being too schematic.

Discipline, for Ellison, is a form of action within certain perspectives. Discipline is, first of all, theatrical action. Ellison quotes Yeats: "If we cannot imagine ourselves as different from what we are and assume the second self, we cannot impose a discipline upon ourselves, though we may accept one from others. Active virtue, as distinct from the passive acceptance of a current code, is the wearing of a mask. It is the condition of an arduous full life." Or again, Ellison: "Let us make up our faces and our minds." Masks must be chosen; and they must work. Secondly, discipline as action is social in the sense of trained self-control; the roles played with notable control by many American Negroes represent a discipline undergone by all human beings in varying degrees as they join society. Thirdly, discipline is artistic action, a willed playfulness which explores chaos, creating relationships among shifting identities and ordering the relations of various identities-in-process with one another and with various sets of social circumstances.

The disciplines of theatrical, social, and artistic action operate, ideally, within perspectives conscious of ironies but never on that account incapacitating the actor, since Ellison's disciplined doubleness affirms life. Personal growth *is* discipline developing. Society, in this perspective, is duplicitous but undisciplined, hence confused —inevitably, to some degree, since conceptions lag behind the flow of events. Art, in battling individual and social confusions, seeks to reform conceptions by creating forms fit to show the way home. And home, finally, is America for Ellison. As it is for Everyman because Ellison's America is pluralist and protean, a delicately poised unity of divergencies—a paradigm of world development.

This seems to me to be Ellison's position in bald summary. Within this framework the "problem of the Negro writer in America" becomes simply one instance of the problem faced by every writer when he has to make sense out of his own experiences in various subcultures. The question remains as to whether Negro American subcultures provide settings conducive to the development of well-articulated identities. By minimizing obstacles and limits Ellison's essays leave the impression that free will is axiomatic, that "discipline" is not only a personal opportunity but a sufficient condition for civility in general. We might all be free if we would. From this position the most important question to be asked about any individual's situation is "How does he cope with it?" The importance ascribed to identity problems tends to equalize all circumstances. What really counts is the quality of perspective. "Men determine their own social weather," says Ellison, "and human fate is a creation of human confusion."

Confusion is dangerous, certainly, and anyone knowing even roughly where and when he has been and is, is someone who must cry out against confusion. Clarity is, at the least, a salvation for intellectuals: experience becomes more acceptable when patterned. And clarity probably serves all men well, although the real thing is so rare that its social consequences are conjectural. But when a man has developed Ellison's rare kind of insight, he rouses hopes that he will outline a moral anatomy of social confusion, estimating which illusions held where are how dangerous, locating our various plights precisely. This is what I miss in *Shadow and Act*.

Nor does Ellison tell us about his own caves of chaos and the particular dragons he slew in finding the treasures of possibility. Well, why should he? To borrow one of his epigraphs: "That which we do is what we are. That which we remember is, more often than not, that which we would like to have been; or that which we hope to be. Thus our memory and our identity are ever at odds; our history ever a tall tale told by inattentive idealists."

Black Boys and Native Sons

by Irving Howe

. . . What astonishes one most about *Invisible Man* is the apparent freedom it displays from the ideological and emotional penalties suffered by Negroes in this country—I say "apparent" because the freedom is not quite so complete as the book's admirers like to suppose. Still, for long stretches *Invisible Man* does escape the formulas of protest, local color, genre quaintness and jazz chatter. No white man could have written it, since no white man could know with such intimacy the life of the Negroes from the inside; yet Ellison writes with an ease and humor which are now and again simply miraculous.

Invisible Man is a record of a Negro's journey through contemporary America, from South to North, province to city, naïve faith to disenchantment and perhaps beyond. There are clear allegorical intentions (Ellison is "literary" to a fault) but with a book so rich in talk and drama it would be a shame to neglect the fascinating surface for the mere depths. The beginning is both nightmare and farce. A timid Negro boy comes to a white smoker in a Southern town: he is to be awarded a scholarship. Together with several other Negro boys he is rushed to the front of the ballroom, where a sumptuous blonde tantalizes and frightens them by dancing in the nude. Blindfolded, the Negro boys stage a "battle royal," a free-for-all in which they pummel each other to the drunken shouts of the whites. Practical jokes, humiliations, terror—and then the boy delivers a prepared speech of gratitude to his white benefactors. At the end of this section, the boy dreams that he has opened the briefcase given him together with his scholarship to a Negro college and that he finds an inscription reading: "To Whom It May Concern: Keep This Nigger-Boy Running."

From "Black Boys and Native Sons" in *A World More Attractive*, by Irving Howe (New York: Horizon Press, 1963), pp. 98–122. Copyright © 1963 by Irving Howe. Reprinted by permission of the author and the publisher.

Most of the original essay concerned the influence of Richard Wright on the work of James Baldwin.

He keeps running. He goes to his college and is expelled for having innocently taken a white donor through a Negro ginmill which also happens to be a brothel. His whole experience is to follow this pattern. Strip down a pretense, whether by choice or accident, and you will suffer penalties, since the rickety structure of Negro respectability rests upon pretense and those who profit from it cannot bear to have the reality exposed (in this case, that the college is dependent upon the Northern white millionaire). The boy then leaves for New York, where he works in a white-paint factory, becomes a soapboxer for the Harlem Communists, the darling of the fellow-travelling bohemia, and a big wheel in the Negro world. At the end, after witnessing a frenzied race riot in Harlem, he "finds himself" in some not entirely specified way, and his odyssey from submission to autonomy is complete.

Ellison has an abundance of that primary talent without which neither craft nor intelligence can save a novelist: he is richly, wildly inventive; his scenes rise and dip with tension, his people bleed, his language sings. No other writer has captured so much of the hidden gloom and surface gaiety of Negro life.

There is an abundance of superbly rendered speech: a West Indian woman inciting her men to resist an eviction, a Southern sharecropper calmly describing how he seduced his daughter, a Harlem street-vender spinning jive. The rhythm of Ellison's prose is harsh and nervous, like a beat of harried alertness. The observation is expert: he knows exactly how zootsuiters walk, making stylization their principle of life, and exactly how the antagonism between American and West Indian Negroes works itself out in speech and humor. He can accept his people as they are, in their blindness and hope:—here, finally, the Negro world does exist, seemingly apart from plight or protest. And in the final scene Ellison has created an unforgettable image: "Ras the Destroyer," a Negro nationalist, appears on a horse dressed in the costume of an Abyssinian chieftain, carrying spear and shield, and charging wildly into the police—a black Quixote, mad, absurd, unbearably pathetic.

But even Ellison cannot help being caught up with *the idea* of the Negro. To write simply about "Negro experience," with the esthetic distance urged by the critics of the fifties, is a moral and psychological impossibility, for plight and protest are inseparable from that experience, and even if less political than Wright and less prophetic than Baldwin, Ellison knows this quite as well as they do.

If *Native Son* is marred by the ideological delusions of the thirties, *Invisible Man* is marred, less grossly, by those of the fifties. The middle section of Ellison's novel, dealing with the Harlem Communists, does not ring quite true, in the way a good portion of the writings on this theme during the postwar years does not ring quite true. Ellison makes his Stalinist figures so vicious and stupid that one cannot understand how they could ever have attracted him or any other Negro. That the party leadership manipulated members with deliberate cynicism is beyond doubt, but this cynicism was surely more complex and guarded than Ellison shows it to be. No party leader would ever tell a prominent Negro Communist, as one of them does in *Invisible Man*: "You were not hired [as a functionary] to think"—even if that were what he felt. Such passages are almost as damaging as the propagandist outbursts in *Native Son*.

Still more troublesome, both as it breaks the coherence of the novel and reveals Ellison's dependence on the postwar *Zeitgeist*, is the sudden, unprepared and implausible assertion of unconditioned freedom with which the novel ends. As the hero abandons the Communist Party he wonders, "Could politics ever be an expression of love?" This question, more portentous than profound, cannot easily be reconciled to a character who has been presented mainly as a passive victim of his experience. Nor is one easily persuaded by the hero's discovery that "my world has become one of infinite possibilities," his refusal to be the "invisible man" whose body is manipulated by various social groups. Though the unqualified assertion of self-liberation was a favorite strategy among American literary people in the fifties, it is also vapid and insubstantial. It violates the reality of social life, the interplay between external conditions and personal will, quite as much as the determinism of the thirties. The unfortunate fact remains that to define one's individuality is to stumble upon social barriers which stand in the way, all too much in the way, of "infinite possibilities." Freedom can be fought for, but it cannot always be willed or asserted into existence. And it seems hardly an accident that even as Ellison's hero asserts the "infinite possibilities" he makes no attempt to specify them. . . .

Ralph Ellison in Our Time

by Stanley Edgar Hyman

Ellison's vision is informed by three great truths: a proposition and its two corollaries. They are all so unfashionable at present, in this country at least, that Ellison constitutes a unique voice. . . .

The proposition is that freedom is the recognition of necessity. In this phrasing, by Engels out of Spinoza, it sounds alien and ideological; but in other language it was early discovered by Ellison in the experience of American Negro life, and was confirmed by his later reading of writers as diverse as Emerson and Malraux. In the introduction to *Shadow and Act,* Ellison writes of the jazz musicians he grew up with in Oklahoma City as "artists who had stumbled upon the freedom lying within the restrictions of their musical tradition as within the limitations of their social background." "Wright was able to free himself in Mississippi," Ellison points out, in a debate with Irving Howe . . . , "because he had the imagination and the will to do so."

In art, the necessity that must be recognized to bring freedom is craft, technique. Ellison identifies art as "an instrument of freedom," and defines "the writer's greatest freedom" as "his possession of technique." He writes of the paradoxical necessity that the jazz musician learn "the fundamentals of his instrument and the traditional techniques of jazz," in order "to express his own unique ideas and his own unique voice." Technique, Ellison informs LeRoi Jones, is "the key to creative freedom."

A recognition of necessity similarly brings freedom in life. "Negro American life," Ellison writes in his introduction, is "bearable and human and, when measured by our own terms, desirable." Sometimes he defines this consciousness as a tragic vision. Ellison told Richard G. Stern in an interview in 1961 that American Negroes share "certain tragic attitudes toward experience and to-

"Ralph Ellison in Our Time," by Stanley Edgar Hyman. From *The New Leader,* Vol. XLVII, No. 22 (October 26, 1964), pp. 21–22. Copyright © 1964 by *The New Leader.* Reprinted by permission of the publisher.

ward our situation as Americans." At other times the recognition
seems closer to stoicism. "But there is also an American Negro tradition," Ellison reminds Howe, "which teaches one to deflect racial
provocation and to master and contain pain. It is a tradition which
abhors as obscene any trading on one's own anguish for gain or
sympathy; which springs not from a desire to deny the harshness
of existence but from a will to deal with it as men at their best
have always done."

Most characteristically, Ellison describes this consciousness as
neither tragic nor stoic, but as "a tragicomic confrontation of life."
He sees this as best exemplified by the blues. "Being initiates,"
Ellison writes, "Negroes express the joke of it in the blues." The
blues, he adds elsewhere, "are, perhaps, as close as Americans can
come to expressing the spirit of tragedy." In another essay Ellison
talks of "the secular existentialism of the blues." "They are the
only consistent art in the United States," he writes, "which constantly remind us of our limitations while encouraging us to see
how far we can actually go."

Ellison makes clear that the freedom he talks of is not an escape
into the imagination, a flight *from* life, but a freedom *in* life. "The
work of art," he writes, "is a social action in itself." It leads to
further social action in the real world by broadening the scope of
possibility for its readers. The aim of *Invisible Man* was "to explore the full range of American Negro humanity"; if it succeeds
even partially in that great aim, no reader, Negro or white, remains
unaltered by the book. If American life contains "the very essence
of the terrible," a Negro writer can assist the process of transforming it by "defining Negro humanity." This is, of course, Kenneth
Burke's dramatistic concept of symbolic action, in which art is a
naming that transforms attitudes, and attitudes in turn eventuate
in actions.

The first corollary that follows from the proposition that freedom
is the recognition of necessity is that consequently the writer's
responsibility is to write. "The real question," Ellison observes in
answering Howe, is: "How does the Negro writer participate *as a
writer* in the struggle for human freedom?" In response to Howe's
statement that "there may of course be times when one's obligation as a human being supersedes one's obligation as a writer,"
Ellison replies: "I think that the writer's obligation . . . is best
carried out through his role as writer."

I first discovered this truth for myself in the career of Henry
Thoreau, and I argued the same unpopular view in "Henry

Thoreau in Our Time" in 1946 (the essay is reprinted in *The Promised End* [1]). Now I am delighted to see that Ellison not only supports Thoreau but often sounds like him. "It is not necessary for even the most unimaginative of us to be consumed by flame in order to envision hellfire," Ellison writes in connection with Stephen Crane, "the hot head of a match against the fingernail suffices." "I could escape the reduction imposed by unjust laws and customs," Ellison tells Howe sternly, "but not that imposed by ideas which defined me as no more than the *sum* of those laws and customs." (The only change Thoreau would have made in that sentence would have been to italicize the "me".)

It is unfortunate that all this had to be stated in controversy with so limited an opponent as Howe (who is not really interested in literature, and has no dimmest understanding of symbolic action), since this resulted in defining the issues far too narrowly. By the nature of Howe's charges Ellison was forced to emphasize his esthetic differences with Wright, rather than his esthetic indebtedness to Wright; he was forced to talk about activism in the Freedom Movement, rather than the fact that art and the imagination *inspired* the Freedom Movement.

The second corollary that follows from Ellison's proposition is that fraternity in the world of the imagination is the necessary preparation for fraternity in society. "I learned very early," Ellison told Stern in the interview reprinted in *Shadow and Act*, "that in the realm of the imagination all people and their ambitions and interests could meet." As *Moby Dick* and *Huckleberry Finn* are "great dramas of interracial fraternity," so are they social forces as real as sit-ins. "The way home we seek," Ellison said when he received the National Book Award in 1953, "is that condition of man's being at home in the world, which is called love, and which we term democracy." Jazz similarly creates "images of black and white fraternity," not only simply, in the mixed band and the unsegregated club, but more complexly in jazz's essential nature as a marriage of cultural traditions, and thus "the most authoritative rendering of America in music."

Ellison and I have been friends for almost a quarter of a century. In *Shadow and Act* he praises me once or twice, then in one essay identifies me as "an old friend and intellectual sparring partner" and does his best to beat my brains out. I would be faithless to that friendship and tradition, and would earn my readers' distrust in

1 *The Promised End,* by Stanley Edgar Hyman (Cleveland: World, 1963).

addition, if I failed to point out that the great virtues of the book are accompanied by many faults. These essays and reviews are a mixed lot, not rewritten, and they vary considerably in quality. The two occasions when Ellison is reduced to counting the Negro characters in the works of American writers are not on the level of sophistication of the rest of the book; a previously unpublished piece turns out to be a 1944 attack on Gunnar Myrdal for ignoring the class struggle and for taking essentially the line that Ellison himself now takes; the old chicken joke at the end of the piece about Charlie Parker is ruinous.

A more important criticism is that these essays, by their occasional nature, their glancing references to books and authors, do not offer the full confrontation of Melville or Dostoevsky or Malraux in Ellison's terms that he owes us and that only he can do. Faulkner's *Intruder in the Dust,* by an accident of journalism, is tackled only in the film version. Beyond that, Ellison has limits: he is too respectful of received opinion; he is not at his best in polemic; he is reluctant to recognize the African elements in American Negro culture. If Ellison's prose sometimes has great beauty and eloquence, it sometimes has great clumsiness; if his similes are at times effective, they are more often strained and far-fetched.

But these are the prices to be paid for the novelist's life, for what Ellison calls (in reference to Jimmy Rushing's blues style) the "romantic lyricism" of the Southwest, for the autodidact's fresh eye. In the closest he comes to self-justification, Ellison writes: "Understatement depends, after all, upon commonly held assumptions and my minority status rendered all such assumptions questionable." Ultimately, Ellison's faults are insignificant weighed against his virtues. *Shadow and Act* is a monument of integrity, a banner proclaiming "the need to keep literary standards high." In his insight into the complexity of American experience, Ralph Ellison is the profoundest cultural critic that we have, and his hard doctrine of freedom, responsibility, and fraternity is a wisdom rare in our time.

"Creating the Uncreated Features of His Face"

Indivisible Man

by James Alan McPherson

July, 1969

Ralph Ellison, a pair of high-powered binoculars close to his eyes, sits by the window of his eighth-floor Riverside Drive apartment, looking down. Across the street, in the long strip of green park which parallels the Hudson River, two black boys are playing basketball. "I watch them every afternoon," he says, and offers the binoculars to me. I look down and recognize the hope of at least two major teams, ten years hence, developing. Perhaps future sociologists will say that they possess superior athletic abilities because of biological advantages peculiar to blacks; but perhaps by then each of these black boys will have gained enough of a sense of who he is to reply: "I'm good at what I do because I practiced it all my life." The encouragement of this sort of self-definition has become almost a crusade with Ellison. But I also recognize that if I ran down and waved my arms and shouted to them: "Did you know that Ralph Ellison watches you playing every afternoon?" they would continue to shoot at the basket and answer: "Who is Ralph Ellison?"

"He spoke at Tougaloo last year," a black exchange student at Santa Cruz told me. "I can't stand the man."

"Why?"

"I couldn't understand what he was saying. He wasn't talking to *us*."

"Did you read his book?"

"No. And I don't think I will, either. I can't stand the man."

If you ask him about the Tougaloo experience, Ellison will laugh and then tell an anecdote about the stuttering black student who said: "Mr. E-l-li-s-s-s-*on*, I r-r-*ead* your b-b-o*ok The* Inv-v-v-si-b-b-

ble M-m-*man*. B-b-but after he-e-e-ar*ing* you tonight I f-f-*feel* like
I j-j-ju-*ust* hear-r-*rd* J-j-je-*sus* C-c-ch-r-r-*rist* d-d-d-runk on *Thunder-
bird Wine!*" And if you laugh along with him, and if you watch
Ellison's eyes as you laugh, you will realize that he is only testing a
deep scar to see if it has healed.

Ellison's difficulty, one cause of all the cuts, is that matter of self-
definition. At a time when many blacks, especially the young, are
denying all influences of American culture, Ellison, as always, dog-
gedly affirms his identity as a Negro-American, a product of the
blending of both cultures. But more than this, he attempts to explore most of the complex implications of this burden in his fiction,
his essays, his speeches, and his private life. He is nothing as simple
as a "brown skinned aristocrat" (as Richard Kostelanetz characterized him in a *Shenandoah* essay-portrait last summer); rather, he is
a thinking black man who has integrated his homework into the
fabrics of his private life. "I don't recognize any white culture," he
says. "I recognize no American culture which is not the partial
creation of black people. I recognize no American style in literature,
in dance, in music, even in assembly-line processes, which does not
bear the mark of the American Negro." And he means it. For this
reason he has difficulty reconciling some of the ideas of black nationalists, who would view black culture as separate from the
broader American culture. To these people he says: "I don't recognize any black culture the way many people use the expression."
And Ellison is one of the few black intellectuals who have struggled
to assess the influence of the black on American culture and the
relationships between the two. But, until fairly recently, not many
blacks—perhaps even college-educated blacks—knew that he existed.
In 1952 he published his first novel, *Invisible Man*, which won
a National Book Award; and this at a time when the white critical
Establishment was less eager to recognize literary achievement by
black Americans. Now, almost nineteen years later, he is still the
only black American who has received this honor. The novel has
gone through twenty paperback printings and was judged, in a
1965 *Book Week* poll of two hundred authors, critics, and editors,
"the most distinguished single work published in the last twenty
years." A second book, a collection of essays and interviews called
Shadow and Act, was published in 1964 and is essential reading for
any attempt at understanding Ellison, the man or the artist. While
Invisible Man is a story of one man's attempt to understand his
society and himself, the essays outline Ellison's own successful

struggle to master the craft of the writer and to understand, and then affirm, the complexities of his own rich cultural experience.

He likes to call himself a college dropout because he completed only three years of a music major at Tuskegee Institute before coming to New York in 1936. Before that he was a shoeshine boy, a jazz musician, a janitor, a free-lance photographer, and a man who hunted game during the Depression to keep himself alive.

Today he is a member, and a former vice president, of the National Institute of Arts and Letters; a member of New York's Century club and the American Academy of Arts and Sciences; and a trustee of the John F. Kennedy Center for the Performing Arts. He is a former teacher at Bard, Rutgers, and Chicago and presently Albert Schweitzer Professor in the Humanities at New York University. He has an interest in noncommercial television which began with his work on the Carnegie Commission on Educational Television, and continues with his trusteeships in the Educational Broadcasting Corporation, and the National Citizens' Committee for Broadcasting. Among his awards are listed the Russwurm Award, the Medal of Freedom (awarded by President Johnson), five honorary Ph.D's, and one of the highest honors which France can bestow on a foreign writer: Chevalier de l'Ordre des Arts et Lettres, awarded to him in 1970 by the French Minister of Cultural Affairs, André Malraux. But all these experiences seem to have equal weight in his mind; all seem to have given equal access to information, equal opportunity for observation of the culture. And he is as likely to begin a discussion with some observation made when he was a shoeshine boy as he is to mention the first names of some of America's most respected writers and critics.

His success does not prove, as one writer says, that "a fatherless American Negro really does have the opportunity to become the author of one of America's greatest novels as well as an aristocratic presence and an all but universally respected literary figure." Ellison's achievements are too enormous to be reduced to a sociological cliché, a rhetorical formulation. If anything, his success proves that intelligence, perseverance, discipline, and love for one's work are, together, too great a combination to be contained, or even defined, in terms of race.

Although he lives in New York and has access to literary and intellectual areas, Ellison seems to have very limited contact with the black writers who also live there. Yet his shadow lies over all their writers' conferences, and his name is likely to be invoked, and defamed, by any number of the participants at any conference. One man has said that he would like to shoot Ellison. Another, whom Ellison has never met, has for almost ten years blamed Ellison for his not receiving the last Prix de Rome Award, given by the American Academy of Arts and Letters. On the other hand, a growing number of young black writers, among them Ernest J. Gaines, Cecil Brown, Michael Harper, Ishmael Reed, and Al Young, are quick to admit their respect for him.

He reads the work of black writers, dismisses some of it, and is always willing to give an endorsement. And although he is very protective of his time, his telephone number is listed in the Manhattan directory, and he will usually grant an interview or a few hours of conversation in the afternoon (his working day usually ends at 4:00 P.M.) to anyone who is insistent.

"A fellow called me one morning," Ellison chuckles, lighting up a cigar, "said he just had to see me. So I consented. I went to the door, and there was a brown-skinned fellow from the Village. He brought a bottle of wine, several records, and four attempts at short stories. I looked at these things, and they weren't really stories. So I asked: 'What do you want me to tell you?' He said: 'Well, what I want you to do is to tell me, should I just write, or should I tell the truth?' " Ellison pauses to laugh deep in his chest. "I said: 'Tell the truth.' "

"He came to Oberlin in April of 1969," a black girl in Seattle recalled. "His speech was about how American black culture had blended into American white culture. But at the meeting with the black caucus after the speech, the black students said: 'You don't have anything to tell us.' "

"What did he say?"

"He just accepted it very calmly. One girl said to him: 'Your book doesn't mean anything because in it you're shooting down Ras the Destroyer, a rebel leader of black people.' "

"What was his answer?"

"He said: 'Remember now, this book was written a long time ago. This is just one man's view of what he saw, how he interpreted what he saw. I don't make any apologies for it.' Well, she went on to tell him: 'That just proves that you're an Uncle Tom.' "

Another of Ellison's problems, one peculiar to any black who attempts to assert his own individuality in his own terms, is that he challenges the defense mechanisms of the black community. Because of a history of enforced cohesiveness, some blacks have come to believe in a common denominator of understanding, even a set number of roles and ideas which are assumed to be useful to the community. Doctors, lawyers, teachers, social workers, some orthodox thinkers, some orthodox writers are accepted—as long as they do not insist on ideas which are foreign to the community's own sense of itself. But when a black man attempts to think beyond what has been thought before, or when he asserts a vision of reality which conflicts with or challenges the community's conception, there is a movement, sometimes unconscious, to bring him back into line or, failing that, to ostracize him. The "mass man" of sociological terminology is the "right-on man" of black slang, gliding smoothly and simplistically, and perhaps more comfortably, over questionable assumptions, and reducing himself to a cliché in the process. For a black thinker, such as Ellison, this assertion of individual vision is especially painful because the resultant ostracism carries with it the charge of "selling out" or "trying to be white." Yet a white thinker who challenges assumptions held by whites about themselves is not charged with "trying to be black." The underlying assumption is that whites have a monopoly on individuality and intelligence, and in order for a black man to lay claim to his own he must, necessarily, change color.

In response to charges by attackers that he is a "token Negro" because he is very often the only black serving on cultural commissions, Ellison says: "All right, if you don't want me on, I'll resign. But you had better put a *cardboard Negro* in my place because when decisions are made which will affect black people you had better make sure that those people who make the decisions remember that you exist and are forced to make sure that some of your interests are being met."

This impulse toward leveling, however, is not confined to the black community. It is a minority-group reaction. And while Ellison remembers a black professor at Tuskegee who tore up a leather-bound volume of Shakespeare's plays to discourage his interest in literature, he also remembers a white professor friend who said: "Ah, here's Ralph again, talking about America. There's no goddamn America out there."

"At Oberlin," the Seattle girl said, "one of the ideas they couldn't accept was Ellison's statement that black styles had historically been incorporated into American life. He went on to say that in the future, don't be surprised if white people begin to wear Afros because that's now a part of American popular culture. Well, the kids went out screaming, 'Who is he to insult what we wear? No honky could wear an Afro. They're stealing what is ours.' "

One year later disenchanted white youth, on both coasts and in between, are sporting their versions of the Afro. . . .

He is as practiced a listener as he is a speaker, and gives even the most naïvely put question thorough consideration before responding. He is a bit guarded at first, perhaps unwinding from a day at his desk, perhaps adjusting to the intellectual level of his guest. Then he begins talking, occasionally pausing to light a cigar, occasionally glancing out the window at the street, the park, the river beyond. After a while you both are trading stories and laughing while Mrs. Ellison makes noises in the kitchen, just off the living room. A parakeet flutters into the room. Ellison calls it, imitating its chirps, and the bird comes and hovers near his hand. "Have you ever heard a dog talk?" he asks.

"No."

We go into his study, and he plays a tape of a dog clearly imitating the rhythm and pitch of a human voice saying "hello." We listen again, and laugh again. Mrs. Ellison calls us to dinner. It is difficult enjoying the food and digesting his conversation at the same time.

"Ralph, stop talking and let him eat," Mrs. Ellison says.

After dinner we move back into the living room and continue the conversation. Finally Ellison's dog, Tucka Tarby, comes into the room and walks back and forth between us. Then you realize that it is well after midnight and that you have put a serious dent in the essential personal rhythm of a writer's day. Tucka has been patient, waiting for his evening walk. Ellison puts on an army jacket, and we go down in the elevator. This is an old building, just on the edge of Harlem, and most of the tenants are black. The lobby has colored tiles, a high ceiling, and live flowers protected by glass. "I've lived here for eighteen years," he says. "But it wasn't until 1964 that some of the people found out I was a writer." Tucka pulls us up 150th Street toward Broadway. We shake hands, and he and the dog walk off into the Harlem night.

"I think that what made it hard for him," the Seattle girl said, "was that LeRoi Jones was coming to Oberlin that next day. The kids figured that Jones the Master is coming, so let's get rid of this cat. But I think he's very gutsy, in a day like today with all these so-called militants trying to run him into the ground, coming to Oberlin saying to the kids: 'You are American, not African.' "

"Did anyone come to his defense?"

"One of the teachers stopped the meeting at one point and said: 'Would you please listen to what the man has to say? You're sitting here criticizing, and some of you haven't even read the damn book.' "

Among his peers Ellison's presence or even the mention of his name causes the immediate arming of intellectual equipment. There can be no soft-pedaling, no relaxation of intellect where he is involved. At Brown University in November of 1969, novelists and critics gathered at the annual Wetmore Lecture to discuss form, the future of the novel, and each other. Critic Robert Scholes opened one discussion on form by reading from Ellison's acceptance speech before the National Book Award Committee. "Ah, Ellison," Leslie Fiedler said, throwing his arm out in a gesture of dismissal. "He's a black Jew."

Ellison chuckles. "Leslie's been trying to make me a Jew for years," he says. "I have to look at these things with a Cold Oklahoma Negro Eye. But someone should have said that *all* us old-fashioned Negroes are Jews." . . .

Ellison is not only interested in the fiction written by young black writers; he is concerned about young black people in general: what they are thinking, what they are doing, what their ambitions are. But his knowledge of them is limited to sessions during speaking engagements, letters, and what he hears from the media. "A hell of a lot of them are reading my book," he observes with obvious pleasure. "I have a way of checking this. And for a long time they didn't read much of anything."

Yet he worries that despite the increased educational opportunities available to them, young black people are becoming too involved in, and almost symbolic of, the campus reactions against intellectual discipline, the life of the mind. "It's too damn bad," he says. "You see that men are now analyzing the song of the whales, the talk of dolphins, planning to go to the moon; computer technology is becoming more and more humanized and miniaturized; great efforts are being made to predetermine sex, to analyze cells, to control the life process in the human animal. And all of this is done with the *mind*. And indeed," he goes on, "the irony is that we've never really gotten away from that old *body* business; the Negro as symbolic of *instinctual* man. Part of my pride in being what I am is that as a dancer, as a physical man . . ."—and again

that distant chuckle comes from deep within his chest—"I bet you
I can outdance, outriff most of these intellectuals who're supposed
to have come back." Now he is serious again. *"But that isn't the
problem, damnit! I was born doing this!* It's a glorious thing to
know the uses of the body and not to be afraid of it. But *that has
to be linked to the mind.* I don't see any solution for literary art.
If you're a dancer, fine. If you're a musician, fine. But what are you
going to do as a writer, or what are you going to do as a critic?"
He sighs, as if he were weighed down by these considerations.

"I find this very interesting," he continues, "but not new. When
I think about Tuskegee and people with whom I went to school,
I know that over and over again they really did not extend themselves because they didn't have the imagination to look thirty
years ahead to a point where there would be a place for them in
the broader American society, had they been prepared."

He says: "I understand ambition; I understand the rejection of
goals because they're not self-fulfilling. I've turned down too many
things starting as a youngster."

He looks out the window toward the Hudson, then continues
in a lower tone. "I was married once before, and one reason that
marriage came to an end was that my in-laws were disgusted with
me, thought I had no ambition, because I didn't want a job in
the Post Office. And here I was with a dream of myself writing the
symphony at twenty-six which would equal anything Wagner had
done at twenty-six. This is where my ambitions were. So I can
understand people getting turned off on that level. But what I
can't understand is people who do not master a technique or
discipline which will get them to a point where they can actually
see that it's not what they want or that something else is demanded. But over and over again I see black kids who are dropping out or rejecting intellectual discipline as though what exists
now will always exist and as though they don't have the possibility
of changing it by using these disciplines as techniques to affirm
their sense of what a human life should be. It's there where I get
upset."

He has a habit of pausing whenever the discussion begins to
touch areas pregnant with emotion, as if careful of remaining
within a certain context. But on some subjects he is likely to continue. "I also get upset when I see announcements of prizes and
medical discoveries and scientific advances, and I don't see any
black names or black faces. I believe that we are *capable*," he says.
"I believe that there are enough unique features in our background

to suggest solutions to problems which seem very, very far removed from our social situation."

The duality of cultural experience which Ellison insists on in his writing is acted out in his professional and personal life. He is just as much at home, just as comfortable, in a Harlem barbershop as he is as a panelist before the Southern Historical Association exchanging arguments with C. Vann Woodward, Robert Penn Warren, and William Styron. He is a novelist well respected by his peers (when his name is mentioned in almost any literary circle, there will invariably be an inquiry about his current project), and he brings to bear the same respect for craft in an introduction to the stories of Stephen Crane as he uses to evaluate the work of black artist Romare Bearden. Yet, precisely because of his racial identity, he is also the leading black writer in American letters. And while he disclaims this position as "an accident, part luck and part a product of the confusion over what a black writer is and what an American writer is," the reality is there, nevertheless, and has to be coped with.

Before he accepted the professorship at New York University, Ellison earned a good part of his income from college speaking engagements. He accepted around twenty each year. He tends to favor the East Coast or Midwest and avoids the West Coast, partially because of the great distance and partially because of the political nature of the West. He is very much in demand, although his fee is usually $1500 to $2000. In the past year he has spoken at such colleges as Millsaps, East Texas State, Rockland, Illinois, West Point, and Iowa State University at Ames.

He takes pride in being able to deliver a ninety-minute speech without the aid of notes. He will make some few digressions to illuminate his points, but will always pick up the major thread and carry it through to its preconceived end.

March, 1970

Ralph Ellison stands on a stage broad enough to seat a full symphony orchestra. Before him, packed into a massive new auditorium of gray concrete and glass and deep red carpets, 2700 Ames students strain to hear the words of the man billed as "Ralph Ellison: Writer." Ames is almost an agricultural school, and its students still have fraternity rows, beer parties, frat pins and ties, white shirts and jackets. Most of them are the beardless sons of farmers and girls whose ambitions extend only as far as engagement by the senior year. The American Dream still lingers here, the simple living, the snow, the hamburgers and milk shakes, the country music and crickets and corn. This is the breadbasket of the country, the middle of Middle America. And yet, ninety miles away in Iowa City, students torn from these same roots are about to burn buildings. "When the pioneers got to your part of the country," he tells them, speaking again of the vernacular, the functional level of the American language, "there was no word for 'prairie' in the *Oxford English Dictionary*." His speech is on "The Concept of Race in American Literature." And he delivers just that. But it is abstract, perhaps over the heads of many of the students there (even though parts of it later appeared as a *Time* essay in the issue on "Black America"). Still, the students are quiet, respectful, attempting to digest. Speaking of the ethnic blending which began with the formation of the country, he says: "And, to make it brief, there was a whole bunch of people from Africa who were not introduced by the British, but quite some time before were introduced into what later became South Carolina by the Spanish. Whereupon they immediately began to revolt—" Here loud applause floats down to the lower audience from black students in the second balcony. Ellison pauses. Then continues: "—and went wild, and started passing for Indians. I hear a lot about black people passing for white, but remember, they first started passing for Indians." There is some giggling and laughter at this. But, behind me, I notice a black student cringing.

During the question-and-answer session afterwards, the students ask the usual things: the conflict between Richard Wright and James Baldwin, the order of symbols in *Invisible Man*. One girl wants to know if racial miscegenation is a necessary ingredient of racial integration. He laughs. "Where'd you get that word?" he says. And answers: "I don't think that any of us Americans wants to lose his ethnic identity. This is another thing which has been used to manipulate the society in terms of race. Some few people might want to lose their identities; this has happened. But I would think that the very existence of such strong Negro-American influences in the society, the style, the way things are done, would indicate that there's never been the desire to lose that. There's just too much self-congratulation in so much of Negro-American expression. They wouldn't want to give that up." He says: "The thing that black people have been fighting for for so long was the opportunity to decide whether they *wanted* to give it up or not. And the proof is that in this period when there is absolutely more racial freedom than has ever existed before, you have the

most militant rejection of integration. These are individual decisions which will be made by a few people. But if I know anything
about the human being, what *attracts* a man to a woman has usually
been picked up very early from the first woman he's had contact
with. There is enough of a hold of tradition, of ways of cooking,
of ways of just relaxing, which comes right out of the family circle,
to keep us in certain groups."

At the reception after the speech, the whites dominate all three
rooms; the few black students cluster together in one. Ellison moves
between the two, sometimes almost tearing himself away from the
whites. He talks to the black students about books, LeRoi Jones,
Malcolm X, color, their personal interests. They do not say much.
A white woman brings a book for his autograph; a professor gives
a nervous explanation of the source of the miscegenation question:
the girl has been reading Norman Podhoretz's essay "My Negro
Problem and Ours" in his course. Ellison smiles and shifts back
and forth on his feet like a boxer. Everyone is pleasantly high.
The black students, still in a corner, are drinking Coke. I am leaving, eager to be out in the Iowa snow. We shake hands. "This is
awkward," he says. "Call me Ralph and I'll call you Jim."

Santa Cruz, California
April, 1970
Dear Amelia:
    I was very pleased to have met you during my stay in Ames. Now,
before the Spring Holidays begin, I wish you would tell me your
impressions of Ellison as an artist, as a black man in touch with
young black people, as a man of ideas. . . .

There are thousands and thousands of books in the rooms of
his apartment; and besides the pieces of sculpture, paintings, African violets, self-designed furniture, and other symbols of a highly
cultivated sensibility, are deep drawers and file cabinets which, if
opened, reveal thick sheaves of notes and manuscripts. Ellison's
huge desk, which sits in a study just off the living room, is covered
with books, a red electric typewriter, well-thumbed manuscripts,
and tape equipment. In conversation he always sits away from it,
in the leather-strap chair by the window, looking out on the
Hudson and the street below.

He is a very direct and open man, even though there are silent
levels of intimidating intelligence and unexpressed feeling beneath
much of what he says. And he tends to approach even the most abstract idea from a personal point of view, usually including in any

observation some supportive incident drawn from his own experience.

He talks freely of his mother, who died when he was in his early
twenties, his relatives in Oklahoma, his professional relationships
with other writers and critics, conversations with people on the
subway or in the streets of Harlem; a recent chance meeting with
Kurt Vonnegut in the streets of Manhattan; his respect for Saul
Bellow as an extremely well read novelist. And there is not an
unkind, unprofessional, or imperceptive word for anyone, not even
his most rabid critics. But he does become irritated if you question
too closely his sense of identity as an American writer as opposed
to a black writer, and is likely to react when he senses a too containing category being projected onto him. "Let's put it this way,
Jim," he says, irritation in his voice. "You see, I *work* out of American literature. In order to write the kind of fiction that I write
I would *have* to be in touch with a broader literary culture than
our own particular culture." He pauses, and then says: "This is
not to denigrate what we have done, but in all *candor* we haven't
begun to do what we can do or what we should have done. I think
one reason why we haven't is that we've looked at our relationship
to American literature in a rather negative way. That is, we've
looked at it in terms of our trying to break into it. Well, damn it"
—and his voice rises, and his hand hits the arm of the chair—
"*that literature is built off our folklore to a large extent!*" And
then he laughs that deep honest chuckle, and says: "I ain't con-
ceding that to *nobody!*"

Ames, Iowa
April, 1970

Dear James:

As an artist the man is beautiful. I think that is what was so cap-
tivating about his book. The symbolism that he uses and the combination of literary mechanics that he employs will probably make
his work much more lasting than that of his black contemporaries.
Invisible Man is a classic, and to say any more or less about it would
be an understatement.

As for being in touch with the ideas of young people today, I
think that he is quite aware, but he doesn't have the charisma that
one would expect after hearing his reputation as a speaker and taking into account the acclaim his book has received. Part of my feeling is due to the disappointment of hearing him explain the figure
in *Invisible Man*. So many concerned blacks had read the plight of
the Afro-American into this figure with no face and no name. So
many people saw the author riding to champion the cause of the

black man. Those same people heard him say that the symbol was representative of a universal man. I found that most disheartening.

We are unfortunate at Ames, as well as at many other places across this nation, to have a group of young people who have been introduced to new ideologies and a new rhetoric and are attempting to adopt both when they do not understand either. Therefore, when they see or hear anyone who does not speak in their rhetoric they cannot, do not, and will not try to communicate with him. This was very true of Ellison.

He has a lot to say to a people who will listen to him. Today's youth are angry, and many times this anger closes their ears to a different rationale. Ellison's language and approach, I fear, attach to him the stigma of black bourgeois and conservatism. This figure does not communicate well with the vocal black youth. . . .

Ellison is still a first-novelist, despite his reputation. And that one novel was published over eighteen years ago. He contributes a steady flow of articles to intellectual journals and periodicals, and scholars and critics are rapidly making a permanent place for him in the archives of American literary criticism. But while students continue to read and his critics continue to write, there is the expectation of his long-awaited second novel. So far he has read from it in universities and on Public Television, published sections of it in intellectual journals, allowed a few close friends to read some of it, and has remained strangely silent about publication of the rest. Inestimable numbers of people, black and white, in and out of universities, friends and enemies, await the publication of the complete novel. Whenever his name is mentioned among a group of writers or literati, the immediate response is: "When is his novel coming out?" One man has heard that he has pulled it back from his publisher again for more revisions; another says that Ellison worries about its being dated; a third man says he has heard that Ellison cannot finish it.

Concerning that novel there are many other stories. Perhaps the best one is that which some friends of the Ellisons supposedly heard from the writer's wife. "She says she hears him in his study at night turning pages and laughing to himself. He enjoys the book so much that he isn't in a hurry to share it with the public."

Whether or not this is true, Ellison is extremely reluctant, at first, to discuss the book. A fire in his summer home in Plainfield, Massachusetts, destroyed a year's worth of revisions, he says, and he is presently in the process of revising it again. "I want what I do to be good," he says.

"Are you worried about the quality of it?"

"No," he says. "But you want to be sure when you write so slowly, because if it's not good, if it's just passable, they'll be terribly disappointed."

He has enough typed manuscripts to publish three novels, but is worried over how the work will hold up as a total structure. He does not want to publish three separate books, but then he does not want to compromise on anything essential. "If I find that it is better to make it a three-section book, to issue it in three volumes, I would do that as long as I thought that each volume had a compelling interest in itself. But it seems to me that one of the decisions one has to make about long fiction is whether the effect of *reading* it is lengthy. If you don't get the impression that you're reading a long thing, then you've licked the problem of the battle of time."

The setting of the novel, he says, is roughly around 1955. The form of it, he says, chuckling to himself, is in the direction of a "realism extended beyond realism." There are several time schemes operating within it, and the sections already published heavily suggest that it is complexly involved with the Negro Church and its ritual. In fact, three of its major characters, Bliss, Eatmore, and Hickman, are ministers.

On an afternoon, after a martini and before dinner, if the flow of conversation has been relaxing, and if the mood is right, Ellison might read a few sections from the book. It may take him a while to thumb through several huge black-bound manuscripts, perhaps numbering thousands of pages, to find an appropriate section. But when he does begin to read there is the impression, from the way the rhythms rise and fall and blend and flow out of him, that he is proud of every word. He chuckles as he reads, stops to explain certain references, certain connections, certain subtle jokes about the minister whose sermon he is reading. And in those sermons his voice becomes that of a highly sophisticated black minister, merging sharp biblical images with the deep music of his voice, playing with your ears, evoking latent memories of heated Southern churches and foot-stomping and fanning ladies in long white dresses and sweating elders swaying in the front rows. And suddenly the sermons are no longer comic, and there is no writer reading from his work. You see a minister, and you feel the depth of his religion, and you are only one soul in a huge congregation of wandering souls hearing him ask, over and over: *"Oh Yes, Yes, Yes, Yes, Yes. DO You Love, Ah DO You Love?"*

"Stephen's [Dedalus] problem," he wrote in *Invisible Man,* "like ours, was not actually one of creating the uncreated conscience of his race, but of creating the *uncreated features of his face.*" Ellison is fifty-six. His face does not show very much of it, but enough is visible. He has a receding hairline, a broad forehead, and deep curved lines on either side of his nose running down to the corners of his mouth. It is a handsome brown face, from either point of view, and there is a healthy stubbornness, besides all else inside that forehead, which helps him to protect it. The face can be cold, severe, analytical, pensive, even smiling. But it is not going to change.

"Who Knows but that I Speak for You?"

Ellison's Zoot Suit

by Larry Neal

Well, there is one thing that you have to admit. And that is,
dealing with Ralph Ellison is no easy matter. It is no easy task to
fully characterize the nature of Ellison's life and work. He cannot
be put into any one bag and conveniently dispensed with. Any attempt to do so merely leads to aesthetic and ideological oversimplifications. On the surface, oversimplifications may appear pragmatic
and viable but, in the long run, they weaken us. To overlook the
complex dimensions of a man's ideas, character, and personality is
to do great disservice to the righteous dissemination of knowledge.

Much of the criticism directed against Ellison is personal, over-
simplified, and often not based on an analysis of the man's work
and ideas. A great deal of the criticism emanates from ideological
sources that most of us today reject.

To be very concise, much of the anti-Ellison criticism springs
from a specific body of Marxian and Black neo-Marxian thought.
The literary term used to designate this body of thought is called
"social realism." Some of Ellison's most virulent critics have been
social realists.

One of the most famous of social realists' attacks was the subject
of a literary exchange between Ellison and Irving Howe, a liberal
left-winger and former editor of *Dissent* magazine. In any essay published in the Fall 1963 issue of *Dissent,* Howe accused Baldwin and
Ralph Ellison of abandoning the task of the Negro writer. That
task Howe proposed to be the militant assertion of Negro freedom.
In his assault upon Baldwin and Ellison, Howe evoked Richard
Wright as the embodiment of the truest, most relevant exponent
of Black freedom in fiction. Howe, the knowing white boy, praised
Wright for his penchant toward what is termed "protest" literature
and castigated both Ellison and Baldwin for their failure to carry

on the "protest" tradition as exemplified by Wright's *Native Son*.

Ellison wrote an excellent rebuttal to Howe's piece entitled, "The World and the Jug." Ellison attacked Howe's attempt to rigidly circumscribe the role of the Black writer. He asserted the essential differences in outlook between himself and Richard Wright. Where Wright, in *Black Boy*, saw Black life "void of hope" and bare of tradition, Ellison countered with a very positive vision of Afro-American life. For Ellison, Black people did not exhibit a tradition void of hopes, memories, and personal attachments. They were, instead, profoundly human and blessed with a strong, spiritually sustaining culture. "The World and the Jug" is a finely balanced essay, mean, but eloquently controlled.

Underlying this exchange between Ellison and Howe is the recurring question of the writer's role, especially in the context of the struggle for human liberation. Marxism puts forth the idea that all literature is propaganda, or becomes propaganda when it enters the social sphere. And as propaganda, it is implicitly a reflection of class attitudes. The role of the revolutionary writer in the Marxist context is, therefore, to extol the virtues of the proletariat, to sharpen their class consciousness in order that they may overthrow the ruling classes and finally take control of the "means of production."

Richard Wright was especially influenced by the Marxist ideas he encountered in the Thirties. As a young writer he had joined the John Reed Club in Chicago and was very active in Communist cultural activities. Coming from Mississippi, where he had seen and experienced racial oppression, he sincerely believed that it was his duty to use his writing as a weapon against that oppression. All of his writing, up to and including his masterwork, *Native Son*, is informed by his belief in social revolution. Following Lenin's idea that the revolutionary vanguard must expose the corruption in the Capitalist system, all of Wright's fictional landscapes, with the exception of *The Long Dream*, tend to be very bleak and humorless. Excellent social realist that he was, he was skillful at depicting in exact details the impact of the material world on both the oppressed and the oppressors alike. Now Wright has gone the way of the ancestors, but he is still a major influence in contemporary Black writing. At least we are still feeling the influence of a certain kind of "protest" writing that appears highly reminiscent of Wright, even though most of it does not begin to approach Wright's high level of artistic achievement.

What Ralph Ellison was doing in his exchange with Irving Howe was defending his right to his (Ellison's) own personal vision, while trying not to fall into the bag of depreciating Wright: "Must I be condemned because my sense of Negro Life was quite different?" Ellison asks this question, fully aware that there is an ideological contingent lying in wait to pounce on him for not carrying on in the tradition of Wright. But, ironically, it was Wright himself who rejected the sectarian Marxism of the American Communist Party. Dig his essay in Arthur Koestler's book, *The God That Failed.* And in the forward to George Padmore's *Pan-Africanism or Communism,* Wright implies that the Black man operates on the premise of a personal nationalism, and not along fixed ideological lines:

> . . . The Negro's fundamental loyalty is, therefore, to *himself.* His situation makes this inevitable. [Am I letting awful secrets out of the bag? I'm sorry. The time has come for this problem to be stated clearly so that there is no possibility of further misunderstanding or confusion. The Negro, even when embracing Communism or Western Democracy, is not supporting ideologies; he is seeking to use *instruments* (instruments owned and controlled by men of other races!) for his own ends. He stands outside of those instruments and ideologies; he has to do so, for he is not allowed to blend with them in a natural, organic and healthy manner.]

Like Wright, Ellison was also active in the literary left of the late Thirties and early Forties. And also like Wright, Ellison rejected sectarian Marxism. As far as I can perceive, Ellison had never really internalized Marxism in the first place. This appears to be the case even when he was writing in the left-wing *New Masses.* His work appears always to have been striving for a penetration into those areas of Black life style that exist below the mere depiction of external oppression. He had read Marx, though, as should anyone who is interested in those ideas operative in today's world. But lucky for us, his work never took on the simplistic assertions of the literary Marxist.

Therefore, Ellison's clearly articulated break with naturalism must also be seen in light of his previous awareness that hard-core ideologues, particularly Communists, represented an awesome threat to not only his artistic sensibility, but to his "national" sensibility as well. And it is amazing how fantastically true Ellison's initial impulses have been. If Harold Cruse's *The Crisis of the Negro Intellectual* has any one theme that demands our greatest attention, it is his clear analysis of the detrimental role that the left wing has played in our struggle for self-determination and liberation. Ellison himself is also aware, and this awareness underlies the following remarks he made in an interview that was published in the March 1967 issue of *Harper's Magazine*. He is speaking to several young Black writers:

> . . . They fostered the myth that Communism was twentieth-century Americanism, but to be a twentieth-century American meant, in their thinking, that you had to be more Russian than American and less Negro than either. That's how they lost the Negroes. The Communists recognized no plurality of interests and were really responding to the necessities of Soviet foreign policy and when the war came, Negroes got caught and were made expedient in the shifting of policy. Just as Negroes who fool around with them today are going to get caught in the next turn of the screw.

Ellison has not been forgotten by his enemies both in the white left and the Black left. The Communists were the first to lead the attack against Ellison when *Invisible Man* appeared in 1952. Since then, we have read or heard a number of attacks emanating from Black writers who trace their literary lineage from the so-called progressive movements of the Thirties and Forties. In this connection, the interested reader should dig Harold Cruse's section on Ellison in *The Crisis of the Negro Intellectual*. Cruse's book seems theoretically out of focus in many instances, because it walks such a precarious line between a weakly defined nationalism and a strained neo-Marxism. But, in my opinion, he is strictly on the case when he enters the "debate" between Ellison and his detractors. Here I refer to Cruse's account of the anti-Ellison attack that occurred at a writer's conference at the New School in 1965. Leading the charge against Ellison was Herbert Aptheker, a leading theoretician of the Communist Party; John Henrik Clarke, the editor of several significant anthologies; and John O. Killens, the novelist. Cruse asserts that the writers gathered at the conference were not properly prepared to cope with the questions posed by Ellison's critical and aesthetic methodology. Further, he asserted that ". . . the radical left wing will never forgive Ellison for writing *Invisible Man*."

Why? The answer is quite simple. The literary left, both white and Negro, were fuming over: 1) Ellison's rejection of white controlled left-wing politics; 2) his harsh depiction of the Communists (called the "Brotherhood" in Ellison's novel); 3) the novel's obvious rejection of the aesthetics of social realism. The Communist *Daily Worker* of June 1, 1952, for example, published a review of the book under the following headline:

"RALPH ELLISON'S NOVEL 'INVISIBLE MAN' SHOWS
SNOBBERY, CONTEMPT FOR NEGRO PEOPLE"

The review which followed was written by a Negro left-winger by the name of Abner N. Berry, who opened his piece by stating:

> Written in vein [sic] of middle class snobbishness—even contempt—towards the Negro people, Ellison's work manipulates his nameless hero for 439 pages through a maze of corruption, brutality, anti-communism slanders, sex perversion and the sundry inhumanities upon which a dying social system feeds.

And on the aesthetic level he asserted:

> There are no *real* characters in *Invisible Man*, nor are there any *realistic* situations. The structure, the characters and the situations are *contrived* and resembles *fever fantasy* . . . In effect, it is 439 pages of contempt for humanity, written in an *affected, pretentious,* and *other worldly* style to suit the king pins of world white supremacy. (Emphasis mine, naturally.)

Therefore, along with making the unpardonable sin of obliquely attacking the Party through his characterization of the "Brotherhood" in his novel, Ellison was also being attacked for having developed a new aesthetic universe, one that was seeking to develop its own laws of form and content. Social realism, particularly Marxist socialist realism, does not allow for the free play of fantasy and myth that Ellison was attempting in his novel. Marxist social realism essentially posits the view that the details of a work of art should be predicated on fairly simple structural lines. A work should extol the virtues of the working classes; but, the extolling should take place along Party lines. Hence, not only is the writer's aesthetic range controlled, but his political range as well. And to further worsen matters, this aesthetic ideology is nearly Victorian in the extreme. It seems to emanate from a very square vision of social realities.

Here is John O. Killens in the 1952 edition of the newspaper *Freedom,* commenting on *Invisible Man*:

> Mix a heavy portion of sex and a heavy, heavy portion of violence, a bit of sadism and a dose of redbaiting (Blame the Communists for everything bad) and you have the making of a bestseller today.
>
> Add to this decadent mixture of a Negro theme with Negro characters as Uncle Toms, pimps, sex perverts, guilt-ridden traitors—and you have a publisher's dream.
>
> But how does Ellison present the Negro people? The thousands of exploited farmers in the South represented by a sharecropper who

made both his wife and daughter pregnant. The main character of the book is a young Uncle Tom who is obsessed with getting to the "top" by pleasing the Big, Rich White folks. A million Negro veterans who fought against fascism in World War II are rewarded with a maddening chapter [of] crazy vets running hogwild in a down home tavern. The Negro ministry is depicted by an Ellison character who is a Harlem pastor and at the same time a pimp and a numbers racketeer.

The Negro people need Ralph Ellison's *Invisible Man* like we need a hole in the head or a stab in the back.

It is a vicious distortion of Negro life.

It is remarkable how similar to this novel were Berry's and Killens' reactions. They easily could have been written by the same person. But this is supposed to be 1970. And I would like to believe that we can read *Invisible Man* with more intellectual freedom than is apparent in Abner Berry's and John O. Killens' hopefully sincere, but extremely flaccid critical remarks. Especially today, when the major concerns ramified throughout Ellison's life and work are still very relevant to our contemporary search for new systems of social organization and creative values. Ellison's vision, in some respects, is not that far removed from the ideas of some of the best Black writers and intellectuals working today. That's why I wince somewhat when I reread the following statement that I made in the afterword to *Black Fire*: ". . . The things that concerned Ellison are interesting to read, but contemporary Black youth feel another force in the world today. We know who we are, and are not invisible, *at least not to each other.* We are not Kafkaesque creatures stumbling through a white light of confusion and absurdity . . ."

My statements represent one stage in a long series of attempts, over the last several years, to deal with the fantastic impression that Ellison's work has had on my life. It is now my contention that of all the so-called older Black writers working today, it is Ralph Ellison who is the most engaging. But the major issue separating many, young Black writers from a Ralph Ellison would appear to have very little to do with creative orientation, but much more to do with the question of political activism and the Black writer. Ellison's stance is decidedly non-political ". . . The novel is always a public gesture, though not necessarily a political one." (We'll come back to this point later.) And further, there is a clearly "aristocratic" impulse in his stance, an understandable desire not to be soiled by the riff-raff from all kinds of ideological camps. As we have already noted, Ellison, like Wright, was active in left-wing literary circles in the late Thirties and early Forties. There must have been some psychological torments for him then, since we can glean, even from his early writings, a distinctly "nationalistic" orientation that must have, at times, been at odds with the Party line. Why should this have caused problems?

The answer is very simple. Most serious writers should understand it: The left wing, particularly the Communist Party, represented one of the main means by which a young Black writer could get published. There were perhaps other routes through the Establishment. But for a young Black writer checking out the literary happenings in 1937 (Ellison was about 28 years old when he wrote his first piece for *Challenge,* a Black left-oriented magazine), the Party was very attractive. After all, was not Richard Wright on that side of the street? And did not the Communist Party seem very amenable to young Black talent? I hope that I am not exaggerating, but it seems that, from this perspective, the whole literary atmosphere, for a Black writer, seems to have been dominated by the left.

Never having been a hard-core ideologue in the first place, Ellison appears to have been exceedingly uncomfortable as a leftist polemicist. Some of his journalistic writing for the Communist-oriented *New Masses* strains for political and social relevancy, just as some of ours does. But you can perceive another kind of spirit trying to cut through the Marxist phrase-mongering, another kind of spirit trying to develop a less simplistic, more viable attitude towards not only the usable content of Afro-American culture in America, but more importantly, a sense of the *meaning* of that culture's presence and its manifestations as they impinged upon "white culture." One isolatable political tendency that begins to emerge at the end of Ellison's Marxist period is a nascent, loosely structured form of Black nationalism.

But Ellison was always clever. As Ellison himself notes in the *Harper's* interview quoted above, he never wrote the "official type of fiction." "I wrote," he says, "what might be called propaganda— having to do with the Negro struggle—but my fiction was always trying to be something else: something different even from Wright's fiction. I never accepted the ideology which the New Masses attempted to impose on writers. They hated Dostoevski, but I was studying Dostoevski . . . I was studying [Henry] James. I was also reading Marx, Gorki, Sholokhov, and Isaac Babel. I was reading everything, including the Bible. Most of all, I was reading Malraux . . . This is where I was really living at the time . . . Anyway, I think style is more important than political ideologies."

But there is even a counter-Marxian thrust below the surface of his early political writings. This counter-thrust manifests itself in Ellison's concern with folk culture and life style. So that in the midst of his political writings, it is possible to see him groping for a unique cultural theory, one that is shaped on the basis of cultural imperatives integral to the Black man's experience in America. For example, 1943 found Ellison Managing Editor of the *Negro Quarterly*. The Editor was Angelo Herndon, a Black intellectual of the radical left. Herndon had been arrested in the South for engaging in union activities. The *Negro Quarterly* appears to have been the last attempt on the part of Black intellectuals of that period to fashion an ideological position that was revolutionary, but yet, was not totally dominated by the white Marxist left.

But there was a war going on in 1943. When the war began, America found herself on the side of the Allied Forces, Britain and France. She was also allied with the Russians against the Fascist German state. Now that Socialist Russia was under attack, American Communists began to concentrate on the war effort. In the interim between the Russo-German Pact of 1939 and the formal entry of Russia into the war, there had been a significant shift in Party policy with respect to the "Negro Question." Now that Russia was under attack, the Non-Aggression Pact abrogated, the Communist Party was urging its American Chapter to de-emphasize the struggle for Negro liberation and to, instead, concentrate on the war effort. They correctly reasoned that excessive political activism among Black people would only slow down the industrial war machinery, thus endangering Russia by impeding the progress of the Allied struggle in Europe. All of this put left-wing Black intellectuals in a trick.

Their international perspective forced them to acknowledge the awesome threat that fascism posed to human progress. But they were also acutely aware that an atmosphere of racism and fascism also existed here in America. Then there was the question of Japan. Many Black people felt a vague sense of identification with the powerful Asian nation and secretly wished that she would overcome the white Western powers. And there were other attitudes which grew out of the specific situation of racism in America.

A significant item in this regard is an unsigned editorial in *Negro Quarterly* which, from the import of its style and content, was probably written by Ralph Ellison. The editorial addresses itself to the conflicting attitudes held by Black people towards the war effort. Black people were being segregated in the armed services, and because of racism were not even getting an opportunity to make some bread in the war-related industries. It was the latter situation which had led to A. Philip Randolph's 1941 threat to march on Washington for jobs and fair employment. Under Randolph's pressure, President Franklin D. Roosevelt was forced to sign Executive Order 8802 which was supposed to guarantee Black people equal access to jobs in the war industries. Under these circumstances, it is easy to understand why there were, among Black people, such conflicting attitudes towards the War.

Ellison's writings enumerated these attitudes. They ranged from apathy to all-out rejection of war. Addressing himself to this attitude of rejection, Ellison stated that it sprang from a "type of Negro nationalism which, in a sense, is admirable; it would settle all problems on the simple principle that Negroes deserve equal treatment with all other free human beings . . ." But Ellison concluded that this attitude of total rejection of the war effort was too narrow in scope. It was not just a case of "good white men" against "bad white men." The Negro, he strongly asserted, had a natural stake in the defeat of fascism whether it was national or international. He further proposed that there was another manifestation of "Negro nationalism" that was neither a "blind acceptance" of the War nor an "unqualified rejection" of it. This attitude is "broader and more human than the first two attitudes; and it is *scientific* enough to make use of *both* by *transforming* them into *strategies of struggle.* It is committed to life, it holds that the main task of the Negro people is to work unceasingly toward creating those democratic conditions in which it can live and recreate itself. It believes the historical role of Negroes to be that of integrating the larger American nation and compelling it untiringly toward true freedom. And while it will have none of the slavishness of the first attitude, it is imaginative and flexible enough to die if dying is forced upon it." (Emphasis mine.)

Somehow we are involved here with an attempt at ideological reconciliation between two contending trends in Afro-American thought, *i.e.,* the will toward self-definition, exclusive of the overall white society, and at the same time the desire not to be counted out of the processes of so-called American democracy. This is the precarious balancing act that Ellison is forced to perform while he tries to cut through the ideological prison in which he finds himself encased. He attacks Negro leaders for not having group consciousness, and calls for a "centralization" of Negro political power.

But as we proceed to read the editorial, we begin to encounter

the Ellison who would be himself and write one of the most important novels in history. Towards the end of this editorial, with its
carefully balanced blend of Marxism and Negro nationalism, we
find Ellison making the following blatantly non-Marxist statement:

> A third major problem, and one that is indispensable to the centrali-
> zation and direction of power, is that of learning the meaning of the
> *myths* and *symbols* which abound among the Negro masses. For
> without this knowledge, leadership, no matter how correct its pro-
> gram, will fail. Much in Negro life remains a *mystery;* perhaps the
> *zoot suit conceals* profound political meaning; perhaps the symmetri-
> cal frenzy of the Lindy-hop conceals clues to great potential powers—
> if only Negro leaders would solve this *riddle*. On this knowledge de-
> pends the effectiveness of any slogan or tactic. For instance, it is
> obvious that Negro resentment over their treatment at the hands of
> their allies is justified. This naturally makes for a resistance to our
> stated war aims, even though these aims are essentially correct; and
> they will be accepted by the Negro masses only to the extent that
> they are helped to see the bright star of *their own* hopes through
> the *fog* of their daily experiences. The problem is *psychological;* it
> will be solved only by a Negro leadership that is aware of the psy-
> chological attitudes and incipient forms of action which the black
> masses *reveal* in their emotion-charged *myths, symbols,* and war-
> time *folk-lore*. Only through a skillful and wise manipulation of
> these centers of repressed social energy will Negro resentment, self-
> pity and indignation be channelized to cut through temporary issues
> and become transformed into positive action. This is not to make
> the problem simply one of words, but to recognize . . . that words
> have their own vital importance. (Emphasis mine.)

There is a clear, definite sense of cultural nationalism at work
here. These statements represent an especial attempt on the part of
Ellison to get past the simplistic analysis of folk culture brought to
bear on the subject by Marxist social realists. For rather than locating the mechanisms for organizing political power totally in an
analysis of the Black man's class structure, Ellison turns Marxism on
its head, and makes the manipulation of cultural mechanisms the
basis for Black Liberation.[1] Further, these statements set into mo-
tion a host of themes which are elaborated upon in his later work,
particularly his cultural criticism. Here also we get snatches of a
theory of culture. And some aspect of this theory seems to imply

[1] See Maulana Karenga's seven criteria for culture in *The Quotable Karenga*
(US), 1967. Note that Maulana makes one of the seven criteria for culture Mythology, and the other important one is Creative Motif. Also see Cruse's *Crisis of
the Negro Intellectual* (Morrow), 1967.

that there is an unstated, even noumenal set of values that exists beneath the surface of Black American culture.

These values manifest themselves in a characteristic manner, or an *expressive style*. The Lindy-hop and the zoot suit are, therefore, in this context not merely social artifacts, but they, in fact, mask deeper levels of symbolic and social energy. Ellison perceives this theory as the instrumental basis for a new kind of Negro leader:

> They [the leaders] must integrate themselves with the Negro masses; they must be constantly alert to new concepts, new techniques and new trends among peoples and nations with an eye toward appropriating those which are valid when tested against the reality of Negro life. By the same test they must be just as alert to reject the faulty programs of their friends. When needed concepts, techniques or theories do not exist they must create them. Many new concepts will evolve when the people are closely studied in action . . ." [2]

To some extent, this kind of perception shapes many of the characters in *Invisible Man*. Rinehart comes to mind in this connection. However, there is a specific allusion to the ideas enunciated in this 1943 editorial in the following passage from Mr. Ellison's novel:

> What about those fellows waiting still and silent there on the platform, so still and silent they clash with the crowd in their very immobility, standing noisy in their very silence; harsh as a cry of terror in their quietness? What about these three boys, coming now along the platform, tall and slender, walking stiffly with swinging shoulders in their well-pressed, too-hot-for-summer suits, their collars high and tight about their necks, their identical hats of black cheap felt set upon the crowns of their heads with a severe formality above their conked hair? It was as though I'd never seen their like before: Walking slowly, their shoulders swaying, their legs swinging from their hips in trousers that ballooned upward from cuffs fitting snug about their ankles; their coats long and hip-tight with shoulders far too broad to be those of natural western men. These fellows whose bodies seemed—what had one of my teachers said of me?—"You're like one of these African sculptures, distorted in the interest of design." Well, what design and whose?

To the protagonist, they seem like "dancers in a funeral service." (This episode follows the death of Todd Clifton.) Their black faces are described as being "secret." They wear heel-plated shoes and rhythmically tap as they walk. They are said to be "men outside of historical time." That is to say, no current theory of historical de-

---

[2] Sounds very much like the statement Don L. Lee made about "integrating Negroes with Black People."

velopment accurately describes them. But yet, there is a gnawing and persistent feeling, on the part of the unnamed protagonist, that the boys may hold the key to the future liberation. And as he grasps the implications of this idea, he is emotionally shaken:

> . . . But who knew (and now I began to tremble so violently I had to lean against a refuse can)—who knew but they were the *saviors, the true leaders, the bearers* of something precious? The *stewards* of something uncomfortable, burdensome, which they hated because, living outside of history, *there was no one to applaud their value* and they themselves failed to understand it." (Emphasis mine.)

Ellison's 1943 remarks in *Negro Quarterly* concerning Black cultural compulsives were cloaked in the language of politics. But they implicitly penetrate way beyond the sphere of politics. It is obvious from the above-quoted passage that he thought enough of the concept of hidden cultural compulsives in Black American life to *translate* them into art. Further, as we have noted, the concept is rather non-Marxist in texture and in substance. It probably represents, for him, a "leap" not only in political consciousness but in aesthetic consciousness as well. As a result of his experiences with hard-core ideological constructs, Ellison came to feel that politics were essentially inhibiting to an artist, if they could not be subsumed into art. Perhaps, this is what he means when he says in the *Harper's* interview: "Any way, I think style is more important than political ideologies."

I am not sure whether or not I fully concur with Ellison on this point. But there is something in his stance that specifically relates to the current Black Arts movement. The current movement is faced with some of the same problems that confronted Ellison. Only the historical landscape has changed, and the operational rhetoric is different.

I don't think I am exaggerating when I say that some form of nationalism is operative throughout all sections of the Black community. The dominant political orientations shaping the sensibilities of many contemporary Black writers fall roughly into the categories of cultural nationalism and revolutionary nationalism. That is to say, as writers we owe whatever importance we may have to this current manifestation of nationalism. I, for one, tend to believe this is a good situation in which to be. It provides an audience to which to address our work, and also imparts to it a certain sense of contemporaneity and social relevance.

But we are going to have to be careful not to let our rhetoric

obscure the fact that a genuine nationalist revolution in the arts
will fail, if the artistic products of that revolution do not encounter
our audiences in a manner that demands their most profound attention. I'm talking about a Black Art that sticks to the ribs. An art
that through the strength of all of its ingredients—form, content,
craft, and technique—illuminates something specific about the living culture of the Nation; and, by extension reveals something
fundamental about Man on this planet.

Therefore, we have to resist the tendency to "program" our art,
to set unnatural limitations upon it. To do so implies that we ultimately don't trust the intelligence of the national laity, and consequently feel that we must paternally guide them down the course of
righteous Blackness. So very often we defuse the art by shaping it
primarily on the basis of fashionable political attitudes. There is a
tendency to respond to work simply on the sensation it creates.[3] If
Black Art is to survive, in the national sense, it's gonna need more
supporting it than a cluster of new clichés.

II
Translating Politics into Art

There is quite a bit of discussion about the nature of history in
Ellison's *Invisible Man*. Along with the obvious theme of identity,
the nameless narrator is constantly in search of a "useable past." In
order to arrive at an understanding of the complex dimensions of
his American experience, Ellison plunged deep into the murky world
of mythology and folklore, both of which are essential elements in
the making of a people's history. But Ellison's history is non-dia-
lectical. The novel attempts to construct its own universe, based
on its own imperatives, the central ones being the shaping of a personal vision, as in the blues, and the celebration of a collective vision
as is represented by the living culture. And it is the living culture,
with all of its shifting complexities, which constitutes the essential
landscape of the novel. The unnamed narrator questions the "scientific" history of the "Brotherhood" and in one of the most intense

[3] For example: Sam Greenlee's novel, *The Spook Who Sat by the Door*, is an
atrocious novel. It lacks style and a conscious sense of craft. It is clearly more of
a "manual" than a "revolutionary" novel. Its major premise is excellent, but
flawed by Greenlee's inability to bring it off. Its "revolutionary content" is
never firmly rooted in a form that is sustaining below the mere surface of
graphic detail. Where Greenlee could have written a "great" novel, one both
excellently written and revolutionary in stance, he blew the challenge by a glib
adherence to militancy.

sections of the novel asks the following question: ". . . What if Brother Jack were wrong? What if history was a gambler, instead of a force in a laboratory experiment, and the boys his ace in the hole? What if history was not a reasonable citizen, but a madman full of paranoid guile . . . ?"

This discourse follows the death of Todd Clifton, a man who had previously been described as having fallen "outside of history." Tottering between contending political forces, *i.e.*, the rigid dogmas of the "Brotherhood," and the emotionally compelling rhetoric of Ras, the Exhorter, Todd attempts to leap outside of historical time altogether. And he ultimately leaps to his death.

Churning way beneath the surface of the novel's narrative is a fantastically rich and engaging mythic and folkloristic universe. Further, this universe is introduced to us through the music of Louis Armstrong. Louis' music, then, forms the over-all structure for the novel. If that is the case, the subsequent narrative and all of the action which follows can be read as one long blues solo. Critic Albert Murray, a close associate of Ellison's, put it this way:

> *Invisible Man* was *par excellence* the literary extension of the blues. Ellison had taken an everyday twelve-bar blues tune (by a man from down South sitting in a manhole up North in New York, singing and signifying about how he got there) and scored it for full orchestra. This was indeed something different and something more than run-of-the-mill U.S. fiction. It had new dimensions of rhetorical resonance (based on lying and signifying). It employed a startlingly effective fusion of narrating realism and surrealism, and it achieved a unique but compelling combination of the naturalistic, the ridiculous, and the downright hallucinatory.

What is important about Murray's observations here is that it isolates, in *Invisible Man,* a very unique aesthetic. There has been much talk of late about a "black aesthetic," but there has been, fundamentally, a failure to examine those elements of the Black experience in America which could genuinely constitute an aesthetic. With no real knowledge of folk culture—blues, folk songs, folk narratives, spirituals, dance styles, gospels, speech, and oral history—there is very little possibility that a black aesthetic will be realized in our literature.

Ellison, on the other hand, finds the aesthetic all around him. He finds it in memories of Oklahoma background. He finds it in preachers, blues singers, hustlers, gamblers, jazz men, boxers, dancers, and itinerant storytellers. He notes carefully the subtleties of American speech patterns. He pulls the covers off the stereotypes in order to probe beneath the surface where the hard-core mythic truth lies. He keeps checking out style. The way people walk, what they say and what they leave *un*said. If anyone has been concerned with a "black aesthetic" it has certainly got to be Ralph Ellison. And even if you disagree with Ellison's political thrust these days, you have got to dig his consistent concern for capturing the essential truths of the Black man's experience in America.

And where are these essential truths embodied, if not in the folk culture? Do not Stagalee, High John The Conqueror, John Henry, Shine, and the Signifying Monkey reveal vital aspects of our group experience? Or has the current "rediscovery" of African culture obscured the fact that however disruptive slavery must have been to our original African personalities, our fathers and mothers intuitively understood what aspect of it could be rescued and reshaped. And did not this reshaping indicate a *willed* desire to survive and maintain one's own specific outlook on life. Didn't it exhibit a willed desire to survive in the face of danger? What kind of people were they in their weaknesses and their strengths? Haven't we read their slave narratives, and listened carefully to their songs? And hasn't the essential spirit that they breathed into these expressions continued to manifest itself in all meaningful aspects of our struggle? We must address ourselves to this kind of humanity because it is meaningful and within our immediate reach. To do so means understanding something essential about the persistency of tradition, and also understanding the manner in which values are shaped out of tradition. And what's more important, values whose fundamental function was to bind us together into a community of shared feelings and memories in order that we might survive.

Ellison's protagonist, when confronted with possible expulsion from his southern Negro College, suffers deeply at the thought of losing his regional roots. In his longing for a sustainable image of the world that has created him, he transforms an "ordinary" house mother into a ritual goddess. Dig. Here is your black aesthetic at its best:

> Ha! to the gray-haired matron in the final row. Ha! Miss Susie, Miss Susie Gresham, back there looking at that co-ed smiling at that he-ed —listen to me, the bungling bugler of words, imitating the trumpet and the trombone's timbre, playing thematic variations like a baritone horn. Hey! old connoisseur of voice sounds, of voices without messages, of newsless winds, listen to the vowel sounds and the crackling dentals, to the low harsh gutturals of empty anguish, now riding the curve of a preacher's rhythm I heard long ago in a Baptist

church, stripped now of its imagery: No suns having hemorrhages, no moons weeping tears, no earthworms refusing the sacred flesh and dancing in the earth on Easter morn. Ha! singing achievement. Ha! booming success, intoning, Ha! acceptance, Ha! a river of word-sounds filled with drowned passions, floating, Ha! floating, Ha! with wrecks of unachievable ambitions and stillborn revolts, sweeping their ears, Ha! ranged stiff before me, necks stretched forward with listening ears, Ha! a-spraying the ceiling and a drumming the dark-stained after rafter, that seasoned crossarm of torturous timber mellowed in the kiln of a thousand voices; playing, Ha! as upon a xylophone; words marching like the student band, up the campus and down again, blaring triumphant sounds empty of triumphs. Hey, Miss Susie! the sound of words that were no words, counterfeit notes singing achievements yet unachieved, riding upon the wings of my voice out to you, old matron, who knew the voice sounds of the founder and knew the accents and echo of his promise; your gray old head cocked with the young around you, your eyes closed, face ecstatic, as I toss the word sounds in my breath, my bellows, my fountain, like bright-colored balls in a water spout—hear me, old matron, justify now this sound with your dear old nod of affirmation, your closed-eye smile and bow of recognition, who'll never be fooled with the mere content of words, not my words, not these pinfeathered flighters that stroke your lids till they flutter with ecstasy with but the mere echoed noise of the promise. And after the singing and outward marching, you seize my hand and sing out quavering, "Boy, some day you'll make the Founder proud!" Ha! Susie Gresham, Mother Gresham, guardian of the hot young women on the puritan benches who couldn't see your Jordan's water for their private steam; you, relic of slavery whom the campus loved but did not understand, aged, of slavery, yet bearer of something warm and vital and all-enduring, of which in that island of shame we were not ashamed—it was to you on the final row I directed my rush of sound, and it was you of whom I thought with shame and regret as I waited for the ceremony to begin.

This poetic narrative is the prelude to the ceremony where Rev. Homer Barbee, taking the role of tribal poet, ritually consecrates the memory of the Founder. His speech is permeated throughout with myth. The Founder's image is not merely locked into legitimate history, it bobs and weaves between facts, half-remembered truths, and apochrypha. The Founder is perceived by Barbee as a culture hero bringing order out of chaos, bringing wisdom to bear upon fear and ignorance. He is compared to Moses, Aristotle, and Jesus. He is called, by Homer Barbee, "prophet," "godly man," "the great spirit," and "the great sun." In his hardships and moments of danger, he is helped by strange emissaries, one of whom, Barbee says, may have come "direct from above." Another of the Founder's helpers is an old slave who is ridiculed by the town's children:

> He, the old slave, showing a surprising knowledge of such matters— *germology* and *scabology*—Ha! Ha! Ha!—he called it, and what youthful skill of the hands! For he shaved our skull, and cleansed our wound and bound it neat with bandages stolen from the home of an unsuspecting leader of the mob. Ha!

Barbee makes his audience, composed primarily of Black college students, identify with the Founder. No, in fact, under the spell of the ritual sermon, they must *become* the Founder. They must don the mask of the god, so to speak. All of these details are said to be remembered by the students, but yet, Barbee has a compulsive need to reiterate them, to recharge them with meaning by reconsecrating them. His essential role, as ritual priest, is to keep before them the "painful details" of the Founder's life. These are memories that his young audience must internalize, and share fully, if they are to ever realize themselves in the passage from adolescence into maturity. And this is the function of folk culture. This is what Ellison sensed in the blues. In an essay entitled, "Richard Wright's Blues," he notes:

> The blues is an impulse to keep the painful details and episodes of a brutal experience alive in one's aching consciousness, to finger its jagged grain, and to transcend it, not by the consolation of philosophy but by squeezing from it a near-tragic, near-comic lyricism. As a form, the blues is an autobiographical chronicle of personal catastrophe expressed lyrically . . ."

In "Blues People," a review of Imamu Baraka's (LeRoi Jones) book, he makes this statement about the role of the blues singer:

> Bessie Smith might have been a "blues queen" to the society at large, but within the tighter Negro community where the blues were part of the total way of life, and a major expression of an attitude toward life, she was a priestess, a celebrant who affirmed the values of the group and man's ability to deal with chaos.[4]

---

[4] Ellison's review of *Blue's People* is stringently critical, and at times a little beside the point. What he really seems to be doing here is castigating LeRoi Jones for not writing the book that he (Ellison) would have written. The specific thrust of *Blues People* was never really analyzed. Of course Ellison is capable of analyzing the specific ideas in *Blues People,* but he just wanted to write his own essay on the blues. And his essay is worthwhile and meaningful, too. Both works taken together, however, make pertinent reading.

Blues represent a central creative motif throughout *Invisible Man* from the hero's "descent" into the music at the beginning of the novel. The blues allow Trueblood to face up to himself after the disastrous event of making his daughter pregnant. The blues inform the texture of much of the novel's prose:

> . . . My stomach felt raw. From somewhere across the quiet of the campus the sound of a guitar blues plucked from an out-of-tune piano drifted towards me like a lazy, shimmering wave, like the echoed whistle of a lonely train, and my head went over again, against a tree, and I could hear it splattering the flowering vines.

And at another point the hero contemplates the meaning of this blues lyric:

> *She's got feet like a monkee*
> *Legs*
> *Legs, legs like a maaad*
> *Bulldog . . .*

"What does it mean," he thinks.

> . . . And why describe anyone in such contradictory words? Was it a sphinx? Did old Chaplin-pants, old dusty butt, love her or hate her; or was he merely singing? What kind of woman could love a dirty fellow like that, anyway? And how could even *he* love her if she were as repulsive as the song described . . . I strode along hearing the cartman's song become a lonesome, broad-toned whistle now that flowered at the end of each phrase into a tremulous, blue-toned chord. And in its flutter and swoop, I heard the sound of a railroad train highballing it, lonely across the lonely night. He was the Devil's son-in-law, all right, and he was a man who could whistle a three-toned chord . . . God damn, I thought, they're a hell of a people! And I didn't know whether it was pride or disgust that suddenly flashed over me.

Why this emphasis on folklore and blues culture? In a recent issue of the College Language Association (CLA) Journal, George Kent supplies an answer which many of those who consider themselves nationalists should well consider:

> Offering the first drawings of a group's character, preserving situations repeated in the history of the group, describing the boundaries of thought and feeling, projecting the group's wisdom in symbols, expressing its will to survive, embodying those values by which it lives and dies, folklore seemed, as Ellison described it, basic to the portrayal of the essential spirit of black people.

Ellison's fundamental spiritual roots are, therefore, deep in the Black American folk tradition. I think that this awareness of specifically Black contributions to the so-called mainstream of American life gives him a fundamental certainty that no matter how much he praises the writers of the white West, he is still himself: Ralph *Waldo* Ellison. Much of Ellison's concern with the major literary figures of Europe and America emanates from his sincere belief that it is the duty of every writer, Black or white, to be fully aware of the best that has ever been written. For Ellison that has never meant *becoming* a white man. It meant bringing to bear on literature and language the force of one's own sensibility and modes of feeling. It meant learning the craft of fiction, even from white artists, but dominating that craft so much that you don't play like the other feller any more. That trumpet you got in your hand may have been made in Germany, but you sure sound like my Uncle Rufus whooping his coming-home call across the cotton fields. But you got to master the instrument first, Ellison might say. I would agree to that, but add: you got to somehow master *yourself* in the process.

If there is any fundamental difference I have with Mr. Ellison, it is his, perhaps unintentional, tendency to imply that Black writers should confine their range of cultural inquiry strictly to America, and even Europe. For a man who was not exactly parochial about his search for knowledge to subtly impose such attitudes on young writers, is to deny the best aspects of his own development as an artist.

Young writers, on the other hand, should not fall for any specious form of reasoning that limits the range of their inquiry strictly to African and Afro-American subject matter. A realistic movement among the Black Arts community should be about the *extension* of the *remembered* and a *resurrection* of the *unremembered;* should be about an engagement with the *selves* we know and the *selves* we have forgotten. Finally, it should be about a synthesis of the conglomerate of world knowledge; all that is meaningful and moral and that makes one stronger and wiser in order to live as fully as possible, as a human being. What will make this knowledge ours is what we do with it, how we color it to suit our specific needs. Its value to us will depend upon what we bring to bear upon it. In our dispersal, we can "dominate" Western culture, or be "dominated" by it. It all depends on what you feel about yourself. Any Black writer or politician who does not believe that Black people have created something powerful and morally sustaining in their 400 or so years here has declared himself a loser before the war begins. How would we create, even fight, denying the total weight of our particular historical experience *here* in America.

I must emphasize the word "total" because, as Ellison and Albert Murray often explain, there is a tendency among American sociologists and Black creative intellectuals to perceive our history in purely pathological terms. For example, Don L. Lee makes a statement in *Ebony* magazine to the following effect: If you don't know about rats and roaches, you don't know about the Black experience. Why define yourself in purely negative terms, when you know that your very life itself, in its most profound aspects, is not merely a result of the negative. We are not simply, in *all* areas of our sensibilities, merely a set of black reactions to white oppression. And neither should our art be merely an aesthetic reaction to white art. It has finally got to exist as good art also, because in terms of the development of a national art, excellent art is, in and of itself, the best propaganda you can have. By now, we should be free enough to use any viable techniques that will allow us to shape an art that breathes, and is based essentially on our own emotional and cultural imperatives.

However, Ellison almost overwhelmingly locates his cultural, philosophical, and literary sensibility in the West. That's his prerogative, and that prerogative should be protected. But being so-called free individuals, at least on the question of whom one accepts as "literary ancestors," it is possible to extend one's vocabulary and memory in any manner one chooses. It's already being done in music; Coltrane, Sun Ra, Pharaoh Sanders and Leon Thomas indicate devices, procedures, functions, attitudes and concerns that are not vividly indicated in Euro-American culture. They indicate a synthesis and a rejection of Western musical theory all at the same time.[5] Just as aspects of Louis Armstrong's trumpet-playing indicated, in its time, a respect for the traditional uses of the instrument, on the one hand; and on the other, to the squares, it indicated a "gross defilement" of the instrument. I recall once reading an article about a descendant of A. J. Sax, the Belgian instrument-maker. The descendant said something to the effect that he didn't believe his father intended for the instrument to be played the way jazz musicians were playing it. Yeah, you can take the other dude's instruments and play like your Uncle Rufus' hog callings. But there is another possibility also: *You could make your own instrument.* And if you can sing through that

[5] This statement itself requires a whole essay on contemporary black music. Check out my essay in the January 1970 issue of *Negro Digest*. See Amiri Baraka's writings, and James Stewart's essay in *Black Fire*.

instrument, you can impose your voice on the world in an heretofore unthought of manner.

In short, you can create another world view, another cosmology springing from your own specific grounds, but transcending them as your new world realizes itself.

All Black creative artists owe Ellison special gratitude. He and a few others of his generation have struggled to keep the culture alive in their artistic works. We should not be content with merely basking in the glow of their works. We need what they have given us. But the world has changed. Which is as it should. And we have changed in the world. Which is quite natural. Because everybody and everything is change. However, what Ellison teaches us is that it is not possible to move toward meaningful creative ends without somehow taking with you the accumulated weight of your forebears' experiences.

What I think we have to do is to understand our roles as synthesizers; the creators of new and exciting visions out of the accumulated weight of our Western experience. We must also deeply understand the specific reasons, both historically and emotionally, that cause many of us to *feel* that there is a range of ideas beyond those strictly of the West. To be more precise, no philosophical, political, or religious attitude in the world today, Western or Eastern, fully provides the means of mankind's spiritual and psychic liberation. No one system of ethics, oriental or occidental, exists in harmony with the social world from which it springs. Why?

Perhaps, it is because the one central component of Man's sensibility which would allow him to survive on human terms has never been allowed to flower. And that is the artistic sensibility which essentially defines Man as a spiritual being in the world. That is because politicians have never accepted the idea that art was simply a public gesture, hence not political. Therefore, Ellison is incorrect when he says to Irving Howe: "I would have said that it [the novel] is always a public gesture, though not necessarily a political one." This statement is only half-true. The novel is *both* a public gesture and a political gesture. As Ellison knows, burning a Cadillac on the White House Lawn[6] is a public gesture, but it is amusingly political also. The minute a work of art enters the social sphere, it faces the problem of being perceived on all kinds of levels, from the grossly political to the philosophically sublime. It just be's that way, that's

---

[6] See Ellison's short story in *Partisan Review* (Spring, 1963) entitled, "It Always Breaks Out."

all. And Marx hasn't a thing to do with it. But Marxists implicitly understand the relationship between a work's public character and its political character, however minute a work's political characteristics might be. And that is why totalitarian and fascist regimes must suppress all genuine art. "Who is that fool babbling all kinds of ghosts and chimera out of his eyes, ears, hands, feet, and mouth? We can't understand him. He must certainly be enemy."

In a system of strategies, of statement, and counter-statement, art is just one other element in the ring, even when it dons an elaborate mask and pretends not to be saying what it really says. *Invisible Man* is artistically one of the world's greatest novels; it is also one of the world's most successful "political" novels. It is just that Ellison's politics are ritualistic as opposed to secular. Ellison's manipulation of rhetorical imagery in *Invisible Man* is enough to blow the average politician off the stand.

The poet, the writer, is a key bearer of culture. Through myth, he is the manipulator of both the collective conscious and unconscious. If he is good, he is the master of rhetorical imagery. And as such, he is much more psychically powerful than the secular politician. And that is why he is, to some extent, in some societies, feared and suppressed by secular politicians. Sometimes, he is suppressed even by the laity who must finally embrace his art, if it is to live. But the suppression of art, whether it occurs in the West or in the East, whether it occurs under capitalism or socialism, is detrimental to Man's spiritual survival. Without spirit, the substance of all of his material accomplishments means essentially nothing. Therefore, what we might consider is a system of politics and art that is as fluid, as functional, and as expansive as Black music. No such system now exists, we're gonna have to build it. And when it is finally realized, it will be a conglomerate, gleaned from the *whole* of all of our experiences.

> Later now:
> A cool *asante*
> in the hey y'all,
> *habari gani* to yo' mamma,
> this has been your sweet Poppa Stoppa
> running the voodoo down.

The Music of Invisibility

by Tony Tanner

'Could this compulsion to put invisibility down in black and
white be thus an urge to make music of invisibility?'

(Invisible Man)

In the Introduction to his essays *(Shadow and Act)*, Ralph Ellison, recalling the circumstances of his youth, stresses the significance
of the fact that while Oklahoman jazz musicians were developing "a
freer, more complex and driving form of jazz, my friends and I were
exploring an idea of human versatility and possibility which went
against the barbs or over the palings of almost every fence which
those who controlled social and political power had erected to restrict our roles in the life of the country." The fact that these musicians working with "tradition, imagination and the sounds and emotions around them," could create something new which was both
free yet recognizably formed (this is the essence of improvisation)
was clearly of the first importance for Ralph Ellison; the ideas of
versatility and possibility which he and his friends were exploring
provide the ultimate subject-matter, and nourish the style, of his
one novel to date, *Invisible Man* (1952), a novel which in many ways
is seminal for subsequent American fiction. His title may owe something to H. G. Wells's novel *The Invisible Man,* for the alienated
Griffin in Wells's novel also comes to realize "what a helpless absurdity an Invisible Man was—in a cold and dirty climate and a
crowded, civilized city" and there is a very suggestive scene in which
he tries to assemble an identity, which is at the same time a disguise,
from the wigs, masks, artificial noses, and clothes of Omniums, the
large London store. It would not be surprising if Wells's potentially

"The Music of Invisibility," by Tony Tanner. From *City of Words: American
Fiction, 1950–1970* (New York: Harper and Row, Publishers, 1971), pp. 50–64.
Copyright © 1971 by Tony Tanner. Reprinted by permission of the Harper and
Row, Publishers, and Jonathan Cape, Ltd.

very probing little novel about the ambiguity involved in achieving social "identity" had stayed in Ellison's extremely literate memory. But if it did so it would be because Ellison's experience as a Negro had taught him a profounder sort of invisibility than any chemically induced vanishing trick. As the narrator says in the opening paragraph, it is as though he lives surrounded by mirrors of distorting glass, so that other people do not see him but only his surroundings, or reflections of themselves, or their fantasies. It is an aspect of recent American fiction that work coming from members of so-called minority groups has proved to be relevant and applicable to the situation of people not sharing their immediate racial experience or, as it may be, sexual inclination; and *Invisible Man,* so far from being limited to an expression of an anguish and injustice experienced peculiarly by Negroes, is quite simply the most profound novel about American identity written since the war.

The book begins and ends in a small underground room, situated significantly in a "border area." It is there that the unnamed narrator—unnamed because invisible on the social surface—is arranging his memories, structuring his experiences, creating his life. It is important to bear this in mind since the book is not only an account of events but quite as importantly about what the consciousness of the narrator has managed to make of those events, how it has managed to change because of them. His little room is flooded with the light from 1,369 light bulbs, run by free current drained off from the Monopolated Light and Power Company. It is an echo of Hemingway's "clean, well-lighted place" but with many significant differences. The narrator has had experience of electricity before. As a child he had been engaged in one of those grotesque entertainments in which white Southerners make negro youths fight among themselves for coins which they are then invited to pick up from an electrified rug. The narrator discovers that if he is careful he can contain the electricity, but then he is thrown bodily on to the rug by the white men who persist in shouting misleading cues and directions. The agony is intense and it seems that a century will pass before he can roll free.

The whole experience is an early paradigm of the treatment he is to receive all through his adult life. Later in life he is given electric shock "treatment" which is intended to have the effect of a prefrontal lobotomy without acutally cutting into the brain. The white doctor explains his technique, describing how they apply pressure to the centres of nerve control—"our concept is Gestalt." This implies that simply by applying the appropriate pressures they can alter the way a man reads reality, another device for that monitoring of consciousness which is so abhorrent to the American hero. And the electricity is important here. It can be seen as the indispensable force by which society warms and lights its way. That power can be also used to make cruel sport of the individual, to condition him, make him jump to the whim of the man at the controls. The question is, can the narrator find a way to "contain" this power, to use it without being its helpless victim or its ruthless exerciser?

The first time he finds himself in opposition to the existing authorities, Dr Bledsoe, who runs the Uncle Tom-like State College for negroes in the South, tells him, "This is a power set-up, son, and I'm at the controls." The moral would seem to be—control or be controlled; as when, later in his life, he sees two pictures of bull-fighting in a bar in one of which the matador gracefully dominates the bull while in the second he is being tossed on the black bull's horns. There is a black powerhouse close to the white buildings of the college, and while the notion of black power which has since emerged in America is not entirely irrelevant here, Ellison is making the much more profound point that power is what keeps society going at all levels; the lights in the library and the chapel, the machines in the factory and the hospital all derive from the morally neutral force of electricity. Morality starts when man diverts this power to specific ends. The experience of the narrator is that it is usually used for the more or less cynical manipulaton of individuals. Yet electricity is also a source of light, and the achievement of the narrator must be to find a way out of the power set-up altogether (for to be a controller is more pernicious than to be one who is controlled) and tap some of that power for his own private purpose—to "illuminate the blackness of my invisibility," to become aware of his own form.

The odyssey which the narrator, with the aid of 1,369 light bulbs, looks back on takes place on many levels. His travelling is geographic, social, historical and philosophical. In an early dream he finds inside his brief-case an envelope which contains an endless recession of smaller envelopes, the last of which contains the simple message "Keep This Nigger-Boy Running." It is only at the end when he finally burns all the contents of his real brief-case that he can start to control his own momentum. Up to that point his movements are really controlled from without, just like the people in the New York streets who to him seem to walk as though they were directed by "some unseen control." The pattern of his life is one of constraint and eviction; he is alternately cramped and dispossessed.

This is true of his experience in the college, the factory, the hospital, the Party. What he discovers is that every institution is bent on processing and programming the individual in a certain way; yet if a man does not have a place in any of the social structures the danger is that he might fall into chaos.

At his college, in the chapel everybody seems to have eyes of robots and faces like frozen masks (i.e. "fixed" in rigid roles), and the blind preacher telling them "the way" inaugurates a theme of the blindness or warped vision of all the creatures of the given structures of society, whether leaders or led—a point underlined when Brother Jack's glass eye falls out. References to dolls, actors, masks, dummies, and so on, proliferate throughout, and before the narrator is startled or pushed out of his first given role—at the state college— he too is described, by a man of accredited perceptions, as a "mechanical man." The speaker is addressing Mr Norton, a trustee of the college, whom he aptly calls "a trustee of consciousness." He is making the point that such institutions turn out automata, who accept the rigid and restraining role imposed on them as true identity, and defer to the white man's version of reality.

The point about all the representatives of social power that the narrator encounters—teacher, preacher, doctor, factory-owner, Party member, whatever—is that they all seek to control reality and they believe that they can run it according to their plan. To this extent one can say that they have a mechanizing attitude towards reality, and it is no accident that the narrator is constantly getting involved with literal machines (in the factory, the hospital, etc.) as well as with what one might call the mechanizers of consciousness, the servants of church, college or Party. On the other hand there is the point that these institutions, these people at the social controls, do seem to give the individual a role, a place in the scheme of things. At one stage the narrator is enthusiastic about the Party, because it gives the world a meaningful shape and himself an important role in it: "everything could be controlled by our science. Life was all pattern and discipline."

The alternative to the servile docility and rigid regulations of the state college would seem to be the utter chaos of The Golden Day Saloon, which with its fighting and drinking and debauchery seems to be in continuous rehearsal for "the end of the world," as one mad participant proclaims it (see R. W. B. Lewis's fine essay "Days of Wrath and Laughter"[1] for a discussion of the apocalyptic hints in

[1] In *Trials of the Word* (New Haven: Yale University Press, 1965).

the novel). It may be more real, more authentic than the fabricated performances in the chapel at the college, but in its utterly shapeless confusion it offers no opportunities for self-development or self-discovery. Society does indeed impose false surfaces on things; a point well made at the paint factory where the narrator has to mix in a black constituent which nevertheless produces a dazzling Optic White paint used for government buildings. It reminds the narrator of the white painted buildings of the campus; it also reminds him that The Golden Day had once been painted white but that now it was all flaking away. The fact that the paint is called Liberty Paint in conjunction with the suggestion that it is at least in part an optical illusion (the narrator can see a grey in the white which his overseer ignores or cannot detect) is a fairly clear irony; we are in fact "caught" in the official version of reality—the painted surfaces— maintained by the constituted authorities. On the other hand, if you strip all the false paint away you are likely to be confronted with the merely chaotic "truth" of The Golden Day. In the same way, the mechanizers and controllers of reality turn people into automata and manipulable dummies; but can a man achieve any visible shape or role if he refuses to join any of the existing patterns?

This is indeed the narrator's problem. When he is about to be sent away from the college he feels that he is losing the only identity that he has ever known. At this stage he equates a stable niche in the social structure with an identity, and for a long time his quest is for some defining and recognized employment. The matter of the letters from Bledsoe is instructive; they are supposed to be helping him find a job which might enable him to return to his higher education, whereas in fact they are treacherously advancing Bledsoe's scheme of keeping him as far away from college as possible. He feels all along that he is playing a part in some incomprehensible "scheme," but it is only when the younger Emerson shows him one of the letters that he begins to understand. "Everyone seemed to have some plan for me, and beneath that some more secret plan." It is an essential part of his education that he should come to realize that "everybody wanted to use you for some purpose" and that the way they recognize you, on and in their own terms, is not to be confused with your identity.

After his accident in the factory he undergoes what is in effect a process of rebirth—not organically but electrically. From his fall into the lake of heavy water and on to his coming to consciousness with a completely blank mind in a small glass-and-nickel box, and his subsequent struggle to get out, it reads like a mechanized parody of the birth process. The electrical treatment has temporarily erased his earlier consciousness and he cannot say who he is or what his name is. His only concern is to get out of the machine without electrocuting himself. "I wanted freedom, not destruction . . . I could no more escape than I could think of my identity. Perhaps, I thought, the two things are involved with each other. When I discover who I am, I'll be free." This, coming nearly halfway through the book, is a crucial turning-point. The machine is every system by which other people want to manipulate him and regulate his actions. In much the same way the Party gives him a new identity and tries to reprogramme him for its ends. The narrator is not a nihilist—he does not wish to smash the machine, knowing that he will probably be destroyed with it—but he wants to find some sort of freedom from the interlocking systems which make up society, and he realizes that it will have to be mainly an inner freedom. At the end he can look back and see that the individuals from various professions or parties who had sought to direct and use him "were very much the same, each attempting to force his picture of reality upon me and neither giving a hoot in hell for how things looked to me." This is why he wants to be free of all parties, all partial pictures, all the imposed and imprisoning constructs of society. This urge will bring him to a second rebirth near the end—this time a private, self-managed one. But before coming to that we should consider some of the advice and examples he has received from figures who are not on the side of the system-makers, not enlisted among the controllers.

His grandfather on his deathbed has given the advice to "overcome 'em with yeses," and only by the end can the narrator see a possible hidden meaning in this exhortation. Before he leaves for New York, the vet in The Golden Day advises him that, once there, he should play the game without believing it: he explains that he will be "hidden right out in the open" because "they" will not expect him to know anything and therefore will not be able to see him. When asked by the narrator who "they" refers to, he answers, "Why the same *they* we always mean, the white folks, authority, the gods, fate, circumstances—the force that pulls your strings until you refuse to be pulled any more." Three further things he says to the narrator are of particular importance. He tells him that much of his freedom will have to be "symbolic"—a deeper truth perhaps than he knows for the boy who will ultimately find his freedom in the symbols called words. He says, "Be your own father, young man," an Oedipal echo (picking up the description we have already had of the narrator standing where three roads converge) and a warning to the boy that he will have to create an identity, not rely on assuming one already waiting for him. Thirdly, he bids him remember that the world is "possibility." And this anticipates the narrator's encounter with Rinehart which is perhaps the most important "epiphany" in the book.

Before this encounter there is the decisive incident connected with Tod Clifton, the narrator's friend who suddenly drops all Party work and makes himself into a sort of parody Negro. Tod becomes a street-hawker in Harlem, mongering self-mocking black dolls. He is duly killed, as his name forwarns us, by a policeman—the cause of his death being described as "resisting reality." It is Tod who, after a bitter encounter with the black fantatic Ras, speculates that, "I suppose sometimes a man *has* to plunge outside history." History is the temporal dimension of the social structure, its emerging shape, as well as being the accumulation of memories which weigh on us. It is everything that has conditioned society and the individual within it. History we could say is the visible part of society's progress or change, the fraction that shows above the surface. It is worth stressing this because we often see the narrator entering, or falling into, or retreating to, dark subterranean places. It is in a subway, looking at some sharply dressed black boys, that the narrator has his vision of the significance of all those anonymous people who play no part in history, the transitory ones who will never be classified, too silent to be recorded, too ambiguous to be caught in "the most ambiguous words." "What if history was a gambler . . . What if history was not a reasonable citizen, but a madman full of paranoid guile and these boys his agents, his big surprise? For they were outside . . . running and dodging the forces of history instead of making a dominating stand." If history is a gambler—and truth tends to come in underground places in this book—then all those people up on the surface who regard it as a manipulable machine are wrong. Up there they "distort" people in the interests of some abstract "design"; they force people into tight little boxes, just as Tod is literally trapped in the ulimate confinement of the coffin. Having seen this much the narrator is effectively through with all parties of the surface. It remains for him to see whether there is any alternative mode of life.

This is when he encounters Rinehart, or rather the phenomenon of Rinehart, since Rinehart is not a man to be met so much as a strategy to be made aware of. The narrator comes to "know" Rinehart by being mistaken for him when he adopts a safety disguise. After being taken for a number of contradictory Rineharts—from gambler to Reverend—the narrator suddenly understands and appreciates the significance of this figure. "His world was possibility and he knew it. He was years ahead of me and I was a fool . . . The world in which we lived was without boundaries. A vast seething, hot world of fluidity, and Rine the rascal was at home. Perhaps *only* Rine the rascal was at home in it." The realization makes him feel as though he has just been released from a plaster cast; it suggests what life on the surface never suggested: "new freedom of movement." "You could actually make yourself anew. The notion was frightening, for now the world seemed to flow before my eyes. All boundaries down, freedom was not only the recognition of necessity, it was the recognition of possibility." This is as succinct an expression of the discovery earned in this book as one could wish for. But what follows is also important. "And sitting there trembling I caught a brief glimpse of the possibilities posed by Rinehart's multiple personalities and turned away." I stress this because although the narrator learns his most important lesson from the spectacle of Rinehart he does not wish to emulate him.

If we can simplify the structuring of reality implicit in the book for a moment, we could say that just as figures like Norton, Emerson, Bledsoe and Brother Jack are at home on the surface, which is the realm of social rigidification and the mechanistic manipulations of history; just so Rinehart is the figure most at home in the subterranean world, a fluid darkness flowing on underneath history and society, beneath their shaping powers. This lower realm clearly has its potencies and its truths. But a world of no boundaries, a world given over to "the merging fluidity of forms," which the narrator sees when he puts on his dark glasses, such a world can finally only be a chaos. And Ellison himself has made this point very clear in an interview.[2] Rinehart's middle name is "Proteus" and Ellison intended something quite specific by his character.

> Rinehart is my name for the personification of chaos. He is also intended to represent America and change. He has lived so long with chaos that he knows how to manipulate it. It is the old theme of *The Confidence Man.* He is a figure in a country with no solid past or stable class lines; therefore he is able to move about easily from one to the other.

To emulate Rinehart would be to submit to chaos. Rinehart, whose heart is in fact all rind, really represents the ultimate diffusion and

[2] In *Paris Review,* Spring, 1965; reprinted in *Shadow and Act* (London: Secker and Warburg, 1967).

loss of self; a freedom, indeed, which might easily turn into that nightmare of jelly. The narrator, attempting to discover or create his own identity, does not want to dissolve in fluidity. Yet if he rejects both the life-denying mechanical fixities of the surface operators, and the fluid adaptations and adaptive improvisations of a Rinehart, the question emerges—where can he go, what can he do?

Perhaps we can get nearer the answer if we ask, not where will he go, but how will he move? One thing he learns after all his experiences on different levels is that the prevailing notion that success involved rising *upward* is a lie used by society to dominate its members. "Not only could you travel upward toward success but you could travel downward as well; up *and* down, in retreat as well as in advance, crabways and crossways and around in a circle, meeting your old selves coming and going and perhaps all at the same time." This notion of movement is related to that "running and dodging" of the forces of history he had earlier discerned as a possibility, and is of special importance as it provides the plot lines of many of the novels we will be considering. At the height of the Harlem riots the narrator finds himself running from all parties, but with the new realization that he no longer has to run either for or from the Jacks and Emersons and the Bledsoes and Nortons, "but only from their confusion, impatience, and refusal to recognize the beautiful absurdity of their American identity and mine." And just when it seems that he will be killed in the converging forces of that apocalyptic night (which, like the battle royal he was involved in as a child, is in fact engineered by unscrupulous white people so that the rebels and rioters who think they are generating a scheme of their own are in fact fulfilling someone else's) the narrator falls down a hole into the dark chamber of his second rebirth.

First of all he has to burn all the papers in his brief-case to find his way out of the hole: those papers represent all the schemes and treacheries that his various controllers have planned for him. He is in fact burning up his past and all the false roles it has sought to trap him in. With the aid of the light from the flames (i.e. he has learned something from this past experience) he enters another dimensionless room where he loses all sense of time. He has to go down a long dark passage and then he lies down in a state between waking and dreaming. Subsequently he has a dream of being castrated by a group consisting of all those who had sought to direct and control his previous life. But when he wakes, he is beyond them. "They were all up there somewhere, making a mess of the world. Well, let them. I was through and, in spite of the dream, I was whole." At this point he decides to take up residence underground and with this gesture of repudiation—a plague on both your houses —so characteristic of American literature, the book might well have ended. But there is an Epilogue, and in some ways this is the most important part of the book.

As was noted, while writing the book the narrator has been living underground and in a "border area." The point is worth remembering because throughout his life he has been striving to avoid being forced into either of the two extremes of life-style exemplified by Emerson's and Jack's surface New York and Rinehart's Harlem. "I don't belong to anything," he cries at one point. To be able to exist in a border area is to resist being wholly drawn into one or the other, to secure a bit of private freedom on the edge. And what he has been doing in his refuge of secret illumination is best suggested by a sentence he remembers from his school-teacher, talking about *A Portrait of the Artist as a Young Man*. "Stephen's problem, like ours, was not actually one of creating the uncreated conscience of his race, but of creating the *uncreated features of his face*." The narrator has discovered what many American heroes have discovered, that he is not free to reorganize and order the world, but he can at least exercise the freedom to arrange and name his perceptions of the world. He cannot perhaps assert and define himself in action, but sometimes at least he can assert and create himself in some private space not in the grip of historical forces. While running and dodging in the outside world, the hero may be evolving and discovering and defining his true features in his inner world, like this narrator. His most important affirmation may be, not of any pattern in the outside world, but of the patterning power of his own mind.

This is not the artist as hero so much as the hero out of dire necessity having to become an artist. For it is only in the "symbolic" freedom of lexical space that he can both find and be himself. In writing his book the narrator has created his face. He is aware of the paradox involved in the compulsion "to put invisibility down in black and white"—the phrase pointing nicely both to the black and white which make up the legibility of print, and the patterning of symbolic black and white which in the book itself is one of his main strategies for rendering his experience visible. But in the pursuit of this paradox lies his only freedom. He tells the story of a yokel who beat a prizefighter against all the odds because he simply stepped "inside of his opponent's sense of time." Just so the narrator can step out of other people's times and schemes, but only by creating his own in his writing. He has a memory or dream of asking his mother to define freedom and she answers, "I guess now it ain't nothing but knowing how to say what I got up in my head." This is the freedom which the narrator achieves in the act of seeking it in his writing.

But the problem remains of "the next step." He had every reason for going underground: "my problem was that I always tried to go in everyone's way but my own," which meant that he had never been master of his own direction, and "to lose your direction is to lose your face." He has gone into hibernation in his cellar to find direction and face. But he makes another discovery there. "I couldn't be still even in hibernation. Because, damn it, there's the mind, the *mind*. It wouldn't let me rest." Here indeed we find a conflict of urges shared by many American heroes—the desire to hibernate (celebrated definitively in Washington Irving's tale of Rip Van Winkle—one of the first American "outsiders"!), and the inability to remain still in hibernation. Ellison's narrator speaks both of his "craving for tranquillity, for peace and quiet," and of the "ache" to "convince yourself that you do exist in the real world." The difficulty here is that if you remain in hibernation you are likely to stagnate in unseen inertia; but if you rejoin the shared reality of the surface you are going to be forced into role-playing.

Ellison's narrator defends the value of hibernation as a covert preparation for some subsequent action, but after writing his book he is still wrestling with the problem of defining the nature of that ensuing action. "Yes, but what *is* the next phase?" In hibernation you can become visible to yourself, but to remain in hibernation indefnitely is simply to die. So at the end the narrator says, "the old fascination with playing a role returns, and I'm drawn upward again," and ends his book with the confession that perhaps "I've over-stayed my hibernation, since there's a possibility that even an invisible man has a socially responsible role to play." At the same time there is the recognition that "up above there's an increasing passion to make men conform to a pattern." What the narrator seeks is a way of rejoining the reality of the surface without being forced into another man's pattern or made to play a role to fit an alien scheme. In this he is only one of many recent American heroes who seek some other alternative to the twin "deaths" of total inertia and diffusion into role-playing. It is as though they are bound to oscillate between the reality-starvation involved in complete ego-autonomy, as defined by David Rapaport, and the loss of ego-autonomy involved in the other-directed behaviour of Erving Goffman's hollow role-players. . . . Confronting this problem—sometimes an impasse

—is one of the main subjects of recent American fiction. No wonder the Invisible Man says he has "become acquainted with ambivalence."

We could say then that the Invisible Man, like many after him, is seeking a new way of being in reality. We do not see him rejoin the surface; again like many after him, he leaves us with a verbal definition of the nature of his resolve. He has learned a whole new way of looking at reality and his relation to it. As he now sees it "my world has become one of infinite possibilities" and "life is to be lived, not controlled." What he also recognizes, and this is crucial, is that he too is imposing a pattern on reality by writing the book. Of course, his motive is different and it is the sort of pattern which clarifies and extends his own consciousness rather than one which cramps and limits someone else. But it is important to keep the fact in mind: "the mind that has conceived a plan of living must never lose sight of the chaos against which that pattern was conceived. That goes for societies as well as for individuals."

He is including here a recognition of the fact that even to perceive reality is to organize it in a certain way in one's consciousness—that too is a Gestalt principle. This is another reason why the novel is so preoccupied with eyesight and the problems involved in the fact that we live at the intersections of endlessly different paths of vision. Without some patterning we cannot even experience reality, let alone participate in it. What he has learned is that it is always dangerous to start to confuse your own particular patterning with reality itself. From that point of view reality *is* chaos, and we live only in the patterns we derive from it or impose on it. But if you live too long in any one pattern you are likely to become completely sealed off from all contact with reality—like those people D. H. Lawrence describes as living under an umbrella.[3]

> Man must wrap himself in a vision, make a house of apparent form and stability, fixity. In his terror of chaos he begins by putting up an umbrella between himself and the everlasting whirl. Then he paints the underside of his umbrella like a firmament . . . Man fixes some wonderful erection of his own between himself and the wild chaos, and gradually goes bleached and stifled under his parasol. Then comes a poet, enemy of convention, and makes a slit in the umbrella; and lo! the glimpse of chaos is a vision, a window to the sun.

[3] "Chaos in Poetry," reprinted in *Selected Literary Criticism,* edited by Anthony Beal (London: William Heinemann, 1955).

Ellison's narrator has made this discovery in his own way for himself. What he also recognizes is that his book, too, like any work of
art, is a "fixity" of "apparent form." A glimpse of chaos is also a
glimpse of The Golden Day: to achieve any sense of ongoing identity
man needs those houses and umbrellas. Consciousness depends on
architecture. What is important is not to forget the fluidity in which
it stands.

When he has only been in New York for a short time, the Invisible
Man meets a man pushing a cart loaded down with thousands of
abandoned blueprints and scrapped plans for houses and buildings.
As the man says, "Folks is always making plans and changing 'em."
The narrator in his naivety says, "but that's a mistake. You have to
stick to the plan," and the man answers, "you kinda young, daddy-o."
It is a little parable in passing. Human beings are inveterate planners, but plans are just so many clues for arranging which ultimately
go to the scrap heap. What the narrator has to learn is that there
are bound to be plans, but that any one plan you get involved in
may well involve some falsification or constriction of your essential
self. He drops out of all plans for a while to draw up his own. But
once drawn up that too has to be left behind, as it were. The highest
aspiration would seem to be not to get trapped in any one plan,
while recognizing that to achieve any identity is to be involved in
plans. One could envisage for the narrator a continuing life of
moving in and out of plans; like the rest of us oscillating between
chaos and pattern but much more aware of it than most. In that
awareness lies a measure of his freedom.

In this connection his final comment that he is sloughing off his
old skin is an important metaphor. For "skin," read "plan of any
kind." And just as the narrator sheds skins, so Ellison himself "sheds"
styles, an example of what I meant when I said that the activity of
the American hero was often an analogue of the activity of his
author. Ellison is quite explicit about this. In the interview referred
to he describes how he deliberately changed the style of the book as
the narrator moved from the South to the North and from thence
into a more private territory; at first it is more naturalistic, then
expressionistic, and finally surrealistic, each modulation intended to
express both the state of mind of the narrator and the society he is
involved in. As the hero manages to extract himself from a series of
fixed environments, so the author manifests a comparable suppleness
by avoiding getting trapped in one style.

Another statement from Ellison makes this very clear and helps
to explain the extraordinary proliferation—and sometimes convul-

sion of styles which is so especially characteristic of recent American
fiction (it is seldom indeed one finds a serious writer committing
himself to the sort of naturalism which earlier American writers had
helped to develop). Naturalism, Ellison maintains, tends to lead
writers to despair, and it fails to confront the diversity of America.
Instead, he says,

> I was to dream of a prose which was flexible, and swift, confronting
> the inequalities and brutalities of our society forthrightly, but yet
> thrusting forth its images of hope, human fraternity and individual
> self-realization. It would use the riches of our speech, the idiomatic
> expression and the rhetorical flourishes from past periods which are
> still alive among us.

He feels that it must be possible to write a kind of fiction which can
arrive at relevant truths "with all the bright magic of a fairy tale."
Ellison's prose in the novel is heavily foregrounded, demonstrating
quite deliberately an ability to draw on sources as disparate as
Revelations, the blues, classical literature, Dante, Southern white
rhetoric, Harlem slang, and so on. This should not be seen as a
wildly eclectic attempt to import significance but rather as a delighted display of the resources of consciousness and imagination
which he can bring to bear against the pressures of a changing environment. In such a way the American writer procures some verbal
freedom from the conditioning forces which surround him.

Ellison has not at this time published another novel, although one
called *And Hickman Comes* has long been promised. Considering
the wealth of *Invisible Man* one might wonder whether he had not
put all his material into that one book. He has published a book of
essays called *Shadow and Act,* however, and in these he is visibly
concerned with the same basic themes and problems; whether re-
viewing books on the Negro question or peering back into his own
past, he is always exploring the nature of his American identity and
its relations with the reality around him. And like his fictional narrator he particularly resents those who would pre-empt his reality
by defining it in their terms.

Both as a novelist and as an essayist, one of his primary aims in
writing is to challenge any "patterning" of life—whether fictional,
ideological or sociological—which is a falsification of existence as he
has experienced it. Perhaps the best image Ellison has for the American writer is the one he takes from the story of Menelaus and
Proteus. Eidothea's advice to Menelaus is to keep a firm hold on
Proteus until, after all his changes of shape, he appears as himself,

at which point he will reveal the name of the offended god and how they can make their way home without further interruption.

> For the novelist, Proteus stands for both America and the inheritance of illusion through which all men must fight to achieve reality. Our task then is always to challenge the apparent forms of reality . . . and to struggle with it until it reveals its mad, vari-implicated chaos, its false faces, and on until it surrenders its insight, its truth.

What we should notice is that the Invisible Man does not emulate Proteus Rinehart any more than Ellison envisages the American writer capitulating to the Protean reality around him. In many recent American novels we will find the hero in quest of identity confronting a Protean figure whose quick metamorphoses seem to make him enviably well adapted to reality; but the hero seldom takes him for a model, no matter how much he may learn from him, for that way lies chaos, the nightmare jelly, the ultimate dissolution of self. No fixed patterns, then, but not a reversion to Protean fluidity either; instead a struggle with, a resistance to, both, conducted in some "border area" where author and hero alike attempt to create themselves and come into the meaning of their experience. In projecting his situation in these terms, or in this "Gestalt,' Ellison was, to take up the last line of his novel, speaking albeit "on the lower frequencies" for more American writers than he can have realized.

Ralph Ellison and the Uses
of the Imagination

by Robert Bone

We live only in one place at one time, but far from being bound by it, only through it do we realize our freedom. We do not have to abandon our familiar and known to achieve distinction; rather in that place, if only we make ourselves sufficiently aware of it, do we join with others in other places.

(William Carlos Williams)

Some fourteen years ago an unknown writer, no longer young, published a first novel and, to no one's astonishment more than his own, won the National Fiction Award for 1952. There, suddenly, was the novel, and it spoke eloquently enough, but who was the author of *Invisible Man*? We knew only that the curve of his life was a parabola, moving from Oklahoma City to New York by way of Alabama. In the intervening years we have had some fleeting glimpses of the man and his ideas: the acceptance speech itself, an occasional interview, a fragment of his work in progress. We might have noticed his music criticism in the *Saturday Review* or the recent exchange with Irving Howe in *The New Leader*. But basically the man behind the mask remained invisible.

Now, with the publication of *Shadow and Act*,[1] this remarkable man emerges, at least in silhouette, to the public view. The book contains most of Ellison's essays, from the beginning of his literary career to the present. There are seven apprentice pieces, written in the Forties, which reflect the author's social and political con-

[1] New York: Random House, 1964.

cerns, and seven essays on jazz and the blues, which appeared principally in the late Fifties. There are three interviews of the *Paris Review* genre, and three first-rate essays on literary topics. Along the way, we learn a good deal about the author and the forces that have shaped his sense of life.

The formative years in Oklahoma City are sketched in some detail. Ellison was born in 1914, just seven years after Oklahoma was admitted to the Union. In the early days, his adopted grandfather had led a group of settlers from Tennessee to the Oklahoma Territory. Containing such elements, the Negro community of Oklahoma City developed more a Western than a Southern tone. Race relations, like all social relations, were more fluid than in established communities. Frontier attitudes persisted well into the present century, and Ellison was raised in a tradition of aggressiveness and love of freedom. He is proud of his frontier heritage, and to it may be traced his fierce individualism and his sense of possibility.

Oklahoma City was a boomtown in the postwar years—a swirling vortex of social styles and human types. There were many masks which an imaginative adolescent might try on:

> Gamblers and scholars, jazz musicians and scientists, Negro cowboys and soldiers from the Spanish-American and First World Wars, movie stars and stunt men, figures from the Italian Renaissance and literature, both classical and popular, were combined with the special virtues of some local bootlegger, the eloquence of some Negro preacher, the strength and grace of some local athlete, the ruthlessness of some businessman-physician, the elegance in dress and manners of some headwaiter or hotel doorman.[2]

If there was no local writer for a model, there was access to a rich oral literature in the churches, schoolyards, barbershops, and cotton-picking camps. And there was a curious double exposure to the exacting habits of artistic discipline. Through one of the ironies of segregation, the Negro school system placed particular stress on training in classical music. Ellison took up the trumpet at the age of eight and studied four years of harmony in high school. Meanwhile he was exposed to the driving beat of Southwestern jazz, of which Kansas City, Dallas, and Oklahoma City were acknowledged centers. From his boyhood onward, he was caught up in that creative tension between the folk and classical traditions which has remained the richest resource of his art.

In 1933 Ellison enrolled at Tuskegee Institute to study composi-

---

[2] *Shadow and Act*, pp. xv–xvi.

tion under William Dawson, the Negro conductor and composer. In his sophomore year, however, he came upon a copy of *The Waste Land,* and the long transition from trumpet to typewriter had begun. He read widely in American fiction and, initially scorning the moderns, developed a lifelong devotion to the nineteenth-century masters. On coming to New York in 1936 he met Richard Wright, who introduced him on the one hand to the prefaces of Conrad and the letters of Dostoevski, and on the other to the orbit of the Communist party. One evening he accompanied Wright to a fund-raising affair for the Spanish Loyalists, where he met both Malraux and Leadbelly for the first time. It was a notable occasion, symbolic of the times and of the cross-pressures exerted from the first upon his art.

From these cross-pressures Ellison derived his most enduring themes. How could he interpret and extend, define and yet elaborate upon the folk culture of the American Negro and, at the same time, assimilate the most advanced techniques of modern literature? How could he affirm his dedication to the cause of Negro freedom without succumbing to the stridencies of protest fiction, without relinquishing his complex sense of life? In *Shadow and Act,* Ellison returns again and again to these tangled themes: the relationship of Negro folk culture to American culture as a whole, and the responsibility of the Negro artist to his ethnic group.

As instrumentalist and composer, Ellison had faced these issues for the better part of two decades. When he began to write, it was natural for him to draw upon his musical experience for guidelines and perspectives. Not that his approach to writing is merely an extension of an earlier approach to jazz and the blues; they tend, in fact, to reinforce each other. But his experience with jazz was formative; it left a permanent mark upon his style. His controlling metaphors are musical, and if we are to grasp his thought, we must trace his language to its source. There, in the world of Louis Armstrong and Charlie Parker, Bessie Smith and Jimmy Rushing, we may discover the foundations of Ellison's aesthetic.

Music

The essence of jazz is group improvisation. Its most impressive effects are achieved, according to Ellison, when a delicate balance is maintained between the individual performer and the group. The form itself, consisting of a series of solo "breaks" within a framework of standard chord progressions, encourages this balance. "Each true jazz moment," Ellison explains, "springs from a contest in which each artist challenges all the rest; each solo flight, or improvisation, represents (like the successive canvases of a painter) a definition of his identity: as individual, as member of the collectivity, and as a link in the chain of tradition." "True jazz," he concludes, "is an art of individual assertion within and against the group."

Here is a working model for the Negro writer. By balancing conflicting claims upon his art, he can solve his deepest problems of divided loyalty. As an artist with a special function to perform within the Negro group, the writer must be careful to preserve his individuality. He must learn to operate "within and against the group," allowing neither claim to cancel out the other. Similarly on the cultural plane, where the Negro's group identity is at stake. Here the writer can affirm whatever is uniquely Negro in his background while insisting precisely on the American quality of his experience. "The point of our struggle," writes Ellison, "is to be both Negro and American and to bring about that condition in American society in which this would be possible."

Closely related to the question of individual and group identity is that of personal and traditional styles. Every jazz musician must strike a balance between tradition and experimentation, for "jazz finds its very life in an endless improvisation upon traditional materials." It follows that no jazzman is free to repudiate the past. The jam session, where he must display a knowledge of traditional techniques, will see to that. He must master "the intonations, the mute work, manipulation of timbre, the body of traditional styles" before he can presume to speak in his own voice. The path, in short, to self-expression lies through what is given, what has gone before.

As an American Negro writer, Ellison inherits a double obligation to the past. He must become familiar with a folk tradition which is his alone, and with a wider literary culture which he shares. Moreover, he must strive in both dimensions for a proper blend of past and present, given and improvised. In describing his response to his folk tradition, Ellison draws a parallel to the work of Picasso: "Why, he's the greatest wrestler with forms and techniques of them all. Just the same, he's never abandoned the old symbolic forms of Spanish art: the guitar, the bull, daggers, women, shawls, veils, mirrors." Similarly, Ellison appropriates folkloristic elements from Negro culture, embroiders on them, adapts them to his literary aims, and lifts them to the level of a conscious art.

In the wider context of American literature, the same principles apply. Consider Ellison's experimental idiom. Not since Jean

Toomer has a Negro novelist been so inventive of new forms, new language, new technical devices. And yet none has been so deeply immersed in the American literary past. As Ellison struggles toward the realization of a personal style, he is *improvising* on the achievement of our nineteenth-century masters. It is this body of writing, he insists, "to which I was most attached and through which . . . I would find my own voice, and to which I was challenged, by way of achieving myself, to make some small contribution, and to whose composite picture of reality I was obligated to offer some necessary modifications."

Still a third balance must be struck between constraint and spontaneity, discipline and freedom. For the jazzman owes his freedom to the confident possession of technique. From his own struggles with the trumpet, Ellison learned how much the wild ecstatic moment depends on patient hours of practice and rehearsal. Freedom, he perceived, is never absolute, but rooted in its opposite. The game is not to cast off all restraint but to achieve, within the arbitrary limits of a musical tradition, a transcendent freedom. Jazz taught Ellison a respect for limits, even as it revealed the possibility of overcoming limits through technique. It was the blues, however, that taught him to discern in this paradox an emblem of the human condition.

The blues arise out of a tension between circumstance and possibility. The grim reality that gives them birth bespeaks the limits and restrictions, the barriers and thwartings, which the universe opposes to the human will. But the tough response that is the blues bespeaks a moral courage, a spiritual freedom, a sense of human possibility, which more than balances the scales. In Ellison's words, "The blues is an art of ambiguity, an assertion of the irrepressibly human over all circumstances whether created by others or by one's own human failings. They are the only consistent art in the United States which constantly reminds us of our limitations while encouraging us to see how far we can actually go."

The blues begin with personal disaster. They speak of flooded farmlands and blighted crops, of love betrayed and lovers parted, of the black man's poverty and the white man's justice. But what matters is the human response to these events. For the blues are a poetic confrontation of reality. They are a form of spiritual discipline, a means of transcending the painful conditions with which they deal. The crucial feature of the blues response is the margin of freedom it proclaims. To call them an art of ambiguity is to assert that no man is entirely the victim of circumstance. Within limits, there is always choice and will. Thinking of this inner freedom, Ellison speaks of "the secular existentialism of the blues."

This sense of possibility lies at the center of Ellison's art. It explains his devotion to his craft, for what is technique but another name for possibility? It explains his attitude toward protest fiction, for the propaganda novel, in portraying the Negro primarily as victim, gives more weight to circumstances than possibility. Ellison's is a more plastic sensibility. His heroes are not victims but adventurers. They journey toward the possible in all ignorance of accepted limits. In the course of their travels, they shed their illusions and come to terms with reality. They are, in short, picaresque heroes, full of "rash efforts, quixotic gestures, hopeful testings of the complexity of the known and the given."

If circumstance often enough elicits tears, possibility may release a saving laughter. This blend of emotion, mixed in some ancient cauldron of the human spirit, is characteristic of the blues. It is a lyricism better sampled than described. Note in Ellison's example how the painful humiliation of the bird is controlled, or absorbed, or even converted into triumph by a kind of grudging laughter:

> Oh they picked poor robin clean
> They picked poor robin clean
> They tied poor robin to a stump
> Lord, they picked all the feathers
> Round from robin's rump
> Oh they picked poor robin clean

The blues have nothing to do with the consolations of philosophy. They are a means of neutralizing one emotion with another, in the same way that alkalies can neutralize an acid stomach. For the American Negro, they are a means of prophylaxis, a specific for the prevention of spiritual ulcers. It is not a question of laughing away one's troubles in any superficial sense, but of gazing steadily at pain while perceiving its comic aspect. Ellison regards this tragicomic sensibility as the most precious feature of his Negro heritage. From it stems his lyrical intensity and the complex interplay of tragic and comic elements which is the distinguishing mark of his fiction.

If the blues are primarily an expression of personal emotion, they also serve a group need. Perhaps the point can best be made through a comparison with gospel singing. When Mahalia Jackson sings in church, she performs a ritual function. Her music serves "to prepare the congregation for the minister's message, to make it receptive to the spirit and, with effects of voice and rhythm, to evoke a shared community of experience." Similarly in the secular context of the blues. When Jimmy Rushing presided over a Saturday night dance in Oklahoma City, he was acting as the leader of a public rite: "It was when Jimmy's voice began to soar with the spirit of the blues that the dancers—and the musicians—achieved that feeling of communion which was the true meaning of the public jazz dance."

We are dealing here with substitute rituals. During an epoch which has witnessed the widespread breakdown of traditional religious forms, Ellison finds in jazz and the blues, as Hemingway found in the bullfight, a code of conduct and a ceremonial framework for his art. "True novels," he insists, "arise out of an impulse to celebrate human life and therefore are ritualistic and ceremonial at their core." Ellison perceives, in short, the priestly office of the modern artist and assumes the role of celebrant in his own work. Like the blues singer, he is motivated by an impulse to restore to others a sense of the wholeness of their lives.

Finally, specific features of Ellison's literary style may be traced to his musical background. His fondness for paradox and ambiguity, for example, derives from the blues: "There is a mystery in the whiteness of blackness, the innocence of evil and the evil of innocence, though being initiates Negroes express the joke of it in the blues." The changing styles of *Invisible Man* (from naturalism to expressionism to surrealism, as Ellison describes the sequence) are based on the principle of modulation. Chord progressions in jazz are called "changes"; they correspond in speed and abruptness to Ellison's sense of American reality, the swift flow of sound and sudden changes of key suggesting the fluidity and discontinuity of American life.

Literature

Let us now turn from Ellison's musical to his literary heritage. We must begin with the picaresque novel and attempt to explain why this form, which first appeared in Renaissance Spain, should be revived by a contemporary Negro novelist. We must then consider Ellison's affinity for the American transcendentalists, in light of his commitment to the picaresque. Finally, we must examine in some detail two devices that are central to his art.

The picaresque novel emerged toward the end of the feudal and the beginning of the bourgeois epoch. Its characteristic hero, part rogue and part outlaw, transcended all established norms of conduct and violated all ideas of social hierarchy. For with the breakdown of static social relations, a testing of personal limits, a bold confrontation with the new and untried became necessary. Hence the picaresque journey, no longer a religious quest or pilgrimage but a journey toward experience, adventure, personal freedom. It was the journey of the bourgeois soul toward possibility, toward a freedom possessed by neither serf nor lord under the old regime.

It can hardly be an accident that *Invisible Man* and *The Adventures of Augie March* should win the National Fiction Award within two years of one another. Nor that Ellison and Bellow should each acknowledge a major debt to Twain. For *Huckleberry Finn* is the last great picaresque novel to be written by a white Anglo-Saxon American. The genre has been abandoned to the Negro and the Jew who, two generations from slavery or the *shtetl*, experiences for the first time and in full force what Ellison calls the magical fluidity of American life. A century after Hawthorne wrote *The Scarlet Letter,* our minority groups are re-enacting the central drama of that novel: the break with the institutions and authorities of the past and the emergence into an epoch of personal freedom and individual moral responsibility.

Ellison's revival of the picaresque reflects his group's belated access to the basic conditions of bourgeois existence. These consist economically of the freedom to rise and psychologically of "the right and opportunity to dilate, deepen, and enrich sensibility." The Southern Negro who is taught from childhood to "know his place" is denied these basic freedoms. He is deprived of individuality as thoroughly as any serf: "The pre-individualistic black community discourages individuality out of self-defense. . . . Within the ambit of the black family this takes the form of training the child away from curiosity and adventure, against reaching out for those activities lying beyond the borders."

The Great Migration of the Negro masses from Southern farm to Northern city was picaresque in character. In terms of Negro personality, it was like uncorking a bottle of champagne. Traditionally the journey has been made by railroad, and it is no accident that the blues are associated with freight yards, quick get-aways and long journeys in "a side door Pullman car." No accident either that Ellison should emphasize his own wanderings: "To attempt to express that American experience which has carried one back and forth and up and down the land and across, and across again the great river, from freight train to Pullman car, from contact with slavery to contact with the world of advanced scholarship, art and science, is simply to burst such neatly understated forms of the novel asunder."

The bursting forth of Negro personality from the fixed boundaries of southern life is Ellison's essential theme. And it is this, at bottom, that attracts him to the transcendentalists. For what was the central theme of Thoreau, Emerson and Whitman, if not the journeying forth of the soul? These writers were celebrating their emancipation from the Custom House, from the moral and political authority of old Europe. Their romantic individualism was a response to the new conditions created by the Revolution, conditions calling for *self*-government in both the political and moral sphere. Their passion for personal freedom, moreover, was balanced by a sense of personal responsibility for the future of democracy.

Ellison's debt to transcendentalism is manifold, but what is not acknowledged can easily be surmised. He is named, to begin with, for Ralph Waldo Emerson. In this connection he mentions two specific influences: the "Concord Hymn" and "Self-Reliance." The poem presumably inspires him with its willingness to die that one's children may be free; the essay, as we shall see, governs his attitude toward Negro culture. He admires Thoreau, plainly enough, for his stand on civil disobedience and his militant defense of John Brown. Whitman he finds congenial, for such poems as "The Open Road" and "Passage to India" are squarely in the picaresque tradition.

In broader terms, it may be said that Ellison's ontology derives from transcendentalism. One senses in his work an unseen reality behind the surfaces of things. Hence his fascination with guises and disguises, with the con man and the trickster. Hence the felt dichotomy between visible and invisible, public and private, actual and fictive modes of reality. His experience as a Negro no doubt reinforces his ironic awareness of "the joke that always lies between appearance and reality," and turns him toward an inner world that lies beyond the reach of insult or oppression. This world may be approached by means of the imagination; it is revealed during the transcendent moment in jazz or the epiphany in literature. *Transcend* is thus a crucial word in Ellison's aesthetic.

Above all, Ellison admires the transcendentalists for their active democratic faith. They were concerned not only with the slavery question but with the wider implications of cultural pluralism, with the mystery of the one and the many. To these writers, the national motto, *e pluribus unum,* was a serious philosophical concern. Emerson discerned a cosmic model for American democracy in the relationship of soul to Oversoul. Whitman, however, made the classic formulation:

> One's self I sing, a simple separate person,
> Yet utter the word Democracy, the word En-Masse.

Ellison reveals, in his choice of ancestors, the depth of his commitment to American ideals. When he describes jazz as "that embodiment of a superior democracy in which each individual cultivated his uniqueness and yet did not clash with his neighbors," he is affirming the central values of American civilization.

It remains to place Ellison in his twentieth-century tradition. What is involved is a rejection of the naturalistic novel and the philosophical assumptions on which it rests. From Ellison's allusions to certain of his contemporaries—to Stein and Hemingway, Joyce and Faulkner, Eliot and Yeats—one idea emerges with persistent force: *Man is the creator of his own reality.* If a culture shapes its artists, the converse is equally the case: "The American novel is in this sense a conquest of the frontier; as it describes our experience, it creates it." This turn toward subjectivity, this transcendence of determinism, this insistence on an existential freedom, is crucial to Ellison's conception of the artist. It finds concrete expression in his work through the devices of masking and naming.

Masking has its origin in the psychological circumstances of southern life: "In the South the sensibilities of both blacks and whites are inhibited by the rigidly defined environment. For the Negro there is relative safety as long as the impulse toward individuality is suppressed." As soon, however, as this forbidden impulse seeks expression, an intolerable anxiety is aroused. Threatened by his own unfolding personality as much as by the whites, the Negro learns to camouflage, to dissimulate, to retreat behind a protective mask. There is magic in it: the mask is a means of warding off the vengeance of the gods.

Consider the jazz solo, one of the few means of self-expression permitted to the southern Negro. Precisely because it is a solo, and the musician must go it alone, it represents potential danger. Ellison writes of certain jazz musicians: "While playing in ensemble, they carried themselves like college professors or high church deacons; when soloing they donned the comic mask." Louis Armstrong, as Ellison reminds us, has raised masking to the level of a fine art. Musical trickster, con man with a cornet, Elizabethan clown, "he takes liberties with kings, queens, and presidents." In a later development, the bearded mask of the bopster appeared, frankly expressive of hostility, rudeness and contempt. It is a pose which still finds favor among certain Negro writers of the younger generation.

In his own prose, Ellison employs various masking devices, including understatement, irony, *double-entendre* and calculated ambiguity. There is something deliberately elusive in his style, something secret and taunting, some instinctive avoidance of explicit statement which is close in spirit to the blues. His fascination with masquerade gives us two memorable characters in *Invisible Man*: the narrator's grandfather, whose mask of meekness conceals a stubborn resistance to white supremacy, and Rinehart, whom Ellison describes as "an American virtuoso of identity who thrives on chaos and swift change." A master of disguise, Rinehart survives by manipulating the illusions of society, much in the tradition of Melville's Confidence Man, Twain's Duke and Dauphin and Mann's Felix Krull.

Masking, which begins as a defensive gesture, becomes in Ellison's hands a means of altering reality. For if reality is a process of becoming, that process can be partially controlled through manipulation of a ritual object or mask. "Masking," Ellison remarks, "is a play upon possibility," and possibility is precisely the domain of art. To clarify the matter he summons Yeats, a man not ignorant of masks: "If we cannot imagine ourselves as different from what we are and assume the second self, we cannot impose a discipline upon ourselves, though we may accept one from others. Active virtue, as distinct from the passive acceptance of a current code, is the wearing of a mask." Yeats is speaking of morality, of active virtue, but the function of the artist is implicit in his words. Before pursuing the point, however, we must come to terms with a second feature of Ellison's art.

Naming likewise has its origin in negation, in the white man's hypocritical denial of his kinship ties. For the African slaves received from their Christian masters not only European names but a massive infusion of European blood, under circumstances so brutal and degrading as to have been virtually expunged from the national consciousness. At once guilty and proud, the white man has resorted to a systematic *misnaming* in an effort to obscure his crime. Thus the use of the matronymic to conceal the slave's paternity. Thus the insulting epithets which deny not merely kinship but humanity. In some obscene rite of exorcism, the white man says "nigger" when he should say "cousin." And yet the family names persist as symbols of that hidden truth, that broken connection which will have to be restored before the nation, sick from the denial of reality, can regain its mental health.

Having been misnamed by others, the American Negro has attempted from the first to define himself. This persistent effort at self-definition is the animating principle of Negro culture. The earliest appearance of Negro folklore, for example, "announced the

Negro's willingness to trust his own experience, his own sensibilities as to the definition of reality, rather than allow his masters to define these crucial matters for him." Similarly with musical expression: the jazzman who rejects classical technique is affirming his right to define himself in sound. Cultural autonomy, to Ellison, is an elementary act of self-reliance. We have listened too long, he seems to say, to the courtly Muses of white America. "Our names, being the gift of others, must be made our own."

For personal as well as historical reasons, Ellison is fascinated by the distinction between one's given and achieved identity. Named for a famous poet, it was half a lifetime before he could define, let alone accept, the burden of his given name. Acknowledging in retrospect the prescience of his father, he speaks of "the suggestive power of names and the magic involved in naming." We are dealing here with the ritual use of language, with the pressure which language can exert upon reality. This is the special province of the poet, and, broadly speaking, Ellison claims it as his own. He regards the novel as an act of ritual naming; the novelist, as a "moralist-designate" who *names* the central moral issues of his time.

"The poet," writes Ralph Waldo Emerson, "is the Namer or Language-maker." As such, he is the custodian of his language and the guarantor of its integrity. In performance of this function, Ellison has discovered that the language of contemporary America is in certain ways corrupt. "With all deliberate speed," for example, does not mean what it seems to mean when uttered by the Supreme Court of the United States. He proposes a rectification of the language and, therefore, of the nation's moral vision. For accurate naming is the writer's first responsibility: "In the myth, God gave man the task of naming the objects of the world; thus one of the functions of the poet is to insist upon a correspondence between words and ever-changing reality, between ideals and actualities."

As with naming, so with the image-making functions as a whole. The artist, or image-maker, is guardian of the national iconography. And since the power of images for good or evil is immense, he bears an awesome responsibility. If his images are false, if there is no bridge between portrayal and event, no correspondence between the shadow and the act, then the emotional life of the nation is to that extent distorted, and its daily conduct is rendered ineffectual or even pathological. This is the effect of the anti-Negro stereotype, whether in song or statuary, novel or advertising copy, comic strip or film. Images, being ritual objects, or masks, may be manipulated by those who have a stake in the preservation of caste lines. What is required is a rectification of the nation's icons, a squaring of the shadow and the act.

Nor can this be accomplished through the use of counter-stereotypes. Protest fiction, by portraying sociological types, holds its readers at a distance from the human person. But the problem is precisely one of identification. To identify, in the psychological sense, is to become one with. For this process to occur between white reader and Negro character, the writer must break through the outer crust of racial conflict to the inner core of common humanity. He must evoke, by his imaginative power, an act of "painful identification." To succeed requires the utmost in emotional maturity, craftsmanship and skill. For what the artist undertakes, in the last analysis, is the rectification of the human heart.

Politics

If Ellison had remained a jazz musician, he might have been spared a series of political attacks upon his art. No one would have complained, if he had spoken in a jazz idiom, that his riffs were lacking in protest content. No one would have accused him, as he blew up there on the bandstand, of abandoning a posture of clenched militancy. For it is not expected of a Negro jazzman that, like the first trumpet in the Dodger Fan Club, he should sit in the stands during every civil-rights contest and play at appropriate moments, "Da da da datta da: Charge!" So long as he refuses to play for segregated audiences, accepts no gigs from the State Department and does an occasional benefit for SNCC, he is allowed to go about the very difficult business of interpreting Negro experience in sound.

Not so with the Negro novelist, who works in the medium of words. For words have a variety of uses, political exhortation being one. The ideologists, therefore, move in. The question of militancy is raised, bearing not on the novelist's conduct as a citizen or political man but precisely on his creative work, his function as an artist. To those who feel above all else the urgency of the Negro's political struggle, it is not enough that a writer demonstrate his solidarity; he must enlist his image-making powers in the service of the cause. Since no writer who understands the proper uses of imagination can acquiesce in this perversion of his talent, he must prepare to walk that lonesome valley during much of his career, and to accept a good deal of abuse from those who do not recognize the value of his art.

It was predictable enough, given the rising tempo of the civil-rights struggle, that Ellison should be under pressure from the political activists. The Freedom Movement, like all great movements of social liberation, is lacking neither in demagogues nor Philistines. But that so sophisticated a critic and humane a man as Irving Howe should join the attack is scandalous. In an article called "Black Boys and Native Sons," [3] Howe takes Baldwin and Ellison to task for abandoning the "rasping outbursts," "black anger," and "clenched militancy" of Richard Wright. While he sees some signs of hope in Baldwin's recent work, he plainly regards Ellison as unregenerate. Howe's essay prompted a reply from Ellison, and the result was a sharp exchange in *The New Leader*.[4]

One's chief impression of this debate is that the antagonists are arguing at cross-purposes. They shout at one another, but little or no dialogue occurs. Howe's original piece is a monument to tactlessness, and Ellison is understandably provoked into a sometimes angry response. It is a bad show all around, and the issues deserve to be aired in a calmer atmosphere. It is not my intent to mediate, however, for in my opinion Howe is overwhelmingly in the wrong. Nor do I wish to repeat Ellison's arguments which—tone aside—make most of the essential points. I should like rather to explore the philosophical foundations of the controversy. If my argument seems elementary, it is best that we proceed with caution, since, plainly, each of the contestants feels threatened by the other at the center of his being.

Let me begin with a parable. Imagine a Negro writer in the late 1950s (I choose the period advisedly, for Howe describes it as a conservative decade) attempting to decide on a subject for a novel. He has before him two projects, each based on the life of a Dodger baseball hero. The one—call it the Jackie Robinson story—is alive with racial drama: the first Negro ballplayer to make the big time, the insults from the stands, the spikings by opposing players, the mixed reception from his teammates. The other—call it the Roy Campanella story—concerns an athlete who, at the height of his career, spun his car around a curve one icy morning and spent the rest of his life in a wheelchair. Within a year or two his wife divorced him, she, too, a victim of her human frailty.

Suppose, for purposes of argument, that our writer chose to tell the second story. Would that choice suggest to Howe that he was running from reality, the reality of the sharpened spikes? Or is it

[3] *Dissent*, Autumn, 1963.
[4] Dec. 9, 1963, and Feb. 3, 1964. Howe's original piece has been reprinted in *A World More Attractive* (New York: Horizon Press, 1963); Ellison's rejoinder appears in *Shadow and Act* under the title "The World and the Jug."

possible that the Campanella story also contains a reality sufficiently sharp? Nor is there a refusal to confront injustice, for the theme of the second story would have to be injustice on a cosmic scale. Perhaps Howe would attempt a political explanation of our writer's choice. He might propose that during the militant decade of the Thirties such a writer would have turned at once to Jackie Robinson, but that out of his "dependence on the postwar *Zeitgeist*" he turned instead to a subject that was safe. But perhaps these political categories are beside the point. Perhaps our writer chose as he did simply because he felt in that story a deeper sense of human life.

Not all human suffering is racial in origin, that is our initial point. Being Negro, unfortunately, does not release one from the common burdens of humanity. It is for this reason that the blues singer so often deals with other than his racial woes. And it is to this dimension of human, as opposed, to racial, pain that Howe gives insufficient attention. Ultimately, Ellison and Howe are divided over the *locus* of human suffering. One stresses man's position in society; the other, his position in the universe at large.

At issue is a crucial distinction between remediable and irremediable evil. The first, roughly speaking, is the domain of politics and science; the second, of art and religion. One's sense of tragedy is linked to one's perception of irremediable evil. What we have, therefore, in the Howe-Ellison exchange, is a confrontation between Howe's political optimism and Ellison's tragic sensibility. Howe, who still believes in Progress, concentrates on the evil that can be changed to the neglect of that which must be borne.

To the white liberal, racial injustice is a remediable evil. The Negro, however, experiences it in both modes simultaneously. In historical time, things are no doubt getting better, but in one's own lifetime, white oppression is a bitter fact to which one must adjust. The Negro, as Ellison points out, must live with and suffer under the present reality even as he works to change it. Entirely apart from the Movement, he must concern himself with the strategies and techniques of personal survival. It is precisely with this necessity of Negro life that Ellison's art is engaged.

Because of Howe's bias toward remediable evil, it is difficult for him to understand redemptive suffering. Speaking of Richard Wright, he remarks, "He examines the life of the Negroes and judges it without charity or idyllic compensation—for he already knows, in his heart and his bones, that to be oppressed means to lose out on human possibilities." This half-truth, it seems to me, dehumanizes the Negro by depriving him of his human triumph over pain. For as Ellison insists, Negro life is not only a burden but a discipline. Is it idyllic to suggest that Campanella's experience as a Negro might have prepared him in some way for coping with his accident? Was it in any way relevant? Was it, in short, an emotional resource?

If one attends primarily to remediable evil, one may be tempted to make larger claims for politics than history can justify. One may end by making politics the touchstone of a man's humanity: "In response to Baldwin and Ellison, Wright would have said . . . that only through struggle could men with black skins, and for that matter, all the oppressed of the world, achieve their humanity." Perhaps the question of humanity is after all more complex. It would be impertinent to remind Howe, who is a close student of the subject, that in recent Russian history many struggled and were brutalized thereby. But the memoirs of Victor Serge suggest to me that even in the midst of revolution the artist has a special function to perform: to remind the revolution of its human ends.

It will be clear, I trust, that I am speaking out of no hostility to the Freedom Movement or to politics as such. I am arguing not for the abandonment of militancy but for the autonomy of art. There is no need for literature and politics to be at odds. It is only when the aesthete approaches politics as if it were a poem, or when the political activist approaches the poem as if it were a leaflet, that the trouble starts. Phrases like "only through struggle" urge the subordination of art to politics. We must stifle these imperialistic impulses and foster a climate of mutual respect. Emerson distinguishes between the Doer and the Sayer, and refuses to honor one at the expense of the other. "Homer's words," he observes, "are as costly to Homer as Agamemnon's victories are to Agamemnon."

And I would add that Homer's words are as valuable as Agamemnon's victories *to the Greeks.* For I am arguing throughout for the social value of art. When Howe touches on this aspect of the question, he tries invariably to pre-empt all social value for his own position. Ellison, he charges, is pursuing the essentially antisocial goal of "personal realization," while Wright is fulfilling his responsibility to the Negro community. It is a false dichotomy. The Negro writer, who is surely not free of social responsibility, must yet discharge it *in his own fashion,* which is not the way of politics but art; not the lecture platform but the novel and the poem. Without repudiating his sense of obligation to the group, Ellison has tried to express it through services which only the imagination can perform.

What is at issue is the role of the imagination in that complex process which we call civilization. The visionary power, the power of naming, the power of revealing a people to itself are not to be despised. If those who can command these powers are diverted from their proper task, who will celebrate the values of the group, who create those myths and legends, those communal rites which alone endow the life of any group with meaning? These gifts are no less precious to a people (and if you like, no more) than those of personal charisma, theoretical analysis, and political organization which are the special province of the revolutionary. Let us therefore give the imaginative faculty its due, concede its social value, and respect its unique contribution to the process of becoming man.

Culture

At least as important as Ellison's defense of the imagination is his contribution to a theory of American Negro culture. Previous work in the field, whether by Negro or white intellectuals, has stressed the autonomous character of Negro culture, viewing it as an alien or exotic tributary to the mainstream of American life. Ellison proposes a more integrated view. Negro folk culture, to his way of thinking, is an indestructible monument to the national past. Embodying as it does three centuries of American history, it is a bittersweet reminder of what we were and are as a people. Far from being isolated from the mainstream, it marks the channel where the river runs deepest to the sea.

Given the complex interplay of culture and personality, race and social class that shapes the lives of American Negroes, some degree of theoretical clarity, some modicum of sophistication in these matters is essential. Not only racial strategies but one's own sanity and peace of mind are at stake. For every American Negro responds, at some level of his being, to two apparently disjunctive cultural traditions. If this can be shown to be an arbitrary division, false to the realities of American history, not only will the personal tensions ease but the Freedom Movement will be seen in new perspective. Integration will now appear as a mutual attempt, by American whites as well as Negroes, to restore a splintered culture to a state of wholeness.

The problem of dual identity is particularly acute for members of the Negro middle class. Suspended between two cultural traditions, each with its own claims and loyalties, the educated Negro has been caught on the horns of a dilemma. To identify closely with the life-style of the white middle class has generally led to a rejection of

Negro folk culture. Conversely, to identify closely with the life-style
of the Negro masses has implied a disaffection with the dominant
values of American civilization. This conflicting pattern of identification and rejection has produced two broad currents of thought
and feeling which I have elsewhere called assimilationism and Negro
nationalism. Let me describe them briefly, for purposes of contrast
with Ellison's point of view.

Assimilationism is a natural response to the experience of upward
mobility. As the Negro middle class becomes differentiated from the
masses by virtue of income, education, and social status, it looks
back upon its origins with embarrassment and shame. Negro folk
culture, this rising middle class would argue, is the creation of an
illiterate peasantry. It is vulgar and often shocking, permeated with
the smell of poverty, reminiscent of our degradation and our pain.
However well it may attest to what we were, it contains nothing of
enduring value for us or for our children. On the contrary, it is a
major obstacle to integration. The white middle class will accept
us only to the extent that we become like them. It is therefore necessary to expunge every trace of "Negroness" from our behavior.

To these arguments Ellison would counterpose the richness of his
folk tradition. He insists upon the relevance of folk experience to
the conditions of modern urban life and, more important still, to
the condition of being man. The assimilationist demands that in
the name of integration the Negro self be put to death. But Ellison
regards this proposal as a projection of self-hatred. To integrate
means to make whole, not to lop off or mutilate; to federate as
equals, not to merge and disappear. Anything else is a denial not
only of one's racial identity but of one's national identity as well.
For slavery really happened on American soil, and it has made us
both, Negro and white alike, what we are today.

Negro nationalism is a natural response to the experience of rejection. Rebuffed by the whites, the Negro nationalist rebuffs in
turn. Rejecting the white man's civilization as thoroughly corrupt,
visibly in decay and hopelessly compromised by its oppression of the
blacks, he asks in anger and despair, "Why should we integrate into
a burning house?" From this mood of separatism and alienation
flows his attitude toward the folk culture. For here is a system of
values to oppose to those of the white middle class. All that is distinctive in Negro life is thus exalted as a matter of racial pride. Traditionally, this point of view has been fortified by some sort of
African mystique, the current version being the concept of *Négritude.*

Here Ellison would counter with the richness of the dominant tradition. European civilization, of which he is a part, cannot be written off so lightly. Emerson and Einstein, Mozart and Michelangelo, Jefferson and Joyce are part of his tradition, and he has paid for them in blood. He is not about to bargain them away in exchange for *Négritude*. The Negro nationalist demands that for the sake of injured pride the Western self be put to death. But if the injury is real, the remedy is disastrous. What is separatism but the sulking of a rejected child? The American Negro, after all, is no stranger to the affairs of this nation. Nor can he stand aside from its appointed destiny. For if the house burns, one thing is certain: the American Negro will not escape the conflagration.

Assimilationism and Negro nationalism both involve a maiming of the self, an unnecessary loss. Why not combine the best of both traditions? Between these opposite and symmetrical errors, Ellison steers a steady course. On the one hand, he wants in: no one, white or colored, will persuade him that he is an outsider. Talk about the mainstream! He's been swimming in it since 1619. On the other hand, he is not about to trade in his tested techniques of survival on some white man's vague promise: "Be like us and we will accept you, maybe." When he comes in, he brings his chitlins with him. If, in the process, he transforms America into a nation of chitlin eaters, so much the better for our ethnic cooking.

While assimilationism and Negro nationalism make opposite evaluations of Negro folk culture, they both regard it as in some sense un-American. To all such formulations Ellison objects that they abstract distinctive Negro qualities from the concrete circumstances of American life. The American Negro *is* different from his white countrymen, but American history and that alone has made him so. Any serious attempt to understand these differences will, therefore, lead, by a thousand devious paths, across the tracks to white America. Always there is a connection, however hidden; always a link, however brutally severed. It follows that "any viable theory of Negro American culture obligates us to fashion a more adequate theory of American culture as a whole."

To this end, Ellison offers what might be called some "Notes toward a Redefinition of American Culture". There is a gross distortion, he suggests, in America's self-image. It begins with the white man's artificial attempt to isolate himself from Negro life. But Negro life is not sealed off hermetically from the historical process. On the contrary, it is the most authentic expression of that process as it has actually unfolded on the North American continent.

Ellison argues, in effect, that the life-style of the Negro ghetto is
more American than the so-called standard American culture of
white suburbia because the latter, in the very impulse that gave it
birth, denies a vital dimension of American experience. There is no
possibility, he warns, of escaping from the past. What is required
is that we bring our distorted image of ourselves into line with the
historical reality.

Paradoxically, what is most distinctive in Negro life is often most
American. Jazz, for example, is not simply Negro music, but the
definitive rendering of American experience in sound. Similarly
with folklore: "In spilling out his heart's blood in his contest with
the machine, John Henry was asserting a national value as well
as a Negro value." Where do we turn for the truth about American
slavery: to Negro spirituals or the songs of Stephen Collins Foster?
Why is the current slang of American teen-agers drawn from the
speech of the Negro ghetto? Why the persistent vogue for Negro
dance forms, unless we have been growing, from Charleston to
Watusi, steadily less inhibited as a nation?

American culture is still in process of becoming. It is not a
finished form, a house that one day will be rented out to Negroes.
On the contrary, in the process of racial integration the culture
will be radically transformed. This transformation will amount to
a correction of perspective. By degrees, the white man's truncated
version of American reality will be enlarged. The American eye will
be retrained to see sights hitherto ignored or, if seen, misconstrued
for venal ends. Connections formerly obscure will now be plain;
the essential oneness of American civilization will emerge. Ultimately Americans will develop a new image of themselves as a
nation.

"I was taken very early," Ellison remarks, "with a passion to link
together all I loved within the Negro community and all those
things I felt in the world which lay beyond." This passion is the
driving force of his career. It can be felt in his response to jazz as
well as his approach to fiction. It accounts, moreover, for his views
on politics and art. For the linking together which he has in mind
can barely begin in courthouse and in workshop, neighborhood and
school. It must be consummated in some inner realm, where all
men meet on common ground. Such are the links that Ellison would
forge, the new reality he would create, the shattered psyche of the
nation that he would make whole.

Ralph Ellison and the Birth
of the Anti-Hero

by William J. Schafer

. . . on a farm in Vermont where I was reading *The Hero* by
Lord Raglan and speculating on the nature of Negro leadership in the U.S., I wrote the first paragraph of *Invisible Man,*
and was soon involved in the struggle of creating the novel.[1]

From the vantage point of the sixties, Ralph Ellison's *Invisible
Man* seems frighteningly prophetic. The convulsive street warfare
of the last summers proves the tragic truth we have refused to face,
and those episodes of the novel which may seem fantastic or mor-
bidly hyperbolic are daily confirmed by front-page statistics. Ellison's novel, which may once have seemed limited to the special
conditions of the Negro at midcentury (as a "Negro novel") is above
all an *American* novel about us all, black and white together. It
simply extends and develops Richard Wright's aphorism, "The
Negro is America's metaphor." The riot episodes and the figure of
Ras the Destroyer are no longer paper chimeras, impossible in the
light of day. The cultural explosive which Ellison described in imaginative terms now shatters our cities.

The gnomic question which concludes *Invisible Man* reveals the
scope of Ellison's vision: "Who knows but that, on the lower frequencies, I speak for you?" This is spoken out of that tangible darkness the nameless narrator has intensified with 1,369 light bulbs, and
while it is as double-edged and ironic as the rest of his story, it
clearly conveys Ellison's intent. Although his story is founded in

[1] *Writers at Work* (The *Paris Review* Interviews, Second Series) (New York,
1965), p. 328.

observed reality and experienced truth and Ellison answers the
street cry—"Tell it like it is, baby!"—he avoids Richard Wright's
bare naturalism on the one hand and James Baldwin's hypertense
polemic on the other. Ellison subsumes local and temporal questions
of human insight and social justice to more profound inquiries into
the human mind and the justice of the heart. The story is basically
a quest for identity that describes America in the twentieth century
—an epic journey through a labyrinth of freedom, conformity,
denial and possibility. Ultimately Ellison's imagination transforms
and illuminates the mingled tragedy and comedy, enslavement and
freedom inherent in us all.

Technically *Invisible Man* is a *tour de force*, using a whole spec-
trum of fictional techniques to convey a complex authorial attitude
and build a fictional world which transcends realistic description
or simple probability. The action shifts from nitty-gritty realism
to hallucinatory fantasy without a break in the seams of style. It
is a virtuoso performance, moving from unsophisticated methods
to highly complex and subtle modes of narration; Ellison especially
reveals his craftsmanship in his language, which builds from collo-
quial idioms and maintains the rhythm and texture of speech
throughout. It is an extended jazz performance—the voice used as
an instrument (as in Louis Armstrong's finest work), with fluid improvisations on simple themes coalescing into a polished and
organic unity.[2] But the shape of the story itself reveals Ellison's skill
most clearly. The story of *Invisible Man* is fairly simple—the archetypal migration and metamorphosis of a southern rural Negro
progressing to the new found land of Harlem. The tale is related
by a man invisible in his impotent self-knowledge, looking back at
his visible innocence—an emergent adult human looking back at
the broken chrysalis.

But Ellison transforms the story into a parable, breaking with
the predictable patterns of the social protest novel by blending
fantasy and naturalism, moving without transition from one level
of ideas to another and skillfully telescoping the episodes of the
novel by concentrating closely on his protagonist's spiritual and
psychological evolution. By using a relatively simple plot structure,
Ellison is able to concentrate on the *quality* of the experience at
hand.

The plot structure of *Invisible Man* is schematic. The novel uses

[2] This idea is developed at length by Richard Kostelanetz, *"Invisible Man* as
Symbolic History," *Chicago Review*, XIX, No. 2 (1967), 5–26.

a cumulative plot (in M. C. Bradbrook's illuminating terminology),[3] developing the same basic episode over and over in an emotional crescendo: the protagonist struggles idealistically to live by the commandments of his immediate social group, then is undone by the hypocrisy built into the social structure and is plunged into despair. This happens in four large movements: 1) the struggle into college, the failure with Norton and expulsion from the "paradise" of the college; 2) job-hunting in New York, Emerson's disillusioning lecture and the battle and explosion at Liberty Paints; 3) the "resurrection" or reconstruction of the protagonist, his plunge into radical activism and his purge by the Brotherhood; 4) the meeting with Rinehart, the beginning of the riots and the protagonist's confrontation and defeat of Ras, ending in the flight underground. Each episode is a development to a climax followed by a peripeteia. The novel's prologue and epilogue simply frame this series of climaxes and reversals and interpret the emotional collapse of the invisible man in the present tense. While this structure has been cited as a "technical flaw," it moves the reader from individual Negro experience to the convulsion of a whole society:

> The constant technical flaw in *Invisible Man* is that it so frequently comes to an end and Ellison is put at every point to a greater muscularity to make the next scene more intense, more thoroughly revealing of what has already been largely revealed. It is the concomitant of that flaw that *Invisible Man* is a death-driven novel. Its movement is to confirm again and again that the hero doesn't exist, and Ellison's difficulty . . . is to resurrect the hero for each subsequent adventure.[4]

This shattered effect of death, rebirth and redeath makes the novel work, illustrates completely the erasure of an individual, the process by which a man becomes invisible. The novel repeats the essential Negro experience in several ways: the overall four-part pattern might be read (albeit overly allegorically) as "emancipation," "industrialization," "organization" and "disintegration"; or the pattern may portray the violent urbanization of a rural Negro consciousness; but the linking of general Negro experience with an individual viewpoint and voice is accomplished through the repeti-

[3] *Themes and Conventions of Elizabethan Tragedy* (Cambridge, 1960), pp. 41–42.
[4] Marcus Klein, "Ralph Ellison's *Invisible Man*," in *Images of the Negro in American Literature*, ed. Seymour L. Gross and John Edward Hardy (Chicago, 1966), p. 264.

tion of the invisible man's failure and his cumulative descent into despair.

Every effect in the novel is aimed at showing the *inside* of the nameless invisible man; we are well below the skin level, and Ellison does not attempt to explain the Negro's experiences or to blame society for them but to show *how* he is affected, what the view is from inside the prison of blackness and invisibility. Therefore, Ellison eschews the cataloging devices of social protest fiction as well as the meticulous references to history and place—the time and place are the present landscape of the Negro mind, as it has become fused in American consciousness over 350 years. Ellison blurs the scenery to prevent the reader from absorbing the novel either in simple realistic or symbolic terms. The characters are nearly types, never probed deeply by the narrator, and the milieu is significant only insofar as it reflects and refracts the invisible man's mind.

For primarily *Invisible Man* is a study in the psychology of oppression. It is the story of an internal quest—a journey of the soul. The migration is from innocence to experience, not just from sunny south to ghetto and the underground. Ellison develops this story along mythic lines, incorporating elements of common cultural experience in the parable to generalize it further, and the protagonist's progress is finally a pilgrimage of the self. Ellison simply worked from observable American rituals:

> . . . the patterns were already there in society so that all I had to do was present them in a broader context of meaning. In any society there are many rituals of situation which, for the most part, go unquestioned. They can be simple or elaborate, but they are the connective tissue between the work of art and the audience.[5]

The story, then, describes the birth of a hero—in this case, an anti-hero—retold in only slightly shaded terms; the novel is, in fact, a fragment of an epic in form.

The anti-hero of *Invisible Man,* though we come to know him intimately, remains nameless. He is no-man and everyman on a modern epic quest, driven by the message his grandfather reveals in a dream: "To Whom It May Concern . . . Keep This Nigger-Boy Running." His primary search is for a name—or for the self it symbolizes. During his search he is given another name by the Brotherhood, but it is no help. When he becomes a "brother," he finds that brotherhood does not clarify his inner mysteries.

[5] *Writers at Work,* pp. 326–27.

In creating his anti-hero, Ellison builds on epic and mythic conventions. The nameless voyager passes through a series of ordeals or trials to demonstrate his stature. First, he passes through the initiation-rites of our society—the battle royal (exposing the sadistic sexuality of the white southern world) and speechmaking that sends him to college are parts of this rite of passage, and he is tormented into the adult world. He passes this test by demonstrating his servility and naively interpreting his grandfather's dictum: "Live with your head in the lion's mouth. I want you to overcome 'em with yeses, undermine 'em with grins, agree 'em to death and destruction, let 'em swoller you till they vomit or bust wide open." This is the first outlook of the invisible man—the paranoia fostered by "them," the white oppressors; the boy here is Buckeye the Rabbit, the swift clever animal living by its wits beneath the jaws of the killer.

When he arrives at college, he is confronted by the deceit and duplicity of Negroes who have capitulated to a white world; he is broken by the powerful coalition of Bledsoe the Negro president and Norton the white trustee. His second trial shows him that the struggle is not a simple one of black against white, that "they" are more complex than his first experiences showed. He finds that both black and white can be turned against him.

The second phase of his career commences in the trip to New York, an exile from "paradise"; in the city, he finds Bledsoe's seven magic passports to success in the white world, the letters of recommendation, are actually betrayals, variations of the dream-letter: "Keep This Nigger-Boy Running." Thus, his primary illusions are shattered, but there are many more layers to the cocoon in which he sleeps.

For he is first of all a dreamer, a somnambulist, and sleep and dreams figure significantly in his image of himself. As he reassesses himself, his metaphor for new discoveries is the same: ". . . it was as though I had been suddenly awakened from a deep sleep." Yet each sleep and each awakening (little deaths and births) prove to be interlocked layers of his existence, a set of never-ending Chinese boxes. One climactic section of the novel details his second crucial awakening—the "descent into the underworld" which occurs in chapters 10 and 11.

Like the hero of myth and ritual, Ellison's invisible man finally descends from life on the mortal plane into an underworld of death. This is the substance of the entire New York section of the novel. On arriving in the city, he recalls the plucked robin of the old song and imagines himself the victim of a fantasy-letter: "My dear Mr. Emerson . . . The Robin bearing this letter is a former student. Please hope him to death, and keep him running." Then he takes the job at Liberty Paints, keeping white paint white by adding drops of pure black, under the ironic slogan, "If It's Optic White, It's The Right White," which (like "If you're white, all right, if you're black, stay back") has been invented by a Negro, the ancient and malevolent Lucius Brockway. The anti-hero becomes a machine within the machines, and he finds that Brockway, an illiterate "janitor" is the heart of the whole industry. In the boiler room, an inferno, he is betrayed again by a Negro and "killed" through his treachery. But the death is the ritual death of the hero's career— a death which leads to resurrection and a new identity.

After the explosion, the anti-hero awakens in a hospital, where he is resurrected by white doctors using an electroshock machine. Chapter 11 opens with a monstrous image of the demons of this underworld: "I was sitting in a cold, white rigid chair and a man was looking at me out of a bright third eye that glowed from the center of his forehead." The doctors revive him ("We're trying to get you started again. Now shut up!") to the accompaniment of fantastic effects—Beethoven motifs and a trumpet playing "The Holy City" and dreamlike dialogue from the surgeons:

> "I think I prefer surgery. And in this case especially, with this, uh . . . background. I'm not so sure that I don't believe in the effectiveness of simple prayer." . . .
> "The machine will produce the results of a prefrontal lobotomy without the negative effects of the knife." . . .
> "Why not a castration, doctor?"

Then, as he is revived, the doctors construct an heroic identity for him, recapitulating his existence as a Negro, starting with the first folkmyth guises of the clever Negro—Buckeye the Rabbit and Brer Rabbit: ". . . they were one and the same: 'Buckeye' when you were very young and hid yourself behind wide innocent eyes; 'Brer' when you were older." The electrotherapy machine is an emblem of the mechanical society imprisoning the anti-hero: "I could no more escape than I could think of my identity. Perhaps, I thought, the two things are involved with each other. When I discover who I am, I'll be free." This lesson of the resurrection is carried through the rest of the anti-hero's journey.

The apparatus which resurrects the invisible man is a mechanical womb, complete with umbilical cord attached to his stomach which is finally cut by the doctors; he is delivered of the machine, and the doctors pronounce his new name—yet he remains nameless. The doctors, who follow a "policy of enlightened humanitarianism" declare that this New Adam will remain a social and economic victim of the machine: "You just aren't prepared for work under our industrial conditions. Later, perhaps, but not now."

The anti-hero sallies forth after his revival in the underworld "overcome by a sense of alienation and hostility" when he revisits the scene of the middle class Negro arrivals in New York. He is now painfully aware of the hostility of his world, and he reacts not passively ("in the lion's mouth") but aggressively. In a symbolic gesture, he dumps a spittoon on a stranger whom he mistakes for his first nemesis, Bledsoe. The act is that of a crazed messiah: "You really baptized ole Rev!" Then he goes forth for a harrowing of hell.

He joins the Brotherhood, an infernal organization which meets at the Chthonian club. In the Brotherhood, he rises to authority, becomes a respected leader and demagogue and is finally again betrayed by the wielders of power, whites who manipulate Negro stooges for their own ends. But at the end of this episode, the penultimate phase of the hero's career, he meets two important emblematic figures: Ras the Destroyer and Rinehart the fox. Ras, the black nationalist leader, is his crazed counterpart, and he harasses the invisible man until the night of the riots, when he attempts to hang and spear the anti-hero as a scapegoat for the mob—a dying god to appease the violence Ras releases. A contrast is Rinehart, who like Reynard is a master of deception and multiple identities: "Rine the runner and Rine the gambler and Rine the briber and Rine the lover and Rine the reverend." He is a tempter, and the invisible man nearly succumbs to his temptation to freedom without responsibility; he strolls through Harlem disguised as Rinehart, the visible-invisible man who passes undetected through many identities. Ras offers the assurance of one undivided black identity and Rinehart the assurance of many shifting amoral identities—the faces of stability and flux. But the anti-hero avoids both traps, turning Ras's spear on him and shucking the dark glasses and wide hat of Rinehart, than finally dropping literally out of sight underground at the climax of the riot. Ellison has said that he took Rinehart's name from the "suggestion of inner and outer," seeming and being, and that he is an emblem of chaos—"He has lived so long with chaos that he knows how to manipulate it." [6] So Rinehart and Ras both represent chaos, two versions of disorder.

[6] *Ibid.*, p. 333.

Loss of identity, sleeping and blindness are the figures that express the invisible man's confusion and despair as his world disintegrates. Then, after the cultural malaise climaxes in the riot, the final phase of the anti-hero's progress begins, a descent into the tomb—the netherworld across the Styx where heroes rest: "It's a kind of death without hanging, I thought, a death alive. . . . I moved off over the black water, floating, sighing . . . sleeping invisibly." So he remains immortal and waiting, like the heroes of myth who disappear and are believed to wait should the world require them—like King Arthur and Finn MacCool, sleeping giants blended into the landscape. The invisible man, now grown into Jack-the-Bear, turns to New York's sewer system, a black and labyrinthine underground—a fitting anti-hero's mausoleum.

In this black crypt he destroys his old selves one by one as he searches for light, erasing his past—burning his high school diploma, a doll which is a bitter totem of Tod Clifton's demise, the name given him by the Brotherhood, a poison-pen note, all the tokens of his identity. Then he dreams of castration and sees that the retreat has been his crucifixion—he has been cut off from the world of possibility: "Until some gang succeeds in putting the world in a strait jacket, its definition is possibility. Step outside the narrow borders of what men call reality and you step into chaos—ask Rinehart, he's a master of it—or imagination." Imagination in the end redeems the anti-hero and makes his flight from battle a victory, for it gives us his story. In his tomb he is not dead but hibernating, preparing for a spring of the heart, a return which may be either death or resurrection:

> There's stench in the air, which, from this distance underground, might be the smell either of death or of spring—I hope of spring. But don't let me trick you, there *is* a death in the smell of spring and in the smell of thee as in the smell of me.

The Easter of the spirit may be the emergence of the new man—no longer an anti-hero, invisible, nameless and dispossessed, but a true hero—or it may be the death of our culture.

The resurrection motif ties the story in the frame of prologue and epilogue, in the voice from underground:

> . . . don't jump to the conclusion that because I call my home a "hole" it is damp and cold like a grave; there are cold holes and warm holes. Mine is a warm hole. And remember, a bear retires to his hole for the winter and lives until spring; then he comes strolling

out like the Easter chick breaking from its shell. I say all this to assure you that it is incorrect to assume that, because I'm invisible and live in a hole, I am dead. I am neither dead nor in a state of suspended animation. Call me Jack-the-Bear, for I am in a state of hibernation.

Buckeye the Rabbit has grown into the formidable Jack-the-Bear (recalling the Bear's Son of the sagas) as the anti-hero has passed his trials and journeyed on his downward path, reliving the recent history of the Negro. He lies in wait beneath the inferno, under the underworld, listening for the hero's call.

The power of *Invisible Man* comes, as I have said, not from realistic description nor from the probability of the story but from metaphoric or symbolic elements linking the episodes of the anti-hero's progress. A skein of metaphor is joined with the outline of the hero's life to unify Ellison's vision of the American dilemma.

The central metaphor is, of course, that of invisibility—light, darkness and transparency. The novel gives shape to the inside of invisibility—the obverse of white America's distorted mythos of Negro life. The whites "see only my surroundings, themselves, or figments of their imagination, everything and anything except me." Blackness and nil are the Negro's position—*nothing nowhere*. And the novel's metaphor leads to the dilemma of identity, for the black man cannot resign himself to nothingness or embrace invisibility: "Why, if they follow this conformity business they'll end up by forcing me, an invisible man, to become white, which is not a color but the lack of one." Both black and white are negative; Ellison, like Melville, has used the black and white of Manichaeism ambiguously so that the "power of black" is a moral consideration, not a matter of genetics or pigmentation.

A second kind of key imagery is a series of emblems of southern Negro life invoked to describe the history of oppression since 1863. In chapter 13, the newly resurrected anti-hero faces his mythic past and the first demonstration of his new identity when he leads a demonstration against an eviction. He first finds that he cannot deny his southern heritage when he encounters a seller of Carolina yams; the food is "forbidden fruit," because it recalls his unsophisticated country ancestry, but he eats it anyway, rebelling against the pressure of conformity: " 'They're my birthmark,' I said, "I yam what I am.' " Then he sees the old couple being evicted and catalogues their possessions, which chronicle the poor Negro's life for a century:

. . . "knocking bones," used to accompany music at country dances, used in black-face minstrels . . . a straightening comb, switches of false hair, a curling iron . . . High John the Conqueror, the lucky stone . . . rock candy and camphor . . . a small Ethiopian flag, a faded tintype of Abraham Lincoln. . . . In my hand I held three lapsed life insurance policies with perforated seals stamped "Void"; a yellowing newspaper portrait of a huge black man with the caption: MARCUS GARVEY DEPORTED. . . . I read: FREE PA- PERS. *Be it known to all men that my negro Primus Provo, has been freed by me on this sixth day of August, 1859.*

These bits of folk myth and history permeate the novel; the invisible man, in his new aggressive role, does not renounce this culture but embraces it, dreaming at first of flaying Bledsoe with chittlins to humiliate him, but returning to Louis Armstrong's unanswerable question in the end: "What did I do/To be so black/And blue?" As shoddy and worn as the Negro's past is, it is all that he has, and the anti-hero embraces it in his search for identity.

Several totems the anti-hero carries on his journey link him with his past, also. He carries the shiny briefcase awarded him after the battle royal—a leather bribe given to buy the invisible man's allegiance to the *status quo.* When the school superintendent presents it to him, he says, "Consider it a badge of office. Prize it. Keep developing as you are and some day it will be filled with important papers that will help shape the destiny of your people." He carries it as a passport into the white world of busy-ness; it seems a sprig of moly, a talisman, but it turns out to be an albatross. In the end it is filled only with the invisible man's cancelled identity cards, which he burns. Thus does he find the "destiny of your people."

Along with the briefcase he has carried homelier reminders of his heritage—first, the fragments of his landlady's bank:

. . . the cast-iron figure of a very black, red-lipped and wide-mouthed Negro, whose white eyes stared up at me from the floor, his face an enormous grin, his single large black hand held palm up before his chest. . . . the kind of bank which, if a coin is placed in the hand and a lever pressed upon the back, will raise its arm and flip the coin into the grinning mouth.

In a fit of rage, of reflex inconoclasm, he smashes the clichéd image of bigotry. But he feels guilty and carries the fragments with him, unable to free himself of this shattered icon of the past. The earlier images of chittlins and hog maws as the emblems of shame are replaced by the bank and its consolidated image of the penny-bribed darky. With it in the briefcase is the paper dancing doll with all its hateful connotations of the Negro who sells himself as the white man's fool. The shameful past intrudes persistently into the invisible man's present.

The imagery and the outline of the hero's life serve to give a classic shape to *Invisible Man*. If we take Joseph Campbell's summary of the hero's career as a standard, we can see how Ellison moved from reading Lord Raglan and pondering Negro leadership to the form of the novel:

> The mythological hero, setting forth from his commonday hut or castle, is lured, carried away, or else voluntarily proceeds to the threshold of adventure (exile to New York). There he encounters a shadowy presence that guards the passage (Lucius Brockway). The hero may defeat or conciliate this power and go alive into the kingdom of the dark . . . or be slain by the opposition and descend in death (the explosion and "death") . . . Beyond the threshold, then, the hero journeys through a world of unfamiliar yet strangely intimate forces, some of which severely threaten him (tests), some of which give magic aid (helpers). When he arrives at the nadir of the mythological round, he undergoes a supreme ordeal and gains his reward. The triumph may be represented as the hero's sexual union with the goddess-mother of the world [the invisible man's seduction by the white woman, who glowed "as though consciously acting a symbolic role of life and feminine fertility"] . . . The final work is that of the return . . . the hero reemerges from the kingdom of dread . . . The boom that he brings restores the world. . . .[7]

Invisible Man follows this loose form. The epic journey from southern oppression to northern invisibility is shaped by the elements of ritual hero; the anti-hero gains stature and universality by his connection with Negro folk-heroes and through his enactment of a ritual role. Only the last part of the myth is incomplete—Ellison does not decide whether the hero will emerge from underground and whether he will bring elixir or destruction. The last question of the novel is posed the reader: will it be death or spring?

Ellison, like Joseph Campbell, probes the unconscious and searches for symbolic representations for states of mind and spirit. He finds in the Negro consciousness the anxieties and problems which Campbell sees as modern man's condition; the invisible man, like all of us, faces the problem of self and other which is the shaping force behind myth:

[7] *The Hero With a Thousand Faces* (New York, 1949), pp. 245–46.

Man is that alien presence with whom the forces of egoism must
come to terms, through whom the ego is to be crucified and resurrected, and in whose image society is to be reformed. Man, understood however not as "I" but as "Thou": for the ideals and temporal institutions of no tribe, race, continent, social class, or century, can be the measure of the inexhaustible and multifariously
wonderful divine existence that is the life in all of us.[8]

The problem of identity and existence that Ellison poses transcends
the issues of social justice and equity; it is not a question of "the
Negro problem" or "race issues." As this novel shows in its prophecy, we must all know who we are before we can be free—and there
is no freedom for a white "I" until there is freedom for a black
"Thou."

[8] *Ibid.*, p. 391.

Invisible Man: Somebody's Protest Novel

by *Thomas A. Vogler*

> This simply because I had a notion it somehow would be of
> help to that Kurtz whom at the time I did not see—you under-
> stand. He was just a word for me. I did not see the man in
> the name any more than you do. Do you see him? Do you see
> the story? Do you see anything?
>
> (Conrad)

> Oh say can you see . . . ?
>
> (National Anthem)

With Hemingway and Faulkner both dead, this is not a time
of recognized literary giants. The public, and critics too, are too
easily preoccupied with literary giantism, with finding the next
heir to the vacated throne. Publishers want their books to sell, and
are not very timid about making claims. Readers want to feel that
what they are reading is what they ought to be reading, in terms
that can only be reached from the vantage point of a historical
perspective. Our contemporary writers should, however, be looked
on and cherished as partly-realized potential, writers whose work
should not be idolized too much, nor ignored, but read with the
best awareness we can bring to them of their relationships to our
own lives and to the traditions they continue. Melville seemed to
be a distinctly minor writer to his own age. In 1945 all seventeen
of Faulkner's books were out of print. We should be chastened
and warned by examples like these, but not overly frightened in
our attempts to find something of value in our contemporary
writers.

With the belated advent of "Black Literature" it has become

"*Invisible Man*: Somebody's Protest Novel," by Thomas A. Vogler. From the
Iowa Review, I (Spring, 1970), pp. 64–82. Copyright © 1970 by the *Iowa Review*.
Reprinted by permission of the author and publisher.

even more difficult to find a long-term context in which to read
or discuss a novel like *Invisible Man*. Its relevance to the contemporary social problems of Black citizens can be used to reduce
it to the level of a documentary of the Black experience.[1] On the
other hand, its insistence on craft and analysis, its careful avoidance of the explicit advocacy of action, can be passed off by the
activists as the "buggy jiving" of a white middle-class sellout, or
the ravings of a private ego trip. This latter trend is accurately
prophesied at the very end of the novel.[2] Most intolerable, perhaps,
is the approach taken by some critics of both colors, that the novel
is "pure" art, that a Negro writer has finally written his way into
the mainstream of some etherealized literary tradition.[3]

In spite of the present existence of what *Time* magazine calls,
in the jargon of the literary stockmarket, a "modest literary
boom," these are not good times for writers. There are as many
kinds of literary suicide available as there are writers, and the
hardest thing seems to be, not to write the first novel, but to
remain at the craft, writing for one's self and for the one imaginary
reader who will understand, rather than for the publisher, the
editor, the reviewer, the agent, the publicist, and the novelty-
seeking audience they serve. But it is not enough of a problem for
the writer to be in an arena where public relations men largely

[1] "To read such a book, for example, as Ralph Ellison's brilliant novel of
1952, *Invisible Man*, is to find, among one's richest satisfactions, the sense of im-
mersion in all the concrete materialities of Negro life. One hears the very buzz
and hum of Harlem in the racy, pungent speech of his West Indians and his
native hipsters, and all the *grotesquerie* in his opening account of the dreary
little backwater of a remote Southern Negro college has in it a certain kind of
empirically absolute rightness. Indeed, the book is packed full of the acutest observations of the manners and idioms and human styles that comprise the ethos
of Negro life in the American metropolis; and it gives us such a sense of social
fact as can be come by nowhere in the stiffly pedantic manuals of academic
sociology." Nathan A. Scott, Jr., "The Dark and Haunted Tower of Richard
Wright," *Black Expression*, ed. Addison Gayle, Jr. (N.Y., 1969), p. 298.

[2] Cf. Leroi Jones' "The Myth of a Negro Literature," where all Black writers
are committed to mediocrity because "The literary and artistic models were
always those that could be socially acceptable to the white middle class, which
automatically limited them to the most spiritually debilitated imitations of
literature available." (*Black Expression*, p. 192)

[3] Worth noting for its grotesque insistence on this point, while at the same
time contradicting it with a reputed social message ("Ellison's hero . . . is one
of those catastrophic individuals of which society must rid itself before there
can be peace and sanity.") is Nancy Tischler's "Negro Literature and Classic
Form," *Contemporary Literature*, X, No. 3 (Summer 1969).

determine whether his book will sell less than 5,000 or more than 100,000 copies. There is also the problem of the critics, who are committed in their own way to thinking of the literary stock-market. Critics quite easily become obsessed with what is for them the counterpart to the writer's creative urge. This is the desire to find patterns comprehensive enough to include everything that is good, and it is a reasonable enough urge when followed with discrimination. But too easily the pattern becomes a definition of what is good, and good writers get lost or distorted because they do not fit the mold. The critic of contemporary writers is especially vulnerable to this mistake. As Norman Mailer pointed out, it is "naturally wiser for the mind of the expert to masticate the themes of ten writers, rather than approach the difficulties of any one."

In many ways, then, to talk about a contemporary novel like *Invisible Man* involves problems different from those we face when discussing a novelist like Wharton or Fitzgerald. On the other hand, no really good writer can be completely contemporary without serious limitations. The kind of synthesis and evaluation of experience that we expect in a good novel cannot be contemporary with the experience itself. In addition, Ellison has roots in the 19th century that are at least as important as those in the 20th; what he writes is as much influenced by what he has read as it is by what he has seen and lived through. Though Ellison is close to Hemingway in many ways, and even copied his stories by hand in order to develop an understanding of his style, he seems to bear an even more important relationship to Melville. Ellison uses two quotations as epigraphs at the beginning of *Invisible Man*. One, from Melville's *Benito Cereno,* suggests the nature of the change the invisible man undergoes in the novel. The other, from Eliot, suggests the discovery of his invisibility which is an essential part of the change. Before discussing invisibility and change, however, I would like to suggest another passage, also from Melville, which will help to get at some of the more negative aspects of the book— for Ellison, like Melville, understood that fiction must be negative in order to fulfill both its artistic and moral obligations:

> There is the grand truth about Nathaniel Hawthorne. He says NO! in thunder; but the devil himself cannot make him say yes. For all men who say yes, *lie;* and all men who say no,—why they are in the happy condition of judicious, unincumbered travellers in Europe; they cross the frontiers into Eternity with nothing but a carpetbag— that is to say, Ego.

There is a nice comparison here with the invisible man, who crosses his frontier into the darkness with a briefcase containing all the clues to his identity or "Ego"; but the passage also suggests the dark impulse of resistance which continues to permeate contemporary fiction in works like *Invisible Man*. The novelists seem to agree that violence and distortion must be the means of projecting a vision to which society is hostile. They seem further to agree that the contemporary world presents a continued affront to man, and that his response must therefore be at least in part that of the rebel.

There is a standard psychological experiment known to produce neuroses and psychopathic behavior patterns in most domestic or trainable animals. In an experimental environment that bears a striking resemblance to the world of the novel, the animals are trained to react in certain ways to certain stimuli, and then placed in a situation in which the reactions are impossible. The animal then makes what attempts it can to go on acting as it has been trained to do, but with continued frustration a nervous collapse of some kind inevitably follows. With some, the reaction is solipsistic—they refuse to mix with other animals even for eating. Others react by batting their heads against the walls of their cages until they die or are too exhausted to continue. The equivalent experience of conflict between expectations and reality has produced what Ellison calls "the American Negro impulse toward self-annihilation and going underground," which can only be overcome by "a will to confront the world, to evaluate his experience honestly and throw his findings unashamedly into the guilty conscience of America."[4] His *Invisible Man* is a record of that agony, and of the discovery of the realities that must be faced before a genuine identity can be achieved.

> But I think the memoir, which is titled *Invisible Man*, his memoir, is an attempt to describe reality as it really exists rather than in terms of what he had assumed it to be. Because it was the clash between his assumptions, his illusions about reality, and its actual shape which made for his agony.[5]

In the novel we see the kind of training the invisible man is subjected to most clearly in the chapel scene in Chapter 5. Here

[4] "Richard Wright's Blues" (*Black Expression*, p. 325).
[5] "An Interview with Ralph Ellison," *Tamarack Review*, No. 32 (Summer 1964), p. 11.

are Barbee's concluding remarks, holding up Bledsoe as the pattern for the hero to follow:

> His is a form of greatness worthy of your imitation. I say to you, pattern yourselves upon him. Aspire, each of you, to someday follow in his footsteps.

In the next chapter, Bledsoe tries to explain to the invisible man what he calls "the difference between the way things are and the way they're supposed to be," but it is a lesson he is not yet prepared to learn. The invisible man, like most of us, is living in a culture whose incentives, rewards and punishments prevent the development of the kind of personal standards which the public ideals demand for a feeling of self-respect. He is in the situation Paul Goodman describes in *Growing up Absurd,* where the only truly healthy response is to reject those parts of society that threaten his own possibilities for self-respect. But he cannot reject them without knowing what they are, and they are built in so that he is himself responsible for much of what he must go through.

To call a novel a protest novel at this point of history is inevitably to call back the thirties and the great American discovery of social injustice. The roots of much in *Invisible Man* are to be found in this period, in writers like Dos Passos, Steinbeck, Farrell, Hemingway (at least in *For Whom the Bell Tolls*), and especially Richard Wright. During the forties there was a decline in novels dealing primarily with the social themes of the thirties; during this period, however, there was a constant discovery of new areas of social disorganization which novelists adopted for the focus of their works. The war experience was another catastrophe, piled on top of the depression, which the American novelist had to cope with in his attempts to find a view of his place in society. Another discovery during this period—and a much belated one—was of the extent and complexity of the social problems of the Negro, and of the essential part these problems took in any attempt to achieve an overall view of American society. The development of the Negro novel is not adequately explained by a theory of growing liberalism, or a shedding of prejudice which now makes white readers willing to read books they know were written by Blacks. It is not even clear that the early publishers, who disguised the fact that particular novels were written by Blacks, were acting realistically—but that's beside the point. What is clear is that in the 20th century, as in the 19th, the position of the Black citizen in our society is the *focus*

of social and ideological polarities that go far beyond the question
of race relations. It is also the focus for many of the neurotic
fears and desires that are an inevitable part of our gross national
product. From Richard Wright's first novel on, the movement has
not been a shedding of prejudice, but a growing awareness, in
writers and readers alike, of the essential centrality of the Black
problem to any adequate view of American society.

> Negro life is a byproduct of Western civilization, and in it, if only
> one possesses the humanity and humility to see, are to be discovered
> all those impulses, tendencies, life and cultural forms to be found
> elsewhere in Western society.[6]

It is in this way that Black writers have been developing and
expressing an awareness of the universal significance of their position, as Faulkner had earlier found in a single southern county
all the elements necessary to an understanding of human nature
and the movement of history. Ellison is like Faulkner in seeing
the South as a land doomed by the curse of slavery, yet still with
a vestigial aura of Edenic simplicity. But Ellison follows his Black
hero out of the South, as Wright had done, and is much more
concerned than Faulkner with a direct consideration of the implications of the civil war, for all aspects of contemporary society,
both North and South.

It would be too simple a view to consider the function of the
Black protagonist as merely that of another outsider who can serve
as a foil to define weaknesses in the social structure. The situation
of the Black, like that of the writer, is a part of the society and reveals important things about it.

> Anyway, in the beginning I thought that the white world was very
> different from the world I was moving out of and I turned out to be
> entirely wrong. It seemed different. It seemed safer, at least the white
> people seemed safer. It seemed clearer, it seemed more polite, and, of
> course, it seemed much richer from the material point of view. But
> I didn't meet anyone in that world who didn't suffer from the very
> same affliction that all the people I had fled from suffered from and
> that was that they didn't know who they were. They wanted to be
> something that they were not. And very shortly I didn't know who I
> was, either. I could not be certain whether I was really rich or really
> poor, really black or really white, really male or really female, really
> talented or a fraud, really strong or merely stubborn. In short, I had
> become an American.[7]

[6] *Black Expression*, p. 324.
[7] James Baldwin, "Notes for a Hypothetical Novel," *Nobody Knows My Name*
(N.Y., 1961), pp. 148–49.

The final test of the mastery of illusion and reality, and the discovery of an identity, is the ability to *tell* it. This is not the novelist's prerogative, as the examples of Malcolm X and Eldridge Cleaver show, and as Ellison suggests in Brother Tarp's recognition of the "signifying" embodied in his chain link and his pleasure at finally being able to communicate his story to the invisible man ("I'm tellin' it better'n I ever thought I could!"). If Ellison has entered the mainstream of modern art, it is through his fusion of the problems of his Black protagonist with those of the writer, whose search for form and reality is the central problem of most serious writers of fiction in the last 100 or so years. In an eloquent mood, Ellison has spoken to the best hopes of most novelists, of whatever color:

> Life is as the sea, art a ship in which man conquers life's crushing formlessness, reducing it to a course, a series of swells, tides and wind currents inscribed on a chart. Though drawn from the world, "the organized significance of art," writes Malraux, "is stronger than all the multiplicity of the world; . . . that significance alone enables man to conquer chaos and to master destiny." [8]

Invisible Man is not "just" a Negro novel then, and Ellison has been very careful throughout to avoid this tempting limitation, even while giving us a very comprehensive view of race relations in both the South and the North. Look for a moment at Tod Clifton, remembering that it is no accident that *Tod* in German means "death." Tod is part black, part white, symbolically gray like the "Liberty Paint" that goes out of the factory to decorate some important national monument. Tod's death is one of the key turning points of the book, forcing the invisible man to the recognition that we all shall die, leading finally to the recognition that, in an absurd society, it is an error to cater to any but one's own unique absurdity. His reflections on Tod's death are a turning-point from which he intensifies the exploration of his own identity and begins to recognize more fully the possible identities of others. In the crowd at the funeral oration he sees individual faces, marked with suffering that he begins to understand:

> Here are the facts. He was standing and he fell. He fell and he kneeled. He kneeled and he bled. He bled and he died. He fell in a heap like any man and his blood spilled out like any blood; red as any blood, wet as any blood—and it dried in the sun as blood dries. That's all.

[8] *Black Expression,* p. 316.

The specific racial killing of a Black man becomes more than the death of an individual caused by social injustice. It is the death of the best parts of the individual caused by the worst parts of society; it is "OUR HOPE SHOT DOWN," for on the lower frequencies Ellison has been speaking for us all.

In *Invisible Man* we have a full portrait of the element of despair and of the destructive element forced on the Black, the writer, and on us as well if we go along. The question we are deliberately left with, in the end which is also a beginning, is the constructive use to which these elements can be put—the role for the self which has at last been recognized and accepted, the kind of life one can live in a realm of absurdity which is also a realm of possibility. The problem of how all this negation can be put to use is already answered in part by the very existence of the novel. It is emphasized in the beginning and end that the protagonist of the book is also its creator, and that the writing of the book is itself part of the experience, and of the discovery of an identity, which is the subject of the book. What is affirmative in both the structure and the existence of the book is that the invisible man does survive through turning his experience into art. In the same way, the ordinary Black in a hostile society has been able to turn daily injustice and suffering into the folk art of the blues. The novel, like the blues, offers a way of standing apart from one's experience without losing its intensity or its meaning. All Black writers have agreed that the blues have been a survival mechanism for the Negro in America and also that they have been the most important cultural contribution to American art. For Ellison, the blues "is an impulse to keep the painful details and episodes of a brutal experience alive in one's aching consciousness, to finger its jagged grain, and to transcend it, not by the consolation of philosophy, but by squeezing from it a near-tragic, near-comic lyricism." The blues recognizes both the painful and contradictory aspects of experience, turning them into something like a joke. "There is a mystery in the whiteness of blackness, the innocence of evil, and the evil of innocence, though, being initiates, Negroes express the joke of it in the blues." The acceptance is finally achieved only in terms of artistic expression, whether it be in the blues or in the form and creation of a novel. In the book itself, this anology with the blues is continually suggested. In some cases, as in the college chapel scene, the blues can be an expression of hope:

> I closed my eyes as I heard the deep moaning sound that issued from him, and the rising crescendo of the student body joining in.

This time it was music sincerely felt, not rendered for the guests, but for themselves; a song of hope and exaltation. I wanted to rush from the building, but didn't dare. I sat stiff and erect, supported by the hard bench, relying upon it as upon a form of hope.

In other cases, such as the singing at Tod Clifton's funeral, the invisible man comes closer to recognizing the sense of blues that Ellison was getting at in his definition. Here is his reaction to the man who starts the singing:

I looked into the face of the old man who had aroused the song and felt a twinge of envy. It was a worn, old, yellow face and his eyes were closed and I could see a knife welt around his upturned neck as his throat threw out the song. . . . I watched him now, wet-eyed, and I felt a wonder at the singing mass. It was as though the song had been there all the time, and he knew it and aroused it; and I knew that I had known it too, and had failed to release it out of a vague, nameless shame or fear. Even white brothers and sisters were joining in. Something deep had shaken the crowd, and the old man and the man with the horn had done it. They had touched upon something deeper than protest or religion. It was not the words, for they were all the same old slave-borne words: it was as though he'd changed the emotion beneath the words while yet the old longing, resigned, transcendent emotion still sounded above, now deepened by that something for which the theory of brotherhood had given me no name.

The invisible man has found something here that the conscious quest for identity had failed to reveal. It is only after this discovery that he is able to make of his writing the same use that the singer makes of the blues. It is a means of achieving an acute sense of identity and self-recognition that society has been unable to provide.[9]

[9] In "The Discovery of What It Means to Be an American" Baldwin describes what he calls "a species of breakdown," and how he was cured of it by listening to Bessie Smith on records. He wrote *Go Tell It on the Mountain* "armed with two of Bessie Smith records and a typewriter," as the invisible man writes his story listening to Louis Armstrong. There is a passage in Part III of *Go Tell It on the Mountain* where John Grimes undergoes an experience comparable to the invisible man's, in almost the same words that I have quoted from Ellison:

He had heard it all his life, but it was only now that his ears were opened to this sound that came from the darkness, that could only come from darkness, that yet bore such sure witness to the glory of the light. And now in his moaning, and so far from any help, he heard it in himself —it rose from his bleeding, his cracked-open heart. It was a sound of rage and weeping which filled the grave, rage and weeping from time set free, but bound now in eternity; rage that had no language, weeping with no

This discovery of the potential for self-discovery in the blues, or in a novel which approaches them in spirit, comes on the invisible man almost unawares, in spite of the more literary and more conscious quest for identity that he has been pursuing before. Sooner or later it seems that almost every modern work can in some way be read as a search—or more typically a "quest"—for a father or a mother. The two concepts are not interchangeable; they offer primitive but different solutions to man's basic need to reach beyond his own mind and find some fixed point around which to orient his own existence. The search for a father is almost always for a principle of authority, a lawgiver of some kind, even if it is the stern inscrutability of some abstract principle of necessity. In the earlier part of *Invisible Man* we find figures like the Founder and Bledsoe, and the great white father figures of Norton and the other trustees. Even the Brotherhood, at first felt as a fraternity of equality and freedom, is finally seen to be dominated by a harshly paternal theory of history, and Brother Jack turns out to be a disguised father masquerading as a brother. The mother figure typically offers an alternative orientation for experience, and has something that is always missing or of lesser importance in the father figures. The strictness of the father is replaced by the all-embracing acceptance of the mother, who refuses to reject her child no matter how poor, weak or sinful he has become. In *Invisible Man* the landlady Mary who takes up the hero and keeps him and feeds him is such a figure. He is trying to reach Mary's when he falls down the hole at the end, and it is to Mary's that his feet had unconsciously taken him earlier in the book:

> But I was never to reach Mary's. And now I realized that I couldn't return to Mary's, to any part of my old life, I could only approach it from the outside, and I had been as invisible to Mary as I had been to the brotherhood.

The recognition that he can't return to Mary, that the alternative she suggests, with all its religious overtones, is as unattainable as that offered by the series of fathers, is paralleled by the tone and

---

voice—which yet spoke now, to John's startled soul, of boundless melancholy, of the bitterest patience, and the longest night; of the deepest water, the strongest chains, the most cruel lash; of humility most wretched, the dungeon most absolute, of love's bed defiled, and birth dishonored, and most bloody, unspeakable, sudden death. Yes, the darkness hummed with murder; the body in the water, the body in the fire, the body on the tree. John looked down the line of these armies of darkness, army upon army, and his soul whispered, *Who are these?* (p. 228)

structure Ellison uses to handle the theme in the novel. The invisible man's search for a father or a mother is a reflex in him, and therefore an inevitable part of his experience and a necessary part of the novel. But if the novel must go through the quest because its protagonist must go through, it can at least do it in a different way. Ellison has pointed out that "When you are influenced by a body of literature or art from an earlier period, it is usually the form of it that is available to you," and he has openly acknowledged the high degree of literary self-consciousness manifest in the novel. "Let's put it this way—I'm a highly conscious writer. I know what's been done because I've read the books, I've studied them." [10] The consciousness of form and archetype leads to a deliberate and parodic use of such patterns in Ellison's work, and contributes to its enlightened literary humor. The invisible man may be duped into questing after unattainable or irrelevant goals, but he will not let his novel make the same mistake. The more innovative quest in *Invisible Man* is not that for a father or a mother, but the search for a group, a fraternity, a brotherhood of fellow humans in which the invisible man can find his identity and achieve the freedom and dignity which are the real goals of his quest. The final irony of this quest is that the real brotherhood, that of all humans facing death and oppression, can be joined only by renouncing all fictitious bases of brotherhood. In every alternative but this, the invisible man must repress part of his emotions and his humanity—the group of Black boys in the battle-royal, his fellow students, the union, the catch-all fraternity of the Harlem Men's House, the disguised paternal system of the Brotherhood, the Black fraternity of Ras the Exhorter-Destroyer—all of these offer roles which he either cannot accept or which demand that he sacrifice too much of himself to find a genuine identity in membership.

As he moves from one tentative role to another, he attempts to cast off earlier parts of his identity which the new roles cannot accept. Simultaneously with becoming a brother, he tries to discard the bank which is an image of different kinds of dependencies. "Feed me," the bank says on its front, and it reminds us of all the Black entertainers who have publicly distorted themselves into this gross caricature, just as the invisible man's attempts to destroy the bank suggest the corps of jazz musicians who have refused to smile while playing in order to prevent associations with the old

[10] *Tamarack Review*, pp. 5–6.

image from coming back to destroy the dignity of their art. In spite of his attempts, the invisible man cannot get rid of the bank. A white woman, and a white man, force him to retrieve it first out of the garbage and then off the street. So he seals it up in the briefcase with all the other clues to the identity which he refuses to accept. The briefcase is an emblem of himself, a container of images which he hates but cannot lose:

> "What's in that briefcase," they said, and if they'd asked me anything else I might have stood still. But at the question a wave of shame and outrage shook me and I ran.

This is the same question the doctors were asking him earlier, only now he is ready to find the answer. He is forced, in the darkness of his hole, to explore the contents of the briefcase which are the real clues to his identity and the only source of light.

The exploration, as I have already suggested, is undertaken in the act of telling the story. In this exploration the big issues are the problems of politics, of freedom, of brotherhood, of the rejection of a father and the loss of a mother, the distrust of rhetoric and abstractions which dilute experience and disguise reality. All of these issues are elements in the formal pattern and structure of the novel. But all of these are tied together by the central problem of finding his identity. Until he finds it, the invisible man is like a cup of water without the cup; he takes on his identity from whatever shape his environment offers until, finally, he realizes that his once new and clean briefcase, now battered and dirty, is symbolically the container of all the clues that are essential to finding his true identity. This chameleon-like flexibility is one of the most typically American features in the whole book, and it is perhaps our best clue to Ellison's identity as an American writer. From the legendary versatility of Benjamin Franklin, through innumerable characters in Irving, Hawthorne, Melville, Whitman and Twain, there is the concept of a character who can move from one identity to another without effort, preparation or reflection. This concept is so basic that it turns up both in the traditions and idealized national myths—characters like Franklin and Alger—and in the works of writers like Ellison who are rebelling from the hypocrisy of those ideals while still realizing that metamorphosis is a basic fact and possibility of existence. It can be a debased, almost subhuman instrument of survival, as in Faulkner's Snopes family, or it can be a social triumph as in the legendary founder of the invisible man's college. It can be the source of humor, as in *Huckleberry Finn*, or the more cosmic and ironic humor of Melville's *Confidence Man*.[11]

At a crucial point in the novel the invisible man "discovers" this principle of metamorphosis which has been there all along. At first, he is impressed by the world of possibilities opened up before him:

> Well, I *was* and yet I was invisible, that was the fundamental contradiction. I was and yet I was unseen. It was frightening and as I sat there I sensed another frightening world of possibilities. . . . Perhaps I could tell them to hope until I found the basis of something real, some firm ground for action. . . . But until then I would have to move them without myself being moved . . . I'd have to do a Rinehart.

So he tries to Rinehart it; he will find a woman in the Brotherhood and use her to gain inside information about their plans. Unfortunately for the invisible man he picks Sybil for his informant, and she has the enthusiastic frenzy but lacks the information he is looking for.[12] Instead, she merely gives him another lesson in his invisibility. She looks through him and sees nothing but her own fantasy of the Black phallus, the Negro rapist. And since he is now "doing a Rinehart" as he puts it, operating in the world of possibility, he can convince her—or let her convince herself—that she was raped without actually doing it. "SYBIL, YOU WERE RAPED BY SANTA CLAUS SURPRISE" he writes on her bare belly. And the image is a perfect one, for her fantasy of him is no more real than the child's fantasy. She has been taught to believe in the Black sex fantasy as the child is taught to believe in the great magic gift-giver.[13]

There is an interesting example of the precision and economy of Ellison's characterization in this episode. There are two sexual adventures in the book, and they both serve distinct functions. The first adventure occurred when the invisible man was sent downtown to lecture on "The Woman Question," only to find out that

---

[11] It can also be the subject of a book, as in Sister Bernetta Quinn's *Metamorphic Tradition in Modern Poetry*, and Daniel Hoffman's *Form and Fable in American Fiction*.

[12] In classical times sibyls or *sibyllae* were young maidens dwelling in lonely caves or by inspiring springs. Their function was to give forth prophetic utterances while under the influence of an enthusiastic frenzy.

[13] Mailer's essay "The White Negro" is a more sophisticated or Hip version of this same fantasy. Baldwin, in "The Black Boy Looks at the White Boy," acknowledges that "to be an American Negro male is also to be a kind of walking phallic symbol: which means that one pays, in one's own personality, for the sexual insecurity of others."

the real question was the one Ras had asked earlier, when trying
to understand what could move a Black to join the Brotherhood.
What is it, Ras asks, money or women, that is confusing the invisible man's ideology. The woman who seduces him in her apartment is confusing the concept of brotherhood with biology, offering
in fact still another alternative that he must try and then reject
during the novel.

> Why did they have to mix their women into everything? Between
> us and everything we wanted to change in the world they placed a
> woman: socially, politically, economically. Why, godammit, why did
> they insist upon confusing the class struggle with the ass struggle,
> debasing both us and them—all human motives.

This is the other side of the confusion that Ras showed on the
woman question. They both attribute a sexual motivation to a
drive to attain social equality and human dignity.

The principle of invisibility and projected fantasy which we have
seen operating in these episodes—and which the invisible man is
gradually discovering—was announced on the first page of the
novel. It is "a peculiar disposition of the eyes of those with whom
I come in contact. A matter of the construction of their *inner* eyes,
those eyes with which they look through their physical eyes upon
reality." The consequence of this disposition of the inner eye for
the invisible man is not that people see nothing at all when they
look in his direction, for they know that *something* is there. What
they do is look through that something at what they expect to see,
what they think is there—the inner eye sees a fiction that it has
itself created. The first concrete example of this error of vision
comes in the Prologue, when the invisible man bumps into a tall
blond man who insults him and curses him when asked to apolo-
gize. In the fight that follows the white man is almost killed, but
not by the invisible man. "Something in this man's thick head
had sprung out and beaten him within an inch of his life," and
that something was the man's own prejudiced concept of the Nigger
which he had insulted and cursed.

The Prologue also introduces the problem of names which the
reader encounters with almost every character, and the critic suffers while trying to write about the nameless protagonist of the
novel. Thoreau once wrote an essay largely devoted to praising the
system of naming practiced by the American Indians. What Thoreau admired about the system was the idea that everyone had to
wait until he had earned a name through some significant action,

or until he had revealed enough of his basic personality for a name to be chosen that adequately reflected his individuality. The "invisible man" is an earned name in something like the same sense, as "Jack the Bear" is his underground name because he sees his underground time as a period of hibernation. Most of the names we are given for characters in the novel are also earned names, or names which serve as clues to the character's nature or his function in the novel. Sometimes these names are symbolic, like "Tod" Clifton or "Mary." More often they are not so much directly symbolic as suggestive.

For example, when we look at Brother Jack, we should remember that a common slang meaning for "jack" is money. The name emphasizes the financial element in the relationship between the invisible man and the Brotherhood. When Ras ("race") the Exhorter asked whether it was money or women that could blind a Negro to his racial identity, the invisible man was outraged that his purity of motive could be questioned. But the whole scene takes place in front of a garish sign that says "CHECKS CASHED HERE." Brother Jack first showed up when the invisible man was out of money, and his first reason for joining the Brotherhood was for the pay they offered. Without knowing it, at the same time as he is trying to get rid of the bank because it is the image of the paid entertainer debasing himself for money, he is taking on an analogous position within the Brotherhood. This is emphasized at the end, when Brother Jack is disciplining him. ". . . you were not hired to think. Had you forgotten that? If so, listen to me: You were not hired to think."

Rinehart is another significant name, but it can be misleading if one looks to the German *rein* ("pure") for help. "Rind" (or "rine" in the pronunciation of the novel) is a good American slang word. If a person has a lot of rind, it means he has a lot of nerve. If he *is* a rind, it means he is thick-skinned in a sense ranging all the way from not caring what other people think to not caring what happens to them. This is the rind in the Rinehart in the novel, and the invisible man points to it just before hunting up Sybil:

> Now I recognized my invisibility. So I'd accept it, I'd explore it, rine and heart. I'd plunge into it with both feet and they'd gag. Oh, but wouldn't they gag.

As it turns out, however, it is the invisible man who gags on the rind, for he is not cynical enough to keep up the role. "Such games were for Rinehart, not me," he says, and he washes off the lipstick inscription he had meant to leave behind. Meanwhile, by doing a Rinehart, by pretending to agree with the Brotherhood in order to undermine it, he does in effect agree, and becomes a betrayer of the Harlem Brothers while working in his own interests. The irony of this role is that in the very moment of seeing Sybil's fantasy of the Black rapist he is himself attempting to live one. Rinehart, the "spiritual technologist" is like the nameless Black Doctor in Barth's *End of the Road,* offering a "Mythotherapy" for role-paralysis which works only until one must face the consequences of his arbitrary action.

"Emerson" is another important name in *Invisible Man,* and one Ellison is acutely aware of as that of his own namesake. He deliberately uses it to undercut the conventional liberal attitude towards race relations, when the *son* of old Emerson (to suggest the historical continuity) tries to befriend the invisible man. Young Emerson tries to find him a place in the great Liberty Paint company just as Norton had tried to help him find a place in the American society, but both Norton and Emerson have an image of *the* Negro which limits their possibility of sharing any kind of reality with the invisible man. Emerson even wants to find a place for him in his own confused private life; after announcing that he had "a difficult session" with his analyst the evening before, Emerson goes on:

> "Some things are just too unjust for words," he said, expelling a plume of smoke, "and too ambiguous for either speech or ideas. By the way, have you ever been to the Club Calamus?"
>
> "I don't think I've ever heard of it, sir," I said.
>
> "You haven't? It's very well known. Many of my Harlem friends go there. It's a rendezvous for writers, artists and all kinds of celebrities. There's nothing like it in the city, and by some strange twist it has a truly continental flavor."

The fey tone of this speech alone is enough to destroy what little respect we might have had for Emerson, but the Calamus Club reference takes it a bit further. The allusion is to the group of Whitman poems commonly called the Calamus Poems and dealing in a subtle but unmistakeable way with the theme of homosexuality. In other words, here is still another fraternity or Brotherhood that is being offered the invisible man, and as the historical Emerson's ideas are debased in his 20th-century "son," Whitman's androgynously cosmic appetite is reduced to a stylish sexual mys-

tique. Emerson makes it even more explicit later, when he says
". . . I'm Huckleberry, you see. . . ." in hopes that the invisible
man will be another Jim, and perhaps have read Leslie Fiedler. But
the invisible man can't be Jim because he is already too busy being
Huckleberry himself without knowing it.

Characters' names, and the club names, and the names of factories, places and institutions—even the names of things, like the
Sambo doll—can be explored indefinitely in this novel. The Brotherhood has its parties at a place called the Chthonian Club, which
is a classical reference comparable to that of the Sybils. The Chthonian realm belonged to the underground gods and spirits; and
true power for Ellison is an underground influence as we learn
from seeing Bledsoe and Brockway and Brother Jack in action, as
well as the invisible man writing in his hole. Where does Ras get
his name, with its vocal nearness to "race"? He gives it to himself,
as the invisible man gives us the name we must call him by if we
are to know him for what he is.

The invisible man in action is an image collector or symbolist,
gathering up into his briefcase all the concrete emblems and reminders of his experience that can serve as clues to finding his real
name and identity. The book itself is for the reader a similar container of images and clues expanded into actions and events. The
first example of an action-as-image after the Prologue is the battle
royal scene which opens the story. If we explored this scene far
enough, we could find in it a prefiguration of almost everything
else in the novel. Before the battle, the boys are forced to look at
the naked blond dancing for the whites. In the battle we see a
group of half-naked Black boys, blindfolded, fighting each other
in a ring for the entertainment of a group of white citizens. Afterwards, they fight again, still among themselves, for the coins on the
electrified rug. The coins they desire the most, the gold ones, turn
out to be brass, but there are enough dollars to go around. Afterwards, the invisible man steps forward and gives his carefully-
prepared speech (with one prophetic verbal slip) in which he defends the status quo of the Southern Negro who is trying to better
himself through education in segregated schools. These are the
bare bones of the scene, and they are suggestive in themselves. But
if we look closer we can see much more. The naked white girl with
golden hair suggests and prefigures the whole problem of money
and sex. Her golden hair, like the fake golden coins, holds out a
promise of a world which can never exist for the invisible man because it too is brass. The blindfolds on the boys are white blind-

folds, and the darkness they are fighting in is a darkness imposed upon them by the white spectators who represent the whole society:

> They were all there—bankers, lawyers, judges, doctors, fire chiefs, teachers, merchants. Even one of the more fashionable pastors.

They unleash a great deal of violence in their brawl, but it is all directed against themselves, under the control of and for the amusement of this representative audience. During the brawl one of the boys, the invisible man, loosens his blindfold enough so that he can make out a little bit of what is going on. And it is this one who comes forward afterwards to speak to the crowd, as the invisible man is speaking to us in the novel.

In the first few pages of the book, this scene seems to be primarily a description of what happened to a few people at a particular "smoker" in some small unidentified southern town. But as we read through the book, with this scene planted in our memories, we gradually realize that in it is condensed the whole world of the novel and almost all of the American society. The final scene, the race riot in Harlem, is in large part a repetition of the beginning scene, but one which we can more easily relate to the larger context it represents. Instead of the coins on the electrified rug, there is the safe on the third rail showering the streets with sparks. Instead of control being ordinary citizens, it is in Brother Jack who represents their interests in controlling the Blacks. Instead of Tatlock and the invisible man battling it out at the end for supremacy, we have Ras and the invisible man, finally silencing his fanatic appeal to race by throwing a spear through his jaws. The riot is probably the most impressively sustained section of the whole novel. It is still carefully kept to the elements already prefigured in the brawl, yet expanded into a comic apocalypse of enormous proportions. It begins as a drunken orgy of consumer wish-fulfillment which is a fantasy Christmas ("At St. Nicholas the street lights were out.") and fourth of July combined. At the peak of their frenzied rebellion the looters are still being controlled and manipulated by society's official symbol-makers:

> "With all them hats in there and I'm going to come out with anything but a *Dobbs?* Man, are you *mad?* All them new, pretty-colored *Dobbs?*"
> "Git a side of bacon, Joe," a woman called. "Git a side of bacon, Joe, git Wilson's."

Even Ras, who now calls himself the "Destroyer," has made himself up from the scrap heap of cultural detritus as Quixote made himself up from scraps and pieces of the old Romances. He is a composite of cowboy and African movies, equipped with stage-prop lion skin, spear and shield, "one of the kind you see them African guys carrying in the moving pictures. . . ." Although they are rioting against society, no one knows how the riot got started, and the only damage they succeed doing is to themselves in the pathetic burning-down of their own tenement. The only difference, save that of scale, is that at the end the invisible man does not step forward and give a speech prepared for him by the cultural myths, but instead disappears down his hole and creates a book which could only be written after he had recognized his invisibility.

On a smaller scale we can see the same kind of significance at work throughout the novel. In fact, there is a whole scale of images at work at almost every point in *Invisible Man*. Small ones, like the statue of the Founder removing the veil from the slave. but seen in such a way that it is impossible to tell whether it is being removed or put more firmly in place—echoed later by the invisible man's spotlight blindness as he makes his first official Brotherhood speech. Another is the recurring image of the mounted police, controlling the animal power of their black horses through a more efficient power and technique. In the invisible man's Brotherhood office is a map of the world with the figure of Columbus, reminding us that the real America is yet to be discovered, and that although there may be natives there, they will not be the natives we expected to find.

Some of these images seem to be quite clearly intended for the reader alone. Although they are registered through the eyes and consciousness of the invisible man, they are not noted by him as containing any special significance. In the El Toro bar, there are two bullfight posters which are described matter-of-factly along with the other miscellaneous contents of the room. The first poster shows a large black bull, being skillfully controlled by the matador. The other poster shows the tables turned, the bull finally discovering the illusion of the cape and tossing the matador high into the air. This is much like the fight between a prizefighter and a yokel described in. the Prologue, where "the yokel, rolling about in the gale of boxing gloves, struck one blow and knocked science, speed and footwork as cold as a well-digger's posterior. The smart money hit the canvas. The long shot got the nod." The bullfight posters, and their echo of the prizefight, are a silent comment on the dis-

cussion going on in the bar between Brother Jack—who is trying
to discipline him—and the invisible man. They are also a predic-
tion of the outcome of the contest which will be fulfilled later in
the novel.

Another condensed prefiguration is carefully suggested in the
scene where Brother Tarp gives the invisible man his severed chain
link, telling him the story of his limp which the doctors can't
explain. For "saying no" to a man who wanted to take something
from him, Tarp lost his wife, children and land and was sentenced
to a life in prison on a chain gang. Nineteen years later, he said
no again, and kept saying it until he broke the chain and left. Still
limping, and still "looking for freedom," he gives the link to the
invisible man because "it's got a heap of signifying wrapped up in
it and it might help you to remember what we're really fighting
against." At the moment of giving him the link, Tarp stops calling
him son and calls him Brother "for the first time." The ceremony is

> like a man passing on to his son his own father's watch, which the
> son accepted not because he wanted the old-fashioned time-piece
> for itself, but because of the overtones of unstated seriousness and
> solemnity of the paternal gesture which at once joined him with his
> ancestors, marked a high point of his present, and promised a con-
> creteness to his nebulous and chaotic future. And now I remembered
> that if I had returned home instead of coming north my father
> would have given me my grandfather's old-fashioned Hamilton, with
> its long, burr-headed winding stem.

Tarp is both his spiritual father and brother, for they are looking
for freedom together by saying no to slavery which has left its
mark on each of them. Had the invisible man stayed in the South,
in his own father's and grandfather's tradition, he would have remained a "burr-head" and a slave without knowing it.

Although some of these images are like guideposts for the reader,
reminding him of the larger pattern of the novel, the larger ones
are all in some degree meaningful to the invisible man, and there is
a consistent pattern in his reaction to them. After each significant
event, he gives a speech which summarizes his state of development as of that moment in the novel. The most naive speech is the
one he gives after the brawl. In each succeeding recognition he is
at least potentially more aware of who he is and what his experience means until the point where he is able to summarize the whole
in a book which *includes* the other speeches. An example of the
tentative progression of these speeches can be seen in Chapter 13.

After having had his old identity wiped out through the boiler explosion, he begins to find a feeling of his own identity in a self-conscious but unashamed acceptance of some of the shabbier aspects of Harlem life. He eats a yam on the streets, without fear of being seen. When he comes on the eviction, he is at first embarrassed by the naked exposure of all the odds and ends of junk that tell the story of the life this old couple has lived. But gradually, as the furniture and debris pile up, he begins to realize that the belongings of the couple tell the story of his race, going all the way back to the Free Papers dated August, 1859. Even the consciousness of shame instilled in him from the day he was born can't obliterate the feeling of identity he gets from seeing these things:

> And it was as though I myself was being dispossessed of some painful yet precious thing which I could not bear to lose; something confounding, like a rotted tooth that one would rather suffer indefinitely than endure the short, violent eruption of pain that would mark its removal. And with this sense of dispossession came a pang of vague recognition.

The recognition is vague but intense, and the intensity shows up in the speech he makes and his willingness to fight for a feeling he still cannot define or fully accept.

Most of the actions and images I have been discussing have a plausible existence in the real world, and the important thing is the sensitivity of vision we bring to them. No matter how subtly calculated we can afterwards see the effect to be, there is always the impression of a real event while we are reading. There are places in *Invisible Man,* however, where the action seems decidedly secondary to the ideas Ellison is trying to convey, where the priority of the ideas dominates so that we can't read without the attempt to translate the action back into the ideas. In these cases Ellison seems to share Ishmael's attitude towards what he calls "hideous and intolerable allegory," not believing in it at all, yet unable to resist the comic indulgence of his appetite for it.

The clearest example here is in the factory hospital scene, where the doctors try to remake the invisible man into the mechanical man he had been before, the subservient southern Negro who died when he attacked Brockway in the boiler room. When he wakes in the hospital his mind is a blank, and he only gradually becomes aware that the doctors are trying to achieve a machine-induced prefrontal lobotomy that will return him to his previous state. The

whole scene is presented as a return to childhood followed by rebirth, including the cutting of the umbilical cord (the electric
cord attached to the stomach node), followed by an alcohol rub-
down by an efficient nurse. "You're a new man," the doctors point-
edly tell him. On the way home from the hospital the "new man"
is metamorphosed into *the* new man, the Biblical Adam, who even
predicts his own fall. "And I felt that I would fall, *had* fallen," he
says, and then looks across the aisle of the subway car to see "a
young platinum blonde nibbling at a red Delicious apple." [14]

The same serio-comic intent is behind the 1,369 light bulbs that
are made so much of in the Prologue. The light bulbs are his means
of fighting the Monopolated Light and Power Company, and Ellison's way of illustrating the effects of a self-recognition on the
power struggle that occupies most of the novel. After first finding
his own light by burning the papers in the briefcase, he can begin
to take revenge on the power monopoly that he has suffered under
for so long. He is finally out of their control. He can't overthrow
them, but he can undermine and weaken them by draining off part
of their power. No writer would go to this extent for the sake of an
idea alone, and there is a very pointed humor in much of Ellison's
"allegory." The ironic, joking tone of the blues is continually showing through, as well as the pleasure Ellison obviously gets from the
virtuoso manipulation of words. For a final example, consider the
description of eating dessert in the hole. The invisible man is sitting
there. He's blue, he's wondering why he's blue, and thinking what
it means to be blue. And he's listening to Louis Armstrong playing
and singing, "What Did I Do to Be so Black and Blue." He has
just made a big point of being in the great American tradition, and
now he is describing his favorite dessert of sloe gin and ice cream.
As we visualize him pouring the red liquid over the white mound,
we suddenly get the point of the color scheme he has been building
up to emphasize his Americanism, and the submerged but deliberate joke helps to establish the tone of the whole Prologue. The

[14] This scene is reminiscent of Hart Crane's "For the Marriage of Faustus and
Helen," where the poet-Faust imagines meeting Helen in a New York subway:

> And yet, suppose some evening I forgot
> The fare and transfer, yet got by that way
> Without recall—lost yet poised in traffic.
> Then I might find your eyes across an aisle,
> Still flickering with those prefigurations—
> Prodigal, yet uncontested now,
> Half-riant before the jerky window frame.

effect is almost gratuitously clever, but Ellison is a fierce punster, and he can't always restrict himself to the obvious level of "I yam what I am," or turning Brother Tobitts into two bits.

He is also a prophetic writer, and that is why I must conclude with the envelope or frame which makes up the novel's beginning and end. The Prologue gives us a picture of the invisible man after he's finished writing the book, a picture of his present state. He has discovered that he is invisible, and taken the first step that he must take after the discovery. He has preserved his anger and his suffering by embodying it in art, and has even more fully grasped his identity in the process. But what is he to do with his identity after this, and after all the emphasis in the Epilogue on "the possibility that even an invisible man has a socially responsible role to play." We know that he is in hibernation, and we can't help wondering with him whether he will come up to find the smell of death or the smell of spring in the outside air. The invisible man doesn't know; he is prepared for a rebirth, and a new life, but has not yet been born into it. About 35 years ago Henry Roth published *Call It Sleep*. It was an extremely good novel, and for a first novel almost unbelievably good. Those were depression times, and it wasn't a protest novel, so there was not a great reaction, but those few who did appreciate it looked forward with anticipation to Roth's next work. While they waited, however, Roth disappeared, and has only recently been discovered, raising game birds near Augusta, Maine. With the rediscovery and tardy acclaim of *Call It Sleep*, many readers have naturally wondered why Roth has not written anything for so long. It turns out that he has been trying to write off and on, but can't. His problem, he says, is that "There is one theme I like above all others, and that is redemption, but I haven't the fable."

Invisible Man is clearly a prelude to and preparation for something like redemption, and therefore an extremely dangerous and difficult novel to follow. It may be that Ellison has written himself into a corner, or it may be that in his next novel he will find the fable for us. It seems to me that, if any of our contemporary writers can find it and express it, he can. But it has to be there first to be found, and whether it exists or not cannot be answered until it *is* found. Ellison has been working on his second novel for a long time now. Whatever he is doing, there is some evidence that it will be apocalyptic, that it will attempt to show us either the pattern of our redemption or of our destruction and continued frustration. We shouldn't forget that the alternative to a vision of redemption is carefully planted in the Prologue of *Invisible Man*. In his reflection on the brawl with the white man, the invisible man says:

> He, let us say, was lost in a dream world. But didn't *he* control that dream world—which, alas, is only too real!—and didn't *he* rule me out of it? And if he had yelled for a policeman, wouldn't *I* have been taken for the offending one? Yes, yes, yes! Let me agree with you, I was the irresponsible one; for I should have used my knife to protect the higher interests of society. Some day that kind of foolishness will cause us tragic trouble. All dreamers and sleepwalkers must pay the price, and even the invisible victim is responsible for the fate of all. But I shirked that responsibility; I became too snarled in the incompatible notions that buzzed within my brain. I was a coward. . . .

Ralph Ellison and the American
Comic Tradition

by Earl H. Rovit

The most obvious comment one can make about Ralph Ellison's *Invisible Man* is that it is a profoundly comic work. But the
obvious is not necessarily either simple or self-explanatory, and it
seems to me that the comic implications of Ellison's novel are elusive
and provocative enough to warrant careful examination both in
relation to the total effect of the novel itself and the American
cultural pattern from which it derives. It is generally recognized
that Ellison's novel is a highly conscious attempt to embody a
particular kind of experience—the experience of the "outsider"
(in this case, a Negro) who manages to come to some sort of temporary acceptance, and thus, definition, of his status in the universe;
it is not so generally recognized that *Invisible Man* is an integral
link in a cumulative chain of great American creations, bearing an
unmistakable brand of kinship to such seemingly incongruous works
as *The Divinity School Address, Song of Myself, Moby Dick,* and
The Education of Henry Adams. But the latter proposition is, I
think, at least as valid as the former, and unless it is given proper
recognition, a good deal of the value of the novel will be ignored.

First it should be noted that Ellison's commitment to what Henry
James has termed "the American joke" has been thoroughly deliberate and undisguised. Ellison once described penetratingly the
ambiguous *locus* of conflicting forces within which the American
artist has had always to work: "For the ex-colonials, the declaration
of an American identity meant the assumption of a mask, and it
imposed not only the discipline of national self-consciousness, it
gave Americans an ironic awareness of the joke that always lies be-

"Ralph Ellison and the American Comic Tradition" by Earl H. Rovit. From
Wisconsin Studies in Contemporary Literature, 1 (Fall 1960), pp. 34–42. Copyright © 1960 by the Regents of the University of Wisconsin. Reprinted by permission of the Regents of the University of Wisconsin.

tween appearance and reality, between the discontinuity of social tradition and that sense of the past which clings to the mind. And perhaps even an awareness of the joke that society is man's creation, not God's." This kind of ironic awareness may contain bitterness and may even become susceptible to the heavy shadow of despair, but the art which it produces has been ultimately comic. It will inevitably probe the masks of identity and value searching relentlessly for some deeper buried reality, but it will do this while accepting the fundamental necessity for masks and the impossibility of ever discovering an essential face beneath a mask. That is to say, this comic stance will accept with the same triumphant gesture both the basic absurdity of all attempts to impose meaning on the chaos of life, and the necessary converse of this, the ultimate significance of absurdity itself.

Ellison's *Invisible Man* is comic in this sense almost in spite of its overtly satirical interests and its excursions into the broadly farcical. Humorous as many of its episodes are in themselves—the surreal hysteria of the scene at the Golden Day, the hero's employment at the Liberty Paint Company, or the expert dissection of political entanglement in Harlem—these are the materials which clothe Ellison's joke and which, in turn, suggest the shape by which the joke can be comprehended. The pith of Ellison's comedy reverberates on a level much deeper than these incidents, and as in all true humor, the joke affirms and denies simultaneously—accepts and rejects with the same uncompromising passion, leaving not a self-cancelling neutralization of momentum, but a sphere of moral conquest, a humanized cone of light at the very heart of the heart of darkness. *Invisible Man,* as Ellison has needlessly insisted in rebuttal to those critics who would treat the novel as fictionalized sociology or as a dramatization of archetypal images, is an artist's attempt to create a *form.* And fortunately Ellison has been quite explicit in describing what he means by *form;* in specific reference to the improvisation of the jazz-musician he suggests that form represents "a definition of his identity: as an individual, as member of the collectivity, and as a link in the chain of tradition." But note that each of these definitions of identity must be individually exclusive and mutually contradictory on any logical terms. Because of its very pursuit after the uniqueness of individuality, the successful definition of an individual must define out the possibilities of generalization into "collectivity" or "tradition." But herein for Ellison in his embrace of a notion of fluid amorphous identity lies the real morality and humor in mankind's art and men's lives—neither of which have much respect for the laws of formal logic.

At one time during the novel when Ellison's protagonist is enthusiastically convinced that his membership in the Brotherhood is the only effective means to individual and social salvation, he recalls these words from a college lecture on Stephen Dedalus: "Stephen's problem, like ours, was not actually one of creating the uncreated conscience of his race, but of creating the *uncreated features of his face*. Our task is that of making ourselves individuals. The conscience of a race is the gift of its individuals who see, evaluate, record. . . . We create the race by creating ourselves and then to our great astonishment we will have created something far more important: We will have created a culture. Why waste time creating a conscience for something that doesn't exist? For, you see, blood and skin do not think!" This is one of the most significant passages in the novel, and one which must be appreciated within the context of the total form if the subtle pressure of that form is to be adequately weighed. And this can be done only if the Prologue and the Epilogue are viewed as functional elements in the novel which set the tempo for its moral action and modulate ironically upon its emergent meanings.

The Prologue introduces the narrator in his underground hibernation musing upon the events of his life, eating vanilla ice-cream and sloe gin, listening to Louis Armstrong's recording, "What Did I Do to Be so Black and Blue?" and trying to wrest out of the confusions of his experiences some pattern of meaning and/or resilient core of identity. The next twenty-five chapters are a first-person narrative flashback which covers some twenty years of the protagonist's life ending with the beginning, the hero's descent into the underground hole. The concluding Epilogue picks up the tonal patterns of the Prologue, implies that both meaning and identity have been discovered, and dramatically forces a direct identification between the narrator and the reader. Ostensibly this is another novel of the initiation of a boy into manhood—a *Bildungsroman* in the episodic picaresque tradition. The advice of the literature teacher has been realized; the hero has created the features of his face from the malleable stuff of his experience. He who accepts himself as "invisible" has ironically achieved a concrete tangibility, while those characters in the novel who seemed to be "visible" and substantial men (Norton, Brother Jack, and even Tod Clifton) are discovered to be really "invisible" since they are self-imprisoned captives of their own capacities to see and be seen in stereotyped images. However, to read the novel in this way and to go no further is to miss the cream of the jest and the total significance of the whole form which pivots on the ironic fulcrum of the blues theme introduced in the Prologue and given resolution in the Epilogue. As in all seriously comic works the reader is left not with an answer, but with a challenging question—a question which soars beyond the novel on the unanswered notes of Armstrong's trumpet: "What did I do to be so black and blue?"

For the protagonist *is* finally and most comically *invisible* at the end of the novel; he has learned that to create the uncreated features of his face is at best a half-value, and at worst, potentially more self-destructive than not to strive after identity at all. For Ellison ours is a time when "you prepare a face to meet the faces that you meet"—a time when we have learned to shuffle and deal our personalities with a protean dexterity that, as is characterized through Rinehart, is a wholesale exploitation of and surrender to chaos. After the narrator's fall into the coalpit he discovers that his arrogantly naive construction of personality is nothing more than the accumulated fragments in his briefcase: the high-school diploma, Bledsoe's letter, Clifton's dancing doll, Mary's bank, Brother Tarp's iron. And most ironically, even these meager artifacts—the fragments he has shored against his ruin—represent not him, but the world's variegated projections of him. The narrator learns then that his educational romance is a farcical melodrama of the most garish variety; the successive births and rebirths of his life (his Caesarean delivery from college, his birth by electronics at the factory hospital, the christening by the Brotherhood) were not the organic gestations of personality that he idealized so much as they were the cold manipulations of artificial insemination. His final acceptance of his invisibility reminds us of the demand of the Zen Master: "Show me the face you had before you were born."

However, we must note also that this acceptance of invisibility, of amorphous non-identity, is far from a resignation to chaos. The protagonist has successfully rebelled against the imposition of social masks whether externally (like Clifton's) or internally (like Brother Tarp's) bestowed; his is not a surrender of personality so much as a descent to a deeper level of personality where the accent is heavier on possibilities than on limitations. The 1,369 glowing light bulbs in his cellar retreat attest to the increased power and enlightenment which are positive gains from his experience, as well as to the strategic advantages of his recourse to invisibility. The literature teacher unwittingly pointed out the flaw in his exhortation even as he declaimed it: "Blood and skin do not think!" For to think is to be as much concerned with analysis as it is with synthesis; the ironic mind tears radiant unities apart even as it forges them. Accordingly Ellison's narrator assumes the ultimate mask of facelessness and emphasizes the fluid chaos which is the secret substance of form, the dynamic interplay of possibilities which creates limitations. The narrator is backed into the blank corner where he must realize that "the mind that has conceived a plan of living must never lose sight of the chaos against which that pattern was conceived." In accepting himself as the Invisible Man he assumes the historic role which Emerson unerringly assigned to the American poet; he becomes "the world's eye"—something through which one sees, even though it cannot itself be seen.

And here it may be fruitful to investigate briefly the peculiar relationship of Emerson's work to Ellison (whose middle name is propitiously Waldo). In the recently published excerpt from a novel in progress, "And Hickman Arrives," Ellison has his main character, Alonzo Zuber, Daddy Hickman, make some complimentary remarks about Emerson, "a preacher . . . who knew that every tub has to sit on its own bottom." Daddy Hickman, a Negro preacher ("Better known as GOD'S TROMBONE"), is vividly characterized as a wise and shrewd virtuoso of the evangelical circuit who might not unfairly be taken as a modern-day Emerson, preaching eloquently the gospel of humanity. These facts may be significant when we remember that Emerson's work is given short shrift as rhetorical nonsense in *Invisible Man* and his name is bestowed upon a character whose minor function in the novel is to be a self-righteous hypocrite. This shift in attitude may indicate that Ellison has come to realize that there are some major affinities binding him to his famous namesake, and, more important, it may enable us to understand more clearly the remarkable consistency of the American struggle to create art and the relatively harmonious visions which these unique struggles have attained.

Superficially there would seem to be little to link the two men beyond the somewhat labored pun of their names and Ellison's awareness of the pun. The one, an ex-Unitarian minister of respectable, if modest, Yankee background, whose orotund explorations in autobiography gave fullest form to the American dream—whose public pose attained an Olympian serenity and optimistic faith which have caused him to be associated with a wide range of sentimentalities from Mary Baker Eddy to Norman Vincent Peale; the other, an Oklahoma City Negro, born in 1914, ex-Leftist propagandist and editor, who would seem to have belied the Emersonian prophecy of individualism and self-reliance by the very title of his novel, *Invisible Man*. The one, nurtured by the most classical education that America had to offer; the other, a rapt disciple of jazzmen like Charlie Christian and Jimmy Rushing who has attributed to their lyric improvisations his deepest understanding of aesthetic form. The one, white and given to the Delphic utterance; the other, black and adept in the cautery of bitter humor. But in their respective searches for identity, in their mutual concern with defining the possibilities and limitations which give form and shape to that which is human, the poet who called man "a golden impossibility" and the novelist who teaches his protagonist that life is a latent hive of infinite possibilities draw close together in their attempts to find an artistic resolution of the contrarieties of existence.

"Only he can give, who has," wrote Emerson; "he only can create, who is." Experience is the fluxional material from which these all-important values and identities are created, and Emerson's great essays are processive incantations whose ultimate function is to bring identity into being, even as they chant the fundamental fluidity of all forms spontaneously and eternally merging into other forms. When we remember that Emerson once wrote: "A believer in Unity, a seer of Unity, I yet behold two," it may be worth a speculation that the Emerson behind the triumphant artifices of the *Essays* was not a terribly different person from the Invisible Man in the coalpit whose submersion into the lower frequencies had given him an entree to the consciousnesses of all men. This awareness of the absurdity of meaning (and the potential meaningfulness of chaos) is at the heart of Emerson's delight in paradox, his seeming inconsistencies, his "dialogistic" techniques, his highly functional approach to language. "All symbols are fluxional," he declaimed; "all language is vehicular and transitive and is good for conveyance not for homestead." Thus Melville's attempted criticism of Emerson in *The Confidence Man* misses widely the mark; Emerson isn't there when the satire strikes home. Melville, who above all of Emerson's contemporaries should have known better, mistook the Olympian pasteboard mask for a reality and misread the eloquent quest for identity as a pretentious melodrama. For, as Constance Rourke recognized, Emerson is one of our most deft practitioners of the American joke, and the magnitude of his success may be measured by the continued effectiveness of his disguises after more than a hundred years.

But again we must return to the *form* of *Invisible Man* to appreciate how deeply involved Ellison's work is with the most basic American vision of reality. Although it is probably true as some critics have pointed out that the dominating metaphor of the novel—the "underground man" theme—was suggested by Dostoevsky and Richard Wright, it is for our purposes more interesting to note a similar metaphor in Hart Crane's poem, "Black Tambourine":

> The interests of a black man in a cellar
> Mark tardy judgment on the world's closed door.
> Gnats toss in the shadow of a bottle,
> And a roach spans a crevice in the floor.
>
> . . . .:•!
>
> The black man, forlorn in the cellar,
> Wanders in some mid-kingdom, dark, that lies,
> Between his tambourine, stuck on the wall,
> And, in Africa, a carcass quick with flies.

Invisible Man achieves an expert evocation of that "mid-kingdom," that *demi-monde* of constant metamorphosis where good and evil, appearance and reality, pattern and chaos are continually shifting their shapes even as the eye strains to focus and the imagination to comprehend. The Kafkaesque surrealism of the novel's action, the thematic entwinement of black-white and dark-light, and the psychic distance from the plot-development which the use of the Prologue and the Epilogue achieves posit the moral center of the novel in that fluid area where experience is in the very process of being transformed into value. The narrator, the author, and the reader as well are caught in the "mid-kingdom" which seems to me to be the characteristic and unavoidable focus of American literature. For this mid-kingdom, this unutterable silence which is "zero at the bone," seems to me to be the one really inalienable birthright of being an American. Some Americans following Swedenborg named it "vastation"; others gave it no name and lamented the dearth of an American tradition within which the artist could work; at least one commissioned the sculptor Saint-Gaudens to incarnate it in a statue. One way of attempting to describe the sense of being within this mid-kingdom can be most dramatically seen in "The Castaway" chapter of *Moby Dick* where Pip is left floundering in the boundless Pacific. And although the techniques of approaching the experience have been richly various, the experience itself, an incontrovertible

sense of absolute metaphysical isolation, can be found at the core
of the most vital American creations.

"American history," writes James Baldwin in *Notes of a Native
Son,* is "the history of the total, and willing, alienation of entire
peoples from their forebears. What is overwhelmingly clear . . . is
that this history has created an entirely unprecedented people, with
a unique and individual past." The alienation, of course, is more
than sociological and ideological; it seeps down into the very depths
whence the sureties of identity and value are wrought; and it im-
prisons the American in this mid-kingdom where the boundaries—
the distance from the tambourine on the wall to the carcass quick
with flies—cannot be measured in either years or miles. The American seeking himself—as an individual, a member of the collectivity,
a link in the chain of tradition—can never discover or create that
identity in fixed restrictive terms. The past is dead and yet it lives:
note Ellison's use of the narrator's grandfather, the yams, the techniques of the evangelical sermon. Individuals are frozen in mute
isolation, and yet communication is possible between them: the
Harlem riot, the way the narrator listens to music. Ellison's novel
is the unique metaphor of his own thoroughly personal experience,
and yet it makes a fitting link in the chain of the American
tradition.

That Ellison and his narrator are Negroes both is and is not important. From the severe standpoint of art the racial fact is
negligible, although there are doubtless areas of meaning and influence in *Invisible Man* which sociological examination might
fruitfully develop. From the viewpoint of cultural history, however, the racial fact is enormously provocative. It is strikingly clear
that contemporary American writing, particularly the writing of
fiction, is dominated by two categories of writers: members of religious and racial minorities, and writers who possess powerful
regional heritages. Both groups have an instinctive leasehold within
the boundaries of the "mid-kingdom"; the Negro, the Catholic, the
Jew, and the Southerner share the immediate experience of living
on the razor's edge of time, at the very point where traditions come
into desperate conflict with the human need to adapt to change.
And, of equal importance, both groups—in varying degrees—are
marked out on the contemporary scene as being "different"; both
groups cannot avoid the terrible problem of identity, because it is
ever thrust upon them whether they like it or not. These are the
conditions which in the American past have nourished our spas-
modic exfoliations of significant literary activity: the great "Renais-

sance" of the 1840's and '50's, the Twain-James-Adams "alliance" of the late nineteenth century, the post-World War One literary florescence from which we have just begun to break away. But the Lost Generation was the last generation which could practise the necessary expatriation or "fugitivism" in which these factors—the dis-severance from the past and the search for identity—could operate on non-minority or non-regional American writers. Thus Ralph Ellison—and contemporaries like Saul Bellow, Flannery O'Connor, and William Styron—are *inside* the heart of the American experience by the very virtue of their being in some way "outsiders." Like Emerson, himself a royal inhabitant of the mid-kingdom over a century ago, they are challenged to create form, or else succumb to the enveloping chaos within and without.

And the answers which they arrive at—again as with Emerson— are answers which cannot be taken out of the context of their individually achieved forms without being reduced to platitude or non-sense. Form, the creation of a radical, self-defining metaphor, is the one rational technique which human beings have developed to deal adequately with the basic irrationality of existence. The answer which *Invisible Man* gives to the unanswerable demands which life imposes on the human being has something to do with human limitation and a good deal to do with freedom; it has something to do with hatred, and a good deal more to do with love. It defines the human distance between the tambourine and the carcass and it accepts with wonder and dignity the immeasurable gift of life. The black man in the cellar transforms his isolation into elevation without denying the brute facts of existence and without losing his ironic grip on the transiency of the moment. The amorphous ambiguity of the mid-kingdom is for a timeless instant conquered and made fit for habitation. Perhaps tragedy teaches man to become divine, but before man can aspire to divinity, he must first accept completely the responsibilities and limitations of being human. The American experience, cutting away the bonds of tradition which assure man of his humanity, has not allowed a tragic art to develop. But there has developed a rich and vigorous comic tradition to which *Invisible Man* is a welcome embellishment, and it is this art which promises most as a healthy direction into the future.

Ralph Ellison and Afro-American Folk and Cultural Tradition

by George E. Kent

Ralph Ellison stressed connections between Afro-American Folk and Cultural tradition and American culture, since "The heel bone is, after all, connected, through its various linkages, to the head bone," and not to be ignored is "the intricate network of connections which binds Negroes to the larger society." [1] Mindful of this pronouncement I shall sketch in some of Ellison's ideas concerning the value of the folk tradition, explore representative techniques in *Invisible Man,* and offer suggested comments concerning the value and limitations of his method.

Pressed toward a bag of pure Blackness, Ellison was capable of minimizing folk tradition's value for the self-conscious writer, as he does in "Change the Joke and Slip the Yoke," an essay in response to Stanley Edgar Hyman's attempt to create achetypes of Blackness.[2] In "Change the Joke," he contended that the Black writer was "heir to the human experience which is literature," an inheritance which might be more important to him than his own living folk tradition. As for himself, Black folklore became important through literary discovery. Seeing the uses to which folklore is put in the works of James Joyce and T. S. Eliot, Ellison saw the folk tradition, the spirituals, blues, jazz and folk-tales as a stable factor in "the discontinuous, swiftly changing, and diverse American culture . . ." [3] It expresses qualities needful in a world

"Ralph Ellison and Afro-American Folk and Cultural Tradition," by George E. Kent. From *C.L.A. Journal,* Volume XIII, Number 3 (March, 1970), pp. 265–276. Copyright © 1970 by the College Language Association. Reprinted by permission of the College Language Association.

[1] Ralph Ellison, *Shadow and Act* (New York, 1964), p. 253.

[2] Both authors' essays first appeared in *Partisan Review* (Spring, 1958). Ellison's essay is reprinted in *Shadow and Act,* Hyman's in *The Promised End* (Cleveland, 1963).

[3] *Shadow and Act,* p. 58.

which exemplifies to a considerable degree a blues-like absurdity. It offers much to the writer, who can "translate its meanings into wider, more precise vocabularies." [4]

Actually, Ellison usually gave greater emphasis to folk traditions, and some allowance should be made for the fact that the primary goal of "Change the Joke" is to correct Stanley Edgar Hyman's concept of Black folklore. Since 1940, Ellison had been stressing its *ultimate* importance. In "Stormy Weather," a review of Langston Hughes's *The Big Sea,* which was critical of Hughes on other grounds, Ellison commended him for developing the national folk sources of his art.[5] Ellison's essay "Recent Negro Fiction" praised Hughes and Wright: Hughes for taking note of folklore and seeing the connection between his efforts and symbols and images of Negro forms; Wright, for attention to the Southern Negro folk.[6] In 1944, Ellison's short story, "Flying Home," made elaborate use of the Black folklore motif of the Black character who comes to grief in heaven for flying too imaginatively with his angel's wings. The main character, a Black aviator, finds peace only when he comes to terms with the survival values of folk tradition.[7]

In 1945, Ellison's essay entitled "Richard Wright's Blues," [8] revealed a profound understanding of the *blues* as a folk cultural form and the value of its *forms* of response to existence for the self-conscious writer. He also analyzed the oppressive weight of American culture upon the folk, argued their complexity, and made a widely publicized definition of the *blues:*

> The blues is an impulse to keep the painful details and episodes of a brutal experience alive in one's aching consciousness, to finger its jagged grain, and to transcend it, not by the consolation of philosophy but by squeezing from it a near-tragic, near-comic lyricism. As a form, the blues is an autobiographical chronicle of personal catastrophe expressed lyrically.[9]

Later in the same essay, he points out that the blues express "both the agony of life" and the possibility of overcoming it through sheer toughness of spirit. The blues are a valuable form also, in that they emphasize self-confrontation.

[4] *Ibid.,* p. 59.
[5] *New Masses,* 37 (September 24, 1940), 20–21.
[6] *New Masses,* 40 (August 5, 1941), 22–26.
[7] James A. Emanuel and Theodore L. Gross, *Dark Symphony* (New York, 1968), pp. 254–270.
[8] *Shadow and Act,* pp. 77–94.
[9] *Ibid.,* p. 78 f.

Comments upon the folk tradition are scattered among several essays in *Shadow and Act*. Perhaps the most emphatic occurs in Ellison's responses during the 1955 Paris Interview.[10] He called attention to several functions of folklore and described some ways in which folklore worked dramatically in *Invisible Man*. Offering the first drawings of a group's character, preserving situations repeated in the history of the group, describing the boundaries of thought and feeling, projecting the group's wisdom in symbols expressing its will to survive, embodying those values by which it lives and dies, folklore seemed, as Ellison described it, basic to the portrayal of the essential spirit of Black people. In general, Ellison noted that great literature of France, Russia, and Spain was erected upon the humble base of folklore. Folk symbols serve Picasso as an annihilator of time through the use of simple lines and curves, and, for the viewer, a whole culture "may resound in a simple rhythm, an image." But most important, in its relationship to Black experience is Ellison's belief that the Black's folklore "announced the Negro's willingness to trust his own experience, his own sensibilities as to the definition of reality, rather than to allow his masters to define these crucial matters for him." Black American folklore, nonetheless, represents for Ellison an American and Western experience—"not lying at the bottom of it, but intertwined, diffused in its very texture."

Ellison also emphasizes the special qualities of a Black tradition in confronting reality, and describes them at some length in his essay, "The World and the Jug." [11] Suffice it here to say that they cover the gamut of attitudes for defining life positively, surviving oppression and extracting from existence many of its joys.

II

In *Invisible Man*, the whole gamut of Ellison's descriptions of the functions of folklore find their place. However, to be fully suggestive of their power is to bear in mind some specifics concerning the total reach of the novel. In the first place the novel's title is *Invisible Man*, not THE *Invisible Man*. In relationship to its nameless protagonist, the story delivers itself through at least three wave-lengths, none in the form of the novel, completely separable from another: the hero as cosmic man, with the in-

---

[10] *Ibid.*, pp. 167–186. The entire interview merits careful study.
[11] *Shadow and Act*, here and there, pp. 107–143.

escapable duty to gather up and affirm *Reality*, despite social oppression; the hero as victim, struggling with a cultural machinery that would reduce him to negative sign; and the hero as an allegory of Black struggle in American history.

Black cultural and folk tradition frequently involves more than one of the wave-lengths.

In simplest form, we may see the interaction through several characters, who, in varying degrees, are folk or are a part of cultural tradition. In more complex form, the interaction of folk and cultural tradition ranges from motifs to situations, symbols, and strategic appearances of folk art forms: blues, spirituals, and folk rhymes.

The characters contrast with the lostness of the invisible narrator, since they represent Reality confronted. Thus the slave woman envisioned singing spirituals in the prologue is used to comment upon the pain of victimization, but she and her sons also define *freedom*, a basic theme of the novel, as the ability to articulate the self, and as a question that can be answered only by each individual's confrontation with the self. Louis Armstrong and his jazz reflect both an articulated self and a mode of breaking through the ordinary categories of Western clock time. The grandfather who appears at strategic points throughout the novel is a reflector of bitter past and continuing victimization. On the other hand, he is, in Ellison's words, the "ambiguity of the past," a sphinx-like riddle which must be approached creatively and not in the literal minded fashion which actually makes of the invisible narrator an accessory to the Brotherhood's crime of provoking a riot in Harlem. Yet the destruction of whites by yessing and confirming their false sense of reality, which the invisible narrator has imitated with nearly fatal consequences, was a solid survival technique of his grandfather and the folk.

Trueblood and Mary, who have assimilated both folk and general Black cultural tradition, play the most powerful dramatic roles among the folk figures. Trueblood, with whom the invisible narrator inadvertently confronts philanthroper Norton, is several roles. On the simple folk level, he is a person who can face the results of his humanity: becoming an expectant father by both his wife and his daughter.

He achieves a conclusion, which the brainwashed and pragmatic invisible narrator requires most of the novel to grasp: "I ain't nobody but myself." His achievement is dramatized through the rituals of first singing spirituals—and then the blues. Singing the spirituals dramatizes his struggle and pain. But it is the singing of the blues, the folk form which Ellison has celebrated for its ritual of self-confrontation, that enables Trueblood to get himself together. In Chapter Nine, the blues *forms of response* to existence become meaningful to the invisible narrator as a street singer celebrates the *absurdity* of a self committed passionately to a woman with "feet like a monkey" and "legs like a frog," and the narrator, realizing how Bledsoe has duped him, can laugh bitterly at himself by singing, "they picked poor robin clean." But it is Trueblood who exemplifies the real toughness of the tradition, and also the racy humor, the folk story-telling tradition, the highly flavored speech, and the capacity for enjoyment of life.

But Trueblood is also interconnected with American and Western tradition. He is, on one hand, the testimony to the density of reality that Western rationalism evades. And he is, on the other, American and Western scapegoat, frankly admitting the sins of the flesh, the full acknowledgment of which the philanthroper Norton dodges by Platonic and puritanical sublimation. For Norton too has committed incest with his daughter but mentally, rather than physically. And the white Southern community acknowledges its secret sexual longings and Trueblood's role as their substitute bearer of sin by dropping coins into his pocket.

But more broadly still, Trueblood connects finally with Western incest tradition and with Freud.[12] Like Oedipus he has invaded unaware the zone of taboo. For he cohabited with his daughter while dreaming. So, was he guilty? Selma Fraiberg argues persuasively that in Freudian terms he was, since he was the author of the dream which his being conjured up for the purpose of allowing the sexual act. At any rate, Trueblood must bear up while the gods deliberate indefinitely concerning the sins of mortal man.

It will be remembered that Mary Rambo is the Southern migrant —now New York mistress of a boarding house—into whose hands the invisible narrator falls after barely surviving the allegorically represented attempt of the industrial system to eliminate all potential for individuality and reduce him to anonymity. The elaborate role that Ellison had designed for Mary may be examined in the fragment published in Herbert Hill's anthology of contemporary Black literature, *Soon One Morning*.[13] Mary is the warmth, wit,

[12] See Selma Fraiberg, "Two Modern Incest Heroes," *Partisan Review*, XXVIII (1961), pp. 646–661. In this section, I am very much indebted to her essay.
[13] Herbert Hill, *Soon One Morning* (New York, 1963).

coping power, and humanity of the folk tradition as it survives in the modern industrial city. And she is the integration of the bitter past with the present, as can be seen by her possession of such purely survival items as the bank topped by a minstrel figure, "a very black, red lipped and wide mouth Negro, his face an enormous grin, his single large black hand held palm up before his chest." In Chapter Fifteen, where he appears, the invisible narrator tries unsuccessfully to drop the symbols of the past, which must be integrated into his being. Unlike Trueblood, Mary is not merged with Western symbols independent of her, a fact of dramatic significance since the hero's recovery from the industrial onslaught is managed through complete, though temporary, retreat into Blackness. Also, unlike Trueblood, Mary makes a strong positive impact upon the invisible narrator, although he must symbolically leave her and become powerless to return as he mounts higher into the abstractions of rationalism through the Brotherhood and as he retreats into the freely imaginative self.

Another folk figure is Dupre, the leader of Harlem rioters who burn down a tenement building. The dramatic and symbolic function of Dupre and his followers is to reflect the folk ability to move with poise amidst chaos and in contradiction to the flat rational assumptions of the Brotherhood concerning its mission as planners for others. The rioters move with a plan that directly confronts Reality.

The discussion of the foregoing characters illustrates, rather than exhausts, the role of folk or folkish characters. We must turn now to scenes that are informed with folk motifs. Ellison himself has commented upon the early Battle Royal scene as one that he lifted from living rituals and placed in a context of larger meaning.[14] It and the invisible narrator's speech comprise on one wave length the ultimate in oppression and self-victimization, as the invisible protagonist tries to be pragmatic and economic man. In the highest sense of the word, the scene is both horrible and wildly comic.

It involves several motifs from folk tradition, a full explanation of which would comprise a separate essay. On the level of Blackness, there is the manipulation of Blacks to fight each other blindly, education as brainwash, the general white manipulation of reality, and the shaping of misleaders of the people. The narrator, himself, embodies the sardonic folk concept that "what's white is right."

But one of the powerful folk motifs is the racial joke of black

[14] *Shadow and Act*, p. 174.

man and tabooed white woman. The unwritten folk joke, from
which the scene derives, is concerned with a Black looking at
a white woman and expressing sexual desire while a white man
stands by and replies.

> Black.   Oh man, will I ever, ever!
> White.   No Nigger, you will never, never!
> Black.   As long as there's life there's hope!
> White.   Yeah Nigger, and as long as there's trees there's rope.

In the Battle Royal scene, it will be recalled, the Black boys
are forced to watch the nude white woman dance, and are abused if
they look and abused if they do not look. In terms of Blackness,
the ritual is to stamp upon them the symbolic castration they are
supposed to experience in the presence of a white woman.

Ellison, however, makes his connections. He dramatizes the per-
verted responses of the white men, and the American flag tattooed
upon the nude woman's belly as satire upon American corruption of
sexuality. He unites the invisible narrator and the nude blonde as
victims and makes out of her a symbol implying the mystery of
freedom, similar to James Joyce's use of woman in *A Portrait of the
Artist as a Young Man*: "She seemed like a fair bird-girl girdled in
veils calling to me from the angry surface of some gray and threaten-
ing sea." [15]

Perhaps enough attention has been given to the unconstrained
density of reality represented by people, folk and non-folk, of the
Golden Day, the sporting house where the philanthroper Norton
is faced with all the reality that his rational categories have suppressed. I focus instead upon the vesper scene in Chapter Five, a
poem really, in which folk, Black cultural tradition in general, and
Western mythology merge. Ellison, in this chapter, is not without
humor, but he extracts, at times tenderly, a deep pathos for the
uplift dreams that somehow ought to be true. The narrator looks
upon them as his investment in identity. The folk motif is the remembered coming of a Moses to bring freedom and richness to the
barren land, a ritual and myth delivered in the rich rhetoric of the
Black speech tradition. Of course, Homer Barbee, the priest who
summons up pictures of ancestors to validate the myth is blind—a
device for undermining his credibility.

Ellison combines the Black Moses myth with the Biblical Moses
and the rituals traditionally describing the miraculous birth and

[15] *Invisible Man*, p. 23.

survival of the hero. For good measure, the students are also involved in the rites of Horatio Alger. The combination carries the chapter to one of the memorable intensities of the novel. And adding still more to the pathos is the ex-slave matron, Susie Greshman, who brings the warmth and tragic knowledge of the folk—and their high hopes—to this colorful but ineffectual ritual. Anyone who has sat through ceremonies that achieve such a high sense of group communion and shared memories will identify briefly with the invisible narrator despite his terrible delusion.

Such folkish scenes appear also at strategic points in the section of the book devoted to the narrator's Northern experiences, and Ellison exacts from them, at will, humor, pathos, and philosophy. The hero's transition to the impersonal Northern experience evokes memories of folklore deriving from the Southern black's initiation into Northern urban life. The black man-white woman motif arises in a comic scene where the crush of subway traffic jams the narrator against a white woman: "I wanted desperately to raise my hands, to show her it was against my will." I have already referred to the pivotal confrontation with Mary, symbol of all that is positive and something of the negative in folk tradition.

I shall mention briefly additional scenes—all of which function mainly in the exemplification of blackness. In Chapter Eleven, the highly symbolic section which portrays the tendency of industrialism to reduce men to a programmed zero, the Brer Rabbit motif emphasizes the toughness of the Black experience, the indestructibility of a fiber, which is later restored through the care of the folkish Mary Rambo. The numerous folk symbols appearing in different scenes within Chapter Thirteen range in significance from the hero's *elementary* awakening to his heritage through the evoking of the entire Black tradition in the eviction of the ex-slave couple, Mr. and Mrs. Primus Provo, a couple who also embody the bitter fruits harvested by Blacks since securing freedom.

The self-contained and bitter pride of the Provos has an affinity with the feelings evoked in Chapter Thirteen by Brother Tarp, a man who spent nineteen years on the chain gang for opposing white imposition before escaping to New York. Tarp passes on to the invisible narrator a link from the chain broken to secure his freedom. Symbolically, it is a bitter link in the chain of Black tradition, meant to serve as a reminder of roots and inescapable contours in the profile of Black reality. Other images of Blackness appear as warnings as the invisible narrator moves deeper into the Brotherhood: the minstrel fascism of the Brother Wrestrum, who provokes

the Brotherhood trial of the narrator; the minstrel dolls manipulated ritualistically to express the youth organizer Todd Clifton's
deep sense of betrayal, and the allied image of the zoot-suited Black
boys playing their bitter hip satire upon "history" in Chapter
Twenty; and perhaps we may include Ras the Exhorter whose existence and strength (Todd Clifton: ". . . it's on the inside that
Ras is strong . . . dangerous.") are based first upon the urban folk's
hunger for identity and nationhood and second, at least latently, in
the breast of every Black conscious of loss and of deep and sustained
betrayal. With Rinehart, symbol of possibility through imagination and masking, we are back to Western tradition.

However, Ellison has a deep sense of the beauty, as well as the
terror of Black tradition, and therefore acknowledgment of his
rendering the rich folk language of the South, the salty speech of the
Northern urban areas, and the joyful myth making of urban nar-
rators in the Harlem riot scene is probably the proper note on which
to draw toward conclusions.

The first conclusion is that, along with other devices, the folk
tradition affords the Black writer a device for instant movement into
the privacy, tensioned coherence, toughness, terror, and beauty of
Black experience—a method for conjuring up instant Blackness. It
is to be noted that Ellison tends to use folk tradition without making
outside connections in some scenes emphasizing the height of betrayal of Blackness (as in the Primus Provo eviction), in those
portraying dramatic recoil of the narrator from illusions, or in those
especially emphasizing a reverential treatment of folk value. But the
principle is not fixed: the over-riding guide is utility to theme and
dramatic structure. The vesper scene at the Southern college, it will
be recalled, derives from Black folklore and Western mythology.

Folklore does not appear then at any point for its own sake, nor
is folk vision sentimentalized. As reverently as the folk Mary Rambo
is treated, she is not seen as useful to the highest abstract reaches of
personality. This view is in line, by extension, with Ellison's concept
of Southern folk community as a pre-individual community.[16] So
it is not surprising that, once having absorbed what he can from
her and having reached for more abstract levels of personality, the
invisible narrator cannot return. Another example of the non-
sentimental approach is the invisible narrator's newly gained appreciation of soul food, a passage which has been widely quoted for its
humor and evidence of acceptance of identity. But the narrator
realizes that identity on this level is really too simple. Further, as he

---

[16] *Shadow and Act,* p. 90.

continues to eat yams, one turns out to be frost-bitten—not mere sweetness.

Yet there is something of the great performance, the *tour de force*, in Ellison's use of the folklore and cultural tradition that makes for both enlightenment regarding the literary potential of folklore and a certain unease. This response, I think, is inspired by the elaborate system of interconnection with Western symbols and mythology, and our awareness that Blackness is more in need of definition than Western tradition, which has had the attention of innumerable literary masters. It has to do with the degree of faith that one has in the West, and the suspicion that major literary documents from Melville through Faulkner have been whispering to us of its death. And, in the Black tradition, there has been so frequently an ambivalence and a questioning of the West that go deeper than casting a critical eye upon its technology and rationalism.

The questions raised by Larry Neal regarding Ellison's relationship to the West in his critical essays may well be raised regarding the interconnection system in *Invisible Man*, since there is almost a mathematical consistency between Ellison's critical pronouncements and his creative performance. Writing in *Black Theatre*, Neal credited Ellison with a broad theoretical sense of Black folklore tradition and culture, and an awareness of the "explosive tensions underlying the Black man's presence in the United States," but criticized him for overlaying "his knowledge of Black culture with concepts that exist outside it." [17]

Certainly, the result in *Invisible Man*, if one commits himself to a grasp of the depths of the book, is sometimes simultaneously an awe at sheer brilliance of conjunctions and a hunger for further depths of definition of Blackness which this wily genius obviously has the capacity to make. For make no mistake about it, anyone who could throw in those images of Blackness with such rapidity and apparent ease, who could tone their depths as a gifted musician would do, has, as a pressure behind his imagination, an almost god-like knowledge of Blackness. Make no mistake, Ellison paid his dues to culture. At no time does one run into a Blackness that is rhetorical only, as one still frequently does in even very radical writing. But Ellison, himself, admits that the book would have been better if it had had more of Mary Rambo.[18] We would add to Mary, more of

[17] Larry Neal, "Cultural Nationalism and Black Theatre," *Black Theatre*, No. 1, p. 10.
[18] See unused section of hospital scene, Herbert Hill, *Soon One Morning* (New York, 1963).

Bledsoe, more of the campus dreamers, more of the Harlem rioters, and more even of B. P. Rinehart and Ras, the Destroyer. And we would suppose that it is possible to sound the depths of the universe by a fine excess in the examination of Blackness. A William Faulkner, for example, in making us feel the American and Western aspects of his universe, simply asserts himself as the deepest of Southerners, and communicates through symbols most deeply associated with the South. Perhaps the Faulknerian way is one for the future, since neither the spirit of the 1950's nor the temperament and sensibility which Ellison has frequently and emphatically expounded suggest that earlier, in dealing with Blackness, a Black focus would have been successful or that it would have found an audience.

In the end, it is the great fruits at hand which Ellison harvested that must be seized upon. For the young writer, his use of folk tradition provides a veritable textbook which can be adapted, according to one's own sensibility and outlook. For more than any other writer, Ellison grappled with its power, its cryptic messages, its complexity. Particularly noteworthy is his realization that folk tradition cannot seem, in a self-conscious artist, to be an end in itself. That is, the writer cannot simply enclose himself within the womb of folkness or content himself with simple celebration of folkness. True folk forms have already celebrated folk life better than the self-conscious artist can hope to do. But the basic *attitudes* and *forms* of response to existence evolved by the folk are abandoned by us only at our peril. These attitudes and forms of response are then of greatest service as flexible instruments for confronting a darkness that is always changing in its complexity. Ellison exemplified a profound knowledge of all such ramifications.

Violence in Afro-American Fiction:
An Hypothesis

by Stephen B. Bennett and William W. Nichols

In *Black Skin, White Masks* Frantz Fanon comments on the paradoxical condition in which a kind of revolutionary rebirth can result from the life-in-death of total oppression: "There is a zone of nonbeing, an extraordinarily sterile and arid region, an utterly naked declivity where an authentic upheaval can be born. In most cases, the black man lacks the advantages of being able to accomplish this descent into a real hell." [1] It will probably surprise no one to discover that many plays in the contemporary black theatre—the works of LeRoi Jones, Jimmie Garret, Ed Bullins, and Ronald Milner, for example—set out to map that "zone of nonbeing" which leads to revolution. What may be somewhat less obvious is the fact that several of the standard works in Afro-American fiction before the 1960s chart the horror of that same barren region. In fact, we have found in the fiction of Arna Bontemps, Richard Wright, Ralph Ellison, Chester Himes, and James Baldwin the values of what might be called a culture of revolution. Jean-Paul Sartre has described those values in his introduction to Fanon's other book on racism and colonialism, *The Wretched of the Earth*. Summing up the antithetical views of the colonial and the native as seen by the colonial at a time of violent revolution, Sartre says, "We find our humanity on this side of death and despair; he finds it beyond torture and death. . . . The child of violence, at every moment he draws from it his humanity." [2] Such values are to be found in much twentieth-century Afro-American fiction; in fact, they may well

"Violence in Afro-American Fiction: An Hypothesis," by Stephen B. Bennett and William W. Nichols. From *Modern Fiction Studies*, Vol. XVII, No. 2 (Summer, 1971), pp. 221–228. Copyright © 1971 by Purdue Research Foundation, West Lafayette, Indiana. Reprinted by permission of the authors and publisher.

[1] (New York: Grove Press, 1967), p. 10.
[2] (New York: Grove Press, 1963), p. 20.

represent a thematic preoccupation that is one distinguishing characteristic of black literature in America.

If American popular culture has often romanticized violence, our
best-known writers of fiction have emphasized its horror. They have
tended to identify violence with chaos. Frederick J. Hoffman sees
this as a theme in most literature since World War II, and he comments: "This literature seems written on wager: life is possible if
violence does not dispose of it." [3] But this is not really a new development in American fiction. One thinks immediately of Huck Finn,
whose response to repeated killings and brutality is both confusion
and compassion, never understanding or acceptance. Or there is
Hemingway's Nick Adams, who seems to bring something like Huck
Finn's sensibility to World War I. His life is essentially a struggle
to salvage some minimal order from that chaos.[4] In fact, it would
be difficult to find a fiction taught in traditional American literature
courses that links violence with the possibility of meaning in human
experience. The kind of violent self-assertion that provides a sure
ticket to manhood in popular westerns and war movies is simply
not available in the best American novels of initiation.

There is no easy equation between violent assertion and self-
realization in Afro-American fiction either, but the finest black
fiction in America has been as far from the traditional identification
of violence with chaos as it has been from the glorified violence of
American popular culture. Much Afro-American fiction is soaked in
blood; it flatly asserts that the black experience in America is inevitably a violent one. And yet the very omnipresence of violence
in black fiction seems to make necessary a search for meaning in the
violence itself, a search that leads in at least two important directions: toward self-destruction and toward the creative violence of
self-discovery.

Acts of self-destruction in Afro-American fiction can often be understood as final, desperate efforts to salvage dignity in the face of
dehumanizing oppression. . . .

---

[3] *The Mortal No: Death and the Modern Imagination* (Princeton, N.J.: Princeton University Press, 1964), p. 287.
[4] Hemingway's treatment of hunting and bullfighting might seem to offer an
exception to what we are saying about the relationship between violence and
meaning in American literature, but even in "The Short, Happy Life of Francis
Macomber" and *Death in the Afternoon* the problem can be seen as essentially
that of salvaging order in the face of violence. Macomber discovers his masculinity
in the process of overcoming his fear of death. The meaning for Macomber, as
for the good bullfighter, is not so much in the act of violently asserting himself
as in facing with poise the possibility of his own violent death.

The death of Tod Clifton in Ralph Ellison's *Invisible Man* is perhaps the most powerful treatment of this situation in Afro-American fiction. Clifton, the embodiment of black pride and beauty in the novel, is killed by a white policeman; but his death is a willful act of self-destruction nevertheless. Having discovered that he has been manipulated by white leadership in his work with a revolutionary organization, the Brotherhood, Clifton stops working as an organizer. He then gives himself up to the self-abasing act of selling Sambo dolls which, manipulated by invisible strings, are symbols of his own degradation. Arrested for peddling the dolls without a license, Clifton chooses not to accept white-imposed humiliation any longer; and Ellison's narrator describes his suicide as a strangely beautiful ballet movement:

> And I could see the cop bark a command and lunge forward, thrusting out his arm and missing, thrown off balance as suddenly Clifton spun on his toes like a dancer and swung his right arm over and around in a short, jolting arc, his torso carrying forward and to the left in a motion that sent the box strap free as his right foot traveled forward and his left arm followed through in a floating uppercut that sent the cop's cap sailing into the street and his feet flying, to drop him hard, rocking from left to right on the walk as Clifton kicked the box thudding aside and crouched, his left food forward, his hands high, waiting.

He is waiting for the only response he can expect from the white policeman, and he dies of it. But there is beauty in that last symbolic defiance of white oppression, as the naive narrator is told by an observer, a "round-headed, apple-cheeked boy with thickly-freckled nose and Slavic eyes." Even this young epitome of whiteness can recognize the power and dignity in Clifton's final act, and he confers a kind of immortality on him by speaking of him in the present tense as he tells the narrator after Clifton's death: "Your friend sure knows how to use his dukes. Biff, bang! One, two, and the cop's on his ass!"

If Clifton lashes out at his oppressor in his last act, his aggression is more symbolic than real. The decision to sell Sambo dolls suggests that he has come to accept as inevitable the dehumanization and exploitation of black men. However, Clifton's suicidal defiance of police power moves closer than most acts of self-destruction to another kind of violence that is important in twentieth-century Afro-American fiction. Jean-Paul Sartre describes this violence as "neither sound and fury, nor the resurrection of savage instincts nor even the effect of resentment; it is man recreating himself." [5] This creative violence can be distinguished rather easily from the romanticized violence of much popular American culture. This is not the violent act in which a man simply asserts his masculinity or his supremacy, as in the typical western gun battle. Rather, in Afro-American fiction there is a kind of violence in which a character discovers, or perhaps rediscovers, his humanity. . . .

Creative violence is important in Ralph Ellison's *Invisible Man*, especially in the Prologue and Epilogue. Early in the Prologue, the narrator tells of having nearly killed a white man who refused to see him, and he comments: "Most of the time (although I do not choose as I once did to deny the violence of my days by ignoring it) I am not so overtly violent." But at the end of the Prologue, as he considers against the near murder, he has decided that he was not violent enough: he should have killed the man "to protect the higher interests of society." In the Epilogue the narrator returns again to the meaning of violence. He does not deny his need to love, but he has begun to see history as a boomerang: he now feels that the violence of America's suppression of black men will inevitably come back upon it. Addressing white America directly, the invisible man says: "You won't believe in my invisibility and you'll fail to see how any principle that applied to you could apply to me. You'll fail to see it even though death waits for both of us if you don't." In the pessimism of that assertion there are the roots of an optimism that can only be called revolutionary, and the paragraph concludes:

> There's a stench in the air, which, from this distance underground, might be the smell either of death or of spring—I hope of spring. But don't let me trick you, there *is* a death in the smell of spring and in the smell of thee as in the smell of me. And if nothing more, invisibility has taught my nose to classify the stenches of death.

This language of death and spring does not seem to imply personal self-discovery so much as social renewal. In terms of social change, at least, Ellison's narrator seems to have decided that there is potential meaning in death and violence; he has accepted the faith of a revolutionary. . . .

The relationship between fiction and experience is too complex to justify any confident declarations about the nature of American society here, but it is probably fair to say that the implications of this brief analysis, if we are correct, may be as appalling as the conclusions of the Kerner Commission for what they say about the

---

[5] Preface to *The Wretched of the Earth*, p. 18.

black experience in America. Our reading of these works suggests that the kind of apocalyptic rage commonly associated with contemporary black militants has been part of the imaginations of the best black writers in America for some time. It may be that the presence of this terrifying dimension in Afro-American fiction has been one reason for its rather systematic exclusion from anthologies and courses in American literature. It may be too that the increased attention being paid to black literature in America will teach us something crucial about the violence which ravages the heart of our civilization.

Notes on the Editor and Contributors

JOHN HERSEY, novelist and journalist, is the editor of this volume. He has been Master of Pierson College at Yale (1965–70) and teaches writing there. He has won the Pulitzer Prize, has been writer-in-residence at the American Academy in Rome, and is Secretary of the American Academy of Arts and Letters.

SAUL BELLOW, novelist, has been a Guggenheim Fellow, and has taught at the University of Chicago, Bard, and Princeton. He has won the National Book Award twice, for *Herzog* (1965) and *Mr. Sammler's Planet* (1970); received the International Literary Prize in 1965; and is a member of the American Academy of Arts and Letters.

STEPHEN B. BENNETT teaches English at Dawson College, Montreal.

ROBERT BONE, Professor of Literature at Teacher's College, Columbia, is the author of a critical and historical work, *The Negro Novel in America*, and of studies of Richard Wright, James Baldwin, and William Demby. His work-in-progress is *Black Epiphanies: A Survey of the Afro-American Short Story.*

LAWRENCE WASHINGTON CHISHOLM is Professor of American Studies at the State University of New York at Buffalo; he has also taught at Yale. His work in progress concerns "morphologies of culture as developed historically in the United States and elsewhere." He is author of *Fenollosa: The Far East and American Culture.*

IRVING HOWE, critic and historian, has taught at Brandeis and Stanford, and has held a Distinguished Professorship at Hunter College of the City University of New York. He is editor of *Dissent,* has written on Sherwood Anderson and William Faulkner, and is the author of a critical history of the Communist Party, and of, among other works, *A World More Attractive* and *The Decline of the New.*

STANLEY EDGAR HYMAN (1919–1971), literary critic, taught at Bennington and was a staff writer for *The New Yorker* and literary critic for *The New Leader.* He was the author of numerous books of criticism, among them studies of Nathaniel West and Flannery O'Connor.

GEORGE E. KENT, Professor of English at the University of Chicago, is the author of a collection of critical essays, *Blackness and the Adventure of*

Western Culture (1972), and his work-in-progress is *Faulkner and White Racial Consciousness.* He has written studies of Richard Wright, Langston Hughes, Gwendolyn Brooks, Claude McKay, George Lamming, and others.

JAMES ALAN MCPHERSON is the author of *Hue and Cry,* a volume of short stories, for which he won an award from the National Institute of Arts and Letters. He is a Contributing Editor of *The Atlantic.*

LARRY NEAL, poet, is the author of *Black Boogaloo,* and was co-editor of *Black Fire: An Anthology of Afro-American Writing.*

WILLIAM W. NICHOLS, Associate Professor of English at Denison University, has written, among other essays, a study of Thoreau and Douglass, and another, besides the one in this volume, on Ellison, "Ralph Ellison's Black American Scholar" *(Phylon).*

EARL H. ROVIT, Professor of English at the City College of New York, is the author of *Herald to Chaos, Ernest Hemingway,* and *Saul Bellow.* He has also published three novels.

WILLIAM J. SCHAFER, Associate Professor of English, Berea College, has held a Younger Humanist Fellowship of the National Endowment for the Humanities (1971–72); and is the author of *Rock Music,* and co-author, with Johannes Riedel, of *The Art of Ragtime.*

TONY TANNER, Director of English Studies at King's College, Cambridge University, has been a Visiting Professor at Northwestern, Emory, and Stanford. He is the author of *Conrad's Lord Jim, The Reign of Wonder, Saul Bellow,* and *City of Words.*

THOMAS A. VOGLER has taught at Yale and at Cowell College, University of California at Santa Cruz. He has written on Emily Brontë, Virginia Woolf, Hart Crane, and Robert Lowell, and is the author of *Preludes to Vision.*

ROBERT PENN WARREN, novelist, poet, journalist, and critic, has won, among other awards, the Pulitzer Prize, the Bollingen Prize, the National Book Award, and the National Medal for Literature. He is a member of the American Academy of Arts and Letters, has held the chair of poetry at the Library of Congress, and has taught at Louisiana State University and Yale.

Selected Bibliography

Steve Cannon, Lennox Raphael, and James Thompson, "A Very Stern Discipline," *Harper's Magazine*, Vol. 234, No. 1402 (March, 1967), pp. 76–95. An important exchange, originally intended for the short-lived magazine *Umbra*, between Ellison and three young members of a black writers' workshop in New York City's lower East Side. It deals with the situation of the black writer in mid-twentieth-century American culture and with Ellison's particular location within—or, as some would see it, outside of—that situation.

John Corry, "An American Novelist Who Sometimes Teaches," *New York Times Sunday Magazine*, November 20, 1966, pp. 55, 179–185, 196. A workmanlike journalistic profile of Ellison, the man and the writer.

Leon Forrest, "Racial History as a Clue to the Action in *Invisible Man*," *Muhammad Speaks*, XII (September 15, 1972), pp. 28, 30. Praise for Ellison and his work from the editor of the newspaper of the Black Muslims. "A Conversation with Ralph Ellison," *Muhammad Speaks*, XII (December 15, 1972), pp. 29–31. Forrest interviews Ellison on his literary and social views.

William Goede, "On Lower Frequencies: The Buried Men in Wright and Ellison," *Modern Fiction Studies*, XV, 4 (Winter 1969–70), pp. 483–501. An essay—another opinion on the issue of Ellison's literary "ancestors" and "relatives"—speculating about the evolution of the "hibernation symbol" of the underground man in *Invisible Man*, suggesting that Ellison both indirectly used and finally transcended Richard Wright's story "The Man Who Lived Underground."

Floyd R. Horowitz, "An Experimental Confession from a Reader of *Invisible Man*," *C.L.A. Journal*, XIII, 3 (March, 1970), pp. 304–314. An attempt by one who had written earlier about Ellison's novel to reappraise it in view of the history that has intervened since its publication. Mr. Horowitz raises the question whether the identity of the invisible man, as it seems to be resolved in the novel's epilogue, is adequate to the world of action toward which it is aimed, as that world has unfolded.

Ernest Kaiser, "A Critical Look at Ellison's Fiction and at Social and Literary Criticism by and about the Author," *Black World*, XX, 2 (December, 1970), pp. 53–59, 81–97. An attack on Ellison, both as man and as author, by a contributing editor of *Freedomways*, whose Marxist view is that Ellison "uses the myths and rituals of the Black people's folklore to show that Black suffering has always existed and always will exist, no matter what Blacks do."

R. W. B. Lewis, "Ellison's Essays," *New York Review of Books* (January 28, 1965). A perceptive response to *Shadow and Act,* making the point that Ellison's stubborn effort to search out and declare his identity requires of a white reader that he define the limits of his own identity; and that after these reciprocal acts, a productive dialogue becomes possible.

Roger Sale, "The Career of Ralph Ellison," *Hudson Review* (Spring, 1965), pp. 124–128. Sale shows how, in his writing, using "a second language" (after his first, music), Ellison has struggled with words and has achieved "a sense of style expressed simply in the thoroughness and self-consciousness with which an idea is thought all the way through." This essay also gives some perspective to the Ellison-Howe debate.

Eleanor R. Wilner, "The Invisible Black Thread," *C.L.A. Journal,* XIII, 3 (March, 1970), pp. 242–257. The thread which Wilner traces through *Invisible Man* is that of "dignity and identity which runs unseen out of a past where death was the price of black defiance, and where intelligent pride wore the disguise of compliance that secretly scorned, and thereby often tricked, the power that oppressed it." Wilner has different interpretations of Tod Clifton's death from that of the Bennett-Nichols essay in this collection (pp. 171–6); and of the meaning of the narrator's final stance in the epilogue from that suggested in the Rovit essay (pp. 151–9).

THE RUSSIAN EDITION WAS PRINTED
IN ACCORDANCE WITH A DECISION
OF THE NINTH CONGRESS OF THE R.C.P.(B.)
AND THE SECOND CONGRESS OF SOVIETS
OF THE U.S.S.R

ИНСТИТУТ МАРКСИЗМА-ЛЕНИНИЗМА при ЦК КПСС

В. И. ЛЕНИН

СОЧИНЕНИЯ

Издание четвертое

ГОСУДАРСТВЕННОЕ ИЗДАТЕЛЬСТВО
ПОЛИТИЧЕСКОЙ ЛИТЕРАТУРЫ
МОСКВА

V. I. LENIN

COLLECTED WORKS

VOLUME
4
1898 – April 1901

PROGRESS PUBLISHERS
MOSCOW

TRANSLATED BY   JOE FINEBERG   AND GEORGE HANNA
EDITED BY VICTOR JEROME

First printing 1960
Second printing 1964
Third printing 1972
Fourth printing 1977

Printed in the Union of Soviet Socialist Republics

11-17-78

Л $\frac{10102-982}{014(01)-77}$ 54-77

CONTENTS

CONTENTS

1901

ILLUSTRATIONS

PREFACE

Volume Four of the *Collected Works* contains Lenin's
writings for the period February 1898-February 1901.
These writings are devoted to the struggle for the victory of
revolutionary Marxism in the working-class movement and
to the exposure of the anti-revolutionary views of the Narodniks, "legal Marxists," and "economists."

"A Note on the Question of the Market Theory (Apropos
of the Polemic of Messrs. Tugan-Baranovsky and Bulgakov),"
"Once More on the Theory of Realisation," and "Capitalism
in Agriculture (Kautsky's Book and Mr. Bulgakov's Article)" were directed against the "legal Marxists," who sought to
subordinate and adapt the working-class movement to the
interests of the bourgeoisie.

This volume contains Lenin's first writings against "economism": "A Protest by Russian Social-Democrats," articles
for the third issue of *Rabochaya Gazeta*, "A Retrograde Trend
in Russian Social-Democracy," and "Apropos of the *Pro-
fession de foi*," in which he laid bare the opportunism of the
"economists" and showed "economism" to be a variety of
international opportunism ("Bernsteinism on Russian soil").
Against the anti-Marxist positions adopted by the "economists," Lenin contraposed the plan of the unity of socialism with the working-class movement.

Several of the articles in this volume are models of the
journalism of social and political exposure to which Lenin
attached great significance in the struggle against the law-
lessness of the tsarist officials, the struggle to awaken the
consciousness of the broad masses of the people. These
articles are: "Beat—but Not to Death!", "Why Accelerate
the Vicissitude of the Times?" and "Objective Statistics," published under the general heading of "Casual Notes"; "The
Drafting of 183 Students into the Army," the preface to

the pamphlet on the famous Kharkov May Day celebration, 1900, *May Days in Kharkov*, and the article, "Factory Courts," written in connection with the granting of police functions to the Factory Inspectorate.

The volume also contains writings relating to the organisation of the all-Russian illegal Marxist newspaper *Iskra*: "Draft of a Declaration of the Editorial Board of *Iskra* and *Zarya*," "How the 'Spark' Was Nearly Extinguished," and "Declaration of the Editorial Board of *Iskra*."

These documents, as well as the articles, "Our Programme," "A Draft Programme of Our Party," "The Urgent Tasks of Our Movement," and "The Workers' Party and the Peasantry," define the tasks confronting the Marxist organisations and the working-class movement of Russia at the moment when Lenin set about the actual formation of a party to fight under the unitary banner of revolutionary Marxism against opportunism, amateurishness in work, ideological disunity, and vacillation.

The present volume also contains the "Draft Agreement" with the Plekhanovist Emancipation of Labour group on the publication of the newspaper *Iskra* and the magazine *Zarya*, which appears for the first time in a collected edition of Lenin's writings. *Iskra* was launched on the basis of the "Draft Agreement."

V. I. LENIN
1897

ON THE QUESTION OF OUR FACTORY STATISTICS

(PROFESSOR KARYSHEV'S NEW STATISTICAL EXPLOITS) [1]

The Russian reading public displays a lively interest in the question of our factory statistics and in the chief conclusions to be drawn from them. This interest is quite understandable, for the question is connected with the more extensive one of the "destiny of capitalism in Russia." Unfortunately, however, the state of our factory statistics does not correspond to the general interest in their data. This branch of economic statistics in Russia is in a truly sad state, and still sadder, perhaps, is the fact that the people who write about statistics often display an astounding lack of understanding of the nature of the figures they are analysing, their authenticity and their suitability for drawing certain conclusions. Such precisely is the estimate that must be made of Mr. Karyshev's latest work, first published in *Izvestia Moskovskovo Selskokhozyaistvennovo Instituta* (4th year, Book 1) and then as a separate booklet with the high-sounding title *Material on the Russian National Economy. I. Our Factory Industry in the Middle Nineties* (Moscow, 1898). Mr. Karyshev tries, in this essay, to draw conclusions from the latest publication of the Department of Commerce and Manufactures on our factory industry.* We shall make a detailed analysis of Mr. Karyshev's conclusions and, especially, of his methods. We think that an analysis of this sort will have significance, not only in determining the way in which the material is treated by Pro-

---

* Ministry of Finance. Department of Commerce and Manufactures. The Factory Industry of Russia. *List of Factories and Works*, St. Petersburg, 1897, pp. 63+vi+1047.

fessor So-and-So (for this a review of a few lines would suffice), but also in determining the degree of reliability of our
factory statistics, for which deductions they are suitable
and for which they are unsuitable, what the most important
requirements of our factory statistics are and the tasks of
those who study them.

As its name implies, the source used by Mr. Karyshev
contains a list of factories in the Empire for the year 1894-95.
The publication of a full list of all factories (i.e., of *relatively* large industrial establishments, with varying conceptions of what is to be considered large) is not new to our literature. Since 1881 Messrs. Orlov and Budagov have compiled
a *Directory of Factories and Works* the last (third) edition of
which was issued in 1894. Much earlier, in 1869, a list of
factories was printed in the notes accompanying the statistical tables on industry in the first issue of the *Ministry of
Finance Yearbook*. The reports which factory owners are by
law obliged to submit annually to the Ministry provided the
material for all these publications. The new publication of
the Department of Commerce and Manufactures differs
from former publications of this type in its somewhat more
extensive information, but at the same time it has tremendous
shortcomings from which the earlier ones did not suffer
and which greatly complicate its utilisation as material on
factory statistics. In the introduction to the *List* there is a
reference to the unsatisfactory condition of these statistics
in the past which thereby defines the purpose of the publication—to serve precisely as material for statistics and not
merely as a reference book. But the *List*, as a statistical publication, amazes one by the complete absence of any sort of
summarised totals. It is to be hoped that a publication of
this sort, the first of its kind, will also be the last statistical
publication without summaries. The huge mass of raw material in the form of piles of figures is useless ballast in a reference book. The introduction to the *List* sharply criticises
the reports previously submitted to the Ministry by factory
owners on the grounds that they "consisted of confusing information, always one and the same, which was repeated
from year to year and did not allow even the quantity of
goods produced to be accurately determined, whereas production figures as complete and reliable as possible are an urgent

necessity" (p. 1). We shall certainly not say a word in defence of the absolutely outmoded system of our former factory statistics that were purely pre-Reform,* both as to organisation and as to quality. But, unfortunately, there is *scarcely any noticeable* improvement in their present condition. The gigantic *List* just published still does not give us the right to speak of any serious changes in the old system admitted by all to be useless. The reports "did not allow even the quantity of goods produced to be accurately determined."... Indeed, in the latest *List* there is no information whatsoever on the quantity of goods, although Mr. Orlov's *Directory*, for example, gave this information for a very large number of factories, and in some branches of industry for almost all factories, so that in the summarised table there is information on the quantity of the product (for the leather, distilling, brick, cereals, flour milling, wax, lard, flax-scutching, and brewery industries). And it was from the old reports that the *Directory* material was compiled. The *List* does not give any information on machinery employed, although the *Directory* gave this information for some branches of industry. The introduction describes the changes that have occurred in our factory statistics in this way: formerly, factory owners supplied information through the police according to "a brief and insufficiently clear programme" and no one checked the information. "Material was obtained from which no more or less precise conclusions could be drawn" (p. 1). Now a new and much more detailed programme has been compiled and the gathering and checking of factory statistical information have been entrusted to the factory inspectors. At first glance one might think that we now have the right to expect really acceptable data, since a correct programme and provision for checking the data are two very important conditions for successful statistics. In actual fact, however, these two features are still in their former primitively chaotic state. The detailed programme with an explanation is not published in the introduction to the *List*, although statistical methodology requires the publication of the programme according to which the data were gathered. We

---

* The Reform of 1861 which abolished serfdom in Russia.—*Ed.*

shall see from the following analysis of the *List* material that the *basic* questions of programme for factory statistics still remain entirely unclarified. With regard to checking the data, here is a statement by a person engaged in the practical side of this process—Mr. Mikulin, Senior Factory Inspector of Kherson Gubernia,* who has published a book containing an analysis of statistical data gathered according to the new system in Kherson Gubernia.

"It proved impossible to make a factual check of all the figures in the reports submitted by owners of industrial establishments and they were, therefore, returned for correction only in those cases when comparison with the data of similar establishments or with information obtained during an inspection of the establishments showed obvious inconsistencies in the answers. *In any case, responsibility for the correctness of the figures for each establishment contained in the lists rests with those who submitted them*" (*Factory and Artisan Industry in Kherson Gubernia*, Odessa, 1897, preface. Our italics). And so, responsibility for the accuracy of the figures, as before, still rests with the factory owners. Representatives of the Factory Inspectorate were not only unable to check all the figures, but, as we shall see below, were even unable to ensure that they were uniform and could be compared.

Later, we shall give full details of the shortcomings of the *List* and the material it uses. Its chief shortcoming, as we have noted, is the complete absence of summaries (private persons who compiled the *Directory* drew up summaries and expanded them with each edition). Mr. Karyshev, availing himself of the collaboration of two other people, conceived the happy idea of filling this gap, at least in part, and of compiling summaries on our factory industry according to the *List*. This was a very useful undertaking, and every one would have been grateful for its achievement, if ... if Mr. Karyshev, firstly, had published even a few of

---

* *Gubernia, uyezd, volost*—Russian administrative-territorial units. The largest of these was the gubernia, which had its subdivisions in uyezds, which in turn were subdivided into volosts. This system of districting continued under the Soviet power until the introduction of the new system of administrative-territorial division of the country in 1929-30.—*Ed.*

the obtained results in their entirety and if, secondly, he had not displayed, in his treatment of the material, a lack of criticism bordering on high-handedness. Mr. Karyshev was in a hurry to draw conclusions before he had studied the material attentively and before his statistical processing was anything like "thorough,"* so that naturally he made a whole series of the most curious errors.

Let us begin with the first, basic question in industrial statistics: what establishments should come under the heading of "factories"? Mr. Karyshev does not even pose this question; he seems to assume that a "factory" is something quite definite. As far as the *List* is concerned, he asserts, with a boldness worthy of better employment, that in contrast to former publications this one registers not only *large* establishments but *all* factories. This assertion, which the author repeats twice (pp. 23 and 34), *is altogether untrue*. Actually the reverse is the case; the *List* merely registers *larger* establishments as compared with former publications on factory statistics. We shall now explain how it is that Mr. Karyshev could "fail to notice" such a "trifle"; but first let us resort to historical reference. Prior to the middle eighties our factory statistics did not include *any* definitions or rules that limited the concept of factory to the larger industrial establishments. Every type of industrial (and artisan) establishment found its way into "factory" statistics; this, it goes without saying, led to terrific chaos in the data, since the full registration of all such establishments, by the employment of existing forces and means (i.e., without a correct industrial census), is absolutely out of the question. In some gubernias or in some branches of industry hundreds and thousands of the tiniest establishments were included, while in others only the larger "factories" were listed. It was, therefore, natural that the people who first tried to make a scientific analysis of the data contained in our factory statistics (in the sixties) turned all their attention to this question and directed all their efforts to separating the

---

* Contrary to the opinion of the reviewer in *Russkiye Vedomosti*[2] (1898, No. 144), who, apparently, was as little capable of a critical attitude to Mr. Karyshev's conclusions as was Mr. Karyshev of a critical attitude to the *List*'s figures.

branches for which there were more or less reliable data from
those for which the data were absolutely unreliable, to separating establishments large enough to enable the obtainment
of satisfactory data from those too small to yield satisfactory
data. Bushen,* Bok,** and Timiryazev *** provided such
valuable criteria on all these questions that, had they been
carefully observed and developed by the compilers of our
factory statistics, we should now have, in all probability,
some very acceptable data. But in actual fact all these criteria remained, as usual, a voice crying in the wilderness, and
our factory statistics have remained in their former chaotic
state. From 1889 the Department of Commerce and Manufactures began its publication of the *Collection of Data on Factory Industry in Russia* (for 1885 and the following years).
A slight step forward was made in this publication: the small
establishments, i.e., those with an output valued at less
than 1,000 rubles, were excluded. It goes without saying
that this standard was too low and too indefinite; it is ridiculous even to think of the *full* registration of *all* industrial
establishments with an output valued at more than that
amount as long as the information is collected by the police.
As before, some gubernias and some branches of industry
included a mass of small establishments with outputs ranging
in value from 2,000 to 5,000 rubles, while other gubernias and
other branches of industry omitted them. We shall see instances of this further on. Finally, our latest factory statistical system has introduced a completely different formula
for defining the concept "factory." It has been recognised
that "all industrial establishments" (of those "*under the
jurisdiction*" *of the Factory Inspectorate*) are subject to registration "if they employ no fewer than 15 workers, as are also
those employing fewer than 15 workers, if they have a steam-
boiler, a steam-engine, *or other mechanical motive power and*

---

* *Ministry of Finance Yearbook*. First Issue. St. Petersburg, 1869.
** *Statistical Chronicle of the Russian Empire*. Series II, Issue 6.
St. Petersburg, 1872. Material for the factory statistics of European
Russia, elaborated under the editorship of I. Bok.
*** *Statistical Atlas of Main Branches of Factory Industry of
European Russia, with List of Factories and Works*. Three issues. St.
Petersburg, 1869, 1870, and 1873.

machines or factory installations."* We must examine this
definition in detail (the points we have stressed are particularly unclear), but let us first say that this concept of "factory" is something quite new in our factory statistics; until
now no attempt has been made to limit the concept "factory"
to establishments with a definite number of workers, with
a steam-engine, etc. In general, the strict limitation of the
concept "factory" is undoubtedly necessary, but the definition
we have cited suffers, unfortunately, from its extreme lack
of precision, from its unclarity and diffusion. It provides the
following definitions of establishments subject to registration as "factories" in the statistics: 1) The establishment must
come within the jurisdiction of the Factory Inspectorate.
This, apparently, excludes establishments belonging to the
state, etc., metallurgical plants and others. In the *List*,
however, there are many state and government factories
(see Alphabetical List, pp. 1-2), and we do not know whether
they were registered in all gubernias or whether the data per-
taining to them were subject to checking by the Factory
Inspectorate, etc. It must be said, in general, that as long
as our factory statistics are not freed from the web of various
"departments" to which the different industrial establishments
belong, they *cannot be* satisfactory; the areas of departmental
jurisdiction frequently overlap and are subject to changes;
even the implementation of similar programmes by different
departments will never be identical. The rational organisation of statistics demands that complete information
on all industrial establishments be concentrated in one
purely statistical institution to ensure careful observation
of identical methods of gathering and analysing data. So
long as this is not done, the greatest caution must be exercised in dealing with factory statistics that now include and
now exclude (at different times and in different gubernias)
establishments belonging to "another department." Metallurgical plants, for instance, have long been excluded from
our factory statistics; but Orlov, nevertheless, included in

---

* Circular of June 7, 1895, in Kobelyatsky (*Handbook for Members
of the Factory Inspectorate, etc.*, 4th edition. St. Petersburg, 1897,
p. 35. Our italics). This circular is not reprinted in the introduction
to the *List*, and Mr. Karyshev, in analysing the *List* material, did not
go to the trouble of discovering what the *List* meant by "factories"!!

the last edition of his *Directory* quite a number of metallurgical plants (almost all rail production, the Izhevsk and Votkinsk factories in Vyatka Gubernia, and others) that are not included in the *List*, although the latter records metallurgical plants in other gubernias that were previously not included in "factory" statistics (e.g., the Siemens copper-smelting plant in Elisavetpol Gubernia, p. 330). In Section VIII of the introduction to the *List*, iron-working, iron-smelting, iron- and copper-founding and other establishments are mentioned (p. iii), but no indication at all is given of the way in which metallurgical plants are separated from those "subordinated" to the Department of Commerce and Manufactures. 2) Only *industrial* establishments are subject to registration. This definition is not as clear as it seems to be at first glance; the separation of artisan and agricultural establishments requires detailed and clearly defined rules applicable to each branch of industry. Below we shall see confusion in abundance arising out of the absence of these rules. 3) The number of workers in an establishment must be no less than 15. It is not clear whether only workers actually employed in the establishment are counted or whether those working outside are included; it has not been explained how the former are to be distinguished from the latter (this is also a difficult question), whether auxiliary workers should be counted, etc. In the above-mentioned book Mr. Mikulin quotes instances of the confusion arising out of this unclarity. The *List* enumerates many establishments that employ *only* outside workers. It stands to reason that an attempt to list *all* establishments of this type (i.e., all shops giving out work, all people in the so-called handicraft industries who give out work, etc.) can only raise a smile under the present system of gathering information, while fragmentary data for some gubernias and some branches of industry are of no significance and merely add to the confusion. 4) All establishments possessing a steam-boiler or a steam-engine are called "factories." This definition is the most accurate and most happily chosen, because the employment of steam is really typical for the development of large-scale machine industry. 5) Establishments possessing "other" (non-steam) "mechanical motive power" are regarded as factories. This definition is very inaccurate and exceedingly broad; by this definition, establishments employing water, horse, and wind power, even treadmills, may be called factories. Since the registration of all such establishments is not even feasible, there must be confusion, examples of which we shall soon see. 6) Under the heading "factories" are included establishments having "factory installations." This most indefinite and hazy definition negates the significance of all definitions given previously and makes the data chaotic and impossible to compare. This definition will inevitably be understood differently in different gubernias, and what sort of definition is it in reality? A factory is an establishment having factory installations.... Such is the last word of our newest system of factory statistics. No wonder these statistics are so unsatisfactory. We shall give examples from *all* sections of the *List* in order to show that in some gubernias and in some branches of industry the tiniest establishments are registered, which introduces confusion into factory statistics, since there can be no question of recording all such establishments. Let us take Section I: "cotton processing." On pp. 10-11 we come across five "factories" in the villages of Vladimir Gubernia which, for payment, dye yarn and linen belonging to others (*sic!*). In place of the value of the output the sum paid for dyeing is given as from 10 rubles (?) to 600 rubles, with the number of workers from zero (whether this means that there is no information on the number of workers or that there are no *hired* workers, is not known) to three. There is no mechanical motive power. These are peasant dye-houses, i.e., the most primitive artisan establishments that have been registered by chance in one gubernia and, it goes without saying, omitted in others. In Section II (wool processing), in the same Vladimir Gubernia, we find hand "factories" that card wool belonging to others for the payment of 12-48 rubles a year and employ 0 or 1 worker. There is a hand silk factory (Section III, No. 2517) in a village; it employs three workers and has an output valued at 660 rubles. Then more village dye-houses in the same Vladimir Gubernia, employing 0-3 workers for hand work and receiving 150-550 rubles for the treatment of linen (Section IV, treatment of flax, p. 141). There is a bast-mat "factory" in Perm Gubernia, on a hand-work level, employing six workers (Section V), with an output valued at 921 rubles (No. 3936). It goes without saying that there are more than a few such establishments in other gubernias (Kostroma, for instance), but they were not counted as factories. There is a printing-works (Section VI) with one worker and an output value of 300 rubles (No. 4167): in other gubernias only the big printing-works were included, and in still others, none at all. There is a "sawmill" with three workers sawing barrel staves for the payment of 100 rubles (Section VII, No. 6274), and a metal-working hand establishment employing three workers with an output valued at 575 rubles (No. 8962). In Section IX (processing of mineral products) there are very many of the tiniest establishments, brickworks especially, with, for example, only one worker and an output valued at 48-50 rubles, and so on. In Section X (processing of livestock products) there are petty candle, sheepskin processing, leather and other establishments employing hand labour, 0-1-2 workers, with an output valued at a few hundred rubles (pp. 489, 507, et al.). More than anywhere else there are numerous establishments of a purely artisan type in Section XI (processing of foodstuffs), in the oil-pressing and, especially, the flour-milling branches. In the latter industry the strict division of "factories" from petty establishments is most essential; but so far this has not been done and utter chaos reigns in all our factory statistical publications. An attempt to introduce order into the statistics on the factory-type flour-milling establishments was made by the first congress of gubernia statistical committee secretaries (in May 1870),* but it was in vain, and up to the present day the compilers of our factory statistics do not seem to be concerned about the utter uselessness of the figures they print. The *List*, for example, included among the factories windmills employing one worker and realising from 0 to 52 rubles, etc. (pp. 587, 589, *et passim*); water-mills with one wheel, employing one worker and earning 34-80 rubles, etc. (p. 589, *et passim*); and so on. It goes without saying that such "statistics" are simply ridiculous, because another and even several other volumes could be filled with such mills without giving

---

* According to the draft rules drawn up by the congress on the gathering of industrial data, all mills equipped with less than 10 pairs of millstones, but not roller mills, were excluded from the list of factories. *Statistical Chronicle*, Series II, Issue 6, Introduction, p. xiii.

a complete list. Even in the section dealing with the chemical industry (XII) there are tiny establishments such as village pitch works employing from one to three workers, with an output valued at 15-300 rubles (p. 995, et al.). Such methods can go so far as to produce "statistics" similar to those published in the sixties in the well-known *Military Statistical Abstract* that for European Russia listed 3,086 pitch and tar "factories," of which 1,450 were in Archangel Gubernia (employing 4,202 workers, with a total output valued at 156,274 rubles, i.e., an average of fewer than three workers and a little more than 100 rubles per "factory"). Archangel Gubernia seems to have been deliberately left out of this section of the *List* altogether, as though the peasants there do not distil pitch and make tar! We must point out that all the instances cited concern registered establishments that do not come under the definitions given in the circular of June 7, 1895. Their registration, therefore, is *purely fortuitous*; they were included in some gubernias (perhaps, even, in some uyezds*), but in the majority they were omitted. Such establishments were omitted in former statistics (from 1885 onwards) as having an output valued at less than 1,000 rubles.

Mr. Karyshev did not properly understand this basic problem of factory statistics; yet he did not hesitate to make "deductions" from the figures he obtained by his calculations. The first of these deductions is that the number of factories in Russia is decreasing (p. 4, et al.). Mr. Karyshev arrived at this conclusion in a very simple way: he took the number of factories for 1885 from the data of the Department of Commerce and Manufactures (17,014) and deducted from it the number of factories in European Russia given in the *List* (14,578). This gives a reduction of 14.3% —the professor even calculates the percentage and is not bothered by the fact that the 1885 data did not include the excise-paying factories; he confines himself to the remark that the addition of excise-paying establishments would give a greater "reduction" in the number of factories. And the author undertakes to discover in which part of Russia this "process of diminution in the number of establishments" (p. 5) is evolving "most rapidly." In actual fact *there is no process of diminution, the number of*

* See footnote on p. 15.—*Ed.*

factories in Russia is increasing and not decreasing, and the figment of Mr. Karyshev's imagination came from the learned professor's having compared data that are not at all comparable.* The incomparability is by no means due to the absence of data on excise-paying factories for 1885. Mr. Karyshev could have taken figures that included such factories (from Orlov's cited *Directory* that was compiled from the same Department of Commerce and Manufactures lists), and in this way could have fixed the number of "factories" in European Russia at *27,986* for 1879, *27,235* for 1884, *21,124* for 1890, and the "reduction" by 1894-95 (14,578) would have been incomparably greater. The only trouble is that all these figures are quite unsuitable for comparison, because, first, there is no uniform conception of "factory" in old and present-day factory statistical publications, and, secondly, very small establishments are included in the number of "factories" fortuitously and indiscriminately (for certain gubernias, for certain years), and, with the means at the disposal of our statistics, it would be ridiculous even to assume that they could be registered in full. Had Mr. Karyshev taken the trouble to study the definition of "factory" in the *List*, he would have seen that in order to compare the number of factories in that publication with the number of factories in others it would be *necessary to take only establishments employing 15 or more workers*, because it is *only this type* of establishment that the *List* registered *in toto* and without any limitations for all gubernias and all branches of industry. Since such establishments are among the relatively large ones, their registration in previous publications was also more satisfactory. Having thus assured the uniformity of data to be compared, let us compute the number of factories in European Russia employing sixteen** or

---

* In 1889 Mr. Karyshev took data for 1885 (*Yuridichesky Vestnik*,[3] No. 9) drawn from the most loyal reports of the governors, data that included the very smallest flour-mills, oil-presses, brickyards, potteries, leather, sheepskin, and other handicraft establishments, and fixed the number of "factories" in European Russia at *62,801*! We are amazed that he did not calculate the percentage of "reduction" in the number of factories today in relation to this figure.

** We are taking 16 and not 15 workers, partly because the computation of factories with 16 and more workers has already been made

more workers, taking them from the *Directory* for 1879 and
from the *List* for 1894-95. We get the following instructive
figures:

| Source | Year | Total | Number of Factories in European Russia | |
			Employing 16 or more workers	Employing fewer than 16 workers
Directory, 1st edition	1879	27,986 *	4,551	23,435
Directory, 3rd edition	1890	21,124	6,013	15,111
List	1894-95	14,578	6,659 (without print-shops 6,372)	7,919

Therefore, the comparison of those figures which alone can
be considered relatively uniform, comparable, and complete
shows that *the number of factories in Russia is increasing*, and
at a fairly rapid rate: in fifteen or sixteen years (from 1879 to
1894-95) it has increased from 4,500 to 6,400, i.e., by 40 per
cent (in 1879 and 1890 print-shops were not included in the
number of factories). As far as the number of establishments
employing fewer than 16 workers is concerned, it would be
absurd to compare them for these years, since different definitions of "factory" and different methods of excluding
small establishments were employed in all these publications. In 1879 *no* small establishments were excluded; *on
account of this*, the very smallest establishments in branches
closely connected with agriculture and peasant industries
(flour milling, oil pressing, brickmaking, leather, potteries,
and others) were included, but they were omitted in later
publications. By 1890 some small establishments (those with
an output valued at less than 1,000 rubles) were omitted;
this left fewer small "factories." And lastly, in 1894-95, the
mass of establishments employing fewer than 15 workers was
omitted, which resulted in the immediate reduction in the
number of small "factories" to about a half of the 1890 figure.
The number of factories for 1879 and 1890 can be made
comparable in another way—by selecting the establishments

---

in the *Directory* for 1890 (3rd edition, p. x), and partly because the
explanations of the Ministry of Finance sometimes adopt this standard
(see Kobelyatsky, *loc. cit.*, p. 14).

* Some gaps in the information have been filled in approximately:
see *Directory*, p. 695.

with an output valued at no less than 2,000 rubles. This is possible because the totals from the *Directory*, as quoted above, refer to all registered establishments, whereas the *Directory* entered in its *name index* of factories only those with an output valued at no less than 2,000 rubles. The number of establishments of this type may be considered approximately comparable (although there can never be a complete list of these establishments as long as our statistics are in their present state), with the exception, however, of the flour-milling industry. Registration in this branch is of a completely fortuitous character in different gubernias and for different years both in the *Directory* and in the *Collection* of the Department of Commerce and Manufactures. In some gubernias only steam-mills are counted as "factories," in others big water-mills are added, in the third case hundreds of windmills, and in the fourth even horse-mills and treadmills are included, etc. Limitation on the basis of the value of output does not clear up the chaos in statistics on factory-type mills, because, instead of that value the quantity of flour milled is taken, and this, even in very small mills, frequently amounts to more than 2,000 poods a year. The number of mills included in factory statistics, therefore, makes unbelievable leaps from year to year on account of the lack of uniformity in registration methods. The *Collection*, for example, listed 5,073, 5,605 and 5,201 mills in European Russia for the years 1889, 1890, and 1891 respectively. In Voronezh Gubernia the number of mills, 87 in 1889, suddenly increased to 285 in 1890 and 483 in 1892 as a result of the accidental inclusion of windmills. In the Don region the number of mills increased from 59 in 1887 to 545 in 1888 and 976 in 1890, then dropping to 685 in 1892 (at times windmills were included, while at others they were not), etc., etc. The employment of such data is clearly impermissible. We, therefore, take only steam-mills and add to them establishments in other branches of industry with an output value of no less than 2,000 rubles, and the number of factories we get for European Russia in 1879 is about 11,500 and in 1890 about 15,500.* From this, again, it follows that there is *an increase*

---

* It is impossible to obtain the required figure from the data in the *List*, first, because it omits a mass of establishments with an output valued at 2,000 rubles and more owing to their employing fewer than

in the number of factories and not the decrease invented by
Mr. Karyshev. Mr. Karyshev's theory of the "process of diminution in the number of establishments" in the factory
industry of Russia is a pure fable, based on a worse than insufficient acquaintance with the material he undertook to
analyse. Mr. Karyshev, as long ago as 1889 (*Yuridichesky
Vestnik*, No. 9), spoke of the number of factories in Russia,
comparing absolutely unsuitable figures taken from the loyal
reports of the governors and published in the *Returns for
Russia for 1884-85* (St. Petersburg, 1887, Table XXXIX)
with the strange figures of the *Military Statistical Abstract*
(Issue IV. St. Petersburg, 1871), which included among the
"factories" thousands of tiny artisan and handicraft establishments, thousands of tobacco plantations (*sic!* see pp. 345
and 414 of the *Military Statistical Abstract* on tobacco "factories" in Bessarabia Gubernia), thousands of rural flour-
mills and oil-presses, etc., etc. Small wonder that in this way
the *Military Statistical Abstract* recorded over 70,000 "factories" in European Russia in 1866. The wonder is that a man was
found who was so inattentive and uncritical with regard to every printed figure as to take it as a basis for his calculations.*

Here a slight diversion is necessary. From his theory of the
diminution of the number of factories Mr. Karyshev deduces
the existence of a process of the concentration of industry.
It goes without saying that, in rejecting his theory, we do not
by any means reject the conclusion, since it is only Mr.
Karyshev's way of arriving at it that is wrong. To demonstrate this process, we must isolate the biggest establishments.
Let us take, for example, establishments employing 100 or
more workers. Comparing the number of such establishments,
the number of workers they employ, and the total value of
their output with data on all establishments, we get this table:

---

15 workers. Secondly, because the *List* counted the total value of the
output without excise (in which it differed from former statistics).
Thirdly, because the *List*, in some cases, registered, not the total value
of the output, but payment for the processing of raw material.

  * Dealing with the question of the number of factory workers, Mr.
Tugan-Baranovsky has shown the utter uselessness of the *Military
Statistical Abstract* data (see his book, *The Factory, etc.*, St. Petersburg,
1898, p. 336, et seq., and *Mir Bozhy*, ⁴ 1898, No. 4), and Messrs.
N.—on and Karyshev have responded with silence to his direct chall-
enge. They really cannot do anything else but remain silent.

See footnote*	1879			1890			1894-95		
	Number of		Value of output (thous. rubles)	Number of		Value of output (thous. rubles)	Number of		Value of output (thous. rubles)
	Factories	Workers		Factories	Workers		Factories	Workers	
All "factories"	27,986	763,152	1,148,134	21,124	875,764	1,500,871	14,578	885,555	1,345,346
Establishments with 100 or more workers	1,238	509,643	629,926	1,431	623,446	858,588	1,468	655,670	955,233
Percentage of total	—	66.8	54.8	—	71.1	57.2	—	74	70.8

* The same sources. Some data for 1879, as already mentioned, have been added approximately. The general data of the *Directory* and the *List* are incomparable with each other, but here we compare *only percentages* of the total number of workers and of the total value of output, and these data in their totals are much more reliable (as we shall show later) than the data on the total number of factories. The estimate of large establishments is taken from *Capitalism in Russia*, which the present writer is preparing for print.⁵

It can be seen from this table that the number of very large establishments is increasing, as well as the number of workers employed and the value of the output, which constitute an ever greater proportion of the total number of workers and the total value of the output of officially registered "factories." The objection may be raised that if a concentration of industry is taking place, it means that big establishments are squeezing out the smaller, whose number and, consequently, the total number of establishments, is decreasing. But, firstly, this last deduction is not made in respect of "factories" but refers *to all industrial establishments,* and of these we have no right to speak because we have no statistics on industrial establishments that are in the least reliable and complete. Secondly, and from a purely theoretical standpoint, it cannot be said *a priori* that the number of industrial establishments in a developing capitalist society must inevitably and always diminish, since, simultaneous with the process of the concentration of industry, there is the process of the population's withdrawal from farming, the process of growth in the number of small industrial establishments in the backward parts of the country as a result of the break-up of the semi-natural peasant economy, etc.*

Let us return to Mr. Karyshev. He pays almost the greatest attention of all to those data that are the least reliable (i.e., the data on the number of "factories"). He divides up the gubernias into groups according to the number of "factories," he designs a cartogram on which these groups are plotted, he compiles a special table of gubernias having the greatest number of "factories" in each branch of industry (pp. 16-17); he presents a mass of calculations in which the number of factories in each gubernia is shown as a percentage of the total (pp. 12-15). In doing this Mr. Karyshev overlooked a mere bagatelle: he forgot to ask himself *whether the numbers of factories in different gubernias are comparable.* This is a question that must be answered in the negative and, consequently, the greater part of Mr. Karyshev's calculations,

---

* The handicraft census for 1894-95 in Perm Gubernia showed, for example, that with every decade of the post-Reform period more and more small industrial establishments are being opened in the villages. See *Survey of Perm Territory. A Sketch of the State of Handicraft Industry in Perm Gubernia.* Perm, 1896.

comparisons, and arguments must be relegated to the sphere
of innocent statistical exercises. If the professor had acquainted himself with the definition of "factory" given in the circular of June 7, 1895, he would easily have concluded that
such a vague definition *cannot* be applied uniformly in
different gubernias, and a more attentive study of the *List*
itself could have led him to the same conclusion. Let us cite
some examples. Mr. Karyshev selects Voronezh, Vyatka, and
Vladimir gubernias (p. 12) for the number of establishments
in Section XI (processing of food products; this group
contains the greatest number of factories). But the abundance
of "factories" in these gubernias is to be explained primarily
by the *purely fortuitous* registration, specifically in these
gubernias, of small establishments such as were not included
in other gubernias. In Voronezh Gubernia, for instance, there
are many "factories" simply because small flour-mills were
included (of 124 mills only 27 are steam-mills; many of them
are water-mills with 1-2-3 wheels; such mills were not included
in other gubernias, and, indeed, they could not be listed in
full), as well as small oil-presses (mostly horse-driven), which
were not included in other gubernias. In Vyatka Gubernia only
3 out of 116 mills are steam-driven, in Vladimir Gubernia a
dozen windmills and 168 oil-presses were included, of which
the majority were wind- or horse-driven or were worked by
hand. The fact that there were fewer establishments in other gubernias, does not, of course, mean that these gubernias
were devoid of windmills, small water-mills, etc. They were
simply not included. In a large number of gubernias steam-
mills were included almost exclusively (Bessarabia, Eka-
terinoslav, Taurida, Kherson, et al.), and the flour-milling
industry accounted for 2,308 "factories" out of 6,233 in
European Russia, according to Section XI. It was absurd
to speak of the distribution of factories by gubernias without
investigating the *dissimilarity* of the data. Let us take Section
IX, the processing of minerals. In Vladimir Gubernia, for
example, there are 96 brickworks and in the Don region, 31,
i.e., less than a third of the number. The *Directory* (for
1890) showed the opposite: 16 in Vladimir and 61 in the Don
region. It now turns out that, according to the *List*, out of
the 96 brickworks in Vladimir Gubernia only 5 employ 16 or
more workers, while the analogous figures for the Don region

are 26 out of 31. The obvious explanation of this is that in the Don region small brickworks were not so generously classified as "factories" as in Vladimir Gubernia, and that is all (the small brickworks in Vladimir Gubernia are all run on hand labour). Mr. Karyshev does not see any of this (p. 14). In respect of Section X (processing of livestock products) Mr. Karyshev says that the number of establishments is small in almost all gubernias but that "an outstanding exception is Nizhni-Novgorod Gubernia with its 252 factories" (p. 14). This is primarily due to the fact that very many small hand establishments (sometimes horse- or wind-driven) were included in this gubernia and not in the others. Thus, for Mogilev Gubernia the *List* includes only two factories in this section; each of them employs more than 15 workers. Dozens of small factories processing livestock products could have been listed in Mogilev Gubernia, in the same way as they were included in the *Directory* for 1890, which showed 99 factories processing livestock products. The question then arises: What sense is there in Mr. Karyshev's calculations of the distribution by percentages of "factories" so differently understood?

In order to show more clearly the different conceptions of the term "factory" in different gubernias, we shall take two neighbouring gubernias: Vladimir and Kostroma. According to the *List*, there are 993 "factories" in the former and 165 in the latter. In all branches of industry (sections) in the former there are tiny establishments that swamp the large ones by their great number (only 324 establishments employ 16 or more workers). In the latter there are very few small establishments (112 factories out of 165 employ 16 or more workers), although everybody realises that more than a few windmills, oil-presses, small starch, brick, and pitch works, etc., etc., could be counted in this gubernia.*

---

* We have here another instance of the arbitrary determination of the number of "factories" in our "newest" system of factory statistics. The *List* for 1894-95 records 471 factories for Kherson Gubernia (Mr. Karyshev, op. cit., p. 5), but for 1896 Mr. Mikulin suddenly lists as many as 1,249 "factory establishments" (op. cit., p. xiii), among them 773 with mechanical motive power and 109 without, employing more than 15 workers. With this unclarity in the definition of "factory" such leaps are inevitable.

Mr. Karyshev's light-minded attitude towards the authenticity of the figures he uses reaches its peak when he compares the number of "factories" per gubernia for 1894-95 (according to the *List*) with that for 1885 (according to the *Collection*). There is a serious dissertation on the increased number of factories in Vyatka Gubernia, on the "considerably decreased" number in Perm Gubernia, and on the substantially increased number in Vladimir Gubernia, and so on (pp. 6-7). "In this we may see," concludes our author profoundly, "that the above-mentioned process of diminution in the number of factories affects places with a more developed and older industry less than those where industry is younger" (p. 7). Such a deduction sounds very "scientific"; the greater the pity that it is merely nonsensical. The figures used by Mr. Karyshev are quite fortuitous. For example, according to the *Collection*, for 1885-90 the number of "factories" in Perm Gubernia was 1, 001, 895, 951, 846, 917, and 1,002 respectively, following which, in 1891, the figure suddenly dropped to 585. One of the reasons for these leaps was the inclusion of 469 mills as "factories" in 1890 and 229 in 1891. If the *List* gives only 362 factories for that gubernia, it must be borne in mind that it now includes only 66 mills as "factories." If the number of "factories" has increased in Vladimir Gubernia, the *List*'s registration of small establishments in that gubernia must be remembered. In Vyatka Gubernia, the *Collection* recorded 1-2-2-30-28-25 mills from 1887 to 1892 and the *List*, 116. In short, the comparison undertaken by Mr. Karyshev demonstrates over and over again that he is quite incapable of analysing figures from different sources.

In giving the numbers of factories in different sections (groups of industrial branches) and in computing their ratio to the total number, Mr. Karyshev once again fails to notice that there is no uniformity in the number of small establishments included in the various sections (there are, for example, fewer in the textile and metallurgical industries than elsewhere, about one-third of the total number for European Russia, whereas in the industries processing livestock and food products they constitute about two-thirds of the total number). It stands to reason that in this way he is comparing non-comparable magnitudes, with the result that his percentages (p. 8) are devoid of all meaning. In short, on the entire question of the number of "factories" and their distribution Mr. Karyshev has displayed a complete lack of understanding of the nature of the data he has employed and their degree of reliability.

As we go over from the number of factories to the number of workers, we must say, in the first place, that the figures for the total number of workers recorded in our factory statistics are much more reliable than those given for the factories. Of course, there is no little confusion here, too, and no lack of omissions and reductions of the actual number. But in this respect we do not find such great divergence in the type of data used, and the excessive variations in the number of small establishments, which are at times included in the number of factories and at others not, have very little effect on the total number of workers, for the simple reason that even a very large percentage of the smallest establishments gives a very small percentage of the total number of workers. We have seen above that for the year 1894-95, 74 per cent of the workers were concentrated in 1,468 factories (10 per cent of the total number). The number of small factories (employing fewer than 16 workers) was 7,919 out of 14,578, i.e., more than a half, and the number of workers in them was (even allowing an average of 8 workers per establishment) something like 7 per cent of the total. This gives rise to the following phenomenon: while there is a tremendous difference in the number of factories in 1890 (in the *Directory*) and in 1894-95, the difference in the number of workers is insignificant: in 1890 the figure was 875,764 workers for fifty gubernias of European Russia, and in 1894-95 it was 885,555 (counting only workers employed inside the establishments). If we deduct from the first figure the number of workers employed in the rail manufacturing (24,445) and salt-refining (3,704) industries, not included in the *List*, and from the second figure the number of workers in print-shops (16,521), not included in the *Directory*, we get 847,615 workers for 1890 and 869,034 workers for 1894-95, i.e., 2.5 per cent more. It goes without saying that this percentage cannot express the actual increase, since many small establishments were not included in 1894-95, but, in general, the closeness of these figures shows the relative suitability of the over-all data on the total number of workers and their relative reliability. Mr. Karyshev, from whom we have taken the total number of workers, does not make an accurate analysis of precisely which branches of industry were included in 1894-95 as compared with former publications, nor does he point out that the *List* omits many establishments that were formerly included in the number of factories. For his comparison with former statistics he takes the same absurd data of the *Military Statistical Abstract* and repeats the same nonsense about the alleged reduction in the number of workers relative to the population which has already been refuted by Mr. Tugan-Baranovsky (see above). Since the data on the number of workers are more authentic, they are deserving of a more thorough analysis than the data on the number of factories, but Mr. Karyshev has done just the opposite. He does not even group factories together according to the number of workers employed, which is what he should have done in the first place, in view of the fact that the *List* regards the number of workers as an important distinguishing feature of the factory. It can be seen from the data cited above that the concentration of workers is very great.

Instead of grouping factories according to the number of workers employed in them, Mr. Karyshev undertook a much simpler calculation, aimed at determining the average number of workers per factory. Since the data on the number of factories are, as we have seen, particularly unreliable, fortuitous, and dissimilar, the calculations are full of errors. Mr. Karyshev compares the average number of workers per factory in 1886 with the figure for 1894-95 and from this deduces that "the average type of factory is growing larger" (pp. 23 and 32-33), not realising that in 1894-95 only the larger establishments were listed, so that the comparison is incorrect. There is a very strange comparison of the number of workers per factory in the different gubernias (p. 26); Mr. Karyshev obtains the result, for instance, that "Kostroma Gubernia turns out to have a bigger average type of industry than all other gubernias"—242 workers per factory as compared with, for example, 125 in Vladimir Gubernia. It does not enter the learned professor's head that this is due merely to different methods of registration, as we have explained above. Having allowed the difference between the number of large and small establishments in different gubernias to pass unnoticed, Mr. Karyshev invented a very simple way of *evading* the difficulties encountered in this question. Precisely put, he multiplied the average number of workers *per factory for the whole of European Russia* (and then for Poland and the Caucasus) by the number of factories in each gubernia and indicated the groups he thus obtained on a special cartogram (No. 3). This, indeed, is really so simple! Why group factories according to the number of workers they employ, why examine the relative number of large and small establishments in different gubernias, when we can so easily *artificially level out* the "average" size of the factories in various gubernias according to one standard? Why try to find out whether there are many or few small and petty establishments included in the number of factories in Vladimir or Kostroma Gubernia, when we can "simply" take the average number of workers per factory *throughout* European Russia and multiply it by the number of factories in *each* gubernia? What matters it if such a method equates hundreds of fortuitously registered windmills and oil-presses with big factories? The reader, of course, will not notice it, and who knows—he may even believe the "statistics" invented by Professor Karyshev!

In addition to workers employed in the establishment, the *List* has a special category of workers "outside the establishment." This includes not only those working at home to the orders of the factory (Karyshev, p. 20), but also auxiliary workers, and so on. The number of these workers given in the *List* (66,460 in the Empire) must not be regarded as "an indication of how far advanced in Russia is the development of the so-called outside department of the factory" (Karyshev, p. 20), since there can be no question of anything like a complete registration of such workers under the present system of factory statistics. Mr. Karyshev says very thoughtlessly: "66,500 for the whole of Russia with her millions of handicraftsmen and artisans is but a few" *(ibid.)*. Before writing this he had to forget that, if not the greater part, at least a very large part of these "millions of handicraftsmen," as is confirmed by all sources, work for jobbers, i.e., are the selfsame "outside workers." One has only to glance at those pages of the *List* devoted to districts known for their handicraft industries to be convinced of the thoroughly fortuitous and fragmentary nature of the registration of "outside workers." Section II (wool processing) of the *List*, for example, for Nizhni-Novgorod Gubernia counts only 28 outside workers in the town of Arzamas and in the suburban Viyezdnaya Sloboda (p. 89), whereas we know from the *Transactions of the Commission of Inquiry into Handicraft Industry in Russia* (Issues V and VI) that many hundreds (up to a thousand) "handicraftsmen" work there for masters. The *List* does not record any outside workers at all in Semyonov Uyezd, whereas we know from the Zemstvo[6] statistics that over 3,000 "handicraftsmen" work there for masters in the felt boot and insole branches. The *List* records only one "factory" employing 17 outside workers in the accordion industry of Tula Gubernia (p. 395), whereas the cited *Transactions of the Commission, etc.*, as early as 1882, listed between 2,000 and 3,000 handicraftsmen working for accordion factory owners (Issue IX). It is, therefore, obvious that to regard the figure of 66,500 outside workers as being in any way authentic and to discuss their distribution by gubernias and branches of industry, as Mr. Karyshev does, and even to compile a cartogram, is simply ridiculous. The real significance of these figures lies not at all in the determination of the extent to which capitalist work is done in the home (which is determinable only from a complete industrial census that includes all shops and other establishments, as well as individuals giving out work to be done at home), but in the separation of the workers in the establishments, i.e., factory workers in the strict sense from outside workers. Hitherto these two types of workers have often been confounded; frequent instances of such confusion are to be found even in the *Directory* for 1890. The *List* is now making the first attempt to put an end to this state of affairs.

The *List*'s figures relating to the annual output of the factories have been analysed by Mr. Karyshev most satisfactorily of all, mainly because that author at last introduced the grouping of factories by the magnitude of their output and not by the usual "averages." It is true that the author still cannot rid himself of these "averages" (the magnitude of output per factory) and even compares the averages for 1894-95 with those for 1885, a method that, as we have repeatedly said, is absolutely incorrect. We would note that the total figures for the annual output of factories are much more authentic than the total figures for the number of factories, for the reason, already mentioned, of the minor role of the small establishments. According to the *List*, there are, for example, only 245 factories in European Russia with an output valued at more than one million rubles, i.e., only 1.9 per cent, but they account for 45.6 per cent of the total annual output of all factories in European Russia (Karyshev, p. 38), while factories with an output valued at less than 5,000 rubles constitute 30.8 per cent of the total number, but account for only 0.6 per cent of the total output, i.e., a most insignificant fraction. We must here note that in these calculations Mr. Karyshev ignores the difference between the value of the total output (= value of the product) and payment for the processing of raw material. This very important distinction is made for the first time in our factory statistics by the *List*.* It goes without saying that these two magnitudes are absolutely incomparable with each other and that they should have been separated. Mr. Karyshev does not do this, and it is to be supposed that the low percentage of annual output of the small establishments is partly due to the inclusion of establishments that showed only the cost of processing the product and not its value. Below we shall give an example of the error into which Mr. Karyshev falls through ignoring this circumstance. The fact that the *List* differentiates between payment for processing and the value of the product and that it does not include the sum of the excise in the price of production makes it imposstble to compare these figures with those of previous publications. According to the *List*, the output of all the factories of European Russia amounts to 1,345 million rubles, while according to the *Directory* for 1890 it amounted to 1,501 million. But if we subtract the sum of the excise from the second figure (250 million rubles in the distilling industry alone), then the first figure will be considerably greater.

---

* The only thing is that, unfortunately, we have no guarantee that the *List* made this distinction strictly and consistently, i. e., that the value of the product is shown *only* for those factories that actually sell their product, and payment for processing raw material only for those that process material belonging to others. It is possible, for example, that in the flour-milling industry (where the above-mentioned distinction is most frequently met with) the mill owners should have shown either of the figures indiscriminately. This is a problem that requires special analysis.

In the *Directory* (2nd and 3rd editions) factories were distributed in groups according to the amount of annual output (without any indication of the share of each group in the total output), but this distribution cannot be compared with the data in the *List* because of the differences in registration methods mentioned above and in the determining of the magnitude of annual output.

We have yet another fallacious argument of Mr. Karyshev to examine. Here, too, in quoting data on the total annual output of factories in each gubernia, he could not refrain from making comparisons with the data for the years 1885 to 1891, i.e., with the data of the *Collection*. Those data contain no information on productions subject to excise, and for that reason Mr. Karyshev looks only for gubernias in which the total output for 1894-95 is *less* than in previous years. Such gubernias are to be found to the number of eight (pp. 39-40), and apropos of this Mr. Karyshev argues about "the retrograde movement in industry" in the "less industrial" gubernias and says that this "may serve as an indication of the difficult position of the small establishments in their competition with big establishments," and so on. All these arguments would probably be very profound if—if they were not all completely fallacious. And here, too, Mr. Karyshev did not notice that he was comparing absolutely noncomparable and dissimilar data. Let us demonstrate this incomparability by data on each of the gubernias indicated by Mr. Karyshev.* In Perm Gubernia the total output in 1890 was 20.3 million rubles (*Directory*), while in 1894-95 it was 13.1 million rubles; this includes the flour-milling industry, 12.7 million (at 469 mills!) in 1890, and 4.9 million (at 66 mills) in 1894-95. The seeming "reduction," therefore, is simply a matter of the fortuitous registration of different numbers of mills. The number of steam-mills, for example, increased from 4 in 1890 and 1891 to 6 in 1894-95. The "reduction" of

---

* In this case we do not take the data of the *Collection* but those of the *Directory* for 1890, *deducting industries subject to excise*. With the exception of these industries, the *Directory* data do not differ from those of the *Collection*, since they are based on the same reports of the Department of Commerce and Manufactures. In order to expose Mr. Karyshev's error we need detailed data for individual factories and not only for individual industries.

census[7] of the population, taken on January 28, 1897, prove satisfactory and if they are analysed in detail, they will greatly facilitate the taking of an industrial census. As long as there are no such censuses it can only be a question of registering some of the big industrial establishments. It must be conceded that the present system of collecting and processing statistical information on such big establishments ("factories and workers" in the prevailing terminology) is unsatisfactory in the highest degree. Its first shortcoming is the division of factory statistics among various "departments" and the absence of a special, purely statistical institution that centralises the collecting, checking, and classifying of all information on all types of factories. When you analyse the data of our present-day factory statistics you find yourself on territory that is intersected in all directions by the boundaries of various "departments" (which employ special ways and means of registration, and so on). It sometimes happens that these boundaries pass through a certain factory, so that one section of a factory (the iron foundry, for example) comes under the Department of Mines and Metallurgy, while another section (the manufacture of ironware, for example) comes under the Department of Commerce and Manufactures. It can be understood how this makes the use of the data difficult and into what errors those investigators risk falling (and fall) who do not pay sufficient attention to this complicated question. With regard to the checking of the information, it must be said in particular that the Factory Inspectorate will, naturally, never be in a position to check the extent to which all information supplied by all factory owners corresponds to reality. Under a system of the present-day type (i.e., under which the information is not gathered by means of a census conducted by a special staff of agents but by means of questionnaires circulated among factory owners), the chief attention should be paid to ensuring that the central statistical institution have *direct* contact with all factory owners, systematically control the *uniformity* of the returns, and see to their completeness and to the dispatch of questionnaires to *all* industrial centres of any importance—that it thus prevent the fortuitous inclusion of dissimilar data, or different applications and interpretations of the programme. The second basic shortcoming of present-day statistics lies in the fact that the programme for the gathering of information has not been elaborated. If this programme is prepared in offices and is not submitted to the criticism of specialists and (what is particularly important) to an all-round discussion in the press, the information *never can be* in any way complete and uniform. We have seen, for example, how unsatisfactorily even the basic programmatic question—what is a "factory"?—is being solved. Since there is no industrial census, and the system employed is that of gathering information from the industrialists themselves (through the police, the Factory Inspectorate, etc.), the concept "factory" should most certainly be defined with complete accuracy and limited to big establishments of such size as to warrant our expectation that they will be registered *everywhere and in their entirety without omissions*. It appears that the fundamental elements of the definition of a "factory establishment" as at present accepted have been quite well chosen: 1) the number of workers employed *in the establishment* to be no fewer than 15 (the question of separating auxiliary workers from factory workers in the true sense of the word, of determining the average number of workers for the year, etc., to be elaborated); and 2) the presence of a steam-engine (even when the number of workers is smaller). Although extreme caution should be exercised in extending this definition, it is an unfortunate fact that to these distinguishing characteristics have been added other, quite indeterminate ones. If, for instance, the bigger establishments employing water power must not be omitted, it should be shown with absolute accuracy what establishments of this type are subject to registration (using motive power of not less than so many units, or employing not less than a certain number of workers, and so on). If it is considered essential to include smaller establishments in some branches, these branches must be listed very precisely and other definite features of the concept "factory establishments" must be given. Those branches in which "factory" establishments merge with "handicraft" or "agricultural" establishments (felt, brick, leather, flour milling, oil pressing, and many others) should be given special attention. We believe that the two characteristics we have given of the concept "factory" should in no case be extended, because even such relatively big establishments can scarcely be registered without omissions under the existing system of gathering information. A reform of the system may be expressed either in partial and insignificant changes or in the introduction of full industrial censuses. As far as the extent of the information is concerned, i.e., the number of questions asked the industrialists, here, too, a radical distinction has to be made between an industrial census and statistics of the present-day type. It is only possible and necessary to strive for complete information in the first case (questions on the history of the establishment, its relations to neighbouring establishments and the neighbourhood population, the commercial side of affairs, raw and auxiliary materials, quantity and type of the product, wages, the length of the working day, shifts, nightwork and overtime, and so on and so forth). In the second case great caution must be exercised: it is better to obtain relatively little reliable, complete, and uniform information than a lot of fragmentary, doubtful information that cannot be used for comparisons. The only addition undoubtedly necessary is that of questions on machinery in use and on the amount of output.

In saying that our factory statistics are unsatisfactory in the highest degree, we do not by any means wish to imply that their data are not deserving of attention and analysis. Quite the contrary. We have examined in detail the shortcomings of the existing system in order to stress the necessity for a particularly thorough analysis of the data. The chief and basic purpose of this analysis should be the separation of the wheat from the chaff, the separation of the relatively useful material from the useless. As we have seen, the chief mistake made by Mr. Karyshev (and many others) consists precisely in the failure to make such a separation. The figures on "factories" are the least reliable, and under no circumstances can they be used without a thorough preliminary analysis (the separate listing of the bigger establishments, etc.). The number of workers and the output values are much more reliable in the grand totals (it is, however, still necessary to make a strict analysis of which productions were included and in which way, how the output value was computed, etc.). If the more detailed totals are taken, it is possible that the data will prove unsuited for comparison and their use conducive to error. The fables of the reduction of the number of factories in Russia and of the number of factory workers (relative to the population)—fables that have been so zealously disseminated by the Narodniks [8]—can only be explained as due to the ignoring of all these circumstances.

As far as the analysis of the material itself is concerned, it must undoubtedly be based on information on each separate factory, i.e., card-index information. The cards must, first and foremost, be grouped by territorial units. The gubernia is too big a unit. The question of the distribution of industry is so important that the classification must be for individual cities, suburbs, villages, and groups of villages that form industrial centres or districts. Further, grouping by branches of industry is essential. In this respect our latest factory statistical system has, in our opinion, introduced an undesirable change, causing a radical rupture with the old subdivision into branches of industry that has predominated right from the sixties (and earlier). The *List* made a new grouping of industries in twelve sections: if the data are taken by sections only, we get an excessively broad framework embracing branches of production of the most diverse character and throwing them together (felt cloth and rough felt, sawmills and furniture manufacture, notepaper and printing, iron-founding and jewellery, bricks and porcelain, leather and wax, oil-pressing and sugar-refining, beer-brewing and tobacco, etc.). If these sections are subdivided in detail into separate branches we get groups that are far too detailed (see Mikulin, op. cit.), *over three hundred* of them! The old system that had ten sections and about a hundred branches of production (91 in the *Directory* for 1890) seems to us to have been much happier. Furthermore, it is essential to group the factories *according to the number of workers, the type of motive power*, as well as *according to the amount of output*. Such a grouping is particularly necessary from the purely theoretical standpoint for the study of the condition and development of industry and for the separation of relatively useful from useless data in the material at hand. The absence of such a grouping (necessary within the territorial groups and the groups of branches of production) is the most significant shortcoming of our present publications on factory statistics, which allow only "average figures" to be determined, quite often absolutely false and leading to serious errors. Lastly, grouping under all these headings should not be limited to a determination of the number of establishments in each group (or sub-group) but must be accompanied by a calculation of the number of workers and aggregate output in each group, in establishments employing both machine and hand labour, etc. In other words, *combined* tables are necessary as well as *group* tables.

It would be a mistake to think that such an analysis involves an inordinate amount of labour. The Zemstvo statistical bureaus with their modest budgets and small staffs carry out much more complicated work for each uyezd; they analyse 20,000, 30,000 and 40,000 separate cards (and the number of relatively big, "factory" establishments throughout the whole of Russia would probably not be more than 15,000-16,000); moreover, the volume of information on each card is incomparably greater: there are several hundred columns in the Zemstvo statistical abstracts, whereas in the *List* there are less than twenty. Notwithstanding this, the best Zemstvo statistical abstracts not only provide group tables under various headings, but also combined tables, i.e., those showing a combination of various features.

Such an analysis of the data would, firstly, provide the requisite material for economic science. Secondly, it would fully decide the question of separating relatively useful from useless data. Such an analysis would immediately disclose the fortuitous character of data on some branches of industry, some gubernias, some points of the programme, etc. An opportunity would be provided to extract relatively full, reliable, and uniform material. Valuable indications would be obtained of the way in which these qualities can be assured in the future.

Written in August 1898

Published in 1898 in the collection, *Economic Studies and Essays,* by Vladimir Ilyin

Published according to the text in the collection

REVIEW

A. Bogdanov. *A Short Course of Economic Science. Moscow,
1897. Publ. A. Murinova's Bookshop. 290 pp. Price 2 rubles.*

Mr. Bogdanov's book is a remarkable manifestation in
our economic literature; not only is it "no superfluous"
guide among a number of others (as the author "hopes"
in his preface), it is by far the best of them. In this note,
therefore, we intend to call the reader's attention to the
outstanding merits of the book and to indicate a few minor
points which could, in our opinion, be improved upon in
future editions; in view of the lively interest displayed by
our reading public in economic questions, it is to be expected
that further editions of this useful book will soon be forth-
coming.

The chief merit of Mr. Bogdanov's *Course* is the strict
adherence to a definite line from the first page to the last,
in a book that treats of many and very extensive problems.
From the outset the author gives a clear-cut and precise
definition of political economy as "the science that studies
the social relations of production and distribution in their
development" (3), and he never deviates from this point
of view, one that is often but poorly understood by learned
professors of political economy who lapse from "the social
relations of production" to production in general and fill
their ponderous courses with a pile of empty banalities
and examples that have nothing to do with social science.
Alien to the author is the scholasticism that often impels
compilers of textbooks to indulge in "definitions" and in an
analysis of every aspect of each definition; the clarity of

his exposition, actually gains, rather than loses, by this, and the reader gets a clear conception, for example, of such a category as *capital*, both in the social and in the historical sense. In his *Course*, Mr. Bogdanov bases the sequence of his exposition on the view that political economy is the science of the historically developing systems of social production. He begins his *Course* with a brief exposition of "general concepts" (pp. 1-19) of the science and ends with a brief "history of economic views" (pp. 235-90), outlining the subject of the science in Section C: "The Process of Economic Development"; he does not give his outline dogmatically (as is the case with the majority of textbooks), but by means of a characteristic of the periods of economic development in their proper sequence: the periods of primitive clan communism, slavery, feudalism and guilds, and, finally, capitalism. This is precisely what an exposition of political economy should be. The objection may be raised that under these circumstances the author is inevitably compelled to break up one and the same theoretical division (e. g., money) between different periods and thereby repeat himself. But this purely formal shortcoming is more than compensated by the fundamental merits of the historical exposition. And is it really a shortcoming? The repetitions are quite insignificant and are of benefit to the beginner because he is better able to grasp the more important postulates. The treatment of the various functions of money in the various periods of economic development, for example, shows the student clearly that the theoretical analysis of these functions is not based on abstract speculation but on a precise study of what actually happened in the course of the historical development of mankind. It provides a more complete conception of the particular, historically determined, systems of social economy. The whole task of a handbook of political economy is, of course, to give the student of that science the fundamental concepts of the different systems of social economy and of the basic features of each system; the whole task is one of placing in the hands of the student who has mastered the elementary handbook a reliable guide to the further study of the subject, so that, having understood that the most important problems of contemporary social life are intimately bound up with problems of economic science, he may acquire an interest in this study. In ninety-nine cases out of a hundred this is precisely what is lacking in handbooks of political economy. Their shortcoming is due not so much to the fact that they are usually limited to one system of social economy (i.e., the capitalist system) as to their inability to focus the reader's attention on the basic features of that system; they are unable to give a clear definition of its historical significance and to show the process (and the conditions) of its emergence, on the one hand, and the tendencies of its further development, on the other; they are unable to represent the different aspects and different manifestations of contemporary economic life as component parts of a definite system of social economy, as manifestations of the basic features of that system; they are unable to give the reader reliable guidance, because they do not usually adhere to one particular line with complete consistency; and, lastly, they are unable to interst the student, because they have an extremely narrow and incoherent conception of the significance of economic questions and present economic, political, moral, and other "factors" in "poetic disorder." Only the *materialist conception of history* can bring light into this chaos and open up the possibility for a broad, coherent, and intelligent view of a specific system of social economy as the foundation of a specific system of man's entire social life.

The outstanding merit of Mr. Bogdanov's *Course* is that the author adheres consistently to historical materialism. In outlining a definite period of economic development in his "exposition" he usually gives a sketch of the political institutions, the family relations, and the main currents of social thought *in connection* with the basic features of the economic system under discussion. The author explains how the particular economic system gave rise to a certain division of society into classes and shows how *these classes* manifested themselves in the political, family, and intellectual life of that historical period, and how the interests of these classes were reflected in certain schools of economic thought, for example, how the interests of developing capitalism were expressed by the school of free competition and how, at a later period, the interests of the same class were expressed by the school of vulgar economists (284), the apologist school. The author rightly points out the connection between the position of definite classes and the historical school (284), as well as the school of *Katheder*-reformers[9] (the "realistic" or "historico ethical" school), which, with its empty and false conception of the "non-class" origin and significance of juridico-political institutions (288), etc., must be characterised as the school of "compromise" (287). The author connects the theories of Sismondi and Proudhon with the development of capitalism and with good reason relegates them to the category of petty-bourgeois economists; he shows the roots of their ideas in the interests of a specific class in capitalist society, the class that occupies the "middle, transitional place" (279), and recognises without circumlocution the reactionary import of such ideas (280-81). Thanks to the consistency of his views and his ability to examine the different aspects of economic life in their relation to the fundamental features of the economic system under discussion, the author has given a correct assessment of such phenomena as the participation of the workers in the profits of an enterprise (one of the "forms of wages" that "can very rarely prove profitable for the employer" [pp. 132-33]) or the production associations which, "being organised within capitalist relations," "in reality serve only to increase the petty bourgeoisie" (187).

We know that it is precisely these features of Mr. Bogdanov's *Course* that will give rise to more than a few reproaches. It stands to reason that representatives and supporters of the "ethico-sociological" school in Russia[10] will be dissatisfied. Among the dissatisfied there will also be those who assume that "the question of the economic conception of history is purely academic,"* and many others…. But apart from this, one might say partisan, dissatisfaction, the objection will be raised that the posing of questions so extensively has led to the extraordinarily condensed exposition of the *Short Course* which, in the brief

---

* This is the opinion of the *Russkaya Mysl*[11] reviewer (1897; November, bibliographical section, p. 517). And to think that there are such comedians in the world!

space of 290 pages, deals with all periods of economic
development, from the clan community and savagery to
capitalist cartels and trusts, as well as the political and
family life of the world of antiquity and the Middle Ages, and
with the history of economic views. Mr. A. Bogdanov's exposition really is condensed to the highest degree, as he himself states in his preface, wherein he says plainly that his
book is a "conspectus." There is no doubt that some of the
author's terse notes, dealing mostly with facts of a historical character, but sometimes with more detailed problems
of theoretical economics, will not be understood by the
beginner who wishes to learn something of political economy. We, however, do not think that the author should be
blamed for this. We would even say, without fear of being
accused of paradoxes, that such notes should be regarded as
a merit and not a shortcoming of the book under review.
For, indeed, were the author to think of giving a detailed
exposition, explanation and basis for every such note, his
book would have attained immeasurable dimensions quite
out of keeping with the purposes of a short guide. And it
would be impossible to outline, in any course, no matter
how extensive, all the data of modern science on all periods
of economic development and on the history of economic
views from Aristotle to Wagner. Had he discarded all such
notes, his book would positively have been worsened by the
reduction of the scope and significance of political economy.
In their present form these terse notes will, we think, be
of great benefit both to teachers and students who use
the book. Concerning the former this is more than true.
The latter will see from the sum total of these notes
that political economy cannot be studied carelessly, *mir
nichts dir nichts*,* without any previous knowledge, and
without making the acquaintance of very many and very
important problems in history, statistics, etc. Students
will see that they cannot become acquainted with problems
of social economy in its development and its influence on
social life from one or even from several textbooks or courses
that are often distinguished by their "facility of exposi-

---

* As Kautsky aptly remarked in the preface to his well-known
book, *Marx's Oekonomische Lehren*. (*Marx's Economic Teachings.— Ed.*)

tion" as well as by their amazing emptiness, their meaningless phrase-mongering; that the most vitally important
questions of history and present-day reality are indissolubly
bound up with economic questions and that the roots of the
latter are to be found in the social relations of production.
Such, indeed, is the chief purpose of any guidebook—to
give the basic concepts of the subject under discussion
and to show in what direction it is to be studied in greater
detail and why such a study is important.

Let us now turn to the second part of our remarks and
point out those places in Mr. Bogdanov's book that, in our
opinion, stand in need of correction or expansion. We hope
the respected author will not demur at the trivial and even
hole-picking nature of these remarks: in a conspectus individual phrases and even individual words have incomparably
greater significance than in an extensive and detailed exposition.

Mr. Bogdanov, in general, uses only the terminology of
the school of economics to which he adheres. But when he
speaks of the form of value he replaces that term by the
expression "formula of exchange" (p. 39, et seq.). This seems
to us to be an unfortunate expression; the term "form of
value" is really inconvenient in a brief handbook, and it
would probably be better to say instead: form of exchange
or stage of development of exchange, since, otherwise, we
get such expressions as "predominance of the second formula
of exchange" (43) (?). In speaking of capital, the author
was mistaken in omitting the general formula of capital
which would have helped the student to master the fact that
trading and industrial capital are of the same kind.

In describing capitalism, the author omitted the question
of the growth of the commercial-industrial population at
the expense of the agricultural population and that of the
concentration of the population in the big cities; this gap
is felt all the more because the author, in speaking of the
Middle Ages, dealt in detail with the relations between
countryside and town (63-66), while in respect of the modern
town he said only a couple of words about the countryside
being subordinated to it (174).

In discussing the history of industry, the author deter-
minedly placed the "domestic system of capitalist produc-

tion"* "mid-way between artisan production and manufacture" (p. 156, *Thesis* 6). This simplification does not seem to us, in the present case, to be very convenient. The author of *Capital* described capitalist domestic industry in the section on machine industry and attributed it directly to the transforming effect which the latter exerts on old forms of labour. Actually those forms of domestic labour that prevail, both in Europe and in Russia, in the dressmaking industry, for example, cannot by any means be placed "mid-way between artisan production and manufacture." They come *later* than manufacture in the historical development of capitalism and it would have been worth while, we think, to say a few words about this.

In the chapter on the machine period of capitalism,** a noticeable gap is the absence of a paragraph on the reserve army and capitalist over-population, engendered by machine industry, on its significance in the cyclical development of industry, and on its chief forms. The very scanty mention the author makes of these phenomena on pages 205 and 270 are clearly insufficient.

The author's statement that "during the past fifty years" "profit has been increasing more rapidly than rent" (179) is too bold an assertion. Not only Ricardo (against whom Mr. Bogdanov mentions the point), but Marx as well affirms the general tendency of rent to increase with particular rapidity under all and any circumstances (rent may even increase when the price of grain is decreasing). That reduction in grain prices (and in rent under certain circumstances), brought about recently by the competition of the virgin fields of America, Australia, etc., became acute only in the seventies, and Engels' note to the section on rent (*Das Kapital*, III, 2, 259-60 [12]), devoted to the present-day agrarian crisis, is formulated with much greater caution. Engels here postulates the "law" of the growth of rent in civi-

---

* Pp. 93, 95, 147, 156. It seems to us that this term is a successful substitution for the expression "domestic system of large-scale production" that was introduced into our literature by Korsak.

** The strict division of capitalism into a period of manufacture and a period of machine industry is one of the most valuable features of Mr. Bogdanov's *Course*.

lised countries, which explains the "amazing vitality of the class of big landlords,"* and further says only that this vitality "is gradually being exhausted" (*allmählig sich erschöpft*).

The paragraphs devoted to farming are also marked by excessive brevity. The paragraph on (capitalist) rent shows only in the barest outline that it is conditioned by capitalist farming ("In the period of capitalism land remains private property and takes on the role of capital," 127—and that is all!). In order to avoid all sorts of misunderstandings, a few words, in greater detail, should have been said about the emergence of the rural bourgeoisie, the condition of the farm labourers, and the difference in their condition and that of the factory workers (a lower standard of living and requirements, remnants of their attachment to the land or of various *Gesindeordnungen*,* etc.). It is also a pity that the author did not touch on the genesis of capitalist rent. After the mention he made of the *coloni* [13] and dependent peasants and, further, of the rent paid by our peasants, he should have given a brief characteristic of the course taken by the development of rent from labour rent (*Arbeitsrente*) to rent in kind (*Produktenrente*), then to money rent (*Geldrente*), and finally to capitalist rent (cf. *Das Kapital*, III, 2, *Kap.* 47 [14]).

In treating of the supplanting of subsidiary industries by capitalism and the resultant loss of stability experienced by peasant economy, the author expresses himself as follows: "In general the peasant economy becomes poorer—the sum total of values produced decreases" (148). This is most inexact. The process of the ruination of the peasantry by capitalism consists in its dispossession by the rural bourgeoisie, which derives from that same peasantry. Mr. Bogdanov could hardly, for example, describe the decline of peasant farming in Germany without mentioning the *Vollbauer*.** In the place mentioned the author speaks of the peasantry in general, and follows this up immediately with an example from Russian reality; well, to speak of the

---

* Legal injunctions fixing the relations between landowners and serfs.—*Ed.*

** A peasant who is in possession of a full (undivided) plot of land.—*Ed.*

Russian peasantry "in general" is a more than risky business. On the same page the author says: "The peasant either
engages in farming alone or he goes to the manufactory,"
that is, we add on our own part, he becomes either a
rural bourgeois or a proletarian (with a tiny piece of land).
Mention should have been made of this two-sided process.

Lastly, we must mention the absence of examples from
Russian life as a general drawback of the book. On very
many questions (for instance, on the organisation of production in the Middle Ages, the development of machine industry and railways, the growth of the urban population,
crises and syndicates, the difference between manufacto-
ries and factories, etc.) such examples taken from our economic literature would have been of great importance, since
the absence of examples with which he is familiar makes it
much more difficult for the beginner to master the subject.
It seems to us that the filling of these gaps would not greatly
increase the size of the book and would not increase the difficulty of distributing it widely, which is very desirable
in all respects.

Written in February 1898

Published in April 1898
in the magazine *Mir Bozhy*, No. 4

Published according to
the text in the magazine

A NOTE ON THE QUESTION OF THE MARKET THEORY

(APROPOS OF THE POLEMIC of Messrs. TUGAN-BARANOVSKY AND BULGAKOV)

The question of markets in capitalist society, it will be remembered, occupied a highly important place in the theory of the Narodnik economists headed by Messrs. V. V. and N.—on. It is, therefore, perfectly natural that economists who adopt a negative attitude towards the Narodnik theories should deem it essential to call attention to this problem and to explain, first and foremost, the basic, abstract-theoretical points of the "market theory." An attempt to offer such an explanation was undertaken by Mr. Tugan-Baranovsky in 1894 in his book, *Industrial Crises in Modern England*, Chapter I, Part 2, "The Market Theory"; last year, Mr. Bulgakov devoted his book, *Markets under Capitalist Production* (Moscow, 1897), to the same problem. The two authors are in agreement in their basic views; the central feature of both is an exposition of the noteworthy analysis, "the circulation and reproduction of the aggregate social capital," an analysis made by Marx in the third section of Volume II of *Capital*. The two authors agree that the theories propounded by Messrs. V. V. and N.—on on the market (especially the internal market) in capitalist society are completely erroneous and are due either to an ignoring or a misunderstanding of Marx's analysis. Both authors recognise the fact that developing capitalist production creates its own market mainly for *means of production and not for articles of consumption*; that the realisation of the product in general and of surplus-value in particular is fully explicable without the introduction of a foreign market; that the necessity of a foreign market for a capitalist country is not due to the conditions of realisation (as Messrs. V. V. and N.—on assumed), but to historical conditions, and so on. It would seem that Messrs. Bulgakov and Tugan-Baranovsky, being in such complete accord, would have nothing to argue about and that they could direct their joint efforts to a further and more detailed criticism of Narodnik economics. But in actual fact a polemic arose between these two writers (Bulgakov, op. cit., pages 246-57, *et passim*; Tugan-Baranovsky in *Mir Bozhy*, 1898, No. 6, "Capitalism and the Market," apropos of S. Bulgakov's book). In our opinion both Mr. Bulgakov and Mr. Tugan-Baranovsky have gone a bit too far in their polemic and have given their remarks too personal a character. Let us try and discover whether there is any real difference between them and, if there is, which of them has the greater right on his side.

To begin with, Mr. Tugan-Baranovsky charges Mr. Bulgakov with possessing "little originality" and with liking too much *jurare in verba magistri** (*Mir Bozhy*, 123). "The solution I set forth as regards the question of the role of the foreign market for a capitalist country," says Mr. Tugan-Baranovsky, "adopted *in toto* by Mr. Bulgakov, is not taken from Marx at all." We believe this statement to be untrue, for it was *precisely from Marx* that Mr. Tugan-Baranovsky took his solution to the question; Mr. Bulgakov no doubt also took it from the same source, so that the argument should not be about "originality" but about the understanding of a certain postulate of Marx, about the need to expound Marx in one way or in another. Mr. Tugan-Baranovsky says that Marx "does not touch at all on the question of the foreign market in the second volume" (*loc. cit.*). This is not true. In that same (third) section of the second volume, wherein he analyses the realisation of the product, Marx very definitely explains the relationship of foreign trade and, consequently, of the foreign market, to this question. He says the following:

"Capitalist production does not exist at all without foreign commerce. But when one assumes normal annual reproduction on a given scale one also assumes that foreign commerce *only replaces home products* [*Artikel—*

---

* To swear by the words of the master.—*Ed.*

goods]* *by articles of other use- or bodily form*, without affecting value-relations, hence without affecting either the value-
relations in which the two categories 'means of production'
and 'articles of consumption' mutually exchange, or the relations between constant capital, variable capital, and surplus-value, into which the value of the product of each of
these categories may be divided. The involvement of foreign
commerce in analysing the annually reproduced value of
products can therefore only confuse without contributing
any new element of the problem, or of its solution. For this
reason it must be entirely discarded" (*Das Kapital*, II [1],
469. [15] Our italics). Mr. Tugan-Baranovsky's "solution of the
question," namely, "... in any country importing goods from
abroad there may be a surplus of capital; a foreign market is
absolutely essential to such a country" (*Industrial Crises*,
p. 429. Quoted in *Mir Bozhy*, *loc. cit.*, 121)—is merely a para-
phrase of Marx's postulate. Marx says that in analysing realisation foreign trade must not be taken into consideration,
since it only replaces one article by another. In analysing
the question of realisation (Chapter 1 of the second part of
Industrial Crises), Mr. Tugan-Baranovsky says, that a
country importing goods must export them, that is, must
have a foreign market. One may ask, can it be said after this
that Mr. Tugan-Baranovsky's "solution of the question" is
"not taken from Marx at all"? Mr. Tugan-Baranovsky says
further that "Volumes II and III of *Capital* constitute a far
from finished rough draft" and that "for this reason we do not
find in Volume III conclusions drawn from the splendid analysis given in Volume II" (op. cit., 123). This statement too
is inaccurate. In addition to individual analyses of social
reproduction (*Das Kapital*, III, 1, 289), [16] there is an explanation of how and to what extent the realisation of constant capital is "independent" of individual consumption
and "we find in Volume III" a special chapter (the 49th, "Concerning the Analysis of the Process of Production") devoted
to conclusions drawn from the splendid analysis given in
Volume II, a chapter in which the results of the analysis

---

* Interpolations in square brackets (within passages quoted by
Lenin) have been introduced by Lenin, unless otherwise indicated.—*Ed.*

are applied to the solution of the exceedingly important question of the forms of social revenue in capitalist society. Lastly, we must point out the equal inaccuracy of Mr. Tugan-Baranovsky's assertion that "Marx, in Volume III of *Capital* speaks in a quite different manner on the given question," and that in Volume III we "can even find statements that are decisively refuted by that analysis" (op. cit., 123). On page 122 of his article Mr. Tugan-Baranovsky quotes two such passages from Marx that allegedly contradict the basic doctrine. Let us examine them closely. In Volume III Marx says: "The conditions of direct exploitation, and those of realising it, are not identical. They diverge not only in place and time, but also logically. The first are only limited by the productive power of society, the latter by the proportional relation of the various branches of production and the consumer power of society.... The more productiveness develops, the more it finds itself at variance with the narrow basis on which the conditions of consumption rest" (III, 1, 226. Russian translation, p. 189)." Mr. Tugan-Baranovsky interprets these words as follows: "The mere proportional distribution of national production does not guarantee the possibility of marketing the products. The products may not find a market even if the distribution of production is proportional—this is apparently the meaning of the above-quoted words of Marx." No, not this is the meaning of those words. There are no grounds for seeing in them some sort of a *correction* to the theory of realisation expounded in Volume II. Marx is here merely substantiating that contradiction of capitalism which he indicated in other places in *Capital*, that is, the contradiction between the tendency toward the *unlimited* expansion of production and the inevitability of *limited* consumption (as a consequence of the proletarian condition of the mass of the people). Mr. Tugan-Baranovsky will, of course, not dispute the fact that this contradiction is *inherent* in capitalism; and since Marx points to this in the passage quoted, we have no right to look for some other meaning in his words. "The consumer power of society" and the "proportional relation of the various branches of production"—these are not conditions that are isolated, independent of, and unconnected with, each other. On the contrary, a definite condition of consumption is one of the elements of proportionality. In actual fact, the analysis of realisation showed that the formation of a home market for capitalism owes less to articles of consumption than to means of production. From this it follows that Department I of social production (the production of means of production) can and must develop more rapidly than Department II (the production of articles of consumption). Obviously, it does not follow from this that the production of means of production can develop *in complete independence* of the production of articles of consumption and *outside of all connection with it.* In respect of this, Marx says: "As we have seen [Book II, Part III], continuous circulation takes place between constant capital and constant capital.... It is at first independent of individual consumption because it never enters the latter. But this consumption definitely *(definitiv)* limits it nevertheless, since constant capital is never produced for its own sake but solely because more of it is needed in spheres of production whose products go into individual consumption" (III, 1, 289. Russian translation, 242).[18] In the final analysis, therefore, productive consumption (the consumption of means of production) is always bound up with individual consumption and is always dependent on it. Inherent in capitalism, on the one hand, is the tendency toward the limitless expansion of productive consumption, toward the limitless expansion of accumulation and production, and, on the other, the proletarisation of the masses of the people that sets quite narrow limits for the expansion of individual consumption. It is obvious that we have here a contradiction in capitalist production, and in the above-quoted passage Marx simply reaffirms this contradiction.*

---

* The other passage quoted by Mr. Tugan-Baranovsky has precisely the same meaning (III, 1, 231, cf. S. [*Seite*—German for page.— *Ed.*] 232 to the end of the paragraph),[19] as well as the following passage on crises: "The ultimate cause of all real crises always remains the poverty and limited consumption of the masses as opposed to the drive of capitalist production to develop the productive forces as though only the absolute consuming power of society constituted their limit" (*Das Kapital*, III, 2, 21. Russian translation, p. 395).[20] The following observation by Marx expresses the same idea: "Contradiction in the capitalist mode of production: the labourers as buyers of commodities are important for the market. But as sellers of their own commodity—

The analysis of realisation in Volume II does not in any way refute this contradiction (Mr. Tugan-Baranovsky's opinion notwithstanding); it shows, on the contrary, the connection between productive and personal consumption. It stands to reason that it would be a serious error to conclude from this contradiction of capitalism (or from its other contradictions) that capitalism is impossible or unprogressive as compared with former economic regimes (in the way our Narodniks like doing). Capitalism cannot develop except in a whole series of contradictions, and the indication of these contradictions merely explains to us the historically transitory nature of capitalism, explains the conditions and causes of its tendency to go forward to a higher form.

Summarising all that has been said above, we arrive at the following conclusion: the solution of the question of the role of the foreign market as expounded by Mr. Tugan-Baranovsky was taken precisely from Marx; there is no contradiction whatsoever on the question of realisation (or on the theory of markets) between Volumes II and III of *Capital*.

Let us proceed. Mr. Bulgakov accuses Mr. Tugan-Baranovsky of an incorrect assessment of the market theories of pre-Marxian economists. Mr. Tugan-Baranovsky accuses Mr. Bulgakov of uprooting Marx's ideas from the scientific soil in which they grew and of picturing matters as though "Marx's views had no connection with those of his predecessors." This last reproach is absolutely groundless, for Mr. Bulgakov not only did not express such an absurd opinion but, on the contrary, cited the views of representatives of various pre-Marxian schools. In our opinion, both Mr. Bulgakov and Mr. Tugan-Baranovsky, in outlining the history of the question, were wrong in paying too little attention to Adam Smith, who absolutely should have been treated in the greatest detail in a *special* exposition of the "market

---

labour-power—capitalist society tends to keep them down to the minimum price" (*Das Kapital*, II, 303). [21] We have already spoken of Mr. N.—on's incorrect interpretation of this passage in *Novoye Slovo*, [22] 1897, May. (See present edition, Vol. 2, *A Characterisation of Economic Romanticism*, pp. 168-69.—*Ed.*) There is no contradiction whatsoever between all these passages and the analysis of realisation in Section III of Volume II.

theory"; "absolutely" because it was precisely Adam Smith who was the founder of that fallacious doctrine of the division of the social product into variable capital and surplus-value (wages, profit and rent, in Adam Smith's terminology), which persisted until Marx and which, not only prevented the solution of the question of realisation, but did not even pose it correctly. Mr. Bulgakov says in all justice that "with incorrect premises and a false formulation of the problem itself, these disputes [on the market theory, that arose in economic literature] could only lead to empty, scholastic discussions" (op. cit., p. 21, note). The author, incidentally, devoted only one page to Adam Smith, omitting the brilliant, detailed analysis of Adam Smith's theory given by Marx in the 19th chapter of Volume II of *Capital* (§ II, *S*. 353-83),[22] and instead dwelt on the theories of the secondary and unoriginal theoreticians, J. S. Mill and von Kirchmann. As far as Mr. Tugan-Baranovsky is concerned, he *ignored Adam Smith altogether* and, as a result, in his outline of the views of later economists *omitted their fundamental error* (that of repeating Adam Smith's above-mentioned error). It goes without saying that under these circumstances the exposition could not be satisfactory. We shall confine ourselves to two examples. Having outlined his Scheme No. 1 that explains simple reproduction, Mr. Tugan-Baranovsky says: "But the case of simple reproduction assumed by us does not, of course, give rise to any doubts; the capitalists, according to our assumption, consume all their profits, so it is obvious that the supply of commodities will not exceed the demand" (*Industrial Crises*, p. 409). This is wrong. It was not at all "obvious" to former economists, for they could not explain even the simple reproduction of social capital, and, indeed, it cannot be explained unless it is understood that the value of the social product is divided into *constant capital*+variable capital+surplus-value, and in its material form into two great departments—means of production and articles of consumption. For this reason even this case gave Adam Smith cause for "doubts," in which, as Marx showed, he got tangled up. If the later economists repeated Smith's *error* without sharing his *doubts*, this only shows that they had taken a step backwards in theory as far as the present question is concerned. It is likewise incorrect for Mr. Tugan-Baranovsky to state: "The Say-Ricardo doctrine is correct theoretically; if its opponents had taken the trouble to make numerical computations of the way commodities are distributed in capitalist economy, they would easily have understood that their refutation of this theory contains a logical contradiction" (*loc. cit.*, 427). No. The Say-Ricardo doctrine is incorrect theoretically—Ricardo repeated Smith's error (see his *Works*, translated by Sieber, St. Petersburg, 1882, p. 221), and Say put the finishing touches to it by maintaining that the difference between the gross and the net product of society is fully subjective. And however hard Say-Ricardo and their opponents had applied themselves to "numerical computations," they would never have reached a solution, because this is not merely a matter of figures, as Bulgakov has rightly remarked in respect of another passage in Mr. Tugan-Baranovsky's book (Bulgakov, *loc. cit.*, p. 21, note).

We now come to another subject for dispute between Messrs. Bulgakov and Tugan-Baranovsky—the question of numerical schemes and their significance. Mr. Bulgakov maintains that Mr. Tugan-Baranovsky's Schemes, "owing to their departure from the model [i.e., from Marx's Scheme], to a great extent lose their power of conviction and do not explain the process of social reproduction" (*loc. cit.*, 248); and Mr. Tugan-Baranovsky says that "Mr. Bulgakov does not properly understand what such schemes are intended for" (*Mir Bozhy*, No. 6 for 1898, p. 125). In our opinion the truth in this case is entirely on Mr. Bulgakov's side. It is more likely that Mr. Tugan-Baranovsky "does not properly understand what the schemes are intended for" when he assumes that they "prove the deduction" (*ibid.*). Schemes alone cannot prove anything: they can only *illustrate* a process, *if its separate elements have been theoretically explained.* Mr. Tugan-Baranovsky compiled his own Schemes which differed from Marx's (and which were incomparably less clear than Marx's), at the same time omitting a theoretical explanation of those elements of the process that they were supposed to illustrate. The basic postulate of Marx's theory, that the social product does not consist of only variable capital+surplus-value (as Adam Smith, Ricardo, Proudhon, Rodbertus, and others thought), but of constant capital + the above two parts—this postulate is not explained at all by Mr. Tugan-Baranovsky, although he adopted it in his Schemes. The reader of Mr. Tugan-Baranovsky's book is *unable to understand* this basic thesis of the new theory. Mr. Tugan-Baranovsky did not in any way show why it is essential to divide social production into two departments (I: means of production and II: articles of consumption), although, as Mr. Bulgakov justly remarked, "in this one division there is greater theoretical meaning than in all former arguments about the market theory" (*loc. cit.*, p. 27). This is why Mr. Bulgakov's exposition of the Marxian theory is much clearer and more correct than Mr. Tugan-Baranovsky's.

In conclusion, examining Mr. Bulgakov's book in greater detail, we must note the following. About a third of the book is devoted to questions of the "differences in the turnover of capital" and of the "wages fund." The sections under these headings seem to us to be the least successful. In the first of these the author tries to add to Marx's analysis (see p. 63, note) and delves into very intricate computations and schemata to illustrate how the process of realisation takes place with differences in the turnover of capital. It seems to us that Mr. Bulgakov's final conclusion (that, in order to explain realisation with differences in the turnover of capital, it is necessary to assume that the capitalists in both departments have reserves, cf. p. 85) follows naturally from the general laws of the production and circulation of capital, so that there was no need to assume different cases of relations of the turnover of capital in Departments I and II and to draw up a whole series of diagrams. The same must be said of the second of the abovementioned sections. Mr. Bulgakov correctly points out Mr. Herzenstein's error in asserting that he had found a contradiction in Marx's theory on this question. The author rightly says that "if the turnover period of all individual capitals is made to equal one year, at the beginning of the given year the capitalists will be the owners both of the entire product of the preceding year and of a sum of money equal to its value" (pp. 142-43). But Mr. Bulgakov was entirely wrong to take (p. 92, et seq.) the purely scholastic presentation of the problem by earlier economists (whether wages are derived

from current production or from the production of the preceding working period); he created additional difficulties
for himself in "dismissing" the statement by Marx, who
"seems to contradict his basic point of view," "arguing as
though" "wages are not derived from capital but from current production" (p. 135). But Marx did not pose the question
in this way at all. Mr. Bulgakov found it necessary to "dis-
miss" Marx's statement because he tried to apply to Marx's
theory a completely alien formulation of the question. Once
it has been established how the entire process of social production takes place in connection with the consumption of
the product by different classes of society, how the capitalists contribute the money necessary for the circulation of
the product—once all this has been explained, the question
of whether wages are derived from current or preceding production loses all serious significance. Engels, publisher of
the last volumes of *Capital*, therefore, said in the preface to
Volume II that arguments like that of Rodbertus, for example, as to "whether wages are derived from capital or income,
belong to the domain of scholasticism and are definitely set-
tled in Part III of the second book of *Capital*" (*Das Kapital*,
II, *Vorwort*, *S.* xxi). [24]

Written at the end of 1898
Published in January 1899
in the magazine *Nauchnoye
    Obozreniye*, [25] No. 1
Signed: *Vladimir Ilyin*

Published according to the
text in the magazine

REVIEW

Parvus. *The World Market and the Agricultural Crisis.*
Economic essays. Translated from the German by L. Y. St. Pe-
tersburg, 1898. Publ. O. N. Popova (Educational Library, Series 2,
No. 2). 142 pp. Price 40 kopeks.

This book, by the gifted German journalist who writes
under the pseudonym of Parvus, consists of a number of essays describing some of the phenomena of modern world
economy, with the greatest attention paid to Germany. Parvus' central theme is the development of the world market
and he describes mainly the recent stages of this development
in the period of the decline of England's industrial hegem-
ony. Of the greatest interest are his remarks on the role
being played by the old industrial countries that serve as
a market for the younger capitalist countries: England, for
example, swallows up an ever-growing amount of German
manufactured goods and at the present time takes from one-
fifth to a quarter of the total German export. Parvus employs
the data of commercial and industrial statistics to describe
the peculiar division of labour between the various capitalist countries, some of whom produce mainly for the colonial
market and others for the European market. In the chapter
headed "Towns and Railways" the author makes an extremely interesting attempt to describe the most important
"forms of capitalist towns" and their significance in the general system of capitalist economy. The remaining and greater part of the book (pp. 33-142) is devoted to questions
concerning the contradictions in present-day capitalist
agriculture and the agrarian crisis. Parvus first explains
the influence of industrial development on grain prices, on
ground rent, etc. He then outlines the theory of ground rent
developed by Marx in Volume III of *Capital* and explains

the basic cause of capitalist agrarian crises from the standpoint of this theory. Parvus adds data on Germany to the
purely theoretical analysis of this question and comes to
the conclusion that "the last and basic cause of the agrarian
crisis is increased ground rent due exclusively to capitalist
development and the consequent increased price of land."
"Eliminate these prices," says Parvus, "and European
agriculture will again be able to compete with the Russian
and American." "Its [private property's] only weapon against
the agrarian crisis is, with the exception of fortuitous favourable combinations on the world market, the auctioning of
all capitalist landed properties" (141). The conclusion drawn
by Parvus, therefore, coincides, by and large, with Engels'
opinion; in Volume III of *Capital* Engels pointed to the fact
that the present-day agricultural crisis makes the ground
rents formerly obtained by European landowners impossble.[26] We strongly recommend to all readers who are interested
in the questions mentioned above to acquaint themselves
with Parvus' book. It is an excellent reply to the current
Narodnik arguments on the present agricultural crisis which
are constantly to be met with in the Narodnik press and which
suffer from a most essential shortcoming: the fact of the crisis is examined in disconnection from the general development of world capitalism; it is examined, not from the standpoint of definite social classes, but solely for the purpose of
deducing the petty-bourgeois moral on the viability of small
peasant farming.

The translation of Parvus' book, can, on the whole, be
considered satisfactory, although in places awkward and
heavy turns of speech are to be met with.

Written in February 1899   Published according to
                                           the text in the magazine
Published in March 1899
in the magazine *Nachalo*, [27] No. 3
     Signed: *Vl. Ilyin*

own arguments are frequently too sweeping and general. This must be said, in particular, of the chapter on handicraft industries. The style of the book suffers, at times, from mannerisms and haziness.

Written in February 1899

Published in March 1899
in the magazine *Nachalo*, No. 3
Signed: *Vl. Ilyin*

Published according to
the text in the magazine

REVIEW

Commercial and Industrial Russia. Handbook for Merchants and Factory Owners. Compiled under the editorship of A. A. Blau, Head of the Statistical Division of the Department of Commerce and Manufactures. St. Petersburg, 1899. Price 10 rubles.

The publishers of this gigantic tome set themselves the aim of "filling a gap in our economic literature" (p. i), that is, to give at one and the same time the addresses of commercial and industrial establishments throughout Russia and information on the "condition of the various branches of industry." No objection could be made to such a combination of reference and scientific-statistical material, were both the one and the other sufficiently complete. In the book named above, unfortunately, the directory completely overwhelms the statistical material, the latter being incomplete and insufficiently analysed. First of all, this publication compares unfavourably with previous publications of the same nature, since it does not give statistical data for *each individual* establishment or enterprise included in its lists. As a result, the lists of establishments and enterprises, occupying 2,703 huge columns of small print, lose all their scientific significance. In view of the chaotic state of our commercial and industrial statistics it is extremely important to have data precisely on each individual establishment or enterprise, since our official statistical institutions never make anything like a tolerable analysis of these data but confine themselves to announcing totals in which relatively reliable material is mixed up with absolutely unreliable material. We shall now show that this last remark applies equally to the book under review; but first let us mention the following original method employed by the compilers. Printing the addresses of establishments and enterprises in each branch of production, they gave the number of establishments and the sum of their turnover for the whole of Russia only; they calculated the average turnover for one establishment in each branch and indicated with a special symbol those having a turnover greater or less than the average. It would have been much more to the purpose (if it was impossible to print information on each individual establishment) to fix a number of categories of establishments and enterprises that are similar for each branch of commerce and industry (according to the amount of turnover, the number of workers, the nature of the motive power, etc.) and to distribute all establishments according to these categories. It would then at least have been possible to judge the completeness and comparability of the material for different gubernias and different branches of production. As far as factory statistics, for example, are concerned, it is enough to read the phenomenally vague definition of this concept on page 1 (footnote) of the publication under review and then glance over the lists of factory owners in some branches to become convinced of the heterogeneity of the statistical material published in the book. It is, therefore, necessary to exercise great caution in dealing with the summarised factory statistics in Section I, Part I of *Commercial and Industrial Russia* (Historical-Statistical Survey of Russian Industry and Trade). We read here that in 1896 (partly also in 1895) there were, throughout the Russian Empire, 38,401 factories with an aggregate output of 2,745 million rubles, employing 1,742,181 workers; these data include excise-paying and non-excise-paying industries and mining and metallurgical enterprises. We are of the opinion that this figure cannot, without substantial verification, be compared with the figures of our factory statistics for previous years. In 1896 a number of branches of production were registered that formerly (until 1894-95) had not come under the heading of "factories": bakeries, fisheries, abattoirs, print-shops, lithograph shops, etc., etc. The value of the total output of all mining and metallurgical establishments in the Empire was fixed at 614 million rubles by original methods about which we are told only that the value of pig-iron is, apparently, repeated in the value of iron and steel. The total number of workers in the mining and metallurgical industries is, on the contrary, apparently underestimated: the figure for 1895-96 was given as 505,000. Either this is an error or many branches have been omitted. From the figures scattered throughout the book it can be seen that for only a few branches in this department the number of workers is 474,000, not including those engaged in coal-mining (about 53,000), salt-mining (about 20,000), stone-quarrying (about 10,000), and in other mining industries (about 20,000). There were more than 505,000 workers in all the mining and metallurgical industries of the Empire in 1890, and precisely these branches of production have developed particularly since that time. For example: in five branches of this division for which historical-statistical data are given in the text of the book (iron founding, wire drawing, machine building, gold- and copper-ware manufacturing) there were, in 1890, 908 establishments, with a total output valued at 77 million rubles and employing 69,000 workers, while in 1896 the figures were—1,444 establishments, with a total output valued at 221.5 million rubles, employing 147,000 workers. By assembling the historical-statistical data scattered throughout the book, which, unfortunately, do not cover all branches of production but only a certain number (cotton processing, chemical production, and more than 45 other branches), we can obtain the following information for the Empire as a whole. In 1890 there were 19,639 factories, with a total output valued at 929 million rubles, employing 721,000 workers, and in 1896 there were 19,162 factories, with a total output valued at 1,708 million rubles, employing 985,000 workers. If we add two branches subject to excise—beet-sugar and distilling— (1890-91—116,000 workers and 1895-96—123,000 workers), we get the number of workers as 837,000 and 1,108,000 respectively, *an increase of nearly one-third in a period of six years.* Note that the decrease in the number of factories is due to the differences in the registration of flour-mills: in 1890, among the factories, 7,003 mills were included (156 million rubles, 29,638 workers), while in 1896 only 4,379 mills (272 million rubles, 37,954 workers) were included.

Such are the data that can be extracted from the publication under review and which allow us to get some conception of the industrial boom in Russia in the nineties. It will be possible to deal with this question in greater detail when the full statistical data for 1896 have been published.

Written in February 1899

Published in March 1899
In the magazine *Nachalo*, No. 3
Signed: *Vl. Ilyin*

Published according to the
text in the magazine

ONCE MORE ON THE THEORY OF REALISATION

My "Note on the Question of the Market Theory (Concerning the Polemic of Messrs. Tugan-Baranovsky and Bulgakov)" was published in the number of *Nauchnoye Obozreniye* for January of the present year (1899) and was followed by P. B. Struve's article, "Markets under Capitalist Production (Apropos of Bulgakov's Book and Ilyin's Article)." Struve "rejects, to a considerable extent, the theory proposed by Tugan-Baranovsky, Bulgakov, and Ilyin" (p. 63 of his article) and expounds his own conception of Marx's theory of realisation.

In my opinion, Struve's polemic against the above-mentioned writers is due not so much to an essential difference of views as to his mistaken conception of the content of the theory he defends. In the first place, Struve confuses the market theory of bourgeois economists who taught that products are exchanged for products and that production, therefore, should correspond to consumption, with Marx's theory of realisation which showed by analysis *how* the reproduction and circulation of the aggregate social capital, i.e., the realisation of the product in capitalist society, takes place.* Neither Marx nor those writers who have expounded his theory and with whom Struve has entered into a polemic deduced the harmony of production and consumption from this analysis, but, on the contrary, stressed forcefully the contradictions that are inherent in capitalism and that are bound to make their appearance in the course of capitalist

---

* See my *Studies*, p. 17, et al. (See present edition, Vol. 2, *A Characterisation of Economic Romanticism*, p. 151, et al.—*Ed.*)

realisation.* Secondly, Struve confuses the abstract theory of realisation (with which his opponents dealt exclusively) with concrete historical conditions governing the realisation of the capitalist product in some one country and some one epoch. This is just the same as confusing the abstract theory of ground rent with the concrete conditions of the development of capitalism in agriculture in some one country. These two basic delusions of Struve engendered a whole series of misunderstandings which can only be cleared up by an analysis of the individual propositions of his article.

1. Struve does not agree with me when I say that in expounding the theory of realisation we must give Adam Smith special emphasis. "If it is a matter of going back to Adam," he writes, "then we should not stop at Smith but at the physiocrats."³² But this is not so. It was precisely Adam Smith who did not confine himself to admitting the truth (known also to the physiocrats) that products are exchanged for products but raised the question of how the different component parts of social *capital* and the product are replaced (realised) according to their value.** For this reason Marx, who fully recognised that in the theory of the physiocrats, i.e., in Quesnay's *Tableau économique*, some postulates were, "for their time, brilliant"***; who recognised that in the analysis of the process of reproduction Adam Smith had, in some respects, taken a step backwards as compared with the physiocrats (*Das Kapital*, I², 612, *Anm.* 32³⁴), nevertheless devoted only about a page and a half to the physiocrats in his review of the history of the question of realisation (*Das Kapital*, II¹, *S.* 350-51³⁵), whereas he devoted

---

* *Ibid.*, pp. 20, 27, 24, et al. (See present edition, Vol. 2, pp. 155, 163-64, 160-61.—*Ed.*)

** Incidentally, in my article in *Nauchnoye Obozreniye* the term "stoimost" (value) was everywhere changed to "tsennost." This was not my doing, but the editor's. I do not regard the use of any one term as being of particularly great importance, but I deem it necessary to state that I used and always use the word "stoimost."

*** Frederick Engels, *Herrn E. Dühring's Umwälzung der Wissenschaft, Dritte Auflage* (Frederick Engels, *Herr Eugen Dühring's Revolution in Science [Anti-Dühring]*, third ed.—*Ed.*), p. 270, ³³ from the chapter written by Marx.

over thirty pages to Adam Smith (*ibid.*, 351-83") and
analysed in detail Smith's basic error which was inherited
by the entire subsequent political economy. It is, therefore,
necessary to pay greater attention to Adam Smith in order
to explain the bourgeois economists' theory of realisation,
since they all repeated Smith's mistake.

2. Mr. Bulgakov quite correctly says in his book that
bourgeois economists confuse simple commodity circulation with capitalist commodity circulation, whereas Marx
established the difference between them. Struve believes
that Mr. Bulgakov's assertion is based on a misunderstanding. In my opinion it is just the opposite, the misunderstanding is not Mr. Bulgakov's but Struve's. And how, indeed, has Struve refuted Mr. Bulgakov? In a manner most
strange: he refutes his postulate by repeating it. Struve says:
Marx cannot be regarded as a champion of that theory
of realisation according to which the product can be realised inside the given community, because Marx "made a sharp
distinction between simple commodity circulation and
capitalist circulation" (!! p. 48). But that is precisely what Mr.
Bulgakov said! This is precisely why Marx's Theory is not
confined to a repetition of the axiom that products are exchanged for products. That is why Mr. Bulgakov is correct in
regarding the disputes between bourgeois and petty-bourgeois economists on the possibility of over-production to be
"empty and scholastic discussions": the two disputants
confused commodity and capitalist circulation; both of
them repeated Adam Smith's error.

3. Struve is wrong in giving the theory of realisation
the name of the theory of proportional distribution. It is
inaccurate and must inevitably lead to misunderstandings.
The theory of realisation is an abstract* theory that shows
how the reproduction and circulation of the aggregate social capital takes place. The essential premises of this
abstract theory are, firstly, the exclusion of foreign trade,
of the foreign markets. But, by excluding foreign trade, the
theory of realisation does not, by any means, postulate
that a capitalist society has ever existed or could ever

---

* See my article in *Nauchnoye Obozreniye*, p. 37. (See p. 55 of this
volume.—*Ed.*)

exist without foreign trade.* Secondly, the abstract theory of realisation assumes and must assume the proportional distribution of the product between the various branches of capitalist production. But, in assuming this, the theory of realisation does not, by any means, assert that in a capitalist society products are always distributed or could be distributed proportionally.** Mr. Bulgakov rightly compares the theory of realisation with the theory of value. The theory of value presupposes and must presuppose the equality of supply and demand, but it does not by any means assert that this equality is always observed or could be observed in capitalist society. The law of realisation, like every other law of capitalism, is "implemented only by not being implemented" (Bulgakov, quoted in Struve's article, p. 56). The theory of the average and equal rate of profit assumes, in essence, the same proportional distribution of production between its various branches. But surely Struve will not call it a theory of proportional distribution on these grounds.

4. Struve challenges my opinion that Marx justly accused Ricardo of repeating Adam Smith's error. "Marx was wrong," writes Struve. Marx, however, quotes directly a passage from Ricardo's work (II^1, 383).[37] Struve ignores this passage. On the next page Marx quotes the opinion of

---

* *Ibid.*, p. 38. (See p. 56 of this volum.—*Ed.*) Cf. *Studies*, p. 25 (see present edition, Vol. 2, p. 162.—*Ed.*): "Do we deny that capitalism needs a foreign market? Of course not. But the question of a foreign market has absolutely nothing to do with the question of realisation."

** "Not only the products ... which replace surplus-value, but also those which replace variable ... and constant capital ... all these products are realised in the same way, in the midst of 'difficulties,' in the midst of continuous fluctuatiens, which become increasingly violent as capitalism grows" [*Studies*, p. 27 (see present edition, Vol. 2, p. 164.—*Ed.*)]. Perhaps Struve will say that this passage is contradicted by other passages, e. g., that on p. 31 (see present edition, Vol. 2, p. 164.—*Ed.*): "... the capitalists *can* realise surplus-value"? This is only a seeming contradiction. Since we take an abstract theory of realisation (and the Narodniks put forward precisely an abstract theory of the impossibility of realising surplus-value), the deduction that realisation is possible becomes inevitable. But while expounding the abstract theory, it is necessary to indicate the contradictions that are inherent in the actual process of realisation. This was done in my article.

Ramsay, who had also noted Ricardo's error. I also indicated another passage from Ricardo's work where he says forthrightly: "The whole produce of the land and labour of every country is divided into three portions: of these, one portion is devoted to wages, another to profits, and the other to rent" (here constant capital is erroneously omitted. See Ricardo's *Works*, translated by Sieber, p. 221). Struve also passes over this passage in silence. He quotes only one of Ricardo's comments which points out the absurdity of Say's argument on the difference between gross and net revenue. In Chapter 49, Volume III of *Capital*, where deductions from the theory of realisation are expounded, Marx quotes precisely this comment of Ricardo, saying the following about it: "By the way, we shall see later"—apparently, this refers to the still unpublished Volume IV of *Capital*[38]—"that Ricardo nowhere refuted Smith's false analysis of commodity-price, its reduction to the sum of the values of the revenues (*Revenuen*). He does not bother with it, and accepts its correctness so far in his analysis that he 'abstracts' from the constant portion of the value of commodities. He also falls back into the same way of looking at things from time to time" (i.e., into Smith's way of looking at things. *Das Kapital*, III, 2, 377. Russian translation, 696). [39] We shall leave the reader to judge who is right: Marx, who says that Ricardo repeats Smith's error,* or Struve, who says that Ricardo "knew perfectly well [?] that the whole social product is not exhausted by wages, profit, and rent," and that Ricardo "unconsciously [!] wandered away from the parts of the social product that constitute production costs." Is it possible to know *perfectly well* and at the same time *unconsciously* wander away?

5. Struve not only did not refute Marx's statement that Ricardo had adopted Smith's error, but repeated that very error in his own article. "It is strange ... to think,"

---

* The correctness of Marx's assessment is also seen with particular clarity from the fact that Ricardo shared Smith's fallacious views on the accumulation of an individual capital. Ricardo thought that the accumulated part of the surplus-value is expended entirely on wages, whereas it is expended as: 1) constant capital and 2) wages. See *Das Kapital*, I[2], 611-13, Chapter 22, § 2.[40] Cf. *Studies*, p. 29, footnote. (See present edition, Vol. 2, p. 167.—*Ed.*)

he writes, "that any one division of the social product into categories could have substantial importance for the general comprehension of realisation, especially since all portions of the product that is being realised actually take on the form of revenue (gross) in the process of realisation and the classics regarded them as revenues" (p. 48). That is precisely the point—*not* all the portions of the product in realisation take on the form of revenue (gross); it was precisely this mistake of Smith that Marx explained when he showed that a part of the product being realised does not and cannot ever take on the form of revenue. That is the part of the social product which replaces the constant capital that serves for the production of means of production (the constant capital in Department I, to use Marx's terminology). Seed grain in agriculture, for instance, never takes on the form of revenue; coal used for the extraction of more coal never takes on the form of revenue, etc., etc. The process of the reproduction and circulation of the aggregate social capital cannot be understood unless that part of the gross product which can serve only as capital, the part that can never take on the form of revenue, is separated from it.* In a developing capitalist society this part of the social product must necessarily grow more rapidly than all the other parts of the product. Only this law will explain one of the most profound contradictions of capitalism: the growth of the national wealth proceeds with tremendous rapidity, while the growth of national consumption proceeds (if at all) very slowly.

6. Struve "cannot at all understand" why Marx's differentiation between constant and variable capital "is essential to the theory of realisation" and why I "particularly insist" on it.

Struve's lack of comprehension is, on the one hand, the result of a simple misunderstanding. In the first place, Struve himself admits one point of merit in this differentiation—that it includes not only revenues, but the whole product. Another point of merit is that it links up the analysis of the process of realisation logically with the

---

* Cf. *Das Kapital*, III, 2, 375-76 (Russian translation, 696),[41] on distinguishing the gross product from gross revenue.

analysis of the process of production of an individual capital. What is the aim of the theory of realisation? It is
to show *how* the reproduction and circulation of the aggregate social capital takes place. Is it not obvious from the
first glance that the role of variable capital must be radically different from that of constant capital? Products that
replace variable capital must be exchanged, in the final
analysis, for *articles of consumption* for the workers and
meet their usual requirements. The products that replace
constant capital must, in the final analysis, be exchanged
for *means of production* and must be employed as capital
for fresh production. For this reason the differentiation between constant and variable capital is absolutely essential
for the theory of realisation. Secondly, Struve's misunderstanding is due to his having, here also, arbitrarily and erroneously understood the theory of realisation as showing that
the products are distributed proportionally (see, especially,
pp. 50-51). We have said above and say again that such a
conception of the content of the theory of realisation is fallacious.

Struve's failure to understand is, on the other hand, due
to the fact that he deems it necessary to make a distinction
between "sociological" and "economic" categories in Marx's
theory and makes a number of general remarks against that
theory. I must say, first, that none of this has anything whatsoever to do with the theory of realisation, and, secondly,
that I consider Struve's distinction to be vague and that I
see no real use for it. Thirdly, that I consider not only debat-
able, but even directly incorrect, Struve's assertions that
"it is indisputable that the relation of the sociological principles" of his theory to the analysis of market phenomena
"was not clear to Marx himself," that "the theory of value,
as expounded in Volumes I and III of *Capital*, undoubtedly
suffers from contradiction."* All these statements of Struve

---

* In opposition to this last statement of Struve let me quote the
latest exposition of the theory of value made by K. Kautsky, who
states and proves that the law of the average rate of profit "does not
abolish the law of value but merely modifies it" (*Die Agrarfrage, S.*
67-68). (*The Agrarian Question*, pp. 67-68.—*Ed.*) We would point
out, incidentally, the following interesting statement made by Kautsky
in the introduction to his excellent book: "If I have succeeded in developing new and fruitful ideas in this work I am grateful, first and

are mere empty words. They are not arguments but decrees. They are the anticipated results of the criticism of Marx which the Neo-Kantians[42] intend to undertake.* If we live long enough we shall see what the criticism brings. In the meantime we assert that this criticism has provided nothing on the theory of realisation.

---

foremost, to my two great teachers for this; I stress this the more readily since there have been, for some time, voices heard even in our circles that declare the viewpoint of Marx and Engels to be obsolete.... In my opinion this scepticism depends more on the personal peculiarities of the sceptics than on the qualities of the disputed theory. I draw this conclusion, not only from the results obtained by analysing the sceptics' objections, but also on the basis of my own personal experience. At the beginning of my ... activities I did not sympathise with Marxism at all. I approached it quite as critically and with as much mistrust as any of those who now look down with an air of superiority on my dogmatic fanaticism. I became a Marxist only after a certain amount of resistance. But then, and later, whenever I had doubts regarding any question of principle, I always came to the ultimate conclusion that it was I who was wrong and not my teachers. A more profound study of the subject compelled me to admit the correctness of their viewpoint. Every new study of the subject, therefore, every attempt to re-examine my views served to strengthen my conviction, to strengthen in me my recognition of the theory, the dissemination and application of which I have made the aim of my life."

* Incidentally, a few words about this (future) "criticism," on which Struve is so keen. Of course, no right-minded person will, in general, object to criticism. But Struve, apparently, is repeating his favourite idea of fructifying Marxism with "critical philosophy." It goes without saying that I have neither the desire nor the opportunity to deal here at length with the philosophical content of Marxism and therefore confine myself to the following remark. Those disciples of Marx who call,"Back to Kant," have so far produced exactly nothing to show the necessity for such a turn or to show convincingly that Marx's theory gains anything from its impregnation with Neo-Kantianism. They have not even fulfilled the obligation that should be a priority with them—to analyse in detail and refute the negative criticism of Neo-Kantianism made by Engels. On the contrary, those disciples who have gone back to pre-Marxian materialist philosophy and not to Kant, on the one hand, and to dialectical idealism, on the other, have produced a well-ordered and valuable exposition of dialectical materialism, have shown that it constitutes a legitimate and inevitable product of the entire latest development of philosophy and social science. It is enough for me to cite the well-known work by Mr. Beltov in Russian literature and *Beiträge zur Geschichte des Materialismus* (Stuttgart, 1896)[43] [*Essays on the History of Materialism* (Stuttgart, 1896).—*Ed.*] in German literature.

7. On the question of the significance of Marx's Schemes in the third section of *Capital* II, Struve maintains that the abstract theory of realisation can be well explained by the most varied methods of dividing the social product. This amazing assertion is to be fully explained by Struve's basic misunderstanding—that the theory of realisation "is completely exhausted" (??!) by the banality that products are exchanged for products. Only this misunderstanding could have led Struve to write such a sentence: "The role played by these masses of commodities [those being realised] in production, distribution, etc., whether they represent capital (*sic!!*) and what sort of capital, constant or variable, is of absolutely no significance to the essence of the theory under discussion" (51). It is of no significance to Marx's theory of realisation, a theory that consists in the analysis of the reproduction and circulation of the aggregate social *capital*, whether or not commodities constitute capital!! This amounts to saying that as far as the essence of the theory of ground rent is concerned, there is no significance in whether or not the rural population is divided into landowners, capitalists, and labourers, since the theory is reduced, as it were, to an indication of the differing fertility of the different plots of land.

Only because of the same misunderstanding could Struve have asserted that the "natural relations between the elements of social consumption—social *metabolism*—can best be shown," not by the Marxian division of the product, but by the following division: means of production+articles of consumption+surplus-value (p. 50).

What is this social metabolism? Primarily it is the exchange of means of production for articles of consumption. How can this exchange be shown if surplus-value is especially *separated from* means of production and *from* articles of consumption? After all, surplus-value is embodied either in means of production or in articles of consumption! Is it not obvious that such a division, which is logically groundless (in that it confuses division according to the natural form of the product with division by elements of value), *obscures* the process of social metabolism?*

---

* Let us remind the reader that Marx divides the aggregate social product into two departments according to the natural form of the

8. Struve says that I ascribed to Marx the bourgeois-apologetic theory of Say-Ricardo (52), the theory of harmony between production and consumption (51), a theory that is in howling contradiction to Marx's theory of the evolution and eventual disappearance of capitalism (51-52); that, therefore, my "perfectly correct argument" that Marx, in both the second and third volumes, stressed the contradiction, inherent in capitalism, between the unlimited expansion of production and the limited consumption on the part of the masses of the people, "jettisons that theory of realisation ... whose defender" I am "in other cases."

This statement of Struve is likewise untrue and derives likewise from the above-mentioned misunderstanding to which he has become subject.

Whence comes Struve's assumption that I do not understand the theory of realisation as an analysis of the process of reproduction and circulation of the aggregate social capital, but as a theory which says only that products are exchanged for products, a theory which preaches the harmony of production and consumption? Struve could not have shown by an analysis of my articles that I understand the theory of realisation in the second way, for I have stated definitely and directly, that I understand it in the first way. In the article, "A Characterisation of Economic Romanticism," in the section devoted to an explanation of Smith's and Sismondi's error, I say: "The whole question is *how* realisation takes place—*that is*, the replacement of all parts of the social product. Hence, the point of departure in discussing social capital and revenue—or, what is the same thing, the realisation of the product in capitalist society—must be the distinction between ... *means of production* and *articles of consumption*" (*Studies*, 17).* "The problem of realisation consists in analysing the *replacement* of all parts of the social product in terms of value and in terms of material form" (*ibid.*, 26).** Is not Struve repeating this when he

---

product: I—means of production and II—articles of consumption. In each of these departments the product is divided into three parts according to elements of value: 1) constant capital, 2) variable capital, and 3) surplus-value.

   * See present edition, Vol. 2, p. 152.—*Ed.*
  ** *Ibid.*, p. 162.—*Ed.*

says—supposedly against me—that the theory which interests us "shows the mechanism of realisation ... insofar as that realisation is effected" (*Nauchnoye Obozreniye*, 62)? Am I contradicting *that* theory of realisation which I defend when I say that realisation is effected "in the midst of difficulties, in the midst of continuous fluctuations, which become increasingly violent as capitalism grows, in the midst of fierce competition, etc."? (*Studies*, 27)*; when I say that the Narodnik theory "not only reveals a failure to understand this realisation, but, in addition, reveals *an extremely superficial understanding of the contradictions inherent in this realisation*" (26-27)**; when I say that the realisation of the product, effected not so much on account of articles of consumption as on account of means of production, "is, of course, a contradiction, but the sort of contradiction that exists in reality, that springs from the very nature of capitalism" (24),*** a contradiction that "fully corresponds to the historical mission of capitalism and to its specific social structure: the former" (the mission) "is to develop the productive forces of society (production for production); the latter" (the social structure of capitalism) "precludes their utilisation by the mass of the population" (20)****?

9. Apparently there are no differences of opinion between Struve and me on the question of the relations between production and consumption in capitalist society. But if Struve says that Marx's postulate (which asserts that consumption is not the aim of capitalist production) "bears the obvious stamp of the polemical nature of Marx's whole system in general," that "it is tendentious" (53), then I most decidedly challenge the appropriateness and justification of such expressions. It is a fact that consumption is not the aim of capitalist production. The contradiction between this fact and the fact that, in the final analysis, production is bound up with consumption, that it is also dependent on consumption in capitalist society—this contradiction does not spring from a doctrine but from reality. Marx's theory of realisation

---

* See present edition, Vol. 2, p. 164.—*Ed.*
** *Ibid.*, p. 163.—*Ed.*
*** *Ibid.*, p. 160.—*Ed.*
**** *Ibid.*, p. 156.—*Ed.*

has, incidentally, tremendous scientific value, precisely
because it shows how this contradiction occurs, and because
it puts this contradiction in the foreground. "Marx's system"
is of a "polemical nature," not because it is "tendentious,"*
but because it provides an exact picture, in theory, of all
the contradictions that are present in reality. For this
reason, incidentally, all attempts to master "Marx's system"
without mastering its "polemical nature" are and will continue
to be unsuccessful: the "polemical nature" of the system is
nothing more than a true reflection of the "polemical nature"
of capitalism itself.

10. "What is the real significance of the theory of realisation?" asks Mr. Struve and answers by quoting the opinion
of Mr. Bulgakov, who says that the possible expansion of
capitalist production is actually effected even if only by a
series of crises. "Capitalist production is increasing throughout the world," says Mr. Bulgakov. "This argument," objects
Struve, "is quite groundless. The fact is that the real 'expansion of capitalist production' is not by any means effected in
that ideal and isolated capitalist state which Bulgakov
presupposes and which, by his assumption, is sufficient
unto itself, but in the arena of world economy where the
most differing levels of economic development and differing forms of economic existence come into collision" (57).

Thus, Struve's objection may be summed up as follows:
In actual fact realisation does not take place in an isolated,
self-sufficing, capitalist state, but "in the arena of world
economy," i.e., by the marketing of products in other countries. It is easy to see that this objection is based on an error.
Does the problem of realisation change to any extent if we
do not confine ourselves to the home market ("self-sufficing"
capitalism) but make reference to the foreign market, if we
take several countries instead of only one? If we do not
think that the capitalists throw their goods into the sea or
give them away gratis to foreigners—if we do not take
individual, exceptional cases or periods, it is obvious that we
must accept a certain equilibrium of export and import.

---

* The classical example of gentlemen à la A. Skvortsov who sees
tendentiousness in Marx's theory of the average rate of profit could
serve as a warning against the use of such expressions.

If a country exports certain products, realising them "in the arena of world economy," it imports other products in their place. From the standpoint of the theory of realisation it must necessarily be accepted that "foreign commerce only replaces home products [*Artikel*—goods] by articles of other use- or bodily form" (*Das Kapital*, II, 469. ⁴⁴ Quoted by me in *Nauchnoye Obozreniye*, p. 38*). Whether we take one country or a group of countries, the essence of the process of realisation does not change in the slightest. In his objection to Mr. Bulgakov, therefore, Struve repeats the old error of the Narodniks, who connected the problem of realisation with that of the foreign market.**

In actual fact these two questions have nothing in common. The problem of realisation is an abstract problem that is related to the general theory of capitalism. Whether we take one country or the whole world, the basic laws of realisation, revealed by Marx, remain the same.

The problem of foreign trade or of the foreign market is an historical problem, a problem of the concrete conditions of the development of capitalism in some one country and in some one epoch.***

11. Let us dwell for a while on the problem that has "long interested" Struve: what is the real scientific value of the theory of realisation?

It has exactly the same value as have all the other postulates of Marx's abstract theory. If Struve is bothered by the circumstance that "perfect realisation is the ideal of capitalist production, but by no means its reality," we must remind him that all other laws of capitalism, revealed by Marx, also depict only the ideal of capitalism and not its reality. "We need present," wrote Marx, "only the inner organisation of the capitalist mode of production, in its ideal average (*in ihrem idealen Durchschnitt*), as it were" (*Das Kapital*, III, 2, 367; Russian translation, p. 688). ⁴⁵ The theory of capital assumes that the worker receives the full value of his labour-power. This is the ideal of capitalism,

---

but by no means its reality. The theory of rent presupposes that the entire agrarian population has been completely divided into landowners, capitalists, and hired labourers. This is the ideal of capitalism, but by no means its reality. The theory of realisation presupposes the proportional distribution of production. This is the ideal of capitalism, but by no means its reality.

The scientific value of Marx's theory is its explanation of the process of the reproduction and circulation of the aggregate social capital. Further, Marx's theory showed how the contradiction, inherent in capitalism, comes about, how the tremendous growth of production is definitely not accompanied by a corresponding growth in people's consumption. Marx's theory, therefore, not only does not restore the apologetic bourgeois theory (as Struve fancies), but, on the contrary, *provides a most powerful weapon against apologetics.* It follows from the theory that, *even* with an ideally smooth and proportional reproduction and circulation of the aggregate social capital, the contradiction between the growth of production and the narrow limits of consumption is inevitable. But in reality, *apart from this*, realisation does not proceed in ideally smooth proportions, but only amidst "difficulties," "fluctuations," "crises," etc.

Further, Marx's theory of realisation provides a most powerful weapon against the petty-bourgeois reactionary criticism of capitalism, as well as against apologetics. It was precisely this sort of criticism against capitalism that our Narodniks tried to substantiate with their fallacious theory of realisation. Marx's conception of realisation inevitably leads to the recognition of the historical progressiveness of capitalism (the development of the means of production and, consequently, of the productive forces of society) and, thereby, it not only does not obscure the historically transitory nature of capitalism, but, on the contrary, explains it.

12. "In relation to an ideal or isolated, self-sufficing capitalist society," asserts Struve, extended reproduction would be impossible, "since the necessary additional workers can nowhere be obtained."

I certainly cannot agree with Struve's assertion. Struve has not proved, and it cannot be proved, that it is impossible

to obtain additional workers from the reserve army. Against
the fact that additional workers can be obtained from
the natural growth of the population, Struve makes the un-
substantiated statement that "extended reproduction, based
on the natural increase in the population, may not be arith-
metically identical with simple reproduction, but from the
practical capitalist standpoint, i.e., economically, may
fully coincide with it." Realising that the impossibility of
obtaining additional workers cannot be proved theoretically,
Struve evades the question by references to historical and
practical conditions. "I do not think that Marx could solve
the historical [?!] question on the basis of this absolutely
abstract construction."... "Self-sufficing capitalism is the
historically [!] inconceivable limit." ... "The intensification
of the labour that can be forced on a worker is extremely
limited, not only in actual fact, but also logically." ... "The
constant raising of labour productivity cannot but weaken
the very compulsion to work." ...

The illogicality of these statements is as clear as daylight! None of Struve's opponents has ever or anywhere
given voice to the absurdity that an historical question can
be solved with the aid of abstract constructions. In the
present instance Struve himself did not propound an historical question, but one that is an absolute abstraction, a
purely theoretical question, "in relation to an ideal capitalist society" (57). Is it not obvious that he is simply evading the question? I, of course, would not dream of denying
that there exist numerous historical and practical conditions
(to say nothing of the immanent contradictions of capitalism)
that are leading and will lead to the destruction of capitalism rather than to the conversion of present-day capitalism
into an ideal capitalism. But on the purely theoretical
question "in relation to an ideal capitalist society" I still
retain my former opinion that there are no theoretical
grounds for denying the possibility of extended reproduction
in such a society.

13. "Messrs. V. V. and N.—on have pointed out the
contradictions and stumbling-blocks in the capitalist development of Russia, but they are shown Marx's Schemes
and told that capital is always exchanged for capital..."
(Struve, op. cit., 62).

This is sarcasm in the highest degree. The pity is that matters are depicted in an absolutely false light. Anyone who reads Mr. V. V.'s *Essays on Theoretical Economics* and Section XV of the second part of Mr. N.—on's *Sketches* will see that both these writers raised precisely the abstract-theoretical question of realisation—the realisation of the product in capitalist society in general. This is a fact. There is another circumstance which is also a fact; other writers, those who opposed them, "deemed it essential to explain, *first and foremost*, the basic, *abstract-theoretical* points of the market theory" (as is stated in the opening lines of my article in *Nauchnoye Obozreniye*). Tugan-Baranovsky wrote on the theory of realisation in the chapter of his book on crises, which bears the subtitle, "The Market Theory." Bulgakov gave his book the subtitle, "A Theoretical Study." It is therefore a question of who confuses abstract-theoretical and concrete-historical questions, Struve's opponents or Struve himself?

On the same page of his article Struve quotes my statement to the effect that the necessity for a foreign market is not due to the conditions of realisation but to historical conditions. "But," Struve objects (a very typical "but"!), "Tugan-Baranovsky, Bulgakov, and Ilyin have examined only the abstract conditions of realisation and have not examined the historical conditions" (p. 62).

The writers mentioned did not explain historical conditions for the precise reason that they took it upon themselves to speak of abstract-theoretical and not concrete-historical questions. In my book, *On the Question of the Development of Capitalism in Russia* ("The Home Market for Large-Scale Industry and the Process of Its Formation in Russia"),* the printing of which has now (March 1899) been completed, I did not raise the question of the market theory but of a home market for Russian capitalism. In this case, therefore, the abstract truths of theory play only the role of guiding principles, a means of analysing concrete data.

---

* The reference is to *The Development of Capitalism in Russia* (see present edition, Vol. 3).—*Ed.*

14. Struve "wholly supports" his "point of view" on the theory of "third persons" which he postulated in his *Critical Remarks*. I, in turn, wholly support what I said in this connection at the time *Critical Remarks* appeared. [46]

In his *Critical Remarks* (p. 251) Struve says that Mr. V. V.'s argument "is based on a complete theory, an original one, of markets in a developed capitalist society." "This theory," says Struve, "is correct insofar as it confirms the fact that surplus-value cannot be realised by consumption, either by the capitalists or the workers, and presupposes consumption by third persons." By these third persons "in Russia" Struve "presumes the Russian agricultural peasantry" (p. 61 of the article in *Nauchnoye Obozreniye*).

And so, Mr. V. V. propounds a complete and original theory of markets in a developed capitalist society, and the Russian agricultural peasantry is pointed out to him! Is this not confusing the abstract-theoretical question of realisation with the concrete-historical question of capitalism in Russia? Further, if Struve acknowledges Mr. V. V.'s theory to be even partly correct, he must have overlooked Mr. V. V.'s basic theoretical errors on the question of realisation, he must have overlooked the incorrect view that the "difficulties" of capitalist realisation are confined to surplus-value or are specially bound up with that part of the value of the product—he must have overlooked the incorrect view that connects the question of the foreign market with the question of realisation.

Struve's statement that the Russian agricultural peasantry, by the differentiation within it, creates a market for our capitalism is perfectly correct (in the above-mentioned book I demonstrated this thesis in detail by an analysis of Zemstvo statistical data). The theoretical substantiation of this thesis, however, relates in no way to the theory of the realisation of the product in capitalist society, but to the theory of the formation of capitalist society. We must also note that calling the peasants "third persons" is not very fortunate and is likely to cause a misunderstanding. If the peasants are "third persons" for capitalist industry, then the industrial producers, large and small, the factory owners and workers, are "third persons" for capitalist farming. On the other hand, the peasant farmers ("third persons") create a market for capitalism only to the extent that they are differentiated into the classes of capitalist society (rural bourgeoisie and rural proletariat), i.e., only insofar as they cease to be "*third*" persons and become *active* persons in the capitalist system.

15. Struve says: "Bulgakov makes the very subtle remark that no difference in principle can be discerned between the home and the foreign market for capitalist production." I fully agree with this remark: in actual fact a tariff or political frontier is very often quite unsuitable as a line drawn between the "home" and "foreign" markets. But for reasons just indicated I cannot agree with Struve that "the theory asserting the necessity for third persons ... arises out of this." One demand does arise directly out of this: do not stop at the traditional separation of the home and foreign markets when analysing the question of capitalism. This distinction, groundless from a strictly theoretical point of view, is of particularly little use for such countries as Russia. It could be replaced by another division which distinguishes, for instance, the following aspects of capitalist development: 1) the formation and development of capitalist relations within the bounds of a certain fully populated and occupied territory; 2) the expansion of capitalism to other territories (in part completely unoccupied and being colonised by emigrants from the old country, and in part occupied by tribes that remain outside the world market and world capitalism). The first side of the process might be called the development of capitalism in depth and the second its development in breadth.* Such a division would include the whole process of the historical development of capitalism: on the one hand, its development in the old countries, where for centuries the forms of capitalist relations up to and including large-scale machine industry have

---

* It goes without saying that the two sides of the process are actually closely united, and that their separation is a mere abstraction, merely a method of investigating a complicated process. My book mentioned above is devoted entirely to the first side of the process. See Chapter VIII, Section V.

been built up; on the other hand, the mighty drive of developed capitalism to expand to other territories, to populate and plough up new parts of the world, to set up colonies and to draw savage tribes into the whirlpool of world capitalism. In Russia this last-mentioned capitalist tendency has been and continues to be seen most clearly in our outlying districts whose colonisation has been given such tremendous impetus in the post-Reform, capitalist period of Russian history. The south and south-east of European Russia, the Caucasus, Central Asia, and Siberia serve as something like colonies for Russian capitalism and ensure its tremendous development, not only in depth but also in breadth.

Finally, the division proposed is convenient because it clearly determines the range of questions which precisely is embraced by the theory of realisation. It is clear that the theory applies only to the first side of the process, only to the development of capitalism in depth. The theory of realisation (i.e., the theory which examines the process of the reproduction and circulation of the aggregate social capital) must necessarily take an isolated capitalist society for its constructions, i.e., must ignore the process of capitalist expansion to other countries, the process of commodity exchange between countries, because this process does not provide anything for the solution of the question of realisation and only transfers the question from one country to several countries. It is also obvious that the abstract theory of realisation must take as a prerequisite an ideally developed capitalist society.

In regard to the literature of Marxism, Struve makes the following general remark: "The orthodox chorus still continues to dominate, but it cannot stifle the new stream of criticism because true strength in scientific questions is always on the side of criticism and not of faith." As can be seen from the foregoing exposition, we have satisfied ourselves that the "new stream of criticism" is not a guarantee against the repetition of old errors. No, let us better remain "under the sign of orthodoxy"! Let us not believe that orthodoxy means taking things on trust, that orthodoxy precludes critical application and further development, that it permits historical problems to be obscured by abstract schemes. If there are orthodox disciples who are guilty of these truly grievous sins, the blame must rest entirely with those disciples and not by any means with orthodoxy, which is distinguished by diametrically opposite qualities.

Written in March 1899

Published in August 1899
in the magazine *Nauchnoye
Obozreniye*, No. 8
Signed: *V. Ilyin*

Published according to the
text in the magazine

REVIEW

Karl Kautsky. *Die Agrarfrage. Eine Uebersicht über die Tendenzen der modernen Landwirtschaft und die Agrarpolitik u.s.w.** *Stuttgart, Dietz, 1899.*

Kautsky's book is the most important event in present-day economic literature since the third volume of *Capital*. Until now Marxism has lacked a systematic study of capitalism in agriculture. Kautsky has filled this gap with "The Development of Agriculture in Capitalist Society," the first part (pp. 1-300) of his voluminous (450-page) book. He justly remarks in his preface that an "overwhelming" mass of statistical and descriptive economic material on the question of agricultural capitalism has been accumulated and that there is an urgent need to reveal the "basic tendencies" of economic evolution in this branch of the economy in order to demonstrate the varied phenomena of agricultural capitalism as "partial manifestations of one common [integral] process" (*eines Gesammtprozesses*). It is true that agricultural forms and the relations among the agricultural population in contemporary society are marked by such tremendous variety that there is nothing easier than to seize upon a whole mass of facts and pointers taken from any inquiry that will "confirm" the views of the given writer. This is precisely the method used in a large number of arguments by our Narodnik press which tries to prove the viability of petty peasant economy or even its superiority over large-scale production

---

* Karl Kautsky. *The Agrarian Question*. A Review of the Tendencies in Modern Agriculture and Agrarian Policy, etc.— *Ed.*

ers and capitalists frequently pass laws that artificially maintain the small peasantry. Petty farming becomes stable when it ceases to compete with large-scale farming, when it is turned into a supplier of labour-power for the latter. The relations between large and small landowners come still closer to those of capitalists and proletarians. Kautsky devotes a special chapter to the "proletarisation of the peasantry," one that is rich in data, especially on the question of the "auxiliary employments" of the peasants, i.e., the various forms of hired labour.

After elucidating the basic features of the development of capitalism in agriculture, Kautsky proceeds to demonstrate the historically transitory character of this system of social economy. The more capitalism develops, the greater the difficulties that commercial (commodity) farming encounters. The monopoly in land ownership (ground rent), the right of inheritance, and entailed estates [47] hamper the rationalisation of farming. The towns exploit the countryside to an ever greater extent, taking the best labour forces away from the farmers and absorbing an ever greater portion of the wealth produced by the rural population, whereby the rural population is no longer able to return to the soil that which is taken from it. Kautsky deals in particularly great detail with the depopulating of the countryside and acknowledges to the full that it is the middle stratum of farmers which suffers least of all from a shortage of labour-power, and he adds that "good citizens" (we may also add: and the Russian Narodniks) are mistaken in rejoicing at this fact, in thinking that they can see in it the beginnings of a rebirth of the peasantry which refutes the applicability of Marx's theory to agriculture. The peasantry may suffer less than other agricultural classes from a shortage of hired labour, but it suffers much more from usury, tax oppression, the irrationality of its economy, soil exhaustion, excessive toil, and underconsumption. The fact that not only agricultural labourers, but even the children of the peasants, flee to the towns is a clear refutation of the views of optimistically-minded pettybourgeois economists! But the biggest changes in the condition of European agriculture have been brought about by the competition of cheap grain imported from America, the Argentine, India, Russia, and other countries. Kautsky made a detailed study of the significance of this fact that arose out of the development of industry in quest for markets. He describes the decline in European grain production under the impact of this competition, as well as the lowering of rent, and makes a particularly detailed study of the "industrialisation of agriculture" which is manifested, on the one hand, in the industrial wage-labour of the small peasants and, on the other, in the development of agricultural technical production (distilling, sugar refining, etc.), and even in the elimination of some branches of agriculture by manufacturing industries. Optimistic economists, says Kautsky, are mistaken in believing that such changes in European agriculture can save it from crisis; the crisis is spreading and can only end in a general crisis of capitalism as a whole. This, of course, does not give one the least right to speak of the ruin of agriculture, but its conservative character is gone for ever; it has entered a state of uninterrupted transformation, a state that is typical of the capitalist mode of production in general. "A large area of land under large-scale agricultural production, the capitalist nature of which is becoming more and more pronounced; the growth of leasing and mortgaging, the industrialisation of agriculture—these are the elements that are preparing the ground for the socialisation of agricultural production...." It would be absurd to think, says Kautsky in conclusion, that one part of society develops in one direction and another in the opposite direction. In actual fact "social development in agriculture is taking the same direction as in industry."

Applying the results of his theoretical analysis to questions of agrarian policy, Kautsky naturally opposes all attempts to support or "save" peasant economy. There is no reason even to think that the village commune, says Kautsky, could go over to large-scale communal farming (p. 338, section, "Der Dorfkommunismus"*; cf. p. 339). "The protection of the peasantry (der Bauernschutz) does not mean protection of the person of the peasant (no one, of course, would object to such protection), but protection of the peasant's property. Incidentally, it is precisely the peasant's property that is the main cause of his impoverishment and

_____
* Village communism.—Ed.

his degradation. Hired agricultural labourers are now quite frequently in a better position than the small peasants. The protection of the peasantry is not protection from poverty but the protection of the fetters that chain the peasant to his poverty" (p. 320). The radical transformation of agriculture by capitalism is a process that is only just beginning, but it is one that is advancing rapidly, bringing about the transformation of the peasant into a hired labourer and increasing the flight of the population from the countryside. Attempts to check this process would be reactionary and harmful: no matter how burdensome the consequences of this process may be in present-day society, the consequences of checking the process would be still worse and would place the working population in a still more helpless and hopeless position. Progressive action in present-day society can only strive to lessen the harmful effects which capitalist advance exerts on the population, to increase the consciousness of the people and their capacity for collective self-defence. Kautsky, therefore, insists on the guarantee of freedom of movement, etc., on the abolition of all the remnants of feudalism in agriculture (e.g., *die Gesindeordnungen,** which place farm workers in a personally dependent, semi-serf position), on the prohibition of child labour under the age of fourteen, the establishment of an eight-hour working day, strict sanitary police to exercise supervision over workers' dwellings, etc., etc.

It is to be hoped that Kautsky's book will appear in a Russian translation.[48]

Written in March 1899
Published in April 1899
in the magazine *Nachalo*, No. 4
Signed: *Vl. Ilyin*

Published according to the text in the magazine

---

* Legislation defining relations between landowners and serfs.—*Ed.*

REVIEW

J. A. Hobson. *The Evolution of Modern Capitalism.* Translated
from the English. St. Petersburg, 1898. Publ. O. N. Popova.
Price 1 rb. 50 kop.

Hobson's book is, strictly speaking, not a study of the evolution of modern capitalism, but a series of sketches, based
mainly on English data, dealing with the most recent industrial development. Hence, the title of the book is somewhat
broad: the author does not touch upon agriculture at all and
his examination of industrial economics is far from complete.
Like the well-known writers Sidney and Beatrice Webb,
Hobson is a representative of one of the advanced trends of
English social thought. His attitude towards "modern capitalism" is critical; he fully admits the necessity of replacing
it by a higher form of social economy and treats the problem
of its replacement with typically English reformist practi-
cality. His conviction of the need for reform is, in the main,
arrived at empirically, under the influence of the recent
history of English factory legislation, of the English labour
movement, of the activities of the English municipalities,
etc. Hobson lacks well-knit and integral theoretical views
that could serve as a basis for his reformist programme and
elucidate specific problems of reform. He is, therefore, at his
best when he deals with the grouping and description of the
latest statistical and economic data. When, on the other
hand, he deals with the general theoretical problems of political economy, he proves to be very weak. The Russian reader
will even find it strange to see a writer with such extensive

knowledge and practical aspirations deserving of full sympathy helplessly labouring over questions like, what is "capital," what is the role of "savings," etc. This weak side of Hobson is fully explained by the fact that he regards John Stuart Mill as a greater authority on political economy than Marx, whom he quotes once or twice but whom he evidently does not understand at all or does not know. One cannot but regret the vast amount of unproductive labour wasted by Hobson in an attempt to get clear on the contradictions of bourgeois and professorial political economy. At best he comes close to the solutions given by Marx long ago; at worst he borrows erroneous views that are in sharp contradiction to his attitude towards "modern capitalism." The most unfortunate chapter in his book is the seventh: "Machinery and Industrial Depression." In this chapter Hobson tried to analyse the theoretical problems of crises, of social capital and revenue in capitalist society, and of capitalist accumulation. Correct ideas on the disproportionateness of production and consumption in capitalist society and on the anarchic character of capitalist economy are submerged in a heap of scholastic arguments about "saving" (Hobson confuses accumulation with "saving"), amidst all sorts of Crusoeisms (suppose "a man working with primitive tools, discovers an implement... saving food," etc.), and the like. Hobson is very fond of diagrams, and in most cases he uses them very ably for graphic illustration of his exposition. But the idea of the "mechanism of production" given in his diagram on page 207 (Chap. VII) can only elicit a smile from the reader who is at all acquainted with the real "mechanism" of *capitalist* "production." Hobson here confuses production with the social system of production and evinces an extremely vague understanding of what capital is, what its component parts are, and into what classes capitalist society is necessarily divided. In Chapter VIII he cites interesting data on the composition of the population according to occupation, and on the changes in this composition in the course of time, but the great flaw in his theoretical arguments on "machinery and the demand for labour" is that he ignores the theory of "capitalist overpopulation" or the reserve army. Among the more happily written chapters of Hobson's book are those in which he examines modern towns and the position of women in modern industry. Citing statistics on the growth of female labour and describing the extremely bad conditions under which this labour is performed, Hobson justly points out that the only hope of improving these conditions lies in the supplanting of domestic labour by factory labour, which leads to "closer social intercourse" and to "organisation." Similarly, on the question of the significance of towns, Hobson comes close to Marx's general views when he admits that the antithesis between town and country contradicts the system of collectivist society Hobson's conclusions would have been much more convincing had he not ignored Marx's teaching on this question too. Hobson would then, probably, have emphasised more clearly the historically progressive role of the cities and the necessity of combining agriculture with industry under the collectivist organisation of economy. The last chapter of Hobson's book, "Civilisation and Industrial Development," is perhaps the best. In this chapter the author proves by a number of very apt arguments the need to reform the modern industrial system along the line of expanding "public control" and the "socialisation of industry." In evaluating Hobson's somewhat optimistic views regarding the methods by which these "reforms" can be brought about, the special features of English history and of English life must be borne in mind: the high development of democracy, the absence of militarism, the enormous strength of the organised trade unions, the growing investment of English capital outside of England, which weakens the antagonism between the English employers and workers, etc.

In his well-known book on the social movement in the nineteenth century, Prof. W. Sombart notes among other things a "tendency towards unity" (title of Chapter VI), i. e., a tendency of the social movement of the various countries, in its various forms and shades, towards uniformity and along with it a tendency towards the spread of the ideas of Marxism. In regard to England Sombart sees this tendency in the fact that the English trade unions are increasingly abandoning "the purely Manchester standpoint." In regard to Hobson's book we can say that under pressure of the demands of life, which is increasingly corroborating Marx's "prognosis," progressive English writers are beginning to

CAPITALISM IN AGRICULTURE

(KAUTSKY'S BOOK AND
MR. BULGAKOV'S ARTICLE)

Written in April–May 1899

Published in January-February
1900 in the magazine *Zhizn* "
Signed: *Vl. Ilyin* .

Published according to the
text in the magazine

FIRST ARTICLE

Nachalo, No. 1-2 (Section II, pp. 1-21), contains an article by Mr. S. Bulgakov entitled: "A Contribution to the Question of the Capitalist Evolution of Agriculture," which is a criticism of Kautsky's work on the agrarian question. Mr. Bulgakov rightly says that "Kautsky's book represents a whole world outlook," that it is of great theoretical and practical importance. It is, perhaps, the first systematic and scientific investigation of a question that has stimulated a heated controversy in all countries, and still continues to do so, even among writers who are agreed on general views and who regard themselves as Marxists. Mr. Bulgakov "confines himself to negative criticism," to criticism of "individual postulates in Kautsky's book" (which he "briefly"—too briefly and very inexactly, as we shall see—reviews for the readers of *Nachalo*). "Later on," Mr. Bulgakov hopes "to give a systematic exposition of the question of the capitalist evolution of agriculture" and thus "also present a whole world outlook" in opposition to Kautsky's.

We have no doubt that Kautsky's book will give rise to no little controversy among Marxists in Russia, and that in Russia, too, some will oppose Kautsky, while others will support him. At all events, the writer of these lines disagrees most emphatically with Mr. Bulgakov's opinion, with his appraisal of Kautsky's book. Notwithstanding Mr. Bulgakov's admission that *Die Agrarfrage** is "a remarkable work," his appraisal is astonishingly sharp, and is written in a tone unusual in a controversy between authors of

---

* *The Agrarian Question.—Ed.*

related tendencies. Here are samples of the expressions Mr. Bulgakov uses: "extremely superficial" ..."equally little of both real agronomics and real economics" ... "Kautsky employs *empty phrases* to evade serious scientific problems" (Mr. Bulgakov's italics!!), etc., etc. We shall therefore carefully examine the expressions used by the stern critic and at the same time introduce the reader to Kautsky's book.

I

Even before Mr. Bulgakov gets to Kautsky, he, in passing, takes a shot at Marx. It goes without saying that Mr. Bulgakov emphasises the enormous services rendered by the great economist, but observes that in Marx's works one "sometimes" comes across even "erroneous views... which have been sufficiently refuted by history." "Among such views is, for example, the one that in agriculture variable capital diminishes in relation to constant capital just as it does in manufacturing industry, so that the organic composition of agricultural capital continuously rises." Who is mistaken here, Marx or Mr. Bulgakov? Mr. Bulgakov has in mind the fact that in agriculture the progress of technique and the growing intensity of farming often lead *to an increase* in the amount of labour necessary to cultivate a given plot of land. This is indisputable; but it is very far from being a refutation of the theory of the diminution of variable capital *relatively* to constant capital, *in proportion* to constant capital. Marx's theory merely asserts that the ratio $\frac{v}{c}$ (v=variable capital, c=constant capital) in general has a tendency to diminish, even when v increases per unit of area. Is Marx's theory refuted if, simultaneously, c increases still more rapidly? Agriculture in capitalist countries, taken by and large, shows a diminution of v and an increase of c. The rural population and the number of workers employed in agriculture are diminishing in Germany, in France, and in England, whereas the number of machines employed in agriculture is increasing. In Germany, for example, from 1882 to 1895, the rural population diminished from 19,200,000 to 18,500,000 (the number of wage-workers in agriculture diminished from 5,900,000 to 5,600,000), whereas the number of machines employed in agriculture increased from 458,369 to 913,391*; the number of steam-driven machines employed in agriculture increased from 2,731 (in 1879) to 12,856 (in 1897), while the total horse power of the steam-driven machinery employed increased still more. The number of cattle increased from 15,800,000 to 17,500,000 and the number of pigs from 9,200,000 to 12,200,000 (in 1883 and 1892 respectively). In France, the rural population diminished from 6,900,000 ("independent") in 1882 to 6,600,000 in 1892; and the number of agricultural machines increased as follows: 1862—132,784; 1882—278,896; 1892—355,795. The number of cattle was as follows: 12,000,000; 13,000,000; 13,700,000 respectively; the number of horses: 2,910,000; 2,840,000; 2,790,000 respectively (the reduction in the number of horses in the period 1882-92 was less significant than the reduction in the rural population). Thus, by and large, the history of modern capitalist countries has certainly not refuted, but has *confirmed* the applicability of Marx's law to agriculture. The mistake Mr. Bulgakov made was that he too hastily raised certain facts in agronomics, without examining their significance, to the level of *general* economic laws. We emphasise "general," because neither Marx nor his disciples ever regarded this law otherwise than as the law of the general tendencies of capitalism, and not as a law for all individual cases. Even in regard to industry Marx himself pointed out that periods of technical change (when the ratio $\frac{v}{c}$ diminishes) are followed by periods of progress on the given technical basis (when the ratio $\frac{v}{c}$ remains constant, and in certain cases may even increase). We know of cases in the industrial history of capitalist countries in which this law is contravened by entire branches of industry, as when large capitalist workshops (incorrectly termed factories) are broken up and supplanted by capitalist domestic industry. There cannot be any doubt that in agriculture the process of development of capitalism is immeasurably more complex and assumes incomparably more diverse forms.

---

* Machines of various types are combined. Unless otherwise stated, all figures are taken from Kautsky's book.

Let us now pass to Kautsky. The outline of agriculture in the feudal epoch with which Kautsky begins is said to be "very superficially compiled and superfluous." It is difficult to understand the motive for such a verdict. We are sure that if Mr. Bulgakov succeeds in realising his plan to give a systematic exposition of the capitalist evolution of agriculture, he will have to outline the main features of the *precapitalist* economics of agriculture. Without this the character of *capitalist* economics and the transitional forms which connect it with feudal economics cannot be understood. Mr. Bulgakov himself admits the enormous importance of "the form which agriculture assumed *at the beginning* [Mr. Bulgakov's italics] of its capitalist course." It is precisely with "the beginning of the capitalist course" of European agriculture that Kautsky begins. In our opinion, Kautsky's outline of feudal agriculture is excellent; it reveals that remarkable distinctness and ability to select what is most important and essential without becoming submerged in details of secondary importance which, in general, are characteristic of this author. In his introduction Kautsky first of all gives an extremely precise and correct presentation of the question. In most emphatic terms he declares: "There is not the slightest doubt—we are prepared to accept this *a priori* (*von vornherein*)—that agriculture does not develop according to the same pattern as industry: it is subject to special laws" (*S.* 5-6). The task is "to investigate whether capital is bringing agriculture under its domination and how it is dominating it, how it transforms it, how it invalidates old forms of production and forms of property and creates the need for new forms" (*S.* 6). Such, and only such, a presentation of the question can result in a satisfactory explanation of "the development of agriculture in capitalist society" (the title of the first, theoretical, part of Kautsky's book).

At the beginning of the "capitalist course," agriculture was in the hands of the *peasantry*, which, as a general rule, was subordinated to the feudal regime of social economy. Kautsky first of all characterises the *system* of peasant farming, the combining of agriculture with domestic industry, and further the elements of decay in this paradise of petty-bourgeois and conservative writers (*à la* Sismondi), the significance of usury and the gradual "penetration into the countryside, deep into the peasant household itself, of the class antagonism which destroys the ancient harmony and community of interests" (*S.* 13). This process, which began as far back as the Middle Ages, has not completely come to an end to this day. We emphasise this statement because it shows immediately the utter incorrectness of Mr. Bulgakov's assertion that Kautsky did not even raise the question of who was the carrier of technical progress in agriculture. Kautsky raised and answered that question quite definitely; anyone who reads his book carefully will grasp the truth (often forgotten by the Narodniks, agronomists, and many others) that the carrier of technical progress in modern agriculture is the *rural bourgeoisie*, both petty and big; and (as Kautsky has shown) the big bourgeoisie plays a more important role in this respect than the petty bourgeoisie.

II

After describing (in Chapter III) the main features of feudal agriculture: the predominance of the three-field system, the most conservative system in agriculture; the oppression and expropriation of the peasantry by the big landed aristocracy; the organisation of feudal-capitalist farming by the latter; the transformation of the peasantry into starving paupers (*Hungerleider*) in the seventeenth and eighteenth centuries; the development of bourgeois peasants (*Grossbauern*, who cannot manage without regular farm labourers and day labourers), for whom the old forms of rural relations and land tenure were unsuitable; the abolition of these forms and the paving of the way for "capitalist, intensive farming" (*S.* 26) by the forces of the bourgeois class which had developed in the womb of industry and the towns—after describing all this, Kautsky goes on to characterise "modern agriculture" (Chapter IV).

This chapter contains a remarkably exact, concise, and lucid outline of the gigantic revolution which capitalism brought about in agriculture by transforming the routine craft of peasants crushed by poverty and ignorance into the scientific application of agronomics, by disturbing the age-long stagnation of agriculture, and by giving (and continuing

to give) an impetus to the rapid development of the productive forces of social labour. The three-field system gave way
to the crop rotation system, the maintenance of cattle and the
cultivation of the soil were improved, the yield increased
and specialisation in agriculture and the division of labour
among individual farms greatly developed. Pre-capitalist
uniformity was replaced by increasing diversity, accompanied
by technical progress in all branches of agriculture. Both
the use of machinery in agriculture and the application of
steam power were introduced and underwent rapid development; the employment of electric power, which, as specialists point out, is destined to play an even greater role in this
branch of production than steam power, has begun. The use
of access roads, land improvement schemes, and the application of artificial fertilisers adapted to the physiology of
plants have been developed; the application of bacteriology
to agriculture has begun. Mr. Bulgakov's assertion that
"Kautsky's data* are not accompanied by an *economic* analysis" is completely groundless. Kautsky shows precisely
the connection between this revolution and the growth of
the *market* (especially the growth of the towns), and the subordination of agriculture to *competition* which *forced* the
changes and specialisation. "This revolution, which has its
origin in urban capital, increases the dependence of the farmer on the market and, moreover, constantly changes market
conditions of importance to him. A branch of production
that was profitable while the local market's only connection
with the world market was a high road becomes unprofitable
and must necessarily be superseded by another branch of
production when a railway is run through the locality. If, for
example, the railway brings cheaper grain, grain production

---

* "All these data," thinks Mr. Bulgakov, "can be obtained from
any (*sic!*) handbook of the economics of agriculture." We do not share
Mr. Bulgakov's roseate views on "handbooks." Let us take from "any" of
the Russian books those of Messrs. Skvortsov (*Steam Transport*) and
N. Kablukov (*Lectures*, half of them reprinted in a "new" book *The
Conditions of Development of Peasant Economy in Russia*). Neither
from the one nor from the other would the reader be able to obtain
a picture of that transformation which was brought about by *capitalism*
in agriculture, because neither even sets out to give a general picture
of the transition from feudal to capitalist economy.

becomes unprofitable; but at the same time a market for milk is created. The growth of commodity circulation makes it possible to introduce new, improved varieties of crops into the country," etc. (*S*. 37-38). "In the feudal epoch," says Kautsky, "the only agriculture was small-scale agriculture, for the landlord cultivated his fields with the peasant's implements. Capitalism first created the possibility for large-scale production in agriculture, which is technically more rational than small-scale production." In discussing agricultural machinery, Kautsky (who, it should be said in passing, points precisely to the specific features of agriculture in this respect) explains the *capitalist* nature of its employment; he explains the influence of agricultural machinery upon the workers, the significance of machinery as a factor of progress, and the "reactionary utopianism" of schemes for restricting the employment of agricultural machinery. "Agricultural machines will continue their transformative activity: they will drive the rural workers into the towns and in this way serve as a powerful instrument for raising wages in the rural districts, on the one hand, and for the further development of the employment of machinery in agriculture, on the other" (*S*. 41). Let it be added that in special chapters Kautsky explains in detail the capitalist character of modern agriculture, the relation between large- and small-scale production, and the proletarisation of the peasantry. As we see, Mr. Bulgakov's assertion that Kautsky "does not raise the question of knowing why all these wonder-working changes were necessary" is entirely untrue.

In Chapter V ("The Capitalist Character of Modern Agriculture") Kautsky expounds Marx's theory of value, profit, and rent. "Without money, modern agricultural production is impossible," says Kautsky, "or, what is the same thing, it is impossible *without capital*. Indeed, under the present mode of production any sum of money which does not serve the purpose of individual consumption can be transformed into capital, i.e., into a value begetting surplus-value and, as a general rule, actually is transformed into capital. Hence, modern agricultural production is capitalist production" (*S*. 56). This passage, incidentally, enables us to appraise the following statement made by Mr. Bulgakov: "I employ this term (capitalist agriculture) in the ordinary sense

(Kautsky also employs it in the same sense), i.e., in the sense of large-scale production in agriculture. Actually, however (*sic!*), when the *whole* of the national economy is organised on capitalist lines, there is no *non*-capitalist agriculture, the *whole* of it being determined by the general conditions of the organisation of production, and only within these limits should the distinction be made between large-scale, entrepreneur farming and small-scale farming. For the sake of clarity a new term is required here also." And so it seems, Mr. Bulgakov *is correcting* Kautsky.... "Actually, however," as the reader sees, Kautsky *does not employ* the term "capitalist agriculture" in the "ordinary," inexact sense in which Mr. Bulgakov employs it. Kautsky understands perfectly well, and says so very precisely and clearly, that under the capitalist mode of production all agricultural production is "as a general rule" capitalist production. In support of this opinion he adduces the simple fact that in order to carry on modern agriculture money is needed, and that in modern society money which does not serve the purpose of individual consumption becomes capital. It seems to us that this is somewhat clearer than Mr. Bulgakov's "correction," and that Kautsky has fully proved that it is possible to dispense with a "new term."

In Chapter V of his book Kautsky asserts, *inter alia*, that both the tenant farmer system, which has developed so fully in England, and the mortgage system, which is developing with astonishing rapidity in continental Europe, express, in essence, one and the same process, viz., *the separation of the land from the farmer*.* Under the capitalist tenant farmer system this separation is as clear as daylight. Under the mortgage system it is "less clear, and things are not so simple; but in essence it amounts to the same thing" (*S.* 86). Indeed, it is obvious that the mortgaging of land is the mortgaging, or sale, of ground rent. Consequently, under the mortgage system, as well as under the tenant farmer system, the recipients of rent (=the landowners) are separated from the

---

* Marx pointed to this process in Volume III of *Capital* (without examining its various *forms* in different countries) and observed that this separation of "land as an instrument of production from landed property and landowner" is "one of the major results of the capitalist mode of production" (III, 2, *S.* 156-57; Russian translation, 509-10). [50]

recipients of the profit of enterprise (=farmers, rural entre-preneurs). "In general, the significance of this assertion of Kautsky is unclear" to Mr. Bulgakov. "It can hardly be consid-ered as proved that the mortgage system expresses the separa-tion of the land from the farmer." "Firstly, it cannot be proved that debt absorbs the *whole* rent; this is possible only by way of exception...." To this we reply: There is no need to prove that interest on mortgage debts absorbs the *whole* rent, just as there is no need to prove that the *actual amount* paid for land leased coincides with rent. It is sufficient to prove that mortgage debts are growing with enormous rapid-ity; that the landowners strive to mortgage all their land, to sell the whole of the rent. The existence of this tendency—a theoretical economic analysis can, in general, deal only with tendencies—cannot be doubted. Consequently, there can be no doubt about the process of separation of the land from the farmer. The combination of the recipient of rent and the recipient of the profit of enterprise in one person is, "from the historical point of view, an exception" (*ist historisch eine Ausnahme, S*. 91).... "Secondly, the causes and sources of the debt must be analysed in each separate case for its signif-icance to be understood." Probably this is either a misprint or a slip. Mr. Bulgakov cannot demand that an economist (who, moreover, is dealing with the "development of agri-culture in capitalist society" *in general*) should investigate the causes of the debt "*in each separate case*" or even expect that he would be able to do so. If Mr. Bulgakov wanted to say that it is necessary to analyse the causes of debt in different countries at different periods, we cannot agree with him. Kautsky is perfectly right in saying that too many monographs on the agrarian question have accumulated, and that the urgent task of modern theory is not to add new mono-graphs but to "investigate the main trends of the capitalist evolution of agriculture as a whole" (*Vorrede, S.* vi*). Among these main trends is undoubtedly the separation of the land from the farmer in the form of an increase in mortgage debts. Kautsky precisely and clearly defined the real significance of mortgages, their progressive historical character (the sep-aration of the land from the farmer being one of the condi-

---

* Foreword, p. vi.—*Ed.*

tions for the socialisation of agriculture, *S.* 88), and the
essential role they play in the capitalist evolution of agriculture.* All Kautsky's arguments on this question are extremely valuable theoretically and provide a powerful
weapon against the widespread bourgeois talk (particularly
in "any handbook of the economics of agriculture") about
the "misfortune" of debts and about "measures of assistance."
..."Thirdly," concludes Mr. Bulgakov, "land leased out may,
in its turn, be mortgaged; and in this sense it may assume the
same position as land not leased out." A strange argument!
Let Mr. Bulgakov point to at least one economic phenomenon, to at least one economic category, that is not interwoven
with others. The fact that there are cases of combined leasing
and mortgaging does not refute, does not even weaken, the
theoretical proposition that the separation of the land from
the farmer is expressed in two forms: in the tenant farmer
system and in mortgage debts.

Mr. Bulgakov also declares that Kautsky's statement
that "countries in which the tenant farmer system is developed are also countries in which large land ownership predominates" (*S.* 88) is "still more unexpected" and "altogether untrue." Kautsky speaks here of the concentration of
land ownership (under the tenant farmer system) and the
concentration of mortgages (under the system in which the
landowners manage their own farms) as conditions that facilitate the abolition of the private ownership of land. On the
question of concentration of land ownership, continues Kautsky, there are no statistics "which would enable one to trace
the amalgamation of several properties in single hands";
but "in general it may be taken" that the increase in the number of leases and in the area of the leased land proceeds
side by side with concentration of land ownership. "Countries in which the tenant farmer system is developed are
also countries in which large land ownership predominates."

---

* The increase in mortgage debts does not always imply that
agriculture is in a depressed state.... The progress and prosperity of
agriculture (as well as its decline) "should find expression in an increase
in mortgage debts—firstly, because of the growing need of capital
on the part of progressing agriculture, and, secondly, because of the
increase in ground rent, which facilitates the expansion of agricultural
credit" (*S.* 87).

It is clear that Kautsky's entire argument applies only to countries in which the tenant farmer system is developed; but Mr. Bulgakov refers to East Prussia, where he "hopes to show" an increase in the number of leases side by side with the break-up of large landed properties—and he thinks that by means of this single example he is refuting Kautsky! It is a pity, however, that Mr. Bulgakov forgets to inform his readers that Kautsky himself points to the break-up of large estates and the growth of peasant tenant farming in the East Elbe province and, in doing so, explains, as we shall see later, the real significance of these processes.

Kautsky points to the concentration of mortgage institutions as proof that the concentration of land ownership is taking place in countries in which mortgage debts exist. Mr. Bulgakov thinks that this is no proof. In his opinion, "It might easily be the case that the deconcentration of capital (by the issue of shares) is proceeding side by side with the concentration of credit institutions." Well, we shall not argue with Mr. Bulgakov on this point.

III

After examining the main features of feudal and capitalist agriculture, Kautsky passes on to the question of "large- and small-scale production" in agriculture (Chapter VI). This chapter is one of the best in Kautsky's book. In it he first examines the"technical superiority of large-scale production." In deciding the question in favour of large-scale production, Kautsky does not give an abstract formula that ignores the enormous variety of agricultural relations (as Mr. Bulgakov, altogether groundlessly, supposes); on the contrary, he clearly and precisely points to the necessity of taking this variety into account in the practical applications of the theoretical law. In the first place, "*it goes without saying*" that the superiority of large-scale over small-scale production in agriculture is inevitable only when "*all other conditions are equal*" (*S.* 100. My italics). In industry, also, the law of the superiority of large-scale production is not as absolute and as simple as is sometimes thought; there, too, it is the equality of "*other conditions*" (not always existing in reality) that ensures the full applicability of the law. In agriculture, however, which is distinguished for the incomparably greater complexity and variety of its relations, the full applicability of the law of the superiority of large-scale production is hampered by considerably stricter conditions. For instance, Kautsky very aptly observes that on the borderline between the peasant and the small landlord estates "quantity is transformed into quality": the big peasant farm may be "economically, if not technically, superior" to the small landlord farm. The employment of a scientifically educated manager (one of the important advantages of large-scale production) is too costly for a small estate; and the management by the owner himself, is very often merely "Junker," and by no means scientific, management. Secondly, large-scale production in agriculture is superior to small production only up to a certain limit. Kautsky closely investigates this limit further on. It also goes without saying that this limit differs in different branches of agriculture and under different social-economic conditions. Thirdly, Kautsky does not in the least ignore the fact that, "*so far,*" there are branches of agriculture in which, as experts admit, small-scale production can compete with large-scale production; for example, vegetable gardening, grape growing, industrial crops, etc. (*S.* 115). But these branches occupy a position quite subordinate to the decisive (*entscheidenden*) branches of agriculture, viz., the production of grain and animal husbandry. Moreover, "even in vegetable gardening and grape growing there are already fairly successful large-scale enterprises" (*S.* 115). Hence, "taking agriculture as a whole (*in Allgemeinen*), those branches in which small-scale production is superior to large-scale production need not be taken into account, and it is quite permissible to say that large-scale production is decidedly superior to small-scale production" (*S.* 116).

After demonstrating the technical superiority of large-scale production in agriculture (we shall present Kautsky's arguments in greater detail later on in examining Mr. Bulgakov's objections), Kautsky asks: "What can small production offer against the advantages of large-scale production?" And he replies: "The greater diligence and greater care of the worker, who, unlike the hired labourer, works for himself, and the low level of requirements of the small independent farmer, which is even lower than that of the agricultural labourer" (*S.* 106); and, by adducing a number of striking facts concerning the position of the peasants in France, England, and Germany, Kautsky leaves no doubt whatever about "overwork and under-consumption in small-scale production." Finally, he points out that the superiority of large-scale production also finds expression in the striving of farmers to form *associations*: "Associated production is large-scale production." The fuss made by the ideologists of the petty bourgeoisie in general, and the Russian Narodniks in particular (e.g., the above-mentioned book by Mr. Kablukov), over the small farmers' associations is well known. The more significant, therefore, is Kautsky's excellent analysis of the role of these associations. Of course, the small farmers' associations are a link in economic progress; but they express *a transition to capitalism (Fortschritt zum Kapitalismus) and not toward collectivism*, as is often thought and asserted (*S.* 118). Associations do not diminish but enhance the superiority (*Vorsprung*) of large-scale over small-scale production in agriculture, because the big farmers enjoy greater opportunities of forming associations and take greater advantage of these opportunities. It goes without saying that Kautsky very emphatically maintains that communal, collective large-scale production is superior to capitalist large-scale production. He deals with the experiments in collective farming made in England by the followers of Robert Owen* and with analogous communes in the United States of North America. All these experiments, says Kautsky, *irrefutably prove* that it is quite possible for workers to carry on large-scale modern farming collectively, but that for this possibility to become a reality "a number of definite economic, political, and intellectual conditions" are necessary. The transition of the small producer (both artisan and peasant) to collective production is hindered by the extremely low development of solidarity and discipline, the isolation, and the "property-owner fanaticism," noted not only among West-European peasants, but, let us add,

---

* On pages 124-26 Kautsky describes the agricultural commune in Ralahine, of which, incidentally, Mr. Dioneo tells his Russian readers in *Russkoye Bogatstvo*,[51] No. 2, for this year,

also among the Russian "commune" peasants (recall
A. N. Engelhardt and G. Uspensky). Kautsky categorically declares that "it is absurd to expect that the peasant in *modern society* will go over to communal production"
(*S.* 129).

Such is the extremely rich content of Chapter VI of
Kautsky's book. Mr. Bulgakov is particularly displeased
with this chapter. Kautsky, we are told, is guilty of the
"fundamental sin" of confusing various concepts; "technical
advantages are confused with economic advantages." Kautsky
"proceeds from the false assumption that the *technically*
more perfect mode of production is also *economically* more
perfect, i.e., more viable." Mr. Bulgakov's emphatic statement is altogether groundless, of which, we hope, the reader
has been convinced by our exposition of Kautsky's line of
argument. Without in the least confusing technique with
economics,* Kautsky rightly investigates the question of
the relation of large-scale to small-scale production in agriculture, *other conditions being equal*, under the capitalist
system of production. *In the opening sentence of the first
section of Chapter VI Kautsky points precisely to this con-*

---

* The only thing Mr. Bulgakov could quote in support of his
claim is the *title* Kautsky gave to the first section of his Chapter VI:
"(a) The *Technical* Superiority of Large-Scale Production," although
this section deals with both the technical and the economic advantages
of large-scale production. But does this prove that Kautsky *confuses*
technique with economics? And, strictly speaking, it is still an open
question as to whether Kautsky's title is inexact. The point is that
Kautsky's object was to contrast the content of the first and second
sections of Chapter VI: in the first section (a) he deals with the technical
superiority of large-scale production in capitalist agriculture, and
here, in addition to machinery, etc., he mentions, for instance, credit.
"A peculiar sort of technical superiority," says Mr. Bulgakov ironically.
But *Rira bien qui rira le dernier*! (He laughs best who laughs last.—*Ed.*)
Glance into Kautsky's book and you will see that he has in mind, principally, the progress made in the *technique* of credit business (and
further on in the technique of trading), which is accessible *only* to
the big farmer. On the other hand, in the second section of this chapter
(b) he compares the quantity of labour expended and the rate of consumption by the workers in large-scale production with those in small-
scale production. Consequently, in this part Kautsky examines *the
purely economic difference* between small- and large-scale production.
The *economics* of credit and commerce is the same for both; but the
technique is different.

nection between the level of development of capitalism and the degree of the general applicability of the law of the superiority of large-scale agriculture: "The more capitalist agriculture becomes, the more it develops the qualitative difference between the techniques of small- and large-scale production" (*S.* 92). This qualitative difference did not exist in pre-capitalist agriculture. What then can be said of this stern admonition to which Mr. Bulgakov treats Kautsky: "In point of fact, the question should have been put as follows: what significance in the competition between large- and small-scale production can any of the specific features of either of these forms of production have *under the present social-economic conditions*?" This "correction" bears the same character as the one we examined above.

Let us see now how Mr. Bulgakov refutes Kautsky's arguments in favour of the technical superiority of large-scale production in agriculture. Kautsky says: "One of the most important features distinguishing agriculture from industry is that in agriculture production in the proper sense of the word [*Wirtschaftsbetrieb*, an economic enterprise] is usually connected with the household (*Haushalt*), which is not the case in industry." That the larger household has the advantage over the small household in the saving of labour and materials hardly needs proof.... The former purchases (note this! *V. I.*) "kerosene, chicory, and margarine wholesale; the latter purchases these articles retail, etc." (*S.* 93). Mr. Bulgakov "corrects": "Kautsky did not mean to say that this was technically more advantageous, but that it *cost less*"!... Is it not clear that in this case (as in all the others) Mr. Bulgakov's attempt to "correct" Kautsky was more than unfortunate? "This argument," continues the stern critic, "is also very·questionable in itself, because under certain conditions the value of the product may not include the value of the scattered huts, whereas the value of a common house is included, even with the interest added. This, too, depends upon social-economic conditions, which—and not the alleged technical advantages of large-scale over small-scale production—should have been investigated."... In the first place, Mr. Bulgakov forgets the trifle that Kautsky, after comparing the significance of large-scale production with that of small-scale production, *all other conditions being equal,* proceeds to examine these conditions in detail. Consequently, Mr. Bulgakov wants to throw different questions together. Secondly, how is it that the value of the peasants' huts does not enter into the value of the product? Only because the peasant "does not count" the value of the timber he uses or the labour he expends in building and repairing his hut. Insofar as the peasant still conducts a natural economy, he, of course, may "not count" his labour; there is no justification for Mr. Bulgakov's not telling his readers that *Kautsky very clearly and precisely points this out on pp. 165-67 of his book* (Chapter VIII, "The Proletarisation of the Peasant"). But we are now discussing the "social-economic condition" of capitalism and not of natural economy or of simple commodity production. Under capitalist social conditions "not to count" one's labour means to work for nothing (for the merchant or another capitalist); it means to work for incomplete remuneration for the labour-power expended; it means to lower the level of consumption below the standard. As we have seen, Kautsky fully recognised and correctly appraised *this* distinguishing feature of small production. In his objection to Kautsky, Mr. Bulgakov repeats the usual trick and the usual mistake of the bourgeois and petty-bourgeois economists. These economists have deafened us with their praises of the "viability" of the small peasant, who, they say, need not count his own labour, or chase after profit and rent, etc. These good people merely forget that such arguments confuse the "social-economic conditions" of natural economy, simple commodity production, and capitalism. Kautsky excellently explains all these mistakes and *draws a strict distinction* between the various systems of social-economic relations. He says: "If the agricultural production of the small peasant is not drawn into the sphere of commodity production, if it is merely a part of household economy, it also remains outside the sphere of the centralising tendencies of the modern mode of production. However irrational his parcellised economy may be, no matter what waste of effort it may lead to, he clings to it tightly, just as his wife clings to her wretched household economy, which likewise produces infinitely miserable results with an enormous expenditure of labour-power, but which represents the only sphere in which she is not subject to another's rule and is free from exploitation" (*S.* 165). The situation changes when natural economy is supplanted by commodity economy. The peasant then has to sell his produce, purchase implements, and *purchase land.* As long as the peasant remains *a simple commodity producer,* he can be satisfied with the standard of living of the wage-worker; he needs neither profit nor rent; he can pay a higher price for land than the capitalist entrepreneur (*S.* 166). But simple commodity production is supplanted by *capitalist production.* If, for instance, the peasant has mortgaged his land, he must also obtain the rent which he has sold to the creditor. At this stage of development the peasant can only formally be regarded as a simple commodity producer. *De facto,* he usually has to deal with the *capitalist*—the creditor, the merchant, the industrial entrepreneur—from whom he must seek "auxiliary employment," i.e., to whom he must sell his labour-power. At this stage—and Kautsky, we repeat, compares large-scale with small-scale farming in capitalist society—the possibility for the peasant "not to count his labour" means only one thing to him, namely, to work himself to death and continually to cut down his consumption.

Equally unsound are the other objections raised by Mr. Bulgakov. Small-scale production permits of the employment of machinery within narrower limits; the small proprietor finds credit more difficult to obtain and more expensive, says Kautsky. Mr. Bulgakov considers these arguments false and refers to—peasant associations! He completely ignores the evidence brought forward by Kautsky, whose appraisal of these associations and their significance we quoted above. On the question of machinery, Mr. Bulgakov again reproaches Kautsky for not raising the "more general economic question: What, upon the whole, is the economic role of machinery in agriculture [Mr. Bulgakov has forgotten Chapter IV of Kautsky's book!] and is it as inevitable an instrument in agriculture as in manufacturing industry?" Kautsky clearly pointed to the capitalist nature of the use of machinery in modern agriculture (*S.* 39, 40, et seq.); noted the specific features of agriculture which create "technical and economic difficulties" for the employment of machinery in agriculture (*S.* 38, et seq.); and adduced data on the growing employment of machinery (*S.* 40), on its technical significance (42, et seq.), and on the role of steam and electricity. Kautsky indicated the size of farm necessary, according to agronomic data, for making the fullest use of various machines (94), and pointed out that according to the German census of 1895 the employment of machinery steadily and rapidly increases from the small farms to the big ones (2 per cent in farms up to two hectares, 13.8 per cent in farms of 2 to 5 hectares, 45.8 per cent in farms of 5 to 20 hectares, 78.8 per cent in farms of 20 to 100 hectares, and 94.2 per cent in farms of 100 and more hectares). Instead of these figures, Mr. Bulgakov would have preferred "general" arguments about the "invincibility" or non-invincibility of machines!...

"The argument that a larger number of draught animals per hectare is employed in small-scale production is unconvincing... because the relative intensity of animal maintenance per farm... is not investigated"—says Mr. Bulgakov. We open Kautsky's book at the page that contains this argument and read the following: "The large number of cows in small-scale farming [per 1,000 hectares] is to no small extent also determined by the fact that the peasant engages more in animal husbandry and less in the production of grain than the big farmer; but this does not explain the difference in the number of horses maintained" (page 96, on which are quoted figures for Saxony for 1860, for the whole of Germany for 1883, and for England for 1880). We remind the reader of the fact that in Russia the Zemstvo statistics reveal the same law expressing the superiority of large-scale over small-scale farming: the big peasant farms manage with a smaller number of cattle and implements per unit of land.*

Mr. Bulgakov gives a far from complete exposition of Kautsky's arguments on the superiority of large-scale over small-scale production in capitalist agriculture. The superiority of large-scale farming does not only lie in the fact that there is less waste of cultivated area, a saving in livestock and implements, fuller utilisation of implements,

---

* See V. Y. Postnikov, *Peasant Farming in South Russia.* Cf. V. Ilyin, *The Development of Capitalism*, Chapter II, Section I. (See present edition, Vol. 3.—*Ed.*)

wider possibilities of employing machinery, and more opportunities for obtaining credit; it also lies in the commercial superiority of large-scale production, the employment in the latter of scientifically trained managers (Kautsky, *S*. 104). Large-scale farming utilises the co-operation of workers and division of labour to a larger extent. Kautsky attaches particular importance to the scientific, agronomic education of the farmer. "A scientifically well-educated farmer can be employed only by a farm sufficiently large for the work of management and supervision to engage fully the person's labour-power" (*S*. 98: "The size of such farms varies, according to the type of production," from three hectares of vineyards to 500 hectares of extensive farming). In this connection Kautsky mentions the interesting and extremely characteristic fact that the establishment of primary and secondary agricultural schools benefits the big farmer and not the peasant by providing the former with employees (the same thing is observed in Russia). "The higher education that is required for fully rationalised production is hardly compatible with the peasants' present conditions of existence. This, of course, is a condemnation, not of higher education, but of the peasants' conditions of life. It merely means that peasant production is able to exist side by side with large-scale production, not because of its higher productivity, but because of its lower requirements" (*S*. 99). Large-scale production must employ, not only peasant labourers, but also urban workers, whose requirements are on an incomparably higher level.

Mr. Bulgakov calls the highly interesting and important data which Kautsky adduces to prove "overwork and underconsumption in small-scale production" "a few [!] casual [??] quotations." Mr. Bulgakov "undertakes" to cite as many "quotations of an opposite character." He merely forgets to say whether he also undertakes to make *an opposite assertion* which he would prove by "quotations of an opposite character." This is the whole point! Does Mr. Bulgakov undertake to assert that large-scale production in capitalist society differs from peasant production in the prevalence of overwork and the lower consumption of its workers? Mr. Bulgakov is too cautious to make such a ludicrous assertion. He considers it possible to avoid the fact of the peasants' overwork and lower consumption by remarking that "in some places peasants are prosperous and in other places they are poor"!! What would be said of an economist who, instead of generalising the data on the position of small- and large-scale production, began to investigate the difference in the "prosperity" of the population of various "places"? What would be said of an economist who evaded the overwork and lower consumption of handicraftsmen, as compared with factory workers, with the remark that "in some places handicraftsmen are prosperous and in other places they are poor"? Incidentally, a word about handicraftsmen. Mr. Bulgakov writes: "Apparently Kautsky was mentally drawing a parallel with *Hausindustrie*,* where there are no technical limits to overwork [as in agriculture], but this parallel is unsuitable here." Apparently, we say in reply, Mr. Bulgakov was astonishingly inattentive to the book he was criticising, for Kautsky did not "mentally draw a parallel" with *Hausindustrie*, but *pointed to it directly and precisely on the very fist page of that part of the chapter* which deals with the question of overwork (Chapter VI, b, *S.* 106): "As in domestic industry (*Hausindustrie*), the work of the children of the family in small peasant farming is even more harmful than wage-labour for others." However emphatically Mr. Bulgakov decrees that this parallel is unsuitable here, his opinion is nevertheless entirely erroneous. In industry, overwork has no technical limits; but for the peasantry it is "limited by the technical conditions of agriculture," argues Mr. Bulgakov. The question arises: who, indeed, confuses technique with economics, Kautsky or Mr. Bulgakov? What has the technique of agriculture, or of domestic industry, to do with the case when facts prove that the small producer in agriculture and in industry drives his children to work at an earlier age, works more hours per day, lives "more frugally," and cuts down his requirements to such a level that he stands out in a civilised country as a real "barbarian" (Marx's expression)? Can the economic similarity of such phenomena in agriculture and in industry be denied on the grounds that agriculture has a large number of specific features (which Kautsky does not forget in the least)? "The

---

* Domestic industry.— *Ed.*

small peasant could not put in more work than his field requires even if he wanted to," says Mr. Bulgakov. But the
small peasant can and does work fourteen, and not twelve,
hours a day; he can and does work with that super-normal
intensity which wears out his nerves and muscles much more
quickly than the normal intensity. Moreover, what an incorrect and extreme abstraction it is to reduce all the peasant's
work to field work! You will find nothing of the kind in Kautsky's book. Kautsky knows perfectly well that the peasant
also works in the household, works on building and repairing
his hut, his cowshed, his implements, etc., *"not counting"*
all this additional work, for which a wage-worker on a big
farm would demand payment at the usual rate. Is it not clear
to every unprejudiced person that overwork has *incomparably wider limits* for the peasant—for the small farmer—
than for the small industrial producer if he is *only* such? The
overwork of the small farmer is strikingly demonstrated as
a universal phenomenon by the fact that all bourgeois writers unanimously testify to the "diligence" and "frugality"
of the peasant and accuse the workers of "indolence" and
"extravagance."

The small peasants, says an investigator of the life of the
rural population in Westphalia quoted by Kautsky, overwork
their children to such an extent that their physical development is retarded; working for wages has not such bad sides.
A small Lincolnshire farmer stated the following to the parliamentary commission which investigated agrarian conditions in England (1897): "I have brought up a family and
nearly worked them to death." Another said: "I and my
children have been working eighteen hours a day for several
days and average ten to twelve during the year." A third:
"We work much harder than labourers, in fact, like slaves."
Mr. Read described to the same commission the conditions
of the small farmer, in the districts where agriculture in the
strict sense of the word predominates, in the following manner: "The only way in which he can possibly succeed is this,
in doing the work of two agricultural labourers and living at
the expense of one ... as regards his family, they are
worse educated and harder worked than the children of the
agricultural labourers" (Royal Commission on Agriculture, Final Report, pp. 34, 358. Quoted by Kautsky,

S. 109). Will Mr. Bulgakov assert that not less frequently
a day labourer does the work of two peasants? Particularly
characteristic is the following fact cited by Kautsky showing that "the peasant art of starvation (*Hungerkunst*) may
lead to the economic superiority of small production": a
comparison of the profitableness of two peasant farms in
Baden shows a deficit of 933 marks in one, *the large one*,
and a surplus of 191 marks in the other, which was *only
half the size* of the first. But the first farm, which was conducted exclusively with the aid of hired labourers, had to feed
the latter properly, at a cost of nearly one mark (about 45
kopeks) per person per day; whereas the smaller farm was
conducted exclusively with the aid of the members of the
family (the wife and six grown-up children), whose maintenance *cost only half the amount* spent on the day labourers: 48 pfennigs per person per day. If the family of the small
peasant had been fed as well as the labourers hired by the big
farmer, the small farmer would have suffered a deficit of
1,250 marks! "His surplus came, not from his full corn bins,
but from his empty stomach." What a huge number of similar examples would be discovered, were the comparison of
the "profitableness" of large and small farms accompanied
by calculation of the consumption and work of peasants and
of wage-workers.* Here is another calculation of the higher
profit of a small farm (4.6 hectares) as compared with a big
farm (26.5 hectares), a calculation made in one of the special
magazines. But how is this higher profit obtained?—asks
Kautsky. It turns out that the small farmer is assisted by his
children, assisted from the time they begin to walk; whereas
the big farmer has to spend money on his children (school,
gymnasium). In the small farm even the old people, over
70 years of age, "take the place of a full worker." "An ordinary
day labourer, particularly on a big farm, goes about his work
and thinks to himself: 'I wish it was knocking-off time.'
The small peasant, however, at all events in all the busy
seasons, thinks to himself: 'Oh, if only the day were an hour
or two longer.'" The small producers, the author of this
article in the agricultural magazine says didactically, make

---

* Cf. V. Ilyin, *The Development of Capitalism in Russia*, pp. 112,
175, 201. (See present edition, Vol. 3, pp. 168-70, 244-46, 273-75.—*Ed.*)

better use of their time in the busy seasons: "They rise earlier, retire later and work more quickly, whereas the labourers employed by the big farmer do not want to get up earlier, go to bed later or work harder than at other times." The peasant is able to obtain a net income thanks to the "simple" life he leads: he lives in a mud hut built mainly by the labour of his family; his wife has been married for 17 years and has worn out only one pair of shoes; usually she goes barefoot, or in wooden sabots; and she makes all the clothes for her family. Their food consists of potatoes, milk, and on rare occasions, herring. Only on Sundays does the husband smoke a pipe of tobacco. "These people did not realise that they were leading a particularly simple life and did not express dissatisfaction with their position.... Following this simple way of life, they obtained nearly every year a small surplus from their farm."

IV

After completing his analysis of the interrelations between large- and small-scale production in capitalist agriculture, Kautsky proceeds to make a special investigation of the "limits of capitalist agriculture" (Chapter VII). Kautsky says that objection to the theory that large-scale farming is superior to small-scale is raised mainly by the "friends of humanity" (we almost said, friends of the people...) among the bourgeoisie, the pure Free Traders, and the agrarians. Many economists have recently been advocating small-scale farming. The statistics usually cited are those showing that big farms are not eliminating small farms. And Kautsky quotes these statistics: in Germany, from 1882 to 1895, it was the area of the medium-sized farms that increased most; in France, from 1882 to 1892, it was the area of the smallest and biggest farms that increased most; the area of the medium-sized farms diminished. In England, from 1885 to 1895, the area of the smallest and the biggest farms diminished; it was the area of the farms ranging from 40 to 120 hectares (100 to 300 acres), i.e., farms that cannot be put in the category of small farms, which increased most. In America, the average area of farms is diminishing: in 1850 it was 203 acres; in 1860—199 acres; in 1870—153 acres; in 1880—134 acres; and in 1890—137 acres. Kautsky makes a closer examination of the American statistics and, Mr. Bulgakov's opinion notwithstanding, his analysis is extremely important from the standpoint of *principle*. The main reason for the diminution in the average farm area is the break-up of the large plantations in the South after the emancipation of the Negroes; in the Southern States the average farm area diminished by more than one-half. "Not a single person who understands the subject will regard these figures as evidence of the victory of small-scale over *modern* [=capitalist] large-scale production." In general, an analysis of American statistics *by regions* shows a large variety of relations. In the principal "wheat states," in the northern part of the Middle West, the average farm area *increased* from 122 to 133 acres. "Small-scale production becomes predominant only in those places where agriculture is in a state of decline, or where pre-capitalist, large-scale production enters into competition with peasant production" (135). This conclusion of Kautsky is very important, for it shows that if certain conditions are not adhered to, the handling of statistics may become merely *mishandling*: a distinction must be drawn between capitalist and pre-capitalist large-scale production. A *detailed* analysis must be made for separate districts that differ materially from one another in the forms of farming and in the historical conditions of its development. It is said, "Figures prove!" But one must analyse the figures to see what they prove. They only prove *what they directly say*. The figures do not speak directly of the scale on which production is carried on, but of the *area* of the farms. It is possible, and in fact it so happens, that "with intensive farming, production can be carried on upon a larger scale on a small estate than on a large estate extensively farmed." "Statistics that tell us only about the area of farms tell us nothing as to whether the diminution of their area is due to the actual diminution of the scale of farming, or to its intensification" (146). Forestry and pastoral farming, these first forms of capitalist large-scale farming, permit of the largest area of estates. Field cultivation requires a smaller area. But the various systems of field cultivation differ from one another in this respect: the exhaustive, extensive system of farming (which has prevailed in America up to now) permits of huge farms (up to 10,000 hectares, such as the *bonanza farms** of Dalrymple, Glenn, and others. In our steppes, too, peasant farms, and particularly merchants' farms, attain such dimensions). The introduction of fertilisers, etc., necessarily leads to a diminution in the area of farms, which in Europe, for instance, are smaller than in America. The transition from field farming to animal husbandry again causes a diminution in the area of farms: in England, in 1880, the average size of livestock farms was 52.3 acres, whereas that of field farms was 74.2 acres. That is why the transition from field farming to animal husbandry which is taking place in England *must* give rise to a tendency for the area of farms to diminish. "But it would be judging very superficially if the conclusion were drawn from this that there has been a decline in production" (149). In East Elbe (by the investigation of which Mr. Bulgakov hopes some time to refute Kautsky), it is precisely the introduction of intensive farming that is taking place: the big farmers, says Sering, whom Kautsky quotes, are increasing the productivity of their soil and are selling or leasing to peasants the remote parts of their estates, since with intensive farming it is difficult to utilise these remote parts. "Thus, large estates in East Elbe are being reduced in size and in their vicinity small peasant farms are being established; this, however, is not because small-scale production is superior to large-scale, but because the former dimensions of the estates were adapted to the needs of extensive farming" (150). The diminution in farm area in all these cases usually leads to an increase in the quantity of products (per unit of land) and frequently to an increase in the number of workers employed, i.e,, to an actual *increase* in the scale of production.

From this it is clear how little is proved by general agricultural statistics on the *area* of farms, and how cautiously one must handle them. In industrial statistics we have *direct* indices of the scale of production (quantity of goods, total value of the output, and number of workers employed), and, besides, it is easy to distinguish the different branches. Agricultural statistics hardly ever satisfy these necessary conditions of evidence.

---

* These words are in English in the original.—*Ed*.

Furthermore, the monopoly in landed property limits agricultural capitalism: in industry, capital grows as a result of *accumulation*, as a result of the conversion of surplus-value into capital; *centralisation*, i.e., the amalgamation of several small units of capital into a large unit, plays a lesser role. In agriculture, the situation is different. The whole of the land is occupied (in civilised countries), and it is possible to enlarge the area of a farm only by *centralising* several lots; this must be done in such a way as to form *one continuous area*. Clearly, enlarging an estate by purchasing the surrounding lots is a very difficult matter, particularly in view of the fact that the small lots are partly occupied by agricultural labourers (whom the big farmer needs), and partly by small peasants who are masters of the art of maintaining their hold by reducing consumption to an unbelievable minimum. For some reason or other the statement of this simple and very clear fact, which indicates the limits of agricultural capitalism, seemed to Mr. Bulgakov to be a mere "phrase" (??!!) and provided a pretext for the most groundless rejoicing: "And so [!], the superiority of large-scale production comes to grief [!] at the very first obstacle." First, Mr. Bulgakov misunderstands the law of the superiority of large-scale production, ascribing to it excessive abstractness, from which Kautsky is very remote, and then turns his misunderstanding into an argument against Kautsky! Truly strange is Mr. Bulgakov's belief that he can refute Kautsky by referring to Ireland (large landed property, but without large-scale production). The fact that large landed property is one of the conditions of large-scale production does not in the least signify that it is a sufficient condition. Of course, Kautsky could not examine the historical and other causes of the specific features of Ireland, or of any other country, in a general work on capitalism in agriculture. It would not occur to anyone to demand that Marx, in analysing the general laws of capitalism in industry, should have explained why small industry continued longer in France, why industry was developing slowly in Italy, etc. Equally groundless is Mr. Bulgakov's assertion that concentration "could" proceed gradually: it is not as easy to enlarge estates by purchasing neighbouring lots as it is to add new premises to a factory for an additional number of machines, etc.

In referring to this purely fictitious possibility of the gradual concentration, or renting, of land for the purpose of forming large farms, Mr. Bulgakov paid little attention to the really specific feature of agriculture in the process of concentration—a feature which Kautsky indicated. This is the latifundia, the concentration of several estates in the hands of a single owner. Statistics usually register the number of individual estates and tell us nothing about the process of concentration of various estates in the hands of big landowners. Kautsky cites very striking instances, in Germany and Austria, of such concentration which leads to a special and higher form of large-scale capitalist farming in which several large estates are combined to form a single economic unit managed by a single central body. Such gigantic agricultural enterprises make possible the combination of the most varied branches of agriculture and the most extensive use of the advantages of large-scale production.

The reader will see how remote Kautsky is from abstractness and from a stereotyped understanding of "Marx's theory," to which he remains true. Kautsky warned against this stereotyped understanding, even inserting a special section on the doom of small-scale production in industry in the chapter under discussion. He rightly points out that even in industry the victory of large-scale production is not so easy of achievement, and is not so uniform, as those who talk about Marx's theory being inapplicable to agriculture are in the habit of thinking. It is sufficient to point to capitalist domestic industry; it is sufficient to recall the remark Marx made about the extreme variety of transitional and mixed forms which obscure the victory of the factory system. How much more complicated this is in agriculture! The increase in wealth and luxury leads, for example, to millionaires purchasing huge estates which they turn into forests for their pleasures. In Salzburg, in Austria, the number of cattle has been declining since 1869. The reason is the sale of the Alps to rich lovers of the hunt. Kautsky says very aptly that if agricultural statistics are taken in general, and uncritically, it is quite easy to discover in the capitalist mode of production a tendency to transform modern nations into hunting tribes!

Finally, among the conditions setting the limits to capitalist agriculture, Kautsky also points to the fact that the shortage of workers—due to the migration of the rural population—compels the big landowners to allot land to labourers, to create a small peasantry to provide labour-power for the landlord. An absolutely propertyless agricultural labourer is a rarity, because in agriculture rural economy, in the strict sense, is connected with household economy. Whole categories of agricultural wage-workers own or have the use of land. When small production is eliminated too greatly, *the big landowners try to strengthen or revive it* by the sale or lease of land. Sering, whom Kautsky quotes, says: "In all European countries, a movement has recently been observed towards... settling rural labourers by allotting plots of land to them." Thus, within the limits of the capitalist mode of production it is impossible to count on small-scale production being entirely eliminated from agriculture, for the capitalists and agrarians themselves strive to revive it when the ruination of the peasantry has gone too far. Marx pointed to this rotation of concentration and parcellisation of the land in capitalist society as far back as 1850, in the *Neue Rheinische Zeitung.*[52]

Mr. Bulgakov is of the opinion that these arguments of Kautsky contain "an element of truth, but still more of error." Like all Mr. Bulgakov's other verdicts, this one has also extremely weak and nebulous grounds. Mr. Bulgakov thinks that Kautsky has "constructed a theory of proletarian small-scale production," and that this theory is true for a very limited region. We hold a different opinion. The agricultural wage-labour of small cultivators (or what is the same thing, the agricultural labourer and day labourer with an allotment) is *a phenomenon characteristic, more or less, of all capitalist countries.* No writer who desires to describe capitalism in agriculture can, without violating the truth, leave this phenomenon in the background.* Kautsky, in Chapter VIII of his book, viz., "The Proletarisation of the Peasant," adduces extensive evidence to prove that in Germany, in

---

* Cf. *The Development of Capitalism in Russia*, Chapter II, Section XII, p. 120. (See present edition, Vol. 3, p. 178.—*Ed.*) It is estimated that in France about 75 per cent of the rural labourers own land. Other examples are also given.

particular, proletarian small-scale production is general.
Mr. Bulgakov's statement that other writers, including
Mr. Kablukov, have pointed to the "shortage of workers" *leaves
the most important thing in the background*—the enormous
difference in principle between Mr. Kablukov's theory and
Kautsky's theory. Because of his characteristically *Klein-
bürger* * point of view, Mr. Kablukov "constructs" out of
the shortage of workers the theory that large-scale production
is unsound and that small-scale production is sound. Kautsky
gives an accurate description of the facts and indicates their
true significance in modern class society: the class interests
of the landowners compel them to strive to allot land to the
workers. As far as class position is concerned, the agricultural wage-workers with allotments are situated between the
petty bourgeoisie and the proletariat, but closer to the latter.
In other words, Mr. Kablukov develops one side of a complicated process into a theory of the unsoundness of large-scale
production, whereas Kautsky analyses the special forms of
social-economic relations created by the interests of large-
scale production at a certain stage of its development and
under certain historical conditions.

V

We shall now pass to the next chapter of Kautsky's book,
the title of which we have just quoted. In this chapter
Kautsky investigates, firstly, the "tendency toward the parcellisation of landholdings," and, secondly, the "forms of
peasant auxiliary employments." Thus, here are depicted
those extremely important trends of capitalism in agriculture that are typical of the overwhelming majority of capitalist countries. Kautsky says that the break-up of landholdings leads to an increased demand for small plots on the part
of small peasants, who pay a higher price for the land than
the big farmers. Several writers have adduced this fact
to prove that small-scale farming is superior to large-scale
farming. Kautsky very appropriately replies to this by comparing the price of land with the price of houses: it is well
known that small and cheap houses are *dearer* per unit of

---

* Petty-bourgeois.— *Ed.*

capacity (per cubic foot, etc.) than large and costly houses.
The higher price of small plots of land is not due to the
superiority of small-scale farming, but to the particularly
oppressed condition of the peasant. The enormous number of
dwarf farms that capitalism has called into being is seen from
the following figures: in Germany (1895), out of 5,500,000
farms, 4,250,000, i.e., more than three-fourths, are of an
area of less than five hectares (58 per cent are less than two
hectares). In Belgium, 78 per cent (709,500 out of 909,000)
are less than two hectares. In England (1895), 118,000 out
of 520,000 are less than two hectares. In France (1892),
2,200,000 (out of 5,700,000) are less than one hectare;
4,000,000 are less than five hectares. Mr. Bulgakov thinks
that he can refute Kautsky's argument that these dwarf
farms are very irrational (insufficient cattle, implements,
money, and labour-power which is diverted to auxiliary oc-
cupations) by arguing that "very often" (??) the land is spade-
tilled "with an incredible degree of intensity," although ...
with "an extremely irrational expenditure of labour-power."
It goes without saying that this objection is totally groundless, that individual examples of excellent cultivation of the
soil by small peasants are as little able to refute Kautsky's
general characterisation of this type of farming as the above-
quoted example of the greater profitableness of a small farm
is able to refute the thesis of the superiority of large-scale
production. That Kautsky is quite right in placing these
farms, *taken as a whole*,* in the proletarian category is seen
from the fact, revealed by the German census of 1895, that
very many of the small farmers cannot dispense with subsidiary earnings. Of a total of 4,700,000 persons obtaining an
independent livelihood in agriculture, 2,700,000, or *57 per
cent*, have subsidiary earnings. Of 3,200,000 farms of less
than two hectares each, only 400,000, or *13 per cent*, have no
subsidiary incomes! In the whole of Germany, out of

---

* We emphasise "taken as a whole," because it cannot, of course,
be denied that in certain cases even these farms having an insignificant area of land can provide a large quantity of products and a large
income (vineyards, vegetable gardens, etc.). But what would we say
of an economist who tried to refute the reference to the lack of horses
among Russian peasants by pointing, for instance, to the vegetable
growers in the suburbs of Moscow who may sometimes carry on rational
and profitable farming without horses?

5,500,000 farms, *1,500,000* belong to agricultural and industrial wage-workers (+704,000 to artisans). And after this Mr. Bulgakov presumes to assert that the theory of proletarian small landholdings was "constructed" by Kautsky!* Kautsky thoroughly investigated the forms assumed by the proletarisation of the peasantry (the forms of peasant auxiliary employment) (*S.* 174-93). Unfortunately, space does not permit us to deal in detail with his description of these forms (agricultural work for wages, domestic industry— *Hausindustrie*, "the vilest system of capitalist exploitation"— work in factories and mines, etc.). Our only observation is that Kautsky makes the same appraisal of *auxiliary employment* as that made by Russian economists. Migratory workers

---

* In a footnote to page 15, Mr. Bulgakov says that Kautsky, believing that grain duties were not in the interest of the overwhelming majority of the rural population, repeats the mistake committed by authors of the book on grain prices.[53] We cannot agree with this opinion either. The authors of the book on grain prices made a large number of mistakes (which I indicated repeatedly in the above-mentioned book); but there is no mistake whatever in admitting that high grain prices are not in the interests of the mass of the population. What is a mistake is the *direct* deduction that the interests of the masses coincide with the interests of the whole social development. Messrs. Tugan-Baranovsky and Struve have rightly pointed out that the *criterion* in appraising grain prices must be whether, more or less rapidly, through capitalism, they eliminate labour-service, whether they stimulate social development. This is a question of fact which I answer differently from the way Struve does. I do not at all regard it as proved that the development of capitalism in agriculture is retarded by low prices. On the contrary, the particularly rapid growth of the agricultural machinery industry and the stimulus to specialisation in agriculture which was given by the reduction of grain prices show that low prices *stimulate* the development of capitalism in Russian agriculture (cf. *The Development of Capitalism in Russia*, Chapter III, Section V, p. 147, footnote 2). (See present edition, Vol. 3, pp. 212-13.—*Ed.*) The reduction of grain prices has a profound transforming effect upon all other relations in agriculture.

Mr. Bulgakov says: "One of the important conditions for the intensification of farming is the raising of grain prices." (The same opinion is expressed by Mr. P. S. in the "Review of Home Affairs" column, p. 299 in the same issue of *Nachalo*.) This is inexact. Marx showed in Part VI of Volume III of *Capital*[54] that the productivity of additional capital invested in land may diminish, *but may also increase*; with a reduction in the price of grain, rent may fall, *but it may also rise*. Consequently, intensification may be due—in different historical periods and in different countries—to altogether different conditions, irrespective of the level of grain prices.

are less developed and have a lower level of requirements than urban workers; not infrequently, they have a harmful effect on the living conditions of the urban workers. "But for those places from which they come and to which they return they are pioneers of progress.... They acquire new wants and new ideas" (S. 192), they awaken among the backwoods peasants consciousness, a sense of human dignity, and confidence in their own strength.

In conclusion we shall deal with the last and particularly sharp attack Mr. Bulgakov makes upon Kautsky. Kautsky says that in Germany, from 1882 to 1895 it was the smallest (in area) and the largest farms that grew most in number (so that the parcellisation of the land proceeded at the expense of the medium farms). Indeed, the number of farms under one hectare increased by 8.8 per cent; those of 5 to 20 hectares increased by 7.8 per cent; while those of over 1,000 hectares increased by 11 per cent (the number of those in the intervening categories hardly increased at all, while the total number of farms increased by 5.3 per cent). Mr. Bulgakov is extremely indignant because the percentage is taken of the biggest farms, the number of which is insignificant (515 and 572 for the respective years). Mr. Bulgakov's indignation is quite groundless. He forgets that these farms, insignificant in number, are the largest in size and that they *occupy nearly as much land as* 2,300,000 to 2,500,000 dwarf farms (up to one hectare). If I were to say that the number of very big factories in a country, those employing 1,000 and more workers, increased, say, from 51 to 57, by 11 per cent, while the total number of factories increased 5.3 per cent, would not that show an increase in large-scale production, notwithstanding the fact that the *number* of very large factories may be insignificant as compared with the total number of factories? Kautsky is fully aware of the fact that it was the peasant farms of from 5 to 20 hectares which grew most in total area (Mr. Bulgakov, p. 18), and he deals with it in the ensuing chapter.

Kautsky then takes the changes in area in the various categories in 1882 and 1895. It appears that the largest increase (+563,477 hectares) occurred among the peasant farms of from 5 to 20 hectares, and the next largest among the biggest farms, those of more than 1,000 hectares (+94,014), whereas the area of farms of from 20 to 1,000 hectares *diminished* by 86,809 hectares. Farms up to one hectare increased their area by 32,683 hectares, and those from 1 to 5 hectares, by 45,604 hectares.

And Kautsky draws the following conclusion: the diminution in the area of farms of from 20 to 1,000 hectares (more than balanced by an increase in the area of farms of 1,000 hectares and over) is due, not to the decline of large-scale production, but to its intensification. We have already seen that intensive farming is making progress in Germany and that it frequently requires a diminution in the area of farms. That there is intensification of large-scale production can be seen from the growing utilisation of steam-driven machinery, as well as from the enormous increase in the number of agricultural non-manual employees, who in Germany are employed only on large farms. The number of estate managers (inspectors), overseers, bookkeepers, etc., increased from 47,465 in 1882 to 76,978 in 1895, i.e., by 62 per cent; the percentage of women among these employees increased from 12 to 23.4.

"All this shows clearly how much more intensive and more capitalist large-scale farming has become since the beginning of the eighties. The next chapter will explain why simultaneously there has been such a big increase in the area of middle-peasant farms" (*S.* 174).

Mr. Bulgakov regards this description as being "in crying contradiction to reality," but the arguments he falls back on again fail to justify such an emphatic and bold verdict, and not by one iota do they shake Kautsky's conclusion. "In the first place, the intensification of farming, if it took place, would not in itself explain the relative and absolute diminution of the cultivated area, the diminution of the total proportion of farms in the 20- to 1,000-hectare group. The cultivated area could have increased simultaneously with the increase in the number of farms. The latter need merely (*sic!*) have increased somewhat faster, so that the area of each farm would have diminished."*

---

* Mr. Bulgakov adduces data, in still greater detail, but they add nothing whatever to Kautsky's data, since they show the same increase in the number of farms in one group of big proprietors and a reduction in the land area.

We have deliberately quoted in full this argument, from which Mr. Bulgakov draws the conclusion that "the diminution in the size of farms owing to the growth of intensive farming is pure fantasy" (sic!), because it strikingly reveals the very mistake of mishandling "statistics" against which Kautsky seriously warned. Mr. Bulgakov puts ridiculously strict demands upon the statistics of the *area* of farms and ascribes to these statistics a significance which they never can have. Why, indeed, should the cultivated area have increased "somewhat"? Why "should not" the intensification of farming (which, as we have seen, sometimes leads to the sale and renting to peasants of parts of estates remote from the centre) have shifted a certain number of farms from a higher category to a lower? Why "should it not" have diminished the cultivated area of farms of from 20 to 1,000 hectares?* In industrial statistics a reduction in the *output* of the very big factories would have indicated a decline in large-scale production. But the diminution in *area* of large estates by 1.2 per cent does not and *cannot indicate* the volume of production, which very often increases with a decrease in the area of the farm. We know that the process of livestock breeding replacing grain farm-ing, particularly marked in England, is going on in Europe as a whole. We know that sometimes this change causes a decrease in the farm area; but would it not be strange to draw from this the conclusion that the smaller farm area implied a decline in large-scale production? That is why, incidental-ly, the "eloquent table" given by Mr. Bulgakov on page 20, showing the reduction in the number of large and small farms and the increase in the number of medium farms (5 to 20 hec-tares) possessing animals for field work, proves nothing at all. This may have been due to a change in the system of farming.

That large-scale agricultural production in Germany has become more intensive and more capitalist is evident, first-ly, from the increase in the number of *steam-driven* ma-chines employed: from 1879 to 1897 their number increased

---

* There was a reduction in this category from 16,986,101 hectares to 16,802,115 hectares, i.e., by a whole ... 1.2 per cent! Does not this speak in favour of the "death agony" of large-scale production seen by Mr. Bulgakov?

fivefold. It is quite useless for Mr. Bulgakov to argue in his objection that the number of *all* machines *in general* (and not steam-driven machines only) owned by small farms (up to 20 hectares) is much larger than that owned by the large farms; and also that in America machines are employed in extensive farming. We are not discussing America now, but Germany, where there are no *bonanza farms.** The following table gives the percentage of farms in Germany (1895) employing steam ploughs and steam threshing machines:

Farms	Per cent of farms employing	
	steam ploughs	steam threshing machines
Under 2 hectares	0.00	1.08
2 to 5 "	0.00	5.20
5 to 20 "	0.01	10.95
20 to 100 "	0.10	16.60
100 hectares and over	5.29	61.22

And now, if the total number of steam-driven machines employed in agriculture in Germany has increased fivefold, does it not prove that large-scale farming has become more intensive? Only it must not be forgotten, as Mr. Bulgakov forgets on page 21, that an increase in the size of enterprises in agriculture is not always identical with an increase in the area of farms.

Secondly, the fact that large-scale production has become more capitalist is evident from the increase in the number of agricultural non-manual employees. It is useless for Bulgakov to call this argument of Kautsky a "curiosity": "an increase in the number of officers, side by side with a reduction of the army"—with a reduction in the number of agricultural wage-workers. Again we say: *Rira bien qui rira le dernier!*** Kautsky not only does not forget the reduction in the number of agricultural labourers, but shows it

---

* These words are in English in the original.—*Ed.*

** What is indeed a curiosity is Mr. Bulgakov's remark that the increase in the number of non-manual employees testifies, perhaps, to the growth of agricultural industry, *but not* (!) to the growth of intensive large-scale farming. Until now we have thought one of the most important forms of increased intensification to be the growth of industry in agriculture (*described in detail and appraised by Kautsky in Chapter X*).

in detail in regard to a number of countries; only this fact has absolutely nothing to do with the matter in hand, because the rural population as a whole is diminishing, while the number of proletarian small farmers is increasing. Let us assume that the big farmer abandons the production of grain and takes up the production of sugar-beet and the manufacture of sugar (in Germany in 1871-72, 2,200,000 tons of beets were converted into sugar; in 1881-82, 6,300,000 tons; in 1891-92, 9,500,000 tons, and in 1896-97, 13,700,000 tons). He might even sell, or rent, the remote parts of his estate to small peasants, particularly if he needs the wives and children of the peasants as day labourers on the beet plantations. Let us assume that he introduces a steam plough which eliminates the former ploughmen (on the beet plantations in Saxony—"models of intensive farming"*—steam ploughs have now come into common use). The number of wage-workers diminishes. The number of higher grade employees (bookkeepers, managers, technicians, etc.) necessarily increases. Will Mr. Bulgakov deny that we see here an increase in intensive farming and capitalism in large-scale production? Will he assert that nothing of the kind is taking place in Germany?

To conclude the exposition of Chapter VIII of Kautsky's book, viz., on the proletarisation of the peasants, we need to quote the following passage. "What interests us here," says Kautsky, after the passage we have cited above, quoted also by Mr. Bulgakov, "is the fact that the proletarisation of the rural population is proceeding in Germany, as in other places, notwithstanding the fact that the tendency to parcellise medium estates has ceased to operate there. From 1882 to 1895 the total number of farms increased by 281,000. By far the greater part of this increase was due to the greater number of proletarian farms up to one hectare in area. The number of these farms increased by 206,000.

"As we see, the development of agriculture is quite a special one, quite different from the development of industrial and trading capital. In the preceding chapter we pointed out that in agriculture the tendency to centralise farms does not lead to the complete elimination of small-scale pro-

---

* Kärger, quoted by Kautsky, *S*. 45.

duction. When this tendency goes too far it gives rise to an opposite tendency, so that the tendency to centralise and the tendency to parcellise alternate with each other. Now we see that both tendencies can operate side by side. There is an increase in the number of farms whose owners come into the commodity market as proletarians, as sellers of labour-power.... All the material interests of these small farmers as sellers of the commodity labour-power are identical with the interests of the industrial proletariat, and their land owner-ship does not give rise to antagonism between them and the proletariat. His land more or less emancipates the peasant small holder from the dealer in food products; but it does not emancipate him from the exploitation of the capitalist entrepreneur, whether industrial or agricultural" (*S*. 174).

———

In the following article we shall deal with the remain-ing part of Kautsky's book and give the work a general ap-praisal; in passing, we shall examine the objections Mr. Bulgakov raises in a later article.

———

SECOND ARTICLE

I

In Chapter IX of his book ("The Growing Difficulties of Commercial Agriculture") Kautsky proceeds to analyse the *contradictions* inherent in capitalist agriculture. From the objections which Mr. Bulgakov raises against this chapter, which we shall examine later, it is evident that the critic has not quite properly understood the general significance of these "difficulties." There are "difficulties" which, while being an "obstacle" to the full development of rational agriculture, at the same time *stimulate the development* of capitalist agriculture. Among the "difficulties" Kautsky points, for example, to the depopulation of the countryside. Undoubtedly, the migration from the countryside of the best and most intelligent workers is an "obstacle" to the full development of rational agriculture; but it is equally indubitable that the farmers combat this obstacle by *developing technique*, e.g., by introducing machinery.

Kautsky investigates the following "difficulties": a) ground rent; b) right of inheritance; c) limitation of right of inheritance; entailment (*fideicommissum*, *Anerbenrecht*)[55]; d) the exploitation of the countryside by the town; e) depopulation of the countryside.

Ground rent is that part of surplus-value which remains after the average profit on invested capital is deducted. The monopoly of landed property enables the landowner to appropriate this surplus, and the price of land (=capitalised rent) *keeps* rent at the level it has once reached. Clearly, rent "hinders" the complete rationalisation of agriculture: under the tenant farmer system the incentive to improvements, etc., becomes weaker, and under the mortgage system the major part of the capital has to be invested, not in production, but in the purchase of land. In his objection Mr. Bulgakov points out, first, that there is "nothing terrible" in the growth of mortgage debts. He forgets, however, that Kautsky, not "in another sense," but precisely in this sense, has pointed to the necessary increase in mortgages even when agriculture is prospering (see above, First Article, II). Here, Kautsky does not raise the question as to whether an increase in mortgages is "terrible" or not, but asks what difficulties prevent capitalism from accomplishing its mission. Secondly, in Mr. Bulgakov's opinion, "it is hardly correct to regard increased rent only as an obstacle.... The rise in rent, the possibility of raising it, serves as an independent incentive to agriculture, stimulating progress of technique and every other form" of progress ("process" is obviously a misprint). Stimuli to progress in capitalist agriculture are: population growth, growth of competition, and growth of industry; rent, however, is a tribute exacted by the landowner from social development, from the growth of technique. It is, therefore, incorrect to state, that the rise in rent is an "*independent* incentive" to progress. Theoretically, it is possible for capitalist production to exist in the absence of private property in land, i.e., with the land nationalised (Kautsky, *S.* 207), when absolute rent would not exist at all, and differential rent would be appropriated by the state. This would not weaken the incentive to agronomic progress; on the contrary, it would greatly increase it.

"There can be nothing more erroneous than to think that it is in the interest of agriculture to force up (*in die Höhe treiben*) the prices of estates or artificially to keep them at a high level," says Kautsky. "This is in the interest of the present (*augenblicklichen*) landowners, of the mortgage banks and the real estate speculators, but not in the interest of agriculture, and least of all in the interest of its future, of the future generation of farmers" (*S.* 199). As to the price of land, it is capitalised rent.

The second difficulty confronting commercial agriculture is that it necessarily requires private property in land. This leads to the situation in which the land is either split up on passing to heirs (such parcellisation even

leading in *some places* to technical retrogression) or is bur-
dened by mortgages (when the heir who receives the land
pays the co-heirs money capital which he obtains by a mortgage on the land). Mr. Bulgakov reproaches Kautsky for
"overlooking, in his exposition, the positive side" of the mobilisation of the land. This reproach is absolutely groundless; for in the historical part of his book (in particular
Chapter III of Part I, which deals with feudal agriculture
and the reasons for its supersession by capitalist agriculture), as well as in the practical part,* Kautsky clearly pointed
out to his readers the positive side and the historical necessity of private property in land, of the subjection of agriculture to competition, and, consequently, of the mobilisation of the land. The other reproach that Mr. Bulgakov
directs at Kautsky, namely, that he does not investigate the
problem of "the different degrees of growth of the population
in different places," is one that we simply cannot understand.
Did Mr. Bulgakov really expect to find studies in demog-
raphy in Kautsky's book?

Without dwelling on the question of entailment, which,
after what has been said above, represents nothing new, we
shall proceed to examine the question of the exploitation of
the countryside by the town. Mr. Bulgakov's assertion that
Kautsky "does not contrapose the positive to the negative
sides and, primarily, the importance of the town as a market
for agricultural produce," is in direct contradiction to the
facts. Kautsky deals very definitely with the importance of
the town as a market for agriculture *on the very first page*
of the chapter which investigates "modern agriculture"
(*S*. 30, et seq.). It is precisely to "urban industry" (*S*. 292)
that Kautsky ascribes the principal role in the transformation of agriculture, in its rationalisation, etc.**

That is why we cannot possibly understand how Mr. Bulgakov could repeat in his article (page 32, *Nachalo*, No. 3)
these very ideas *as if in opposition to Kautsky!* This is a

---

* Kautsky emphatically expressed his opposition to every medieval restriction upon the mobilisation of the land, to entailment
(*fideicommissum, Anerbenrecht*), and to the preservation of the medieval peasant commune (*S*. 332), etc.

** Cf. also *S*. 214, where Kautsky discusses the role urban capital
plays in the rationalisation of agriculture.

particularly striking example of this stern critic's false exposition of the book he is subjecting to criticism. "It must not be forgotten," Mr. Bulgakov says to Kautsky admonishingly, that "part of the values [which flow to the towns] returns to the countryside." Anyone would think that Kautsky forgets this elementary truth. As a matter of fact Kautsky distinguishes between the flow of values (from the countryside to the town) with or without an equivalent return much more clearly than Mr. Bulgakov attempts to do. In the first place, Kautsky examines the "flow of commodity values from the country to the town without equivalent return (*Gegenleistung*)" (*S.* 210) (rent which is spent in the towns, taxes, interest on loans obtained in city banks) and justly regards this as the economic exploitation of the countryside by the town. Kautsky further discusses the question of the efflux of values with an equivalent return, i.e., the exchange of agricultural produce for manufactured goods. He says: "From the point of view of the law of value, this efflux does not signify the exploitation of agriculture*; actually, however, in the same way as the above-mentioned factors, it leads to its agronomic (*stofflichen*) exploitation, to the impoverishment of the land in nutritive substances" (*S.* 211).

As for the agronomic exploitation of the countryside by the town, here too Kautsky adheres to one of the fundamental propositions of the theory of Marx and Engels, i.e., that the antithesis between town and country destroys the necessary correspondence and interdependence between agriculture and industry, and that with the transition of capitalism to a higher form this antithesis must disappear.**

---

* Let the reader compare Kautsky's clear statement as quoted above with the following "critical" remark by Mr. Bulgakov: "If Kautsky regards the giving of grain to the non-agricultural population by direct grain producers as exploitation," etc. One cannot believe that a critic who has read Kautsky's book at all attentively could have written that "if"!

** It goes without saying that the opinion that it is necessary to abolish the antithesis between town and country in a society of associated producers does not in the least contradict the admission that the attraction of the population to industry from agriculture plays a *historically* progressive role. I had occasion to discuss this elsewhere (*Studies*, p. 81, footnote 69). (See present edition, Vol. 2, p. 229.—*Ed.*)

Mr. Bulgakov thinks that Kautsky's opinion on the agronomic exploitation of the country by the town is a "strange" one; that, "at all events, Kautsky has here stepped on the soil of absolute fantasy" (*sic*!!!). What surprises us is that Mr. Bulgakov ignores the fact that Kautsky's opinion, which he criticises, is identical with one of the fundamental ideas of Marx and Engels. The reader would be right in concluding that Mr. Bulgakov considers the idea of the abolition of the antithesis between town and country to be "absolute fantasy." If such indeed is the critic's opinion, then we emphatically disagree with him and go over to the side of "fantasy" (actually, not to the side of fantasy, of course, but to that of a more profound criticism of capitalism). The view that the idea of abolishing the antithesis between town and country is a fantasy is not new by any means. It is the ordinary view of the bourgeois economists. It has even been borrowed by several writers with a more profound outlook. For example, Dühring was of the opinion that antagonism between town and country "is inevitable by the very nature of things."

Further, Mr. Bulgakov is "astonished" (!) at the fact that Kautsky refers to the growing incidence of epidemics among plants and animals as one of the difficulties confronting commercial agriculture and capitalism. "What has this to do with capitalism...?" asks Mr. Bulgakov. "Could any higher social organisation abolish the necessity of improving the breeds of cattle?" We in our turn are astonished at Mr. Bulgakov's failure to understand Kautsky's perfectly clear idea. The old breeds of plants and animals created by natural selection are being superseded by "improved" breeds created by artificial selection. Plants and animals are becoming more susceptible and more demanding; with the present means of communication epidemics spread with astonishing rapidity. Meanwhile, farming remains individual, scattered, frequently small (peasant) farming, lacking knowledge and resources. Urban capitalism strives to provide all the resources of modern science for the development of the technique of agriculture, but it leaves the social position of the producers at the old miserable level; it does not systematically and methodically transplant urban culture to the rural districts. No higher social organisation will abolish the necessity of improving the breeds of cattle (and Kautsky, of course, did not think of saying anything so absurd); but the more technique develops, the more susceptible the breeds of cattle and plants* become, the more the present capitalist social organisation suffers from lack of social control and from the degraded state of the peasants and workers.

The last "difficulty" confronting commercial agriculture that Kautsky mentions is the "depopulation of the countryside," the absorption by the towns of the best, the most energetic and most intelligent labour forces. Mr. Bulgakov is of the opinion that in its general form this proposition "is at all events incorrect," that "the present development of the urban at the expense of the rural population in no sense expresses a law of development of capitalist agriculture," but the migration of the agricultural population of industrial, exporting countries overseas, to the colonies. I think that Mr. Bulgakov is mistaken. The growth of the urban (more generally: industrial) population *at the expense of* the rural population is not only a present-day phenomenon but a general phenomenon which expresses *precisely the law* of capitalism. The theoretical grounds of this law are, as I have pointed out elsewhere,** first, that the growth of social division of labour wrests from primitive agriculture an increasing number of branches of industry,*** and,

---

* That is why in the practical part of his book Kautsky recommends the sanitary inspection of cattle and of the conditions of their maintenance (*S.* 397).

** *The Development of Capitalism in Russia*, Chapter I, Section II, and Chapter VIII, Section II. (See present edition, Vol. 3.—*Ed.*)

*** Pointing to this circumstance, Mr. Bulgakov says that "the agricultural population may diminish *relatively* [his italics] even when agriculture is flourishing." Not only "may," but *necessarily must* in capitalist society.... "The relative diminution [of the agricultural population] merely (*sic!*) indicates here a growth of new branches of people's labour," concludes Mr. Bulgakov. That "merely" is very strange. New branches of industry do actually withdraw "the most energetic and most intelligent labour forces" from agriculture. Thus, this simple reason is sufficient to enable one to accept Kautsky's general thesis as being *fully correct*: the *relative* diminution of the rural population sufficiently confirms the correctness of the general thesis (that capitalism withdraws the most energetic and most intelligent labour forces from agriculture).

secondly, that the variable capital required to work a given plot of land, on the whole, diminishes (cf. *Das Kapital*, III, 2, *S*. 177; Russian translation, p. 526, [56] which I quote in my book, *The Development of Capitalism*, pp. 4 and 444*). We have indicated above that in certain cases and certain periods we observed an increase in the variable capital required for the cultivation of a given plot of land; but this does not affect the correctness of the general law. Kautsky, of course, would not think of denying that not in every case does the relative diminution of the agricultural population become absolute diminution; that the degree of this absolute diminution is also determined by the growth of capitalist colonies. In relevant places in his book Kautsky very clearly points to this growth of capitalist colonies which flood Europe with cheap grain. ("The flight from the land of the rural population (*Landflucht*) which leads to the depopulation of the European countryside, constantly brings, not only to the towns, but also to the colonies, fresh crowds of robust country dwellers..." *S*. 242.) The phenomenon of industry depriving agriculture of its strongest, most energetic, and most intelligent workers is general, not only in industrial, but also in agricultural, countries; not only in Western Europe, but also in America and in Russia. The contradiction between the culture of the towns and the barbarism of the countryside which capitalism creates inevitably leads to this. The "argument" that "a decrease in the agricultural population side by side with a general increase in the population is inconceivable without the importation of large quantities of grain" is, in Mr. Bulgakov's opinion, "obvious." But in my opinion this argument is not only not obvious, but wrong. A decrease in the agricultural population side by side with a general increase in the population (growth of the towns) is quite conceivable without grain imports (the productivity of agricultural labour increases and this enables a smaller number of workers to produce as much as and even more than was formerly produced). A general increase in the population parallel with a

---

* See present edition, Vol. 3, pp. 40, 561.—*Ed.*

decrease in the agricultural population and a decrease (or a disproportionate increase) in the quantity of agricultural products is also conceivable—"conceivable" because the nourishment of the people has deteriorated under capitalism.

Mr. Bulgakov asserts that the increase of the medium-sized peasant farms in Germany in the period 1882-95, a fact established by Kautsky, which he connected with the other fact that these farms suffer least from a shortage of labour, "is capable of shaking the whole structure" of Kautsky's argument. Let us examine Kautsky's statements more closely.

According to agricultural statistics, the largest increase in area in the period 1882-95 occurred in the farms of from 5 to 20 hectares. In 1882 these farms occupied 28.8 per cent of the total area of all farms and in 1895, 29.9 per cent. This increase in the total area of medium-sized peasant farms was accompanied by a decrease in the area of big peasant farms (20 to 100 hectares; 1882—31.1 per cent, 1895—30.3 per cent). "These figures," says Kautsky, "gladden the hearts of all good citizens who regard the peasantry as the strongest bulwark of the present system. 'And so, it does not move, this agriculture,' they exclaim in triumph; 'Marx's dogma does not apply to it.'" This increase in the medium-sized peasant farms is interpreted as the beginning of a new era of prosperity for peasant farming.

"But this prosperity is rooted in a bog," Kautsky replies to these good citizens. "It arises, not out of the *well-being* of the peasantry, but out of the *depression* of agriculture as a whole" (230). Shortly before this Kautsky said that, "notwithstanding all the technical progress which has been made, *in some places* [Kautsky's italics] there is a decline in agriculture; there can be no doubt of that" (228). This decline is leading, for example, to the revival of feudalism—to attempts to tie the workers to the land and impose certain duties upon them. Is it surprising that backward forms of agriculture should revive on the soil of this "depression"? That the peasantry, which in general is distinguished from workers employed in large-scale production by its lower level of requirements, greater ability to starve, and greater exertion while at work, can hold out longer during a crisis?* "The agrarian crisis affects all agricultural classes that produce commodities; it does not stop at the middle peasant" (S. 231).

One would think that all these propositions of Kautsky are so clear that it is impossible not to understand them. Nevertheless, the critic has evidently failed to understand them. Mr. Bulgakov does not come forward with an opinion: he does not tell us how he explains this increase in the medium-

---

* Kautsky says elsewhere: "The small farmers hold out longer in a hopeless position. We have every reason to doubt that this is an advantage of small-scale production" (S. 134).

In passing, let us mention data fully confirming Kautsky's view that are given by Koenig in his book, in which he describes in detail the condition of English agriculture in a number of typical counties (*Die Lage der englischen Landwirtschaft, etc.* [*The Condition of English Agriculture, etc.*], Jena, 1896, von Dr. F. Koenig). In this book we find *any amount* of evidence of overwork and under-consumption on the part of the small farmers, as compared with hired labourers, but no evidence of the opposite. We read, for instance, that the small farms pay "because of immense (*ungeheuer*) diligence and frugality" (88); the farm buildings of the small farmers are inferior (107); the small landowners (*yeoman farmers* [these words are in English in the original.—*Ed.*]) are worse off than the tenant farmers (149); "their conditions are very miserable (in Lincolnshire), their cottages being worse than those of the labourers employed on the big farms, and some are in a very bad state. The small landowners work harder and for longer hours than ordinary labourers, but they earn less. They live more poorly and eat less meat ... their sons and daughters work without pay and are badly clothed" (157). "The small farmers work like slaves; in the summer they often work from 3 a.m. to 9 p.m." (a report of the Chamber of Agriculture in Boston, S. 158). "Without a doubt," says a big farmer, "the small man (*der kleine Mann*), who has little capital and on whose farm all the work is done by members of his family, finds it easier to cut down housekeeping expenses, while the big farmer must feed his labourers equally well in bad years and good" (218). The small farmers (in Ayrshire) "are extraordinarily (*ungeheuer*) diligent; their wives and children do no less, and often more, work than the day labourers; it is said that two of them will do as much work in a day as three hired labourers" (231). "The life of the small tenant farmer, who must work with his whole family, is the life of a slave" (253). "Taken as a whole... the small farmers have evidently withstood the crisis better than the big farmers; but this does not imply that the small farm is more profitable. The reason, in our opinion, is that the small man (*der kleine Mann*) utilises the unpaid assistance of his family.... Usually ... the whole family of the small farmer works on the farm.... The children are fed and clothed, and only rarely do they get a definite daily wage" (277-78), etc., etc.

sized peasant farms, but he ascribes to Kautsky the opinion
that "the development of the capitalist mode of production
is ruining agriculture." And Mr. Bulgakov exclaims angrily:
"Kautsky's assertion that agriculture is being destroyed is
wrong, arbitrary, unproved, and contradicts all the main
facts of reality," etc., etc.

To this we can only say that Mr. Bulgakov *conveys Kautsky's ideas altogether incorrectly*. Kautsky does not state
that the development of capitalism is ruining agriculture;
he says the opposite. Only by being very inattentive in reading Kautsky's book can one deduce from his words on the
depression (=crisis) in agriculture and on the technical retrogression to be observed *in some places* (*nota bene*) that he
speaks of the "destruction," the "doom" of agriculture. In
Chapter X, which deals especially with the question of overseas competition (i.e., the main reason for the agrarian crisis), Kautsky says: "The impending crisis, of course (*natür-
lich*), need not necessarily (*braucht nicht*) ruin the industry
which it affects. It does so only in very rare cases. As a general rule, a crisis merely causes a change in the existing
property relations in the capitalist sense" (273-74). This
observation made in connection with the crisis in the agricultural industries clearly reveals Kautsky's general view
of the significance of a crisis. In the same chapter Kautsky
again expresses the view in relation to the whole of
agriculture: "What has been said above does not give one
the least right to speak about the doom of agriculture
(*Man braucht deswegen noch lange nicht von einem Unter-
gang der Landwirtschaft zu sprechen*), but where the modern mode of production has taken a firm hold its conservative character has disappeared for ever. The continua-
tion of the old routine (*das Verharren beim Alten*) means
certain ruin for the farmer; he must constantly watch the
development of technique and continuously adapt his methods of production to the new conditions.... Even in the rural districts economic life, which hitherto has with strict
uniformity moved in an eternal rut, has dropped into a state
of constant revolutionisation, a state that is characteristic of the capitalist mode of production" (289).

Mr. Bulgakov "does not understand" how trends toward the
development of productive forces in agriculture can be com-

bined with trends that increase the difficulties of commercial agriculture. What is there unintelligible in this? Capitalism in both agriculture and industry gives an enormous impetus to the development of productive forces; but it is precisely this development which, the more it proceeds, causes the contradictions of capitalism to become more acute and creates new "difficulties" for the system. Kautsky develops one of the fundamental ideas of Marx, who categorically emphasised the progressive historical role of agricultural capitalism (the rationalisation of agriculture, the separation of the land from the farmer, the emancipation of the rural population from the relations of master and slave, etc.), at the same time no less categorically pointing to the impoverishment and oppression of the direct producers and to the fact that capitalism is incompatible with the requirements of rational agriculture. It is very strange indeed that Mr. Bulgakov, who admits that his "general social-philosophic world outlook is the same as Kautsky's,"* should fail to note that Kautsky here develops a fundamental idea of Marx. The readers of *Nachalo* must inevitably remain in perplexity over Mr. Bulgakov's attitude towards these fundamental ideas and wonder how, in view of the identity of their general world outlook, he can say: "*De principiis non est disputandum*"!!?** We permit ourselves not to believe Mr. Bulgakov's statement; we consider that an argument between him and other Marxists is possible precisely because of the community of these "*principia*." In saying that capitalism rationalises agriculture and that industry provides machinery for agriculture, etc., Mr. Bulgakov merely repeats one of these "*principia*." Only he should not have said "quite the opposite" in this connection. Readers might think that Kautsky holds a different opinion, whereas he very emphatically and definitely develops these fundamental ideas of Marx in his book. He says: "It is precisely industry which has created the technical and scientific conditions for new, rational agriculture. It is precisely industry which has revolutionised agriculture by means of machines

---

* As for the philosophic world outlook, we do not know whether what Mr. Bulgakov says is true. Kautsky does not seem to be an adherent of the critical philosophy, as Mr. Bulgakov is.
** In matters of principle there is no disputing.—*Ed.*

and artificial fertilisers, by means of the microscope and the chemical laboratory, giving rise in this way to the technical superiority of large-scale capitalist production over small-scale, peasant production" (*S*. 292). Thus, Kautsky does not fall into the contradiction in which we find Mr. Bulgakov bogged: on the one hand, Mr. Bulgakov admits that "capitalism [i.e., production carried on with the aid of wage-labour, i.e., not peasant, but large-scale production?] rationalises agriculture," while on the other, he argues that "it is not large-scale production which is the vehicle of this technical progress"!

II

Chapter X of Kautsky's book deals with the question of overseas competition and the industrialisation of agriculture. Mr. Bulgakov treats this chapter in a very offhand manner: "Nothing particularly new or original, more or less well-known main facts," etc., he says, leaving in the background the fundamental question of the conception of the agrarian crisis, its essence and significance. And yet this question is of enormous theoretical importance.

The conception of the agrarian crisis inevitably follows from the general conception of agrarian evolution which Marx presented and on which Kautsky enlarges in detail. Kautsky sees the essence of the agrarian crisis in the fact that, owing to the competition of countries which produce very cheap grain, agriculture in Europe has lost the opportunity of shifting to the masses of consumers the burdens imposed on it by the private ownership of land and capitalist commodity production. From now on agriculture in Europe *"must itself bear them* [these burdens], *and this is what the present agrarian crisis amounts to"* (*S*. 239, Kautsky's italics). Ground rent is the main burden. In Europe, ground rent has been raised by preceding historical development to an extremely high level (both differential and *absolute* rent) and is fixed in the price of land.* On the other hand, in

---

* For the process of inflating and fixing rent see the apt remarks of Parvus in *The World Market and the Agricultural Crisis*. Parvus shares Kautsky's main views on the crisis and on the agrarian question generally.

the colonies (America, Argentina, and others), insofar as they remain colonies, we see *free* land occupied by new settlers, either entirely gratis or for an insignificant price; moreover, the virginal fertility of this land reduces production costs to a minimum. Up to now, capitalist agriculture in Europe has quite naturally transferred the burden of excessively high rents to the consumer (in the form of high grain prices); now, however, the burden of these rents falls upon the farmers and the landowners themselves and ruins them.* Thus, the agrarian crisis has upset, and continues to upset, the prosperity which capitalist landed property and capitalist agriculture formerly enjoyed. Hitherto capitalist landed property has exacted an ever-increasing tribute from social development; and it fixed the level of this tribute in the price of land. Now it has to forego this tribute.** Capitalist agriculture has now been reduced to the state of instability that is characteristic of capitalist industry and is compelled to adapt itself to new market conditions. Like every crisis, the agrarian crisis is ruining a large number of farmers, is bringing about important changes in the established property relations, and *in some places* is leading to technical retrogression, to the revival of medieval relations and forms of economy. Taken as a whole, however, it is *accelerating* social evolution, ejecting patriarchal stagnation from its last refuge, and making necessary the further specialisation of agriculture (a principal factor of agricultural progress in capitalist society), the further application of machinery, etc. On the whole, as Kautsky shows by data

---

* Parvus, op. cit., p. 141, quoted in a review of Parvus' book in *Nachalo*, No. 3, p. 117. (See present volume, p. 66.—*Ed*.) We should add that the other "difficulties" of commercial agriculture confronting Europe affect the colonies to an incomparably smaller degree.

** Absolute rent is the result of monopoly. "Fortunately, there is a limit to the raising of absolute rent....Until recent times it rose steadily in Europe in the same way as differential rent. But overseas competition has undermined this monopoly to a very considerable extent. We have no grounds for thinking that differential rent in Europe has suffered as a result of overseas competition, except for a few counties in England.... But absolute rent has dropped, and this has benefited (*zu gute gekommen*) primarily the working classes" (*S*. 80; cf. also *S*. 328).

for several countries, in Chapter IV of his book, *even* in Western Europe, instead of the stagnation in agriculture in the period 1880-90, we see technical progress. We say *even* in Western Europe, because in America, for example, this progress is still more marked.

In short, there are no grounds for regarding the agrarian crisis as an obstacle to capitalism and capitalist development.

REPLY TO Mr. P. NEZHDANOV

In issue No. 4 of *Zhizn*, Mr. P. Nezhdanov examined articles by me and other authors on the market theory. I intend to reply to only one of Mr. Nezhdanov's assertions—that in my article in *Nauchnoye Obozreniye*, issue No. 1 for this year, I "distorted my struggle against the theory of third persons." As far as the other questions are concerned, those raised by Mr. P. Nezhdanov in respect of the market theory and, in particular, of P. B. Struve's views, I shall confine myself to a reference to my article in reply to Struve ("Once More on the Theory of Realisation"; the delay in its publication in *Nauchnoye Obozreniye* was due to circumstances over which the author had no control).

Mr. P. Nezhdanov maintains that "capitalist production does not suffer from any contradiction between production and consumption." From this he concludes that Marx, in recognising this contradiction, "suffered from a serious internal contradiction" and that I am repeating Marx's error.

I believe Mr. Nezhdanov's opinion to be a mistaken one (or one based on a misunderstanding) and cannot see any contradiction in Marx's views.

Mr. P. Nezhdanov's assertion that there is no contradiction between production and consumption in capitalism is so strange that it is only to be explained by the very *special meaning* that he attaches to the concept "contradiction." Mr. P. Nezhdanov is of the opinion that "if there really were a contradiction between production and consumption that contradiction would provide a regular surplus-product" (p. 301; the same in the final theses, p. 316). This is an utterly

arbitrary and, in my opinion, utterly incorrect interpretation. In criticising my assertions on the contradiction between production and consumption in capitalist society, Mr.
P. Nezhdanov should (I think) have told the reader how I
understand that contradiction and should not have limited
himself to an exposition of his own views on the essence and
significance of that contradiction. The whole essence of the
question (which has given rise to Mr. P Nezhdanov's polemic
against me) is that I understand the contradiction under
discussion quite differently from the way in which Mr. P.
Nezhdanov wishes to understand it. I did not say anywhere
that this contradiction should *regularly** produce a surplus-
product; I do not think so and such a view cannot be deduced
from Marx's words. The contradiction between production
and consumption that is inherent in capitalism is due to the
tremendous rate at which production is growing, to the
tendency to unlimited expansion which competition gives it,
while consumption (individual), if it grows at all, grows
very slightly; the proletarian condition of the masses of the
people makes a rapid growth of individual consumption
impossible. It seems to me that any one reading carefully
pages 20 and 30 of my *Studies* (the article on the Sismondists
cited by Mr. P Nezhdanov) and page 40 of *Nauchnoye
Obozreniye* (1899, No. 1)** can convince himself that, from
the outset, I gave *only this meaning* to the contradiction
between production and consumption in capitalism. Indeed,
no other meaning can be ascribed to this contradiction by
one who adheres strictly to Marx's theory. The contradiction
between production and consumption that is inherent in
capitalism consists only in this, that the growth of the national
wealth proceeds side by side with the growth of the people's
poverty; that the productive forces of society increase
without a corresponding increase in consumption by the
people, without the employment of these productive forces
for the benefit of the working masses. The contradiction

---

* I stress *regularly* because the irregular production of a surplus-
product (crises) is inevitable in capitalist society as a result of the
disturbance in proportion between the various branches of industry.
But a certain state of consumption is one of the elements of proportion.

** See present edition, Vol. 2, pp. 155 and 167 and pp. 58-59 of
the present volume.—*Ed.*

under discussion, understood in this sense, is a fact that does not admit of any doubt and that is confirmed by the daily experience of millions of people, and it is the observation of this fact that leads the working men to the views that have found a full scientific expression in Marx's theory. This contradiction does not, by any means, lead inevitably to the regular production of a surplus-product (as Mr. Nezhdanov would like to think). We can quite well imagine (if we argue from a purely theoretical standpoint about an ideal capitalist society) the realisation of the entire product in a capitalist society without any surplus-product, *but we cannot imagine capitalism* without a disparity between production and consumption. This disparity is expressed (as Marx has demonstrated clearly in his Schemes) by the fact that the production of the means of production can and must outstrip the production of articles of consumption.

Mr. Nezhdanov, therefore, was completely mistaken in his deduction that the contradiction between production and consumption must regularly provide a surplus-product, and this mistake led to his unjustly accusing Marx of inconsistency. Marx, on the contrary, remains consistent when he shows:

1) that the product *can* be realised in a capitalist society (it goes without saying that this is true if proportionality between the various branches of industry is assumed); that it would be incorrect to introduce foreign trade or "third persons" to explain this realisation;

2) that the theories of the petty-bourgeois economists (*à la* Proudhon) on the impossibility of realising *surplus-value* are based on a complete misunderstanding of the very process of realisation in general;

3) that even with fully proportional, ideally smooth realisation we cannot imagine capitalism without a contradiction between production and consumption, without the tremendous growth of production being accompanied by an extremely slow growth (or even stagnation and worsening) of consumption by the people. Realisation is due more to means of production than to articles of consumption—this is obvious from Marx's Schemes; and from this, in turn, it follows inevitably that "the more productiveness develops, the more it finds itself at variance with the narrow basis on

which the conditions of consumption rest" (Marx). [57] It is obvious from all the passages in *Capital* devoted to the contradiction between production and consumption* that it is *only in this sense* that Marx understood the contradiction between production and consumption.

Incidentally, Mr. P Nezhdanov is of the opinion that Mr. Tugan-Baranovsky also denies the contradiction between production and consumption in a capitalist society. I do not know whether this is true. Mr. Tugan-Baranovsky himself introduced into his book a scheme showing the possibility of the growth of production accompanied by a contraction of consumption (which, of course, is possible and actual under capitalism). How can one deny that we see here a contradiction between production and consumption, although there is no surplus-product?

In charging Marx (and me) with inconsistency, Mr. P. Nezhdanov also lost sight of the fact that he should have explained, as a basis for his viewpoint, how one should understand the "independence" of the production of means of production from the production of articles of consumption. According to Marx, this "independence" is limited to the following: a certain (and constantly growing) part of the product which consists of means of production is realised by exchanges within the given department, i.e., exchanges of means of production for means of production (or the use of the product obtained, *in natura*,** for fresh production); but in *the final analysis* the manufacture of means of production is necessarily bound up with that of articles of consumption, since the former are not manufactured for their own sake, but only because more and more means of production are demanded by the branches of industry manufacturing articles of consumption.*** The views of the petty-bourgeois economists, therefore, do not differ from those of Marx because the

---

* These passages are quoted in my article in *Nauchnoye Obozreniye*, 1899, No. 1 (see present volume, p. 56, et seq.—*Ed.*) and are repeated in the first chapter of *The Development of Capitalism in Russia*, pp. 18-19. (See present edition, Vol. 3, p. 56-57.—*Ed.*)
** In its natural form.—*Ed.*
*** *Das Kapital*, III, 1, 289. [58] Quoted by me in *Nauchnoye Obozreniye*, p. 40 (see present volume, p. 59.—*Ed.*), and in *The Development of Capitalism*, 17. (See present edition, Vol. 3, p. 55.—*Ed.*)

former recognised in general the connection between production and consumption in a capitalist society while the latter denied in general that connection (which would be absurd). The difference is that the petty-bourgeois economists considered this connection between production and consumption to be *a direct one*, that they thought *production follows consumption*. Marx showed that this connection is *an indirect one*, that it only makes itself felt *in the final analysis*, because in capitalist society *consumption follows production*. But the connection nevertheless exists, even if it is indirect; consumption must, in the final analysis, follow production, and, if the productive forces are driving towards an unlimited growth of production, while consumption is restricted by the proletarian condition of the masses of the people, there is undoubtedly a contradiction present. This contradiction does not signify the impossibility of capitalism,* but it does signify that its transformation to a higher form is a necessity: the stronger this contradiction becomes, the more developed become the objective conditions for this transformation, as well as the subjective conditions, i.e., the workers' consciousness of this contradiction.

The question now arises: what position could Mr. Nezhdanov adopt on the question of the "independence" of the means of production as regards articles of consumption? One of two: either he will completely deny any dependence between them, will assert the possibility of realising means of production that are *in no way connected* with articles of consumption, that are not connected even in "the final analysis" —in which case he will inevitably descend to the absurd, or he will admit, following Marx, that in the final analysis means of production are connected with articles of consumption, in which case he must admit the correctness of my understanding of Marx's theory.

In conclusion, let me take an example to illustrate these abstract arguments with concrete data. It is known that in any capitalist society exceptionally low wages (=the low

---

* *Studies*, p. 20 (see present edition, Vol. 2, p. 155.—*Ed.*); *Nauchnoye Obozreniye*, No. 1, p. 41 (see present volume, p. 60.—*Ed.*); *The Development of Capitalism*, pp. 19-20. (See present edition, Vol.3, p. 58.—*Ed.*) If this contradiction were to lead to "a regular surplus-product," it would signify precisely the impossibility of capitalism.

level of consumption by the masses of the people) often hinder the employment of machinery. What is more, it even happens that machines acquired by entrepreneurs are in disuse because the price of labour drops so low that manual labour becomes more profitable to the owner!* The existence of a contradiction between consumption and production, between the drive of capitalism to develop the productive forces to an unlimited extent and the limitation of this drive by the proletarian condition, the poverty and unemployment of the people, is, in this case, as clear as daylight. But it is no less clear that it is correct to draw one single conclusion from this contradiction—that the development of the productive forces themselves must, with irresistible force, lead to the replacement of capitalism by an economy of associated producers. It would, on the other hand, be utterly incorrect to draw from this contradiction the conclusion that capitalism must *regularly* provide a surplus-product, i.e., that capitalism cannot, in general, realise the product, and can, therefore, play no progressive historical role, and so on.

Written in May 1899

Published in December 1899
in the magazine *Zhizn*
Signed: *Vladimir Ilyin*

Published according to
the text in the magazine

---

* I bring an instance of this phenomenon in the sphere of Russian capitalist agriculture in *The Development of Capitalism in Russia*, page 165. (See present edition, Vol. 3, p. 234.—*Ed.*) Similar phenomena are not individual instances but are the usual and *inevitable* consequences of the basic features of capitalism.

A PROTEST BY RUSSIAN SOCIAL-DEMOCRATS [53]

Written at the end of August-
beginning of September 1899
First published abroad in
December 1899 as the separate
reprints from No. 4-5 of the
magazine *Rabocheye Dyelo* [66]

Published according to the
text in the magazine

Оттискъ изъ № 4-5 „Рабочаго Дѣла".

ПРОТЕСТЪ

РОССІЙСКИХЪ СОЦІАЛЬДЕМОКРАТОВЪ

СЪ ПОСЛѢСЛОВІЕМЪ ОТЪ РЕДАКЦІИ „РАБОЧАГО ДѢЛА

—

Собраніе соціальдемократовъ одной мѣстности (Россіи), въ числѣ семнадцати человѣкъ, приняло ЕДИНОГЛАСНО слѣдующую резолюцію и постановило опубликовать ее и передать на обсужденіе всѣмъ товарищамъ.

Въ послѣднее время среди русскихъ соціальдемократовъ замѣчаются отступленія отъ тѣхъ основныхъ принциповъ русской соціальдемократіи, которые были провозглашены какъ основателями и передовыми борцами—членами Группы „Освобожденія Труда",— такъ и соціальдемократическими изданіями русскихъ рабочихъ организацій 90-хъ годовъ. Ниже приводимое „credo", долженствующее выражать основные взгляды нѣкоторыхъ („молодыхъ") русскихъ соціальдемократовъ, представляетъ изъ себя попытку систематическаго и опредѣленнаго изложенія „новыхъ возрѣній". — Вотъ это „credo" въ полномъ видѣ.

„Существованіе цехового и мануфактурнаго періода на Западѣ наложило рѣзкій слѣдъ на всю послѣдующую исторію, въ особенности на исторію соціальдемократіи. Необходимость для буржуазіи завоевать свободныя формы, стремленіе освободиться отъ сковывающихъ производство цеховыхъ регламентацій, сдѣлали ее, буржуазію, революціоннымъ элементомъ; она повсюду на Западѣ начинаетъ съ liberté, fraternité, égalité (свобода, братство и равенство).

Facsimile of the first page of the reprint of "A Protest by Russian Social-Democrats" from No. 4-5 of *Rabocheye Dyelo*. 1899.

A MEETING OF SOCIAL-DEMOCRATS, SEVENTEEN IN NUMBER, HELD AT A CERTAIN PLACE (IN RUSSIA), ADOPTED *UNANIMOUSLY* THE FOLLOWING RESOLUTION AND RESOLVED TO PUBLISH IT AND TO SUBMIT IT TO ALL COMRADES FOR THEIR CONSIDERATION

A tendency has been observed among Russian Social-Democrats recently to depart from the fundamental principles of Russian Social-Democracy that were proclaimed by its founders and foremost fighters, members of the Emancipation of Labour group[61] as well as by the Social-Democratic publications of the Russian workers' organisations of the nineties. The *Credo* reproduced below, which is presumed to express the fundamental views of certain ("young") Russian Social-Democrats, represents an attempt at a systematic and definite exposition of the "new views." The following is its full text:

"The guild and manufacture period in the West laid a sharp impress on all subsequent history and particularly on the history of Social-Democracy. The fact that the bourgeoisie had to fight for free forms, that it strove to release itself from the guild regulations fettering production, made the bourgeoisie a revolutionary element; everywhere in the West it began with *liberté, fraternité, égalité* (liberty, fraternity, equality), with the achievement of free political forms. By these gains, however, as Bismarck expressed it, it drew a bill on the future payable to its antipode—the working class. Hardly anywhere in the West did the working class, as a class, win the democratic institutions—it made use of them. Against this it may be argued that the working class took part in revolutions. A reference to history will refute this opinion, for, precisely in 1848, when the consolidation of Constitutions took place in the West, the working class represented the urban artisan element, the petty-bourgeois democracy; a factory proletariat hardly existed, while the proletariat employed in large-scale industry (the German weavers depicted by Hauptmann, the weavers of Lyons) represented a wild mass capable only of rioting, but not of advancing any political demands. It can be definitely stated that the Constitutions of 1848 were won by the bourgeoisie and the small urban artisans. On the other hand, the working class (artisans, manufactory workers, printers, weavers, watchmakers, etc.) have been accustomed since the Middle Ages to membership in organisations, mutual benefit societies, religious societies, etc. This spirit of organisation is still alive among the skilled workers in the West, sharply distinguishing them from the factory proletariat, which submits to organisation badly and slowly and is capable only of *lose-organisation* (temporary organisations) and not of permanent organisations with rules and regulations. It was these manufactory skilled workers that comprised the core of the Social-Democratic parties. Thus, we get the picture: on the one hand, the relative ease of political struggle and every possibility for it; on the other hand, the possibility for the systematic organisation of this struggle with the aid of the workers trained in the manufacturing period. It was on this basis that theoretical and practical Marxism grew up in the West. The starting-point was the parliamentary political struggle with the prospect—only superficially resembling Blanquism, but of totally different origin—of capturing power, on the one hand, and of a *Zusammenbruch* (collapse), on the other. Marxism was the theoretical expression of the prevailing practice: of the political struggle predominating over the economic. In Belgium, in France, and particularly in Germany, the workers organised the political struggle with incredible ease; but it was with enormous difficulty and tremendous friction that they organised the economic struggle. Even to this day the economic organisations as compared with the political organisations (leaving aside England) are extraordinarily weak and unstable, and everywhere *laissent à désirer quelque chose* (leave something to be desired). So long as the energy in the political struggle had not been completely exhausted, *Zusammenbruch* was an essential organisational *Schlagwort* (slogan) destined to play an extremely important historical role. The fundamental law that can be discerned by studying the working-class movement is that of the line of least resistance. In the West, this line was political activity, and Marxism, as formulated in the *Communist Manifesto*, was the best possible form the movement could assume. But when all energy in political activity had been exhausted, when the political movement had reached a point of intensity difficult and almost impossible to surpass (the slow increase in votes in the recent period, the apathy of the public at meetings, the note of despondency in literature), this, in conjunction with the ineffectiveness of parliamentary action and the entry into the arena of the ignorant masses, of the unorganised and almost unorganisable factory proletariat, gave rise in the West to what is now called Bernsteinism,[62] the crisis of Marxism. It is difficult to imagine a more logical course than the period of development of the labour movement from the *Communist Manifesto* to Bernsteinism, and a careful study of this whole process can determine with astronomical exactitude the outcome of this "crisis." Here, of course, the issue is not the defeat or victory of Bernsteinism—that is of little interest; it is the radical change in practical activity that has been gradually taking place for a long time within the party.

"The change will not only be towards a more energetic prosecution of the economic struggle and consolidation of the economic organisations, but also, and most importantly, towards a change in the party's attitude to other opposition parties. Intolerant Marxism, negative Marxism, primitive Marxism (whose conception of the class division of society is too schematic) will give way to democratic Marxism, and the social position of the party within modern society must undergo a sharp change. The party *will recognise* society; its narrow corporative and, in the majority of cases, sectarian tasks will be widened to social tasks, and its striving to seize power will be transformed into a striving for change, a striving to reform present-day society on democratic lines adapted to the present state of affairs, with the object of protecting the rights (all rights) of the labouring classes in the most effective and fullest way. The concept 'politics' will be enlarged and will acquire a truly social meaning, and the practical demands of the moment will acquire greater weight and will be able to count on receiving greater attention than they have been getting up to now.

"It is not difficult to draw conclusions for Russia from this brief description of the course of development taken by the working-class movement in the West. In Russia, the line of least resistance will never tend towards political activity. The incredible political oppression will prompt much talk about it and cause attention to be concentrated precisely on this question, but it will never prompt practical action. While in the West the fact that the workers were drawn into political activity served to strengthen and crystallise their weak forces, in Russia, on the contrary, these weak forces are confronted with a wall of political oppression. Not only do they lack practical ways of struggle against this oppression, and hence, also for their own development, but they are systematically stifled and cannot give forth even weak shoots. If to this we add that the working class in our country has not inherited the spirit of organisation which distinguished the fighters in the West, we get a gloomy picture, one that is likely to drive into despondency the most optimistic Marxist who believes that an extra factory chimney stack will by the very fact of its existence bring great welfare. The economic struggle too is hard, infinitely hard, but it is possible to wage it, and it is in fact being waged by the masses themselves. By learning in this struggle to organise, and coming into constant conflict with the political regime in the course of it, the Russian worker will at last create what may be called a form of the labour movement, the organisation or organisations best conforming to Russian conditions. At the present, it can be said with certainty that the Russian working-class movement is still in the amoeba state and has not yet acquired any form. The strike movement, which goes on with any form of organisation, cannot yet be described as the crystallised form of the Russian movement, while the illegal organisations are not worth consideration even from the mere quantitative point of view (quite apart from the question of their usefulness under present conditions).

"Such is the situation. If to this we add the famine and the process of ruination of the countryside, which facilitate *Streikbrecher*-ism,* and, consequently, the even greater difficulty of raising the masses of the workers to a more tolerable cultural level, then ... well, what is there for the Russian Marxist to do?! The talk about an independent workers' political party merely results from the transplantation of alien aims and alien achievements to our soil. The Russian Marxist, so far, is a sad spectacle. His practical tasks at the present time are paltry, his theoretical knowledge, insofar as he utilises it *not as an instrument for research* but as a schema for activity, is worthless for the purpose of fulfilling even these paltry practical tasks. Moreover, these borrowed patterns are harmful from the practical point of view. Our Marxists, forgetting that the working class in the West entered political activity after that field had already been cleared, are much too contemptuous of the radical or liberal opposition activity of all other non-worker strata of society. The slightest attempt to concentrate attention on public manifestations of a liberal political character rouses the protest of the orthodox Marxists, who forget that a number of historical conditions prevent us from being Western Marxists and demand of us a different Marxism, suited to, and necessary in, Russian conditions. Obviously, the lack in every Russian citizen of political feeling and sense cannot be compensated by talk about politics or by appeals to a non-existent force. This political sense can only be acquired through education, i.e., through participation in that life (however un-Marxian it may be) which is offered by Russian conditions. 'Negation' is as harmful in Russia as it was appropriate (temporarily) in the West, because negation proceeding from something organised and possessing real power is one thing, while negation proceeding from an amorphous mass of scattered individuals is another.

"For the Russian Marxist there is only one course: participation in, i.e., assistance to, the economic struggle of the proletariat, and participation in liberal opposition activity. As a 'negator,' the Russian Marxist came on the scene very early, and this negation has weakened the share of his energy that should be turned in the direction of political radicalism. For the time being, this is not terrible; but if the class schema prevents the Russian intellectual from taking an active part in life and keeps him too far removed from opposition circles, it will be a serious loss to all who are compelled to fight for legal forms separately from the working class, which has not yet put forward political aims. The political innocence concealed behind the cerebrations of the Russian Marxist intellectual on political topics may play mischief with him."

We do not know whether there are many Russian Social-Democrats who share these views. But there is no doubt that ideas of this kind have their adherents, and we there-

---

* Strike-breaking —*Ed.*

fore feel obliged to protest categorically against such views and to warn all comrades against the menacing deflection of Russian Social-Democracy from the path it has already marked out—the formation of an independent political working-class party which is inseparable from the class struggle of the proletariat and which has for its immediate aim the winning of political freedom.

The above-quoted *Credo* represents, first, "a brief description of the course of development taken by the working-class movement in the West," and, secondly, "conclusions for Russia."

First of all, the authors of the *Credo* have an entirely false conception of the history of the West-European working-class movement. It is not true to say that the working class in the West did not take part in the struggle for political liberty and in political revolutions. The history of the Chartist movement and the revolutions of 1848 in France, Germany, and Austria prove the opposite. It is absolutely untrue to say that "Marxism was the theoretical expression of the prevailing practice: of the political struggle predominating over the economic." On the contrary, "Marxism" appeared at a time when non-political socialism prevailed (Owenism, "Fourierism," "true socialism") and the *Communist Manifesto* took up the cudgels at once against non-political socialism. Even when Marxism came out fully armed with theory (*Capital*) and organised the celebrated International Working Men's Association,[63] the political struggle was by no means the prevailing practice (narrow trade-unionism in England, anarchism and Proudhonism in the Romance countries). In Germany the great historic service performed by Lassalle was the transformation of the working class from an appendage of the liberal bourgeoisie into an independent political party. Marxism linked up the economic and the political struggle of the working class into a single inseparable whole; and the effort of the authors of the *Credo* to separate these forms of struggle is one of their most clumsy and deplorable departures from Marxism.

Further, the authors of the *Credo* also have an entirely wrong conception of the present state of the West-European working-class movement and of the theory of Marxism, under the banner of which that movement is marching.

To talk about a "crisis of Marxism" is merely to repeat the nonsense of the bourgeois hacks who are doing all they can to exacerbate every disagreement among the socialists and turn it into a split in the socialist parties. The notorious Bernsteinism—in the sense in which it is commonly understood by the general public, and by the authors of the *Credo* in particular—is an attempt to narrow the theory of Marxism, to convert the revolutionary workers' party into a reformist party. As was to be expected, this attempt has been strongly condemned by the majority of the German Social-Democrats. Opportunist trends have repeatedly manifested themselves in the ranks of German Social-Democracy, and on every occasion they have been repudiated by the Party, which loyally guards the principles of revolutionary international Social-Democracy. We are convinced that every attempt to transplant opportunist views to Russia will encounter equally determined resistance on the part of the overwhelming majority of Russian Social-Democrats.

Similarly, there can be no suggestion of a "radical change in the practical activity" of the West-European workers' parties, in spite of what the authors of the *Credo* say: the tremendous importance of the economic struggle of the proletariat, and the necessity for such a struggle, were recognised by Marxism from the very outset. As early as the forties Marx and Engels conducted a polemic against the utopian socialists who denied the importance of this struggle.[64]

When the International Working Men's Association was formed about twenty years later, the question of the importance of trade unions and of the economic struggle was raised at its very first Congress, in Geneva, in 1866. The resolution adopted at that Congress spoke explicitly of the importance of the economic struggle and warned the socialists and the workers, on the one hand, against exaggerating its importance (which the English workers were inclined to do at that time) and, on the other, against underestimating its importance (which the French and the Germans, particularly the Lassalleans, were inclined to do). The resolution recognised that the trade unions were not only a natural, but also an essential phenomenon under capitalism and considered them an extremely important means for organising the working class in its daily struggle against capital and for the abolition of wage-labour. The resolution declared that the trade unions must not devote attention exclusively to the "immediate struggle against capital," must not remain aloof from the general political and social movement of the working class; they must not pursue "narrow" aims, but must strive for the general emancipation of the millions of oppressed workers. Since then the workers' parties in the various countries have discussed the question many times and, of course, will discuss it again and again—whether to devote more or less attention at any given moment to the economic or to the political struggle of the proletariat; but the general question, or the question in principle, today remains as it was presented by Marxism. The conviction that the class struggle must necessarily combine the political and the economic struggle into one integral whole has entered into the flesh and blood of international Social-Democracy. The experience of history has, furthermore, incontrovertibly proved that absence of freedom, or restriction of the political rights of the proletariat, always make it necessary to put the political struggle in the forefront.

Still less can there be any suggestion of a serious change in the attitude of the workers' party towards the other opposition parties. In this respect, too, Marxism has mapped out the correct line, which is equally remote from exaggerating the importance of politics, from conspiracy (Blanquism, etc.), and from decrying politics or reducing it to opportunist, reformist social tinkering (anarchism, utopian and petty-bourgeois socialism, state socialism, professorial socialism, etc.). The proletariat must strive to form independent political workers' parties, the main aim of which must be the capture of political power by the proletariat for the purpose of organising socialist society. The proletariat must not regard the other classes and parties as "one reactionary mass"[65]; on the contrary, it must take part in all political and social life, support the progressive classes and parties against the reactionary classes and parties, support every revolutionary movement against the existing system, champion the interests of every oppressed nationality or race, of every persecuted religion, of the disfranchised sex, etc. The arguments the *Credo* authors advance on this subject merely reveal a desire to obscure the class character of the struggle of the proletariat, weaken this struggle by a meaningless "recognition of society," and reduce revolutionary Marxism to a trivial reformist trend. We are convinced that the overwhelming majority of Russian Social-Democrats will resolutely reject this distortion of the fundamental principles of Social-Democracy. Their erroneous premises regarding the West-European working-class movement led the authors of the *Credo* to draw still more erroneous "conclusions for Russia."

The assertion that the Russian working class "has not yet put forward political aims" simply reveals ignorance of the Russian revolutionary movement. The North-Russian Workers' Union[66] formed in 1878 and the South-Russian Workers' Union[67] formed in 1875 put forward even then the demand for political liberty in their programmes. After the reaction of the eighties, the working class repeatedly put forward the same demand in the nineties. The assertion that "the talk about an independent workers' political party merely results from the transplantation of alien aims and alien achievements to our soil" reveals a complete failure to understand the historical role of the Russian working class and the most vital tasks of Russian Social-Democracy. Apparently, the programme of the authors of the *Credo* inclines to the idea that the working class, following "the line of least resistance," should confine itself to the economic struggle, while the "liberal opposition elements" fight, with the "participation" of the Marxists, for "legal forms." The application of such a programme would be tantamount to the political suicide of Russian Social-Democracy, it would greatly retard and debase the Russian working-class movement and the Russian revolutionary movement (for us the two concepts coincide). The mere fact that it was possible for a programme like this to appear shows how well grounded were the fears expressed by one of the foremost champions of Russian Social-Democracy, P. B. Axelrod, when, at the end of 1897, he wrote of the possibility of the following prospect:

"The working-class movement keeps to the narrow rut of purely economic conflicts between the workers and employers and, in itself, taken as a whole, is not of a political character, while in the struggle for political freedom the advanced strata of the proletariat follow the revolutionary circles and groups of the so-called intelligentsia" (Axelrod, *Present Tasks and Tactics of the Russian Social-Democrats*, Geneva, 1898, p. 19).

Russian Social-Democrats must declare determined war upon the whole body of ideas expressed in the *Credo*, for these ideas lead straight to the realisation of this prospect. Russian Social-Democrats must bend every effort to translate into reality another prospect, outlined by P. B. Axelrod in the following words:

"The other prospect: Social-Democracy organises the Russian proletariat into an independent political party which fights for liberty, *partly side by side and in alliance with* the bourgeois revolutionary groups (if such should exist), and partly by recruiting directly into its ranks or securing the following of the most democratic-minded and revolutionary elements from among the intelligentsia" (*ibid.*, p. 20).

At the time P. B. Axelrod wrote the above lines the declarations made by Social-Democrats in Russia showed clearly that the overwhelming majority of them adhered to the same point of view. It is true that one St. Petersburg workers' paper, *Rabochaya Mysl*,[68] seemed to incline toward the ideas of the authors of the *Credo*. In a leading article setting forth its programme (No. 1, October 1897) it expressed, regrettably, the utterly erroneous idea, an idea running counter to Social-Democracy, that the "economic basis of the movement" may be "obscured by the effort to keep the political ideal constantly in mind." At the same time, however, another St. Petersburg workers' newspaper, *S. Peterburgsky Rabochy Listok*[69] (No. 2, September 1897), emphatically expressed the opinion that "the overthrow of the autocracy ... can be achieved only by a well-organised and numerically strong working-class party" and that "organised in a strong party" the workers will "emancipate themselves, and the whole of Russia, from all political and economic oppression." A third newspaper, *Rabochaya Gazeta*,[70] in its leading article in issue No. 2 (November 1897), wrote: "The fight against the autocratic government for political liberty is the immediate task of the Russian working-class movement." "The Russian working-class movement will increase its forces tenfold if it comes out as a single harmonious whole, with a common name and a well-knit organisation...." "The separate workers' circles should combine into one common party." "The Russian workers' party will be a Social-Democratic Party."

That precisely these views of *Rabochaya Gazeta* were fully shared by the vast majority of Russian Social-Democrats is seen, furthermore, from the fact that the Congress of Russian Social-Democrats [71] in the spring of 1898 formed the Russian Social-Democratic Labour Party, published its manifesto and recognised *Rabochaya Gazeta* as the official Party organ. Thus, the *Credo* authors are taking an enormous step backward from the stage of development which Russian Social-Democracy has already achieved and which it has recorded in the *Manifesto of the Russian Social-Democratic Labour Party*. Since the frenzied persecution by the Russian Government has led to the present situation in which the Party's activity has temporarily subsided and its official organ has ceased publication, it is the task of all Russian Social-Democrats to exert every effort for the utmost consolidation of the Party, to draw up a Party programme and revive its official organ. In view of the ideological vacillations evidenced by the fact that programmes like the above-examined *Credo* can appear, we think it particularly necessary to emphasise the following fundamental principles that were expounded in the *Manifesto* and that are of enormous importance to Russian Social-Democracy. First, Russian Social-Democracy "desires to be and to remain the class movement of the organised working masses." Hence it follows that the motto of Social-Democracy must be: aid to the workers, not only in their economic, but also in their political struggle; agitation, not only in connection with immediate economic needs, but also in connection with all manifestations of political oppression; propaganda, not only of the ideas of scientific socialism, but also of democratic ideas. Only the theory of revolutionary Marxism can be the banner of the class movement of the workers, and Russian Social-Democracy must concern itself with the further development and implementation of this theory and must safeguard it against the distortions and vulgarisations to which "fashionable theories" are so often subjected (and the successes of revolutionary Social-Democracy in Russia have already made Marxism a "fashionable" theory). While concentrating all their present efforts on activity among factory and mine workers, Social-Democrats must not forget that with the expansion of the movement home workers, handicraftsmen, agricultural labourers, and the millions of ruined and starving peasants must be drawn into the ranks of the labouring masses they organise.

Secondly: "On his strong shoulders the Russian worker must and will carry to a finish the cause of winning political liberty." Since its immediate task is the overthrow of the autocracy, Social-Democracy must act as the vanguard in the fight for democracy, and consequently, if for no other reason, must give every support to all democratic elements of the population of Russia and win them as allies. Only an independent working-class party can serve as a strong bulwark in the fight against the autocracy, and only in alliance with such a party, only by supporting it, can all the other fighters for political liberty play an effective part.

Thirdly and finally: "As a socialist movement and trend, the Russian Social-Democratic Party carries on the cause and the traditions of the whole preceding revolutionary movement in Russia; considering the winning of political liberty to be the most important of the immediate tasks of the Party as a whole, Social-Democracy marches towards the goal that was already clearly indicated by the glorious representatives of the old Narodnaya Volya.⁷²" The traditions of the whole preceding revolutionary movement demand that the Social-Democrats shall at the present time concentrate all their efforts on organising the Party, on strengthening its internal discipline, and on developing the technique for illegal work. If the members of the old Narodnaya Volya managed to play an enormous role in the history of Russia, despite the fact that only narrow social strata supported the few heroes, and despite the fact that it was by no means a revolutionary theory which served as the banner of the movement, then Social-Democracy, relying on the class struggle of the proletariat, will be able to render itself invincible. "The Russian proletariat will throw off the yoke of autocracy in order to continue the struggle against capital and the bourgeoisie for the complete victory of socialism with still greater energy."

We invite all groups of Social-Democrats and all workers' circles in Russia to discuss the above-quoted *Credo*

and our resolution, and to express a definite opinion on the
question raised, in order that all differences may be removed and the work of organising and strengthening the
Russian Social-Democratic Labour Party may be accelerated.

Groups and circles may send their resolutions to the
Union of Russian Social-Democrats Abroad which, by
Point 10 of the decision of the 1898 Congress of Russian
Social-Democrats, is a part of the Russian Social-Democratic
Party and its representative abroad.

REVIEW

S. N. Prokopovich. *The Working-Class Movement in the West*[73]

"...to turn to social science and to its alleged conclusion that the capitalist system of society is hastening inexorably to its doom by virtue of the contradictions developing within it. We find the relevant explanations in Kautsky's *Erfurt Programme*" (147). Before dealing with the content of the passage quoted by Mr. Prokopovich, we must take note of a peculiarity highly typical of him and similar reformers of theory. Why is it that our "critical investigator," in turning to "social science," looks for "explanations" in Kautsky's popular booklet and nowhere else? Does he really believe that the whole of "social science" is contained in that little booklet? He knows perfectly well that Kautsky is "a faithful custodian of the traditions of Marx" (I, 187) and that an exposition and a substantiation of the "conclusions" of a certain school of "social science" are to be found precisely in Marx's treatises on political economy; yet he acts as though such a thing were altogether unknown to him. What are we to think of an "investigator" who confines himself to attacks on "custodians" of a theory but who does not once, throughout his book, risk crossing swords openly and directly with the theory itself?

In the passage quoted by Mr. Prokopovich, Kautsky says that the technological revolution and the accumulation of capital are progressing with increasing rapidity, that the expansion of production is made necessary by the fundamental properties of capitalism and must be uninterrupted, while the expansion of the market "has for some time been proceeding too slowly" and that "the time is apparently at hand when the market for European industry will not only cease its further expansion but will even begin to shrink. This event can only mean the bankruptcy of the entire capitalist society." Mr. Prokopovich "criticises" the "conclusions" drawn by "social science" (*i.e.*, Kautsky's citation of *one* of the laws of development evolved by Marx): "The basis thus given for the inevitability of the collapse of capitalist society allots the chief role to the contradiction between 'the constant drive to expand production and the ever slower expansion of the market and, finally, its shrinkage.' It is this contradiction, according to Kautsky, that must bring about the collapse of the capitalist system of society. But [listen well!] the expansion of production presumes the 'productive consumption' of part of the surplus-value—i.e., first its realisation and then its expenditure on machinery, buildings, etc., for new production. In other words, the expansion of production is most closely connected with the existence of a market for the commodities already produced; the constant expansion of production with a market that is relatively shrinking is, therefore, an impossibility" (148). And Mr. Prokopovich is so well satisfied with his excursion into the sphere of "social science" that in the very next line he speaks with condescending disdain of a "scientific" (in inverted commas) substantiation of faith, etc. Such jockeying with criticism would be outrageous, were it not for the fact that it is, more than anything else, amusing. Our good Mr. Prokopovich has heard a knell, but knows not from what bell. Mr. Prokopovich has heard of the abstract theory of realisation that has recently been heatedly discussed in Russian literature in the course of which the role of "productive consumption" has been particularly stressed on account of errors in Narodnik economics. Mr. Prokopovich has not properly understood this theory and imagines that it *denies* (!) the existence in capitalism of those basic and elementary contradictions Kautsky speaks of. To listen to Mr. Prokopovich, we would have to believe that "productive consumption" could develop *quite independently* of individual consumption (in which consumption by the masses plays the dominant role), i.e., that capitalism does not contain within itself any contradiction between production and

consumption. This is simply absurd, and Marx and his Russian supporters* have clearly opposed such misconstructions. Not only does the bourgeois-apologetic theory into which our "critical investigator" has wandered not follow from the fact that "the expansion of production presumes productive consumption," but, on the contrary, from it follows the contradiction between the tendency towards the unlimited growth of production and limited consumption that is inherent precisely in capitalism and that must bring about its collapse.

Apropos of what has been said, it is worth while mentioning the following interesting point. Mr. Prokopovich is a fervent follower of Bernstein, whose magazine articles he quotes and translates for several pages. In his well-known book, *Die Voraussetzungen, etc.*,** Bernstein even recommends Mr. Prokopovich to the German public as his Russian supporter, but he makes a reservation, the substance of which is that Mr. Prokopovich is more Bernsteinian than Bernstein. And, a remarkable thing, Bernstein and his Russian yesman both distort the theory of realisation, but *in diametrically opposite directions*, so that they *cancel each other out*. Firstly, Bernstein regarded as a "contradiction" the fact that Marx turned against Rodbertus' theory of crises and at the same time declared that "the ultimate cause of all real crises is the poverty and limited consumption of the masses." Actually there is no contradiction here at all, as I have had occasion to point out in other places (*Studies*, p. 30,*** *The Development of Capitalism in Russia*, p. 19****). Secondly, Bernstein argues in precisely the same manner as does Mr. V. V. here in Russia, that the tremendous growth of the surplus-product must inevitably mean an increase in the number of well-to-do (or the greater prosperity of the workers),

---

* Cf. my article in *Nauchnoye Obozreniye* for August 1899, especially page 1572 (see pp. 74-93 of this volume, especially p. 84.—*Ed.*), and *The Development of Capitalism in Russia*, p. 16, et seq. (See present edition, Vol. 3, p. 54, et seq.—*Ed.*)

** *The Premises, etc.—Ed.*

*** See present edition, Vol. 2, *A Characterisation of Economic Romanticism*, pp. 167-68.—*Ed.*

**** See present edition, Vol. 3, p. 58.—*Ed.*

since the capitalists themselves and their servants (*sic!*) cannot "consume" the entire surplus-product (*Die Voraussetz- ungen, etc., S.* 51-52). This naïve argument completely ignores the role of productive consumption, *as Kautsky point- ed out in his book against Bernstein* (Kautsky, *Gegen Bern- stein,* II. *Abschnitt,** —the paragraph on "the employment of surplus-value"). And now there appears a Russian Bernstein- ian, recommended by Bernstein, who says exactly the oppo- site, who lectures Kautsky on the role of "productive con- sumption" and then reduces Marx's discovery to the absurdity that productive consumption can develop quite inde- pendently of individual consumption (!), that the realisa- tion of surplus-value by its use for the production of means of production does away with the dependence, in the final anal- ysis, of production on consumption and, consequently, with the contradiction between them! By this example the reader may judge whether Mr. Prokopovich's "loss of a good half of the theoretical premises" is due to the "investigations" or whether our "critical investigator" is "at a loss" due to some other cause.

A second example. Taking up three pages (25-27), our author "investigated" the question of peasant associations in Germany. He gave a list of the various kinds of asso- ciations and statistical data on their rapid growth (especial- ly of dairy associations) and argued: "The artisan has been almost deprived of his roots in the modern economic system, whereas the peasant continues to stand firm [!] in it." How very simple, isn't it really? The undernourishment of the German peasants, their exhaustion from excessive labour, the mass flight of people from the countryside to the towns— all that must be mere invention. It suffices to point to the rapid growth of associations (especially dairy associations that result in depriving the peasants' children of milk and lead to the peasants' greater dependence on capitalists) in order to prove the "stability" of the peasantry. "The de- velopment of capitalist relations in the manufacturing in- dustry ruins the artisan but improves the condition of the peasant. It [the condition?] hinders the penetration of capi- talism into agriculture." This is new! Until now it has been

---

* Kautsky, *Against Bernstein*, Section II.— *Ed.*

believed that it is the development of capitalism in the manufacturing industry that is the main force which gives rise to, and develops, capitalism in agriculture. But Mr. Prokopovich, like his German prototypes, could truly say of himself: *nous avons changé tout ca*—we have changed all that! But would that be true, gentlemen? Have you really changed *anything at all*, have you shown the error in even one of the basic postulates of the theory you have "torn to pieces" and replaced it by a truer postulate? Have you not, on the contrary, returned to the old prejudices?... "On the other hand, the development of the manufacturing industry ensures subsidiary earnings for the peasant."... A return to the doctrine of Messrs. V. V. & Co. on the subsidiary earnings of the peasantry! Mr. Prokopovich does not deem it worth mentioning the fact that in a large number of cases these "earnings" express the conversion of the peasant into a wage-labourer. He prefers to conclude his "investigation" with the high-sounding sentence: "The sap of life has not yet left the peasant class." It is true that Kautsky has shown, precisely in respect of Germany, that agricultural associations are a transition stage on the way *to capitalism*—but, you see, we already know how the terrible Mr. Prokopovich has crushed Kautsky!

We see this resurrection of Narodnik views (Narodnik views of the V. V. hue) not only in the above passage but in many other places in Mr. Prokopovich's "critical investigation." The reader probably knows the fame (a sorry fame) that Mr. V. V. earned for himself by his excessive narrowing and debasing of the theory known as "economic" materialism: this theory, as "adapted" by Mr. V. V., did not postulate that in the final analysis all factors are reduced to the development of the productive forces, but postulated that many extremely important (although in the final analysis secondary) factors could be neglected. Mr. Prokopovich offers us a very similar distortion when he attempts to expose Kautsky as one who does not understand the significance of "material forces" (144), in the course of which Mr. Prokopovich himself light-mindedly confuses "economic organisation" (145) with "economic force" (on 146 and especially 149). Unfortunately we cannot dwell to the needed extent on an analysis of this error of Mr. Prokopovich, but must refer the reader to the above-mentioned book by Kautsky

against Bernstein (*Abschnitt* III, Section *a*), where the
original versions of Mr. Prokopovich's rehashings are discussed at length. We also hope that the reader who peruses
Mr. Prokopovich's book attentively will see quite easily that
the theory torn to pieces by our "critical investigator"
(Mr. Prokopovich, incidentally, here, too, maintains a modest
silence about the views of the founders of the theory and
refrains from examining them, preferring to confine himself
to extracts from the speeches and articles of present-day
adherents of this theory)—that the theory is in no way to
blame for this disgraceful narrowing of "economic" materialism (cf., for example, statements by authoritative Belgian
spokesmen on pp. 74, 90, 92, 100 in the second part).

As far as the extracts quoted by Mr. Prokopovich are concerned, it should be said that he often seizes on individual
passages and gives the reader a distorted impression of views
and arguments that have not been expounded in Russian
literature. On account of this, Mr. Prokopovich's jockeying with criticism creates a most repulsive impression.
In some cases it would be worth the while of those who
read Mr. Prokopovich's book to refer even to a book by
Professor Herkner that has recently been translated into
Russian: *Wage-Labour in Western Europe* (St. Petersburg,
1899, published by the magazine *Obrazovaniye*). For instance,
in a note to page 24 (Part I) Mr. Prokopovich writes that
the Congress of 1892 "adopted a resolution sympathising
with the organisation of producers' associations" and follows
this up with a quotation which, first, does not fully support
the words of the author and, secondly, *breaks off* precisely at
the point where it speaks of the necessity "to conduct a particular struggle against the belief that associations are in a
position to bring any influence to bear on capitalist production relations, etc." (Herkner, Notes, pp. xi-xii, Note
6 to Chapter IX).

Mr. Prokopovich is just as successful in his crushing of
Kautsky on pages 56, 150, 156, 198, and in many other places
as he is in the case we have examined. Mr. Prokopovich's
assertions that Liebknecht, in the sixties, for a time renounced his ideals, betrayed them, etc. (111, 112), are in
no sense to be taken seriously. We have had occasion to see
how well-founded his judgements are, and the following

sentence (once again directed, not against the founder of the theory, but against its "custodian") will, for example, show us to what Pillars of Hercules the insolence and self-assurance of our "investigator" will take him: "We should be acting superficially, if we undertook to criticise this whole conception of the working-class movement from the standpoint of its conformity to the true course taken by the development of this movement—from the standpoint of its *scientific basis* [Mr. Prokopovich's italics]. There is not and cannot be (*sic!*) a grain of science in it" (156). This is what you call categorical criticism! All this Marxism, it isn't even worth criticising, and that's that! Obviously we have before us either a man who is destined to make a great revolution in the science "of which there cannot be even a grain" in the theory that is dominant in Germany, or ... or—how can it be put delicately?—or a man who, when "at a loss," repeats the phrases of others. Mr. Prokopovich prostrates himself with such fervour before this very latest of gods who has pronounced those words for the thousandth time that he has no pity on his own forehead. Bernstein, if you please, "has some shortcomings in his theoretical views" (198) that consist—can you imagine it?—in his belief in the necessity of a scientific theory that defines the aims of the men of action concerned. "Critical investigators" are not subject to this strange belief. "Science will become free," utters Mr. Prokopovich, "only when it is admitted that it must *serve* the aims of a party and not *define* them. It must be recognised that science cannot define the aims of a practical party" (197). Be it noted that Bernstein renounced precisely these views of his follower. "A principled programme inevitably leads to dogmatism and is only a hindrance in the way of the party's sound development.... Theoretical principles are all very well in propaganda but not in a programme" (157). "Programmes are unnecessary; they are harmful." "The individual himself may be a programme if he is sensitive to, and has a fine feeling for, the needs of the times."... The reader probably thinks that I am continuing to quote Mr. Prokopovich. But no, I am now quoting the newspaper *Novoye Vremya*,[74] which recently published articles on a programme that attracted a great deal of attention—not the programme of a party, of course, but of the new Minister for Internal Affairs....

The relationship of the freedom of unprincipledness—excuse me, "freedom of science"—preached by Mr. Prokopovich to the views of the majority of the West-European personalities of whom our valiant critic so valiantly writes, may be seen from the following quotations drawn from that same book by Mr. Prokopovich: "Of course, without a betrayal of principles..." (159). "Not in any way violating one's independence, loyalty to principle...." "I renounce compromise only in the case ... in which it leads to a renunciation of principles or even to the ignoring of principles..." (171). "Introducing no unprincipledness..." (174). "Not, of course, selling one's soul, in the present case, one's principles..." (176). "The principles are now firmly established..." (183). "A compass [is needed] that would rid us of the need to grope our way," against "short-sighted empiricism," against "a thoughtless attitude to principles" (195). "Primary importance attaches to principles, to the theoretical part..." (103, Part II), etc.

In conclusion, two more quotations: "If German Social-Democracy were the expression of socialism and not of the proletariat that is acting in defence of its own interests in present-day society, for the first time recognising its significance, then—since not all Germans are idealists—side by side with this party that pursues idealist aims we should see another, stronger party, a working-class party that represents the practical interests of that part of the German proletariat that is not idealist."... "If socialism were not to play the role of a mere symbol in that movement, a symbol distinguishing one definite organisation, if it were the motive idea, the principle that demands of party members a certain specific service—in that case the socialist party would separate from the general labour party, and the mass of the proletariat, which strives for better living conditions under the existing system and cares little for the ideal future, would form an independent labour party." The reader will again probably think....

Written at the end of 1899

First published in 1928
in Lenin Miscellany VII

Published according to
the manuscript

REVIEW

Karl Kautsky. *Bernstein und das sozialdemokratische Programm. Eine Antikritik**

... In the introduction Kautsky gives voice to some extremely valuable and apt ideas on the conditions that must be satisfied by serious and conscientious criticism if those undertaking it do not wish to confine themselves within the narrow bounds of soulless pedantry and scholasticism, if they do not wish to lose sight of the close and indestructible bonds that exist between the "theoretical reason" and the "practical reason"—not the practical reason of individuals, but of the masses of the population placed in specific conditions. Truth, of course, comes first, says Kautsky, and if Bernstein has become sincerely convinced of the error of his former views, it is his plain duty to give definite expression to his convictions. But the trouble with Bernstein is his lack of precisely this directness and definiteness. His pamphlet is amazingly "encyclopaedic" (as Antonio Labriola has remarked in a French magazine); it touches on a mass of problems, an agglomeration of questions, but *not on any one* of them does it provide an integral and precise exposition of the critic's new views. The critic merely expresses his doubts and abandons difficult and complicated questions without any independent analysis after having scarcely touched upon them. This brings about, Kautsky notes sarcastically, a strange phenomenon: Bernstein's followers understand his

---

* Karl Kautsky. *Bernstein and the Social-Democratic Programme. A Counter-Critique.—Ed.*

book in the most diverse ways, whereas his opponents all understand it in the same way. Bernstein's chief objection to his opponents is that they do not understand him, that they do not want to understand him. The whole series of newspaper and magazine articles that Bernstein has written in answer to his opponents has failed to explain his positive views.

Kautsky begins his counter-criticism with the question of method. He examines Bernstein's objections to the materialist conception of history and shows that Bernstein confuses the concept of "determinism" with that of "mechanism," that he confuses freedom of will with freedom of action, and without any grounds identifies historical necessity with the hopeless position of people under compulsion. The outworn accusation of fatalism, which Bernstein also repeats, is refuted by the very premises of Marx's theory of history. Not everything can be reduced to the development of the productive forces, says Bernstein. Other factors "must be taken into consideration."

Very well, answers Kautsky, that is something every investigator must do, irrespective of what conception of history guides him. Anyone who wants to make us reject Marx's method, the method that has so brilliantly justified itself and continues to justify itself in practice, must take one of two paths: either he must reject altogether the idea of objective laws, of the necessity of the historical process, and in so doing abandon all attempts at providing a scientific basis for sociology; or he must show how he can evolve the necessity of the historical process from other factors (ethical views, for example), he must show this by an analysis that will stand up to at least a remote comparison with Marx's analysis in *Capital*. Not only has Bernstein not made the slightest attempt to do this, but, confining himself to empty platitudes about "taking into consideration" other factors, he *has continued* to use the old materialist method in his book as though he did not declare it to be wanting! As Kautsky points out, Bernstein, at times, even applies this method with the most impermissible crudity and one-sidedness! Further on Bernstein's accusations are levelled against dialectics which, he alleges, lead to arbitrary constructions, etc., etc. Bernstein repeats these phrases (that have already managed to disgust also the Russian readers) without making the slightest attempt to show what is incorrect in dialectics, whether Hegel or Marx and Engels are guilty of methodological errors (and precisely what errors). The only means by which Bernstein tries to motivate and fortify his opinion is a reference to the "tendentiousness" of one of the concluding sections of *Capital* (on the historical tendency of capitalist accumulation). This charge has been worn threadbare: it was made by Eugen Dühring and Julius Wolf and many others in Germany, and it was made (we add on our part) by Mr. Y. Zhukovsky in the seventies and by Mr. N. Mikhailovsky in the nineties—by the very same Mr. Mikhailovsky who had once accused Mr. Y. Zhukovsky of acrobatics for making the selfsame charge. And what *proof* does Bernstein offer in confirmation of this worn-out nonsense? Only the following: Marx began his "investigation" with ready-made conclusions, since in 1867 *Capital* drew the same conclusion that Marx had drawn as early as the forties. Such "proof" is tantamount to fraud, answers Kautsky, because Marx based his conclusions on two investigations and not on one, as he points out very definitely in the introduction to *Zur Kritik* (see Russian translation: *A Critique of Some of the Propositions of Political Economy*[15]). Marx made his first investigation in the forties, after leaving the Editorial Board of the *Rheinische Zeitung*.[16] Marx left the newspaper because he had to treat of material interests and he realised that he was not sufficiently prepared for this. From the arena of public life, wrote Marx about himself, I withdrew into the study. And so (stresses Kautsky, hinting at Bernstein), Marx had doubts regarding the correctness of his judgement of material interests, regarding the correctness of the dominant views on this subject at that time, but he did not think his doubts to be important enough to write a whole book and inform the world about them. On the contrary, Marx set out to study in order to advance from doubtings of the old views to positive new ideas. He began to study French social theories and English political economy. He came into close contact with Engels, who was at that time making a detailed study of the actual state of the economy in England. The result of this joint work, this *first* inquiry, was the well-known conclusions which the two writers expounded very definitely towards the end of the forties.[77] Marx moved to London in 1850, and the favourable conditions there for research determined him "to begin afresh *from the very beginning* and to work through the new material critically" (*A Critique of Some of the Propositions*, 1st edition, p. xi.[78] Our italics). The fruit of this *second* inquiry, lasting many long years, were the works: *Zur Kritik* (1859) and *Das Kapital* (1867). The conclusion drawn in *Capital* coincides with the former conclusion drawn in the forties because the second inquiry confirmed the results of the first. "My views, however they may be judged ... are the result of conscientious investigation lasting many years," wrote Marx in 1859 (*ibid.*, p. xii).[79] Does this, asks Kautsky, resemble conclusions found ready-made long before the investigation?

From the question of dialectics Kautsky goes over to the question of value. Bernstein says that Marx's theory is unfinished, that it leaves many problems "that are by no means fully explained." Kantsky does not think of refuting this: Marx's theory is not the last word in science, he says. History brings new facts and new methods of investigation that require the further development of the theory. If Bernstein had made an attempt to utilise new facts and new methods of inquiry for the further development of the theory, everybody would have been grateful to him. But Bernstein does not dream of doing that; he confines himself to cheap attacks on Marx's disciples and to extremely vague, purely eclectic remarks, such as: the Gossen-Jevons-Böhm theory of marginal utility is no less just than Marx's theory of labour-value. Both theories retain their significance for different purposes, says Bernstein, because Böhm-Bawerk has as much right, *a priori*, to abstract from the property of commodities that they are produced by labour, as Marx has to abstract from the property that they are use-values. Kautsky points out that it is utterly absurd to regard two opposite, mutually exclusive theories suitable for different purposes (and, furthermore, Bernstein does not say for what purposes either of the two theories is suitable). It is by no means a question as to which property of commodities we are, *a priori* (*von Hause aus*), entitled to abstract from; the question is how to explain the principal phenomena of present-day society, based on the *exchange* of products, how to explain the value of commodities, the function of money, etc. Even if Marx's theory may leave a number of still unexplained problems, Bernstein's theory of value is a totally unexplained problem. Bernstein further quotes Buch, who constructed the concept of the "maximum density" of labour; but Bernstein does not give a complete exposition of Buch's views or make a definite statement of his own opinion on that question. Buch, it seems, gets entangled in contradictions by making value depend on wages and wages depend on value. Bernstein senses the eclecticism of his statements on value and tries to defend eclecticism in general. He calls it "the revolt of the sober intellect against the tendency inherent in every dogma to constrict thought within narrow confines." If Bernstein were to recall the history of thought, retorts Kautsky, he would see that the great rebels against the constriction of thought within narrow confines were never eclectics, that what has always characterised them has been the striving for the unity, for the integrity of ideas. The eclectic is too timid to dare revolt. If, indeed, I click my heels politely to Marx and at the same time click my heels politely to Böhm-Bawerk, that is still a long way from revolt! Let anyone name even one eclectic in the republic of thought, says Kautsky, who has proved worthy of the name of rebel!

Passing from the method to the results of its application, Kautsky deals with the so-called *Zusammenbruchstheorie*, the theory of collapse, of the sudden crash of West-European capitalism, a crash that Marx allegedly believed to be inevitable and connected with a gigantic economic crisis. Kautsky says and proves that Marx and Engels never propounded a special *Zusammenbruchstheorie*, that they did not connect a *Zusammenbruch* necessarily with an economic crisis. This is a distortion chargeable to their opponents who expound Marx's theory one-sidedly, tearing out of context odd passages from different writings in order thus triumphantly to refute the "one-sidedness" and "crudeness" of the theory. Actually Marx and Engels considered the transformation of West-European economic relations to be dependent on the maturity and strength of the classes

brought to the fore by modern European history. Bernstein
tries to assert that this is not the theory of Marx, but Kautsky's interpretation and extension of it. Kautsky, however,
with precise quotations from Marx's writings of the forties
and sixties, as well as by means of an analysis of the basic
ideas of Marxism, has completely refuted this truly pettifog-
ging trickery of the Bernstein who so blatantly accused
Marx's disciples of "apologetics and pettifoggery." This part
of Kautsky's book is particularly interesting, the more so,
since some Russian writers (e.g., Mr. Bulgakov in the magazine *Nachalo*) have been in a hurry to repeat the distortion
of Marx's theory which Bernstein offered in the guise of
"criticism" (as does Mr. Prokopovich in his *Working-Class
Movement in the West*, St. Petersburg, 1899).

Kautsky analyses the basic tendencies of contemporary
economic development in particularly great detail in order
to refute Bernstein's opinion that this development is not
proceeding in the direction indicated by Marx. It stands to
reason that we cannot present here a detailed exposition of
the chapter "Large- and Small-Scale Production" and of
other chapters of Kautsky's book which are devoted to a
political-economic analysis and contain extensive numerical
data, but shall have to confine ourselves to a brief mention of
their contents. Kautsky emphasises the point that the question is one of the direction, by and large, of development
and by no means of particularities and superficial manifestations, which *no* theory can take into account in all their great
variety. (Marx reminds the reader of this simple but oft forgotten truth in the relevant chapters of *Capital*.) By a detailed
analysis of the data provided by the German industrial
censuses of 1882 and 1895 Kautsky shows that they are a brilliant confirmation of Marx's theory and have placed beyond
all doubt the process of the concentration of capital and
the elimination of small-scale production. In 1896 Bernstein
(when he himself still belonged to the guild of apologists and
pettifoggers, says Kautsky ironically) most emphatically
recognised this fact, but now he is excessive in his exaggeration of the strength and importance of small-scale production. Thus, Bernstein estimates the number of enterprises
employing fewer than 20 workers at several hundred thousand, "apparently adding in his pessimistic zeal an extra

nought to the figure," since there are only 49,000 such enterprises in Germany. Further, whom do the statistics not
place among the petty entrepreneurs—cabmen, messengers,
gravediggers, fruit hawkers, seamstresses (even though they
may work at home for a capitalist), etc., etc.! Here let us note
a remark of Kautsky's that is particularly important from
the theoretical standpoint—that petty commercial and industrial enterprises (such as those mentioned above) in
capitalist society are often merely one of the forms of relative over-population; ruined petty producers, workers
unable to find employment turn (sometimes temporarily)
into petty traders and hawkers, or rent out rooms or beds
(also "enterprises," which are registered by statistics equally with all other types of enterprise!), etc. The fact that
these employments are overcrowded does not by any means
indicate the viability of petty production but rather the
growth of poverty in capitalist society. Bernstein, however,
emphasises and exaggerates the importance of the petty
"industrial producers" when to do so seems to him to serve his
advantage (on the question of large- and small-scale production), but keeps silent about them when he finds it to his
disadvantage (on the question of the growth of poverty).
    Bernstein repeats the argument, long known to the Rus-
sian public as well, that joint-stock companies "permit"
the fragmentation of capital and "make unnecessary" its
concentration, and he cites some figures (cf. *Zhizn*, No. 3
for 1899) on the number of small shares. Kautsky replies
that these figures prove exactly nothing, since small shares
in any companies might belong to big capitalists (as even
Bernstein must admit). Bernstein does not adduce any evidence, nor can he, to prove that joint-stock companies
increase the number of property-owners, for the joint-
stock companies actually serve to expropriate the gullible
men of small means for the benefit of big capitalists and
speculators. The growth in the number of shares merely
shows that wealth has a tendency to take on the form of
shares; but this growth tells us nothing about the distribution of wealth. In general, Bernstein's attitude to the
question of an increase in the number of wealthy people,
the number of property-owners, is an astonishingly thoughtless one, which has not prevented his bourgeois followers

7*

from praising precisely this part of his book and announcing that it is based on "a tremendous amount of numerical
data." And Bernstein proved himself skilful enough, says
Kautsky ironically, to compress this tremendous amount of
data into two pages! He confuses property-owners with capitalists, although no one has denied an increase in the number of the latter. In analysing income-tax data, he ignores
their fiscal character, and their confusion of income from
property with income in the form of salary, etc. He compares
data for different times that have been collected by different
methods (on Prussia, for example) and are, therefore, not
comparable. He even goes so far as to borrow data on the
growth of property-owners in England (printing these figures
in heavy type, as his trump card) from an article in some
sensational newspaper that was singing the praises of Queen
Victoria's jubilee and whose handling of statistics was the
nec plus ultra of light-mindedness! The source of this information is unknown and, indeed, such information cannot
be obtained on the basis of data on the English income tax,
since these do not permit one to determine the number of
tax-payers and the total income of each tax-payer. Kautsky
adduces data from Kolb's book on the English income tax
from 1812 to 1847 and shows that they, in exactly the same
way as Bernstein's newspaper data, indicate an (apparent)
increase in the number of property-owners—and that, in a
period of the most terrible increase in the most horrible
poverty of the people in England! A detailed analysis of Bernstein's data led Kautsky to the conclusion that Bernstein had
not quoted a single figure that actually proved a growth in
the number of property-owners.

Bernstein tried to give this phenomenon a theoretical
grounding: the capitalists, he said, cannot themselves
consume the entire surplus-value that increases to such a
colossal extent; this means that the number of property-
owners that consume it must grow. It is not very difficult
for Kautsky to refute this grotesque argument that totally
ignores Marx's theory of realisation (expounded many times
in Russian literature). It is particularly interesting that
for his refutation Kautsky does not employ theoretical arguments alone, but offers concrete data attesting to the growth
of luxury and lavish spending in the West-European coun-

tries; to the influence of rapidly changing fashions, which greatly intensify this process; to mass unemployment; to the tremendous increase in the "productive consumption" of surplus-value, i.e., the investment of capital in new enterprises, especially the investment of European capital in the railways and other enterprises of Russia, Asia, and Africa.

Bernstein declares that everyone has abandoned Marx's "theory of misery" or "theory of impoverishment." Kautsky demonstrates that this is again a distorted exaggeration on the part of the opponents of Marx, since Marx propounded no such theory. He spoke of the growth of poverty, degradation, etc., indicating at the same time the counteracting tendency and the real social forces that alone could give rise to this tendency. Marx's words on the growth of poverty are fully justified by reality: first, we actually see that capitalism has a tendency to engender and increase poverty, which acquires tremendous proportions when the above-mentioned counteracting tendency is absent. Secondly, poverty grows, not in the physical but in the social sense, i.e., in the sense of the disparity between the increasing level of consumption by the bourgeoisie and consumption by society as a whole, and the level of the living standards of the working people. Bernstein waxes ironical over such a conception of "poverty," saying that this is a Pickwickian conception. In reply Kautsky shows that people like Lassalle, Rodbertus, and Engels have made very definite statements to the effect that poverty must be understood in its social, as well as in its physical, sense. As you see—he parries Bernstein's irony—it is not such a bad company that gathers at the "Pickwick Club"! Thirdly and lastly, the passage on increasing impoverishment remains perfectly true in respect of the "border regions" of capitalism, the border regions being understood both in the geographical sense (countries in which capitalism is only beginning to penetrate and frequently not only gives rise to physical poverty but to the outright starvation of the masses) and in the political-economic sense (handicraft industries and, in general, those branches of economy in which backward methods of production are still retained).

The chapter on the "new middle estate" is likewise extremely

interesting and, for us Russians, particularly instructive.
If Bernstein had merely wanted to say that in place of
the declining petty producers a new middle estate, the intelligentsia, is appearing, he would be perfectly correct, says
Kautsky, pointing out that he himself noted the importance
of this phenomenon several years before. In all spheres of
people's labour, capitalism increases the number of *office
and professional workers* with particular rapidity and makes
a growing demand for intellectuals. The latter occupy a
special position among the other classes, attaching themselves
partly to the bourgeoisie by their connections, their outlooks,
etc., and partly to the wage workers as capitalism increasingly deprives the intellectual of his independent position,
converts him into a hired worker and threatens to lower his
living standard. The transitory, unstable, contradictory position of that stratum of society now under discussion is
reflected in the particularly widespread diffusion in its midst
of hybrid, eclectic views, a farrago of contrasting principles
and ideas, an urge to rise verbally to the higher spheres and
to conceal the conflicts between the historical groups of the
population with phrases—all of which Marx lashed with his
sarcasm half a century ago.

In the chapter on the theory of crises Kautsky shows
that Marx did not at all postulate a "theory" of the ten-
year cycle of industrial crises, but merely stated a fact.
The change in this cycle in recent times has been noted by
Engels himself. It is said that cartels of industrialists
can counteract crises by limiting and regulating production.
But America is a land of cartels; yet instead of a limitation we see there a tremendous growth of production. Further, the cartels limit production for the home market but
expand it for the foreign market, selling their goods abroad
at a loss and extracting monopoly prices from consumers in
their own country. This system is inevitable under protectionism and there are no grounds for anticipating a change
from protectionism to Free Trade. The cartels close small
factories, concentrate and monopolise production, introduce
improvements, and in this way greatly worsen the condition
of the producers. Bernstein is of the opinion that the speculation which gives rise to crises weakens as the conditions
on the world market change from unforeseeable to foreseeable

and known conditions; but he forgets that it is the "unfore-seeable" conditions in the new countries that give a tremendous impetus to speculation in the old countries. Using statistical data, Kautsky shows the growth of speculation in precisely the last few years, as well as the growth in the symptoms indicating a crisis in the not very distant future.

With regard to the remaining part of Kautsky's book, we must mention his analysis of the muddle people get into through confusing (as does Mr. S. Prokopovich, op. cit.) the economic strength of certain groups with their economic organisations. We must mention Kautsky's statement to the effect that Bernstein ascribes to purely temporary conditions of a given historical situation the dignity of a general law— his refutation of Bernstein's incorrect views on the essence of democracy; and his explanation of Bernstein's statistical error, in comparing the number of industrial workers in Germany with the number of voters and overlooking the mere trifle that not all the workers in Germany (but only males over the age of 25) enjoy the franchise and that not all participate in the elections. We can only strongly recommend to the reader who is interested in the question of the significance of Bernstein's book and in the polemic around it to turn to the German literature and under no circumstances to believe the biased and one-sided reviews by the proponents of eclecticism that dominate in Russian literature. We have heard that part of Kautsky's book here under review will probably be translated into Russian. This is very desirable, but is no substitute for an acquaintanceship with the original.

Written at the end of 1899

First published in 1928
in *Lenin Miscellany VII*

Published according to
the manuscript

ARTICLES FOR "RABOCHAYA GAZETA" [80]

Written in the second half of 1899
First published in 1925
in *Lenin Miscellany III*

Published according
to manuscripts copied
by an unknown hand